AF559660

GLOBALIZATION, GOVERNANCE, AND TECHNOLOGY

Challenges and Alternatives

# GLOBALIZATION, GOVERNANCE, AND TECHNOLOGY

## Challenges and Alternatives

*Editors*

DHIRENDRA K. VAJPEYI

*and*

RENU KHATOR

DEEP & DEEP PUBLICATIONS PVT. LTD.
F-159, Rajouri Garden, New Delhi - 110 027

GLOBALIZATION, GOVERNANCE, AND TECHNOLOGY
Challenges and Alternatives

ISBN 978-81-8450-080-6



Printed in India at MAYUR ENTERPRISES,
WZ Plot No. 3, Gujjar Market, Tihar Village, New Delhi - 110 018.

Published by DEEP & DEEP PUBLICATIONS PVT. LTD.,
F-159, Rajouri Garden, New Delhi - 110 027 • Phone : 25435369, 25440916
E-mail : ddpubs@gmail.com • ddpbooks@yahoo.co.in
*Showroom :*
2/13, Ansari Road, Daryaganj, New Delhi - 110 002 • Telefax : 23245122

# Contents

# Preface

The role of bureaucracy in developing societies continues to be explored and debated by scholars of public administration. More often than not, bureaucracy is the most, if not the only, stable structure, the "steel framework" in developing societies due to the experimental nature of their democratic institutions. Its smooth functioning, under these situations, becomes a necessary precondition to social and economic welfare as well as successful evolution of democratic government. Innovations in technology in general and information technology (IT) in particular in recent years have greatly impacted the style and substantive behavior of bureaucratic governance. Issues related to transparency and accountability have become crucial aspects of the emerging democratic process.

Over the years, scholars of public administration have been most critical of the often corrupt and inefficient nature of bureaucracy but have also been in search of good and effective governance by proposing reforms and restructuring strategies. Many scholars are responsible for contributing to the depth and breadth of the field as it exists today, but only a very few have made a pioneering effort. One such scholar is Professor R.B. Jain, whom I had the pleasure of meeting in 1986 at the International Political Science Association's World Congress meeting in Chicago. I was an Assistant Professor, freshly minted from Purdue University and was badly in need of a scholarly anchor. Professor Jain, as Chair of the IPSA Research Committee on Public Bureaucracy in Developing Societies, (RC 04) invited me to join the group and then entrusted various leadership roles. Last year, when the Board of the Research Committee on Public Bureaucracy in Developing Societies (RC 04) in cooperation with Research Committee on Technology and Development (RC 35) decided to publish a volume to honor Professor Jain, the response was so great that we decided to publish two volumes instead of a single volume. This action-reaction speaks highly of Professor Jain's influence on scholars and impact on the discipline, and is also a glowing testimony to how much he is respected and loved by his colleagues.

A brief glimpse on Professor Jain's many accomplishments is in order as we dedicate this first volume to his scholarly contributions. A National

Fellow of the Indian Council of Social Science Research at the Indian Institute of Public Administration, New Delhi, Professor Jain is a scholar of international repute. Earlier he has been Dean, Faculty of Social Sciences and Professor and Head, Department of Political Science, University of Delhi, Professor and Head, Department of Public Administration, Punjabi University, Patiala, and Professor of Public Administration at the Indian Institute of Public Administration, New Delhi. He has held visiting appointments at various Universities in Canada, USA and Germany and has lectured in all the continents. He has been a former editor of *Indian Journal of Political Science*, and a member of the Editorial Boards of *The Indian Journal of Public Administration* and *Environment and Security* (Canada). He has authored/edited 33 books and published more than 180 articles in referred Journals and compendiums all over the world. It is difficult for a student of bureaucracy to not know of his name and to not have cited his work. Among his recent and most widely read books are: *Governing Development Across Cultures: Challenges and Dilemmas of an Emerging Sub-Discipline in Political Science* (Barbara Budrich, 2007) *Globalization and Good Governance: Pressures for Constructive Reforms* (New Delhi, 2005), and *Public Administration in India: 21st Century Challenges for Good Governance* (2001, and 2002). He is on the panels of consultants and reviewers to various foundations and organizations, and international journals in India and abroad. He has written extensively on Comparative Public Administration, Public Policy and Electoral and Party Reforms, Good Governance, E-governance, Legislative studies, and Political and Bureaucratic Corruption. He has been bestowed with many honors at home and abroad. Most importantly, he has mentored many doctoral students and aspiring young professionals. If leadership is about inspiring others to go where they could not have gone on their own, Professor Jain is a true leader in the field of Public Administration. He has recently been honoured with the Distinguished Member Award by the Indian Institute of Public Administration, New Delhi for his contribution to the discipline of Public Administration.

Contributions for this volume are organized around the theme of globalization, governance and technology since the three intersect to make the complex environment in which bureaucracies are supposed to succeed today. The first drafts of some of the chapters were presented at a conference held in Tampa, Florida jointly organized by IPSA Research Committees 04 and 35 in September of 2005. The theme continued to evolve in 2006 when a few more scholars presented their ideas at the International Political Science Association's World Congress meeting in Fukuoka, Japan. Two additional chapters were sought in 2007 to provide a regional balance to the volume. Professor Jain has always been a visionary person and we hope that this forward looking, visionary theme will do justice to his vision.

During the preparation of this volume, many friends and colleagues have assisted. First and foremost, we profusely thank all the contributors for taking ownership of the theme and engaging in a lively discussion at both conferences. Many others have also helped in various capacities during the conferences by critiquing the papers and challenging the authors to stretch their thought processes. We also thank the Kiran C. Patel Center for Global Solutions at the University of South Florida to host the 2005 meeting which led to the germination of the idea. Thanks to Lisa Fairchild for helping on the first draft of the manuscript. Erin Steurer deserves much credit and special thanks for formatting and revising the manuscript but above all her patience for accommodating our "unreasonable" deadlines. Their assistance has been invaluable. Finally, my personal thanks to my co-editor, Dr. Dhirendra Vajpeyi, for keeping me on track and not letting me buckle down under administrative pressures of the provost's job. It has been gratifying and uplifting to be part of this dedication project.

RENU KHATOR

# List of Contributors

**O.P. Dwivedi**, *Order of Canada*, Ph.D., LL.D. (Hon.), Fellow of the Royal Society of Canada, is University Professor Emeritus, Department of Political Science, University of Guelph, Guelph, Canada. He is a past President of the Canadian Political Science Association (Ottawa), President of the Canadian Asian Studies Association (Montreal), and a former Vice-President of the International Association of Schools and Institutes of Administration, Brussels, Belgium. He has authored, co-authored and edited 33 books and over 120 articles and chapters in books and scholarly journals. Most recently, he was Senior Research Scholar with the Kiran C. Patel Center for Global Solutions, University of South Florida, Tampa, USA (2005-2006).

**Trudy Eden** received her J.D. from Emory University, and her Ph.D. from Johns Hopkins University. She has published a book, *Cooking in America, 1690-1840* (Greenwood, 2006), and articles on food and culture and is currently working on a book-length project on food regulation. She is an associate professor at the University of Northern Iowa.

**Harold Fuhr** is Professor and Chair of International Relations at the Faculty of Economics and Social Sciences at the University of Potsdam, Potsdam, Germany. He holds a Ph.D. from the University of Konstanz, Germany where he also received the venia legendi for political and administrative science. Prof. Fuhr teaches International Relations and Development Politics; his main research interests are international development policies, the changing role of the political sector, and institutional reforms, in particular Latin America and the Near East. Prof. Fuhr has been consultant to *inter alia* the German Federal Ministry for Economic Cooperation and Development (BMZ), the German Society for Technical Assistance (GTZ), the World Bank and UNDP. His latest publication is a co-edited volume *Leadership and Innovation in Subnational Government: Case Studies from Latin America* published in 2004 by the World Bank Institute.

**Kofi Glover** received his Ph.D. in Political Science, in 1975 from Indiana University. Presently he is the Associate Provost at the University of South Florida, Tampa. He is also an adjunct Professor in the

Department of African Studies. His areas of research are comparative, and International Politics.

**Leonardo Patricio Grottola** holds a degree in Political Science from the University of Buenos Aires (UBA). As an assistant researcher at the Instituto de Investigaciones Gino Germani (IIGG/UBA) he is working on several projects on development and institutions. He is also a member of the Public Sector and State Reform Research Program at the IIGG.

**R.B. Jain,** Ph.D. is currently a National Fellow of the Indian Council of Social Science Research (ICSSR), at the Indian Institute of Public Administration, New Delhi. Earlier he has been Dean, Faculty of Social Sciences and Professor and Head, Department of Political Science, University of Delhi, Professor and Head, Department of Public Administration, Punjabi University, Patiala, and Professor of Public Administration at the Indian Institute of Public Administration, New Delhi. He is the President Emeritus of the International Political Science's Research Committee 4 on Public Bureaucracies in Developing Societies and a former Editor of the *Indian Journal of Political Science,* and is presently on the Editorial Board of *Indian Journal of Public Administration, Environment and Security* (Canada), a member of the Board of Centre for Business and Public Service Ethics (Cambridge). He is also associated with many national/international private and public educational institutions and foundations as consultant. He has been a UN expert on Economic Sanctions (1999) and a member of the Advisory Panel on Electoral Reforms and Standards in Public Life of the Government of India's National Commission to Review the working of the Constitution (2000-2003). He has published extensively on legislative studies, comparative public administration, bureaucracy and governance, and is the author/editor of 33 books and more than 180 articles in scholarly journals and chapters in the books published in all the continents.

**Li Jian** is an Assistant Professor of Anthropology at the University of Northern Iowa. He has conducted ethnographic field research in China, Thailand, Laos, and Myanmar. He has published research articles in Human Organization; Culture and Agriculture; China's Ethnic Groups; the Chinese Journal of Schistosomiasis Control; Anthropology News; Journal of SESA; and Journal of China's Central University for Nationalities. His current research focuses on development and health, medical anthropology, and emerging and re-emerging infectious diseases.

**Mora Kantor** holds a degree in Political Science from the University of Buenos Aires (UBA). As an assistant researcher and an Assistant Professor at the Instituto de Investigaciones Gino Germani (IIGG/UBA) she is a member of the Public Sector and State Reform Research Program.

**Renu Khator** received her Ph.D. from Purdue University in 1985. She is currently the Provost and Senior Vice-President at the University of South Florida. She has been the Chair of the International Political Science Association's (IPSA's) Research Committee 4, Public Bureaucracies in Developing Societies since 2003. Dr. Khator has published five books, and articles in numerous scholarly journals in the area of environmental policy and sustainable development. She is the recipient of many prestigious awards, including the *Hind Rattan* (Jewel of India), Outstanding American by Choice by the United States Government, and Outstanding Contributions by the American Foundation for Greek Language and Culture (AFGLC).

**Markus Lederer** is an Assistant Professor at the University of Potsdam, Potsdam, Germany, where he teaches International Relations, International Political Economy, and Development Politics. He holds a MA and a Ph.D. in political science from the University of Munich and has been a visiting scholar at Columbia University in New York. Dr. Lederer has specialized on international financial regulation, in particular money laundering and terrorist finance. He also works on issues of global governance and development politics. His latest publication is a co-edited volume *Criticizing Global Government* published in 2005 by Palgrave.

**Philip Mauceri** received his Ph.D. from Columbia University. He is Professor at the University of Northern Iowa since 1994. His areas of research are political violence, human rights and Latin American Politics. He is the author and co-editor of four books (*Politics in the Andes, Ethnic Conflict and International Relations, State Under Siege: Policy and Development in Peru, The Peruvian Lagyrinth: Polity, Economy and Society*) as well as several articles, and is the recipient of two Fulbright awards (to Colombia and the Dominican Republic).

**Jorge Nef** is Professor in Rural Extension Studies and International Development at the University of Guelph, Canada, and Director of the Institute for the Study of Latin America and the Caribbean (ISLAC) at the University of South Florida, USA. His areas of research include human security, political economy, inter-American relations, global studies, and public policy. He is a current Vice-President of the Canadian Society for the Study of International Development, a past President of the Canadian Association of Latin America and Caribbean Studies, the recipient of many teaching awards and recognitions throughout his career, and inducted into the World Academy of Art and Science (2003).

**Csaba Nikolenyi** received his Ph.D. from the University of British Columbia in 2000. Presently, he is an Associate Professor at Concordia University's Department of Political Science. His current work focuses on the stability of executive coalitions and the formation of pre-electoral alliances in the multiparty systems of post-communist East-Central Europe. His work has been published in a variety of journals including *Party Politics, the Canadian Journal of Political Science, Communist and Post-Communist Studies, Europe-Asia Studies and the Japanese Journal of Political Science*. In 2006, he was appointed as the English Co-Editor of the *Canadian Journal of Political Science*, and he is also an executive member of the Research Committee of Legislative Specialists of the International Political Science Association.

**Dora Orlansky** is a Sociologist (University of Buenos Aires, UBA) with a Ph.D. in Administration (UBA). She is full Professor in State Reform at the Political Science Department (UBA) and Director of the Public Sector and State Reform Research Program at the Instituto de Investigaciones Gino Germani (IIGG-UBA). She has conducted research projects in academic centers in Argentina and elsewhere; has been a consultant for international agencies (UN, IDB, ILO, UNESCO, etc.); held different positions as an adviser for the government of Argentina. Her contributions (more than 70) in different areas of social sciences have been published in Argentina and foreign journals and books. Fellowships and Awards: William and Flora Hewlett Visiting Latin American Scholars Program, Ford Foundation, René Thalmann Fellowship, Fulbright Research Fellowship, Complutense University of Madrid-CICLOS/UBA, Scientific Research (UBA), French Government/Sorbonne, University of Paris, etc.

**Alice Sindzingre** is a Research Fellow currently posted at the French agency for research, the National Centre for Scientific Research (Centre National de la Recherche Scientifique/CNRS, Paris) and affiliated to the University Paris-X-Nanterre (Research Center Economics). She is also Research Associate and Visiting Lecturer at the School of Oriental and African Studies (SOAS, Department of Economics, University of London). She holds a Masters degree in Business Administration from the University Paris IX-Dauphine, a Ph.D. in anthropology from the EDESS (School of Advanced Studies in Social Sciences, Paris) and a post-graduate diploma in economics from ENSAE (National School of Statistics and Economic Administration, Paris). She has conducted research on development economics and political economy mostly in West Africa. She has also served as a consultant for international organizations and governments. She has been a member of the Core Team of the World Development Report 2000/1 of the World Banks, 'Attacking Poverty.' She has published in academic journals on a large range of topics, including poverty, globalization, corruptions, the concept of the developmental state, the political economy of development, and the theory of institutions in relation with development.

**Keshav C. Sharma**, M.A. (Econ. & Public Adm.), M.P.A. (ISS, The Hague), Doctor of Social Sciences (Amsterdam) is now a Professor in the Department of Political and Administrative Studies at the University of Botswana. He has served several universities in Africa, Asia, Europe, the U.K., and the U.S. and has published extensively. He has undertaken consultancies for international organizations and served on the editorial boards of international journals.

**Erin Steurer** is a Graduate Assistant/Teaching Assistant in Environmental Science and Policy program at the University of South Florida, Tampa. Her research interests include globalization, the environment, and the role of international organizations in promoting sustainable development. She is also an Administrative Secretary to RC 04, 'Public Bureaucracies in Developing Societies of IPSA.'

**Reeta Chowdhari Tremblay** is the Dean, Faculty of Arts, and a Professor of Political Science at Memorial University, St. John's, Newfoundland, Canada. She completed her doctoral studies at the University of Chicago. Her areas of research include comparative public policy, comparative federalism, nation-state and secessionist movements in South Asia and Indian popular cinema. She is a member of the editorial boards of several prestigious journals in Political Science and Asian Studies. Her recent publications include *Human Rights: A General Overview* (forthcoming), *Mapping the Political Landscape* (2004, 2006) and several articles and reviews in many journals.

**Dhirendra Vajpeyi** is a Professor of Political Science at the University of Northern Iowa. He has authored, co-authored, or edited fifteen books and numerous articles. His books include *Environmental Policies in the Third World; Technology and Development; Local Government and Politics in the Third World, Indira Gandhi's India; Deforestation, Environment, and Sustainable Development, A Comparative Analysis, Civil-Military Relations, Nation-Building, and National Identity*; and *Local Democracy and Politics in South Asia.* Currently he is Chair of the Research Committee on Technology and Development RC 35 of International Political Science Association. He is also a member of the Executive Board of the Research Committee on Public Bureaucracies in Developing Societies.

# Introduction

## Globalization, Bureaucracy, and Sustainable Development

Dhirendra K. Vajpeyi and Renu Khator

The collapse of the Soviet Union in 1991 drastically changed the political, economic, and security map of not only Europe but proved to be of tremendous importance to the rest of the world. An international economic and security system which had dominated the world since WWII was finally overturned. The disappearance of a formidable competitor—the Soviet Union—also left the United States of America as the sole superpower in the global arena with unprecedented economic and military power. This preponderance gave America tremendous freedom of action which, according to several observers, has led to the "unilateral impulse in American foreign policy" and to the "arrogance of power" (Gilpin 2000) which often means treating others as "instruments in a concert with an American conductor" (Hoffmann 2000: 6). Translated into economic terms it meant an aggressive push to bury the last remnants of already disgraced Marxist utopia of prosperity, and relentlessly invoke the free market visions of Frederick Hayek and Adam Smith to solve the global economic problems which plague most of the world. The Cold War preoccupation with the realist (masculine—coercive) paradigm had, by and large, excluded non-military threats and non-military means to achieve prosperity and security. Other causes of conflicts such as economic disparity between the industrialized countries (North) and the impoverished countries (South) of Asia, Africa, and Latin America, issues related to human rights, environmental degradation, concentration of *defacto* power in the hands of a few, mainly European, (former colonialists) in the United Nations Security Council and other major international political and financial institutions (World Bank, International Monetary Fund [IMF]) took a backseat to the ideological conflict between America and the Soviet Union. Even the 'reluctant American imperialists' (Mallaby 2002: 2-7) and cold war warriors realize that American prosperity and political-military dominance requires a somewhat different approach to placate "too many millions whose dreams are more vulgar, more real—whose raw energies and desires will overwhelm the visions of elites, remaking the future into something frighteningly new" (Kaplan 2000: 48). Hence the need for a more balanced, just, and 'holistic' approach to social, economic, and political issues—ethnic/religious conflicts, terrorism, political instability, poverty, environmental degradation, immigration—became more apparent and urgent. Failure to manage these problems, it was realized, could pose serious threat to the nation-state and could spill over into the international arena. The so-called 'Washington consensus' emerged out of the belief that free flow of goods, ideas, and technology across national borders with minimum state regulations will usher a brave new world of economic prosperity, democracy, and harmony to all. As democracies do not go to war with each other so will the prosperous people not engage in conflicts. The panacea to cure all the ills came to be known as globalization. It has been embraced as the new *mantra*, the buzzword of the 1990s, as well as the continuation of modernization. It has mesmerized the free market champions (the Bhagwatis) and has disenchanted the neo-liberals (the Kaplans), supporters of state sovereignty, and the nationalists. However, despite its new armor and shine it is not a new phenomenon. From time immemorial goods, commerce, ideas, and technologies (from printing press to gun powder) have moved across continents without the Internet, the World Trade Organization (WTO), and the Harvard Business School. What is new is the tempo and the intensity of support and opposition among its promoters and detractors on its nature and impact of the reincarnated concept. It has raised serious questions about the relationship between political and economic realms. It has been viewed as "anything from Internet to a hamburger, from McDonaldization to democratization, from universal civilization to a common destiny of mankind to 'neo-colonialism.' It has become a very emotionally charged issue in public discourse. For some it implies the promise of an international civil society, conducive to a new era of peace and democratization. For others it implies the threat of an American economic domination, and political hegemony with its cultural consequences being a homogenized world resembling a sort of metastasized Disneyland" (Berger and Huntington [eds.] 2002: 2). The following definitions will give us some idea of this schism:

1. "Globalization refers to all those processes by which the peoples of the world are incorporated into a single world society, a global society" (Albrow 1990).

2. "The characteristics of the globalization trend include the internationalizing of production, the new international division of labor, new migratory movements from South to North, the new competitive environment that accelerates these processes and the internationalizing of the state . . . making states into agencies of the globalizing world" (Cox 1993).
3. "Globalization is what we in the Third World have for several centuries called colonialism" (Khor 1995).
4. Globalization is the "widening, deepening, and speeding up of global interconnectedness across economic, technological, cultural, social, and political spheres." (Held *et. al.* 1999: 14).
5. "Globalization promotes integration and the removal of cultural barriers and the negative dimensions of culture. Globalization is a vital step toward both a more stable world and better lives for the people in it" (Rothkapf 1997: 442).
6. "Globalization means an increase in global interdependence along with the awareness of that interdependence" (Hsiao 2002: 49).
7. "Globalization is itself a multilayered and multicentered process" (Akoi 2002: 87-88).
8. Globalization as a "second bourgeois revolution" (Webb 2006: 80).

Above views present the following main facets/aspects of globalization, and its impact on international behavior:

- internationalization of finance,
- increased international trade,
- adoption and application of new technologies,
- reduced role of the sovereign state, and the emergence of non-state actors such as the Non-governmental Organizations (NGOs), and multinational, multilateral agencies (the World Bank, the IMF, General Electric, etc.) in international political and economic affairs,
- increased migration driven by labor demands from South to North,
- homogenization of cultures, emergence of a global culture, and spread of democratic values.

The globalization paradigm is essentially driven by economic concerns and represents "an international culture of business and political leaders" (Berger and Huntington 2002: 3) which without doubt will have impact on social and political aspects of international life. It is basically integrationist and envisions a global society dominated by certain universal core values. However, not everybody has joined the globalization bandwagon. It has produced both pessimists and cheerleaders. Huntington (1996) spoke of the 'clash of civilizations,' Fukuyama (1992) predicted 'the end of history and man,' Korbin (1996) lamented the 'return back to medievalism,' and a French official called it a "cultural Chernobyl" (Berger and Huntington 2002: 2). The cheerleaders feel that the process of political and economic globalization will give humanity a new way to solve economic problems, will bring diverse cultural and economic systems under a cooperative framework. Such integration will create a global village where life will be less 'nasty, brutish, and short.' They chide and belittle the critics of globalization as 'kids,' 'leftwing students,' and 'young people' (Bhagwati 2002: 2-7) maintaining that economic openness does lift more people up than it pushes down (Kitching 2001). The pessimists, or in Kaplan's (2001) words 'tragic realists' have not been as cheerful about the impact of globalization on political and economic spheres as the 'globalists' have been. Several of them dismiss globalization as no more than a fashionable myth; "a constellation of market, technological, ideological and civilizational developments that have nothing in common" (Falk 1997). Gill (1997) denounces globalization's "economism, its economic reductionism, its political cynicism, defeatism, and immobilism," while Appadorai (2001) calls it 'cocacola colonization,' a perceived system in which economic and political power remains in the hands of entrepreneurial class which aims to preserve, as much as possible, its superiority. "It has created a '20-80 society' and the rising tide has not lifted all boats" (Webb 2006: 80). The much-touted trickle down evaporates before it reaches the poorest and the weakest in the society (Vajpeyi 1998: 43-47). According to the World Watch Institute, the world's total income rose from $10.1 trillion in 1970 to approximately $20 trillion in 1994 but not all nations have become richer. The gross domestic product and the availability of basic needs have declined in Asia, Africa, and Latin America (Klare 2000: 134). "Any belief that either the end of major ideological competition or the revolutionary process of economic globalization would prevent conflict has been revealed as utterly wishful thinking" (Annan 2002: 125). This polarized debate on expected global integration, and/or fragmentation presents further fodder to the debate. It has been observed that the growth of transnational corporations and NGOs—because of their 'state'—indifferent nature—and the spread of global capitalism have made the Westphalia state irrelevant to even obsolescent (Ball 1967; Naisbitt 1994; Ohame 1995), and that global capitalism has led to the creation of supra-state governing agencies that are supplanting the territorial nation-states (Cox 1993) and that global corporations will help create a world order beyond nation-states (Reich 1991), a 'world government' with 'global management' (Wilson 1994: 305-318, Webb 2006: 76). It has also been suggested that global capitalism has eroded the sense of community and urban power structure (Mele 1996; Knox 1997) causing the loss of urban jobs. Increased dependency of less developed countries, IMF dictated structural adjustments have exacerbated their (less developed countries) fiscal crisis and have created a serious problem of governability in these nations (Kregel 1998; Vajpeyi 1998: 185-230).

The globalists point out that international security viewed in the framework of globalization emphasizes integration, openness, and cooperation instead of the Cold War competitive-confrontational model. A review of recent literature on globalization challenges these globalist notions by asserting that globalization is not a win-win situation. Global free trade promoters argue that globalization creates jobs, makes business corporations more competitive and efficient, lowers prices for consumers, provides poor countries, through infusions of foreign capital and technology, with the chance to develop economically, creates favorable conditions for democracy and greater respect for human rights (Finnegan 2000: 42), and makes public opinion and debates more open and transparent on critical social issues such as environmental degradation, and violence against women and children. This is also the picture the Americans and their free trade partners present. It has been accepted by businesses, governments, and policy-makers in many Third World countries as the 'Washington consensus.' Critics of this 'consensus,' however, dispute these claims by pointing out that this growth is wasteful, destructive and unjust to weaker sections of the society. The economic policies imposed on developing countries by the World Bank and the IMF have widened the gap between the rich and the poor. The suggested 'structural adjustments' and 'conditionalities' have weakened the economic and political structures of these LDCs. "A small number of people are doing very well indeed, but the vast majority is suffering more than ever. There are wonderful things in the shops now, but who can buy them?" (*Time*, April 24, 2000). The lion's share of private international financial flow has continued to go to capital abundant nations. Most of the developing world has not been as fortunate as China (Assadourian 2005: 44). A few countries might be shinning but most of them are still struggling. "The dark side of globalization in which the new illusions of familiarity are enlisted in the service of a nasty atavism" (*The New Republic* 2000, February 21: 9). "As globalization has intensified, the gap between per capita incomes in rich and poor countries has widened. Although this trend has been around for the past two centuries it has accelerated in recent years" (Cutter *et al.* 2000: 93). "This time, the United States has put its hegemonic weight behind developing the open world economy—creating multilateral institutions, sponsoring trade rounds, opening its own markets to imports, and singing the praises of commercial liberalism" (Ikenberry 2000: 146). It is also pointed out that "economic policy is today, perhaps the most important part of America's interaction with the rest of the world and yet the culture of international economic policy in the world's most powerful democracy is not democratic" (Stiglitz 2000: 60). According to Kofi Annan (2000: 126), "throughout much of the developing world, the awakening to globalization's downside has been one of the resistance and resignation, a feeling that globalization is a false God foisted on weaker states by the capitalist centers of the West. Globalization is seen, not as a term describing objective reality, but as an ideology of predatory capitalism." The above discussion is just a glimpse of disagreements on the nature and the goals of globalization. It is still uncertain as to how the process will play out in the future. Many questions remain unanswered (Sachs 2000: 219-26).

1. Will globalization promote faster economic growth especially for the poorest of the world (4.5 billion people)?

2. Will globalization promote or undermine macroeconomic stability?
3. Will globalization promote growing income inequalities?
4. How will governmental institutions at all levels—regional, national, and international—adjust their powers and responsibilities in view of the emergence of a global market?

Besides these economic questions there are several other aspects of globalization which have come under severe scrutiny.

1. Impact of globalization on ethnic-religious lives of the people and societies.
2. impact on global culture diversity.
3. impact on the environment, human rights, and overall political development and nation-building of emerging economies and political systems, and on international security.
4. Role of the sovereign state in relation to transnational corporations, and international non-governmental organizations.
5. Will it fare better than modernization approach? Does it mean post-modernity, or late modernity or Americanization, rupture, or continuity? (Shami 2001: 221).

Following is a brief discussion of the impact of globalization on several core issues which impinge on the overall human security—economic, political, and socio-cultural.

## ETHNIC CONFLICTS

The causes that contribute to heightened ethnic consciousness and politicization vary from country/region to country/region. Ethno-nationalistic movements can be triggered by domestic and external factors, or a combination of both such as spread of modernity (Hall 1998: 251-67; Harvey 1990; Riggs 1998; Thompson 1983; Vajpeyi 1979; Vajpeyi 1994; Wallerstein 1976: 131-35) which could be introduced from within or adopted from the outside. Development of world commercialism (globalization) is one such factor. According to Friedman, globalization and the development of world capitalism is a major factor which produces ethnic conflicts. It creates losers and winners. The losers oftentimes resent the success of the winners and find justification in vilifying the winners, especially if they belong to other cultures or ethnic and religious groups. Globalization in institutional terms "entails the formation of international communities, however loosely knit, that share common interests" (Friedman 1998: 242). Global systems insofar as they are based on commercial economics tend to be characterized by hegemonic centers in which individualism is developed to such an extent that ethnicity takes on essential characteristics. The world of 'hegemonic' growth is one in which hegemonic classes tend to form as the elites of culturally 'hegemonizing' states and where the multicultured is spatially differentiated and hierarchical (Friedman 1998: 248-49). Globalization also nibbles at the state authority by introducing international corporations and other important political and economic actors in decision-making processes. Ethnic groups that feel that they are being left out or could make better deals without the state raise issues clothed in patriotic-nationalist rhetoric, and attack the national or dominant elites for selling out national interests to outsiders. In doing so they aim to weaken the state, and enhance their bargaining power *vis-à-vis* the state. Tehranian maintains that forces of globalism result in large-scale population migration from areas that are not benefiting from globalization of the world economy. The migrants solidify extreme ethnic groups that have been left out. Tehranian (1998: 289-303) observes that some of the major trends in global conflicts are results of globalization, localization, and indigenization movements, such as that of Islamism."

## RELIGIOUS CONFLICTS

Recent debates and discussions on the nature and impact of globalization, political development, and impending 'clash of civilizations' point out that somehow it was the failure of modernization approach to nation-building which contributed to a large extent "the re-emergence of religious values and fundamentalism in both advanced industrialized societies and non-industrialized societies (Melitza 2000: 75-90; Nandy 1985: 1-10; Taylor 1988) including the powerful 'ultramontane' impact of religion, especially resurgent Islam (Lewis 1990: 47-54; Esposito 1992; Fuller 2002: 48-60). This 'unsecularization of the world' is a side effect of modernization, 'the revenge of God' (Giles 1994) in the post-Cold War era. In my opinion these arguments fail to take into consideration that religion 'embodied in desperate human cultures' has always "served as the foundation for national differences, racial conflicts, class exploitation and the resolution of hostility and the achievement of full humanity for those at the bottom of all societies on the other" (Hopkins 2001: 1). Hindu-Muslim conflicts in India, Protestant-Catholic strife in Ireland, Christian-Jew problems in Europe and elsewhere, wars between animists, Christians, and Muslims in Africa and even Shia-Sunni violence are not new. Inquisitions, holy and just wars have plagued humanity since time immemorial. In the earlier part of the 20$^{th}$ century (1914-1950) the oppressed people of Asia, Latin America, and Africa did use religious ideologies and symbols against colonial powers of Europe. Religion united them against their common enemy but it also divided them. Religious revivals, oftentimes, legitimized their extreme rhetoric and actions. The creation of Pakistan and the new state of Israel were pre-1950. The post-WWII era was characterized by a Cold War between U.S.-led Western Europe, and the Soviet Union-led Eastern Europe. In ideological terms a competition and confrontation ensued between capitalism, free market, democracy on one hand, and planned (command) economy (communism) non-democratic systems on the other. Oftentimes this conflict was presented as a conflict between 'in God we trust' morally good side and the 'atheist' (Godless) evil empire in heavily peppered religious tones. Their determination to superimpose one system over the other exhausted much time and energy. They simply ignored many other global problems if they did not pose any threat to their well-crafted view of the world. Political and military alliances with religious fanatics like Osama bin Laden, Zia of Pakistan, Uzbeks, and Chechens, and Saudis were acceptable. In sum, religious fundamentalism was justified as part of the just and moral war. Hence to argue that religious strifes have been revitalized (Huntington 1997: 47) during the post-Cold War is at best a very weak/explanation of their past (academics and security experts) failure to give sufficient attention to religion's role in the international/national security.

The above discussion raises a related question to the framework of this paper. Has globalization accelerated or originated religious strife? There is no doubt that increased and easily available communication facilities have provided new opportunities not only for international transfer of capital and ideas but also to bin Laden's al Qaeda, and other groups to carry out their political and religious agendas. International immigration not only has physical/geographical consequences for the immigrants and the host societies, it also solidifies religious and ethnic identities of the immigrants. In short, intense increase in ethnic and religious identification is a prelude to confrontation with other groups, and possibly challenges to state authority by inflating their importance and demands. The fear of being inundated and assimilated by more powerful religion becomes real beyond one's own national boundaries. McDonald's, MTV, and Hollywood are viewed as "vicious and insidious attacks on the very foundation of civilizations" (Dougherty 2001: 23). A threat to one's culture becomes a threat to one's God, one's ancestors and one's core identity" (Rothkopf 1997: 443) and prefabrication of cultural and religious past. "The growing pressures of the globalizing economy energized by further squeezing by the World Bank, the International Monetary Fund, U.S. monopoly corporations, and local elites have fostered a persistent resurgence of indigenous grass-root communities, often bolstered by liberation theologies and a politicized spirituality and survival and freedom" (Hopkins 2001: 5).

## GLOBALIZATION, DEMOCRATIZATION, AND SOCIAL CAPITAL

Proponents of democratization from Lipset (1959) to Milton Friedman (1962), World Bank, International Monetary Funders, Jagdish Bhagwati (2002), Gilpin (2000) and many others have consistently maintained that free market at a global level accomplishes three things (Kaplan 2001: 23).

1. weakens the coercive power of the state,
2. creates a more democratic middle class, and
3. transforms political culture by exposing masses to democratic—participant—liberal ideas from abroad.

These tenets have influenced both liberal (Clintonites) and conservatives (Bush) policy-makers in America. "Freedom to trade is the great subversive and liberating force in human history." Free trade, according to free market globalists will usher democracy and respect for human rights in non-democratic countries. Nations and people who trade with each other do not go to war against each other. Big Macs, and Papa Murphy's pizza will have a domino effect on totalitarian systems. Peace through trade, investment, and commerce will be achieved. Opponents of the above arguments point out that capitalist transformations weaken rather than strengthen liberalism (Moore 1993). American policy-makers have held that trade with China will create a freedom loving middle class and respect for human rights. Kaplan points out that no such developments are taking place in China. The Chinese Communist Party "restricts private property, it prohibits independent churches and labor unions, truly autonomous social organizations, and any other civic institutions that might plausibly compete with the state." It monitors email exchanges, blocks access to 'damaging' topics and to western news sources...prosecutes "thousands of people for crimes no greater than practicing breathing exercises...and exercising freedom of expression association or worship" (Kaplan 2001: 23-27). Saudi Arabia is another case in point. It has free trade relations with the West, political and military alliances with Americans and Europeans, but it is neither democratic nor tolerant to the rights of humans—women, non-Muslims and even non-Saudi Arabs. It has supported Taliban and is still one of the major sources of funds to all sorts of shady organizations around the world. Egypt, Kuwait, and Indonesia could be added to this list. Multinational Corporations in the name of globalization demand greater tax and investment freedoms and privileges but put business first, democracy later. Western investment in China far outpaces its investment in India, not that India has fewer skilled people and is less democratic than China or even Singapore. Also, "free trade is not only good economic policy it is good human rights policy" observed U.S. Secretary of State Powell. Then the free trade instead of economic sanctions should have also reformed Saddam's behavior. Also if a positive linkage between globalization and democratization is accepted then one must be prepared to accept challenges and problems which democratization might pose. According to several scholars, the recent third wave of democratization has released pent up ethnic and religious frustrations all over the world. They maintain that "as the level of democracy increases in a heterogeneous state, the opportunities and potential payoffs of ethnic mobilization and protests increase relative to more violent forms of political action" (Gurr 1999: 9). In Latin America in general, and Bolivia and Ecuador in particular, mobilization of indigenous groups is linked with democratization of these societies. A similar situation exists in Eastern Europe and Russia. Recent electoral victory of Hamas in Palestine is another example of democratization and its consequences on unassimilated groups. How post-Taliban Afghanistan and post-Saddam Iraq cope with globalization-democratization will be interesting to watch. In a global economy which is a more and more interconnected one, many of even apparently small religious/ethnic conflicts have the potential of producing strong side effects in the neighboring and even distant countries. Such conflicts also question the legitimacy of governing elites and ultimately weaken the state itself.

### Social Capital

As discussed above, globalization's impact on democratization, redefinition of ethnic and religious identities also generates forces which reshape social capital and help in the emergence of a civil society as a significant political force (Tulchin *et al.* 2002: 116). Social capital is "civic engagement involving both private and public political organizations" (Mauceri 2003: 3; Foley and Edwards 1996: 38-42). Mauceri (2003: 3) maintains that "social capital is the 'glue' of civil society helping to determine the density and bonding of a broad range of social organizations and relationships," however globalization's impact will vary and would have different consequences for different societies.

TABLE 1.1
**Impact of Globalization on Social Capital and Implications for Democracy***

| *Globalization Processes* | *Social Capital Outcome Scenarios* | *Democratic Challenges of Social Capital Outcomes* |
|---|---|---|
| — Market Liberalization | 1. Decline and Atomization | — Collective Action Problems |
| — Communication Revolution | | — Demagoguery/ Opportunism |
| — Consumerism | 2. Issue/Identity Transformation | — Disjunction between issues and institutions: unresponsiveness |
| — Limitations on the State | | — Exclusion/Conformity |

*(Mauceri 2003: 4).

## WEAKENING OF THE SOVEREIGN STATE AND THE ROLE OF BUREAUCRACY

Globalization in the name of integration not only seeks a new configuration of the international system but it also tends to influence the traditional role of the Westphalian sovereign state. Traditionally the state through its regulative, distributive, and coercive powers consolidates different groups in the society. It acts as a judge, jury, and executioner. It determines the economic and social policies to maintain a working balance between competing groups in the society. Globalization by its very nature intrudes into vital spheres of national policies and thereby sets itself as 'competitor' with a great degree of autonomy and freedom. Globalization is seen "as an ever tightening vise increasing the demands on states to provide safety nets while limiting their ability to do so" (Annan 2000: 126). Also, as "globalization proceeds, state roles and structures experience significant transformations. Weberian bureaucracy is becoming New Public Management (NPM), while the Keynesian model that previously formed state-economy relations is losing its hegemony to neo-liberal and monetarist theory" (Sven 2004: 282). The debate between the "proponents of state redundancy *versus* the champions of continuing state potency" presents following arguments (Clarke 1999: 44-45).

1. Since national economies will be part of the global economy the role of the state in defining and managing economic policies will be reduced (Reich 1991: 3; Higgat 1996: 33; Rosenau 1997: 362). George Soros (2002) an ardent supporter of globalization concluded that "international finance and trade have outstripped the capacity of sovereign states to manage the politics of globalization."
2. The success of free open market global economic system depends on free flow of goods and finance across borders. It invites powerful transnational corporations (TNCs) to heavily invest in countries such as China, Mexico, and Thailand, which provide them a hospitable business climate—weak or non-existent labor unions, lax environmental laws, and large tax benefits. In many cases these TNCs have more financial resources than the total annual budget of the host states. Also most of these TNCs are owned by Western/European conglomerates. They receive strong political support from their respective governments. It has also been pointed out that these TNCs invest very little, if any, in delivering and supporting social policies helpful to the weakest in the society, those who might have lost their farmland, or jobs due to the transnationalization of native businesses. In fact they exacerbate and even exploit the vast social and economic inequalities that exist in the world (Epstein and Chen 2002: 29). These developments encroach on the state's power by subverting the state's capacity "to control and protect the international life of society" (Falk 1997: 124-25). It is also expected that in a globalized system trading partners will become political partners, and the economic interdependence would eliminate the potential for political and military conflicts (Annan 2002: 127). It has turned out to be a wishful thinking and a false promise. As discussed earlier, globalization has neither brought economic prosperity to most of the people in the world nor has it ushered democracy especially in those countries which seem to have benefited most from global investment. In many countries—Asia, Africa, and Latin America—the gross domestic product has declined, and especially neglected have been public health, human rights, environmental protection, and other public goods (Soros 2002). "Those at the bottom are not doing so well at all. Some 852

million people go hungry each day, according to a 2004 estimate, equivalent to the combined population of North America, Japan, and Europe and increase of 18 million over the last decade" (Flavin, 2005: 15). The states' capacity to manage these issues has not increased with globalization. A diminished state cannot provide adequate safety nets. There have been more losers in these economies than the winners.

3. The above discussion pointed out the negative impact of globalization on the sovereign states' ability to make policies in their own borders; however, there are those who are not ready to bury the state. They maintain that globalization is not to weaken the state power. It will expand and strengthen the role of the state in an international framework of consensus and compromise based decision-making. A decision by WTO is as much binding on the U.S.A. as it is on Botswana. "This side of the argument is expressed once again in three principal versions:

    1. that all economic and market structures reflect political frameworks and choices;
    2. that the state remains potent in the development of the process of globalization itself; and
    3. that the state remains decisive, notwithstanding the effects and constraints of globalization" (Clarke 1999: 45).

In our view the traditional concept of state sovereignty has been going through change and transformation for a long period of time. With increasing interdependency, the role of the United Nations and many other multilateral agencies, the World Bank, IMF, the WTO, and emerging international NGOs, and concerns about environmental issues have already introduced subtle and not so subtle changes in the behavior of states around the world. Very few countries—even China, Russia and Pakistan—are willing to ignore international public opinion on many global issues related to human rights, terrorism, environmental protection, and so on. In the 21st century the state will be trimmer, relatively more transparent irrespective of purely economically driven globalization. As long as it is realized that "no one wants to reside in a totally closed society like North Korea, but complete integration and openness also bring their perils and achieving a fine balance between accessibility and security will be excruciatingly difficult" (Kennedy 2001: 43).

Pluralistic liberal democratic governance ensures that no one single group, especially the business and commercial interests in collusion with politicians, may keep on dominating the policymaking or regulatory regime while getting away with the degradation of the environment. This is true not only in the North but in developing nations like India and Sri Lanka where the presence of free press and independent judiciary has forced governments to take appropriate regulatory action to control pollution. Of course, it is important to strengthen the system of monitoring and enforcement of laws, and there is a need to shift the present focus on criminal prosecution to a greater reliance on civil penalties and liability. This will require transparency, accountability at all levels, and minimal transaction costs (Ghosh, 2004: 11). And this is attainable when good governance exists. Although "politics determines all," nevertheless it is the operationalization of that politics in the form of good governance that is the key to improving the quality of life, securing human and environmental security, and attaining sustainable growth thereby reducing poverty. The objective of good governance is to create conditions which enable a society to be ensured of healthy food, clean water, and sanitation, education health care, security, and justice so that people may lead dignified and meaningful lives. And one of the keys to attain good governance is the development of a trusted, trustworthy, and caring professional public service guided by honest political leaders. Nothing destroys public credibility in public institutions more than corruption in government; because it destroys confidence, undermines people's faith, diverts public resources to questionable deals, mocks the application of laws and judicial process, and casts deep shadows over the credibility of government policies and programs. Clearly, the prudent way forward for sustainable development and "well-being of all" has to be based on the existence of good governance in a country.

According to German philosopher Hegel, good governance defines the crucial relationship between civil society and the state. Good governance enables "participation of those concerned in the formulation and development of policies and programs and practices to equitable and sustainable system" (Tulchin 2002: 3). In a globalized-democratic context institutional capacity building (macro-level) and strengthening of citizen participation (micro-level) are essential for good governance. "Those who govern are responsive to the wishes and demands of citizens and various groups; formulation, adoption, execution, monitoring, and evaluation of governmental programs . . . which require accountability of those who govern their constituents within a system of laws, rules, regulations, and standards; mobilization of resources to pursue the developmental vision and achieve good outcomes" (LaQuian 2002: 99). In an ideal world if all the requisites of good governance could be achieved a globalized world would be politically, economically, and socially a sustainable system.

It is hoped that globalization will contribute to 'internationalization of the state' and 'of societies' (Goldmann 2001; Friedman 2005) and will increase the "internationality of political decision-making" (Goldman 2001) which will need the harnessing of technologies in general and information technologies (IT) in particular.

## GLOBALIZATION AND SUSTAINABLE DEVELOPMENT

Jorge Nef has argued that the fundamental premise of the dominant international paradigms which have emerged since the World War II (and especially since the collapse of the Soviet Union) is the notion that North is secure and the South is insecure (Nef 2005). Instead in an increasingly interdependent world, the weakness of the South increases the vulnerability of the North. There is a need to change the mental mode within the North which denies and resists any change to its age-old perception that developing nations are the problem. That is why there is a need to redefine or create a new global paradigm which supports human security and well-being of all. And, although the 1972 UN Conference on the Human Environment brought into discussion the concept/term of sustainable development, it was not until the publication of the World Commission on Environment and Development (WCED) Report, *Our Common Future,* in 1987 that this term received a worldwide acceptance and usage. This paradigm has dominated the world scene for about two decades but appears to have declined in its prestige since the World Summit in Johannesburg in 2002. According to Victor (2006: 92), "Sustainable development has become a cover for inaction and a black hole for resources; it is also a wasted opportunity." He further maintains that "governments and the UN system have also marginalized sustainable development by failing to articulate serious objectives and coherent strategies for its implementation" (2006: 94). There is a need to develop a new paradigm which smoothly functions in "global partnership for development" (Victor 2006: 94).

## CONCLUSION

As discussed above globalization is not an autonomous process solely driven by economic imperatives. It is a multidimensional politically driven and economically sustained process, and without a doubt will impact more than one aspect of society and politics:

1. Cultural autonomy will come under severe pressure in this 'reform and openness' (Appadorai 2001) because globalization "seeks a homogenized monoculture of the market to transform people" (Hopkins 2001: 13) often at the expense of local economies and cultures (Gardner 2002: 16).
2. Globalization and democratization will release pent up ethnic frustrations. In a weak state constraints on ethnic conflicts are reduced, mutual uncertainty about intentions increases, and the rivals are prompted to mobilize and take preemptive actions against one another (Gurr 1999: 6) and jeopardize both national and international security. It is to be noted here that no hard evidence links globalization with ethnic conflicts (Byman and VanEveral 1998: 11-21).
3. Increase in international trade (Figure 1.1) and emergence of non-state actors (TNCS, NGOs) will have impact on the behaviors of sovereign states and international security, however, in the absence

FIG. 1.1
**World Exports of Goods, 1950-2003 and of Goods and Services, 1970-2003**

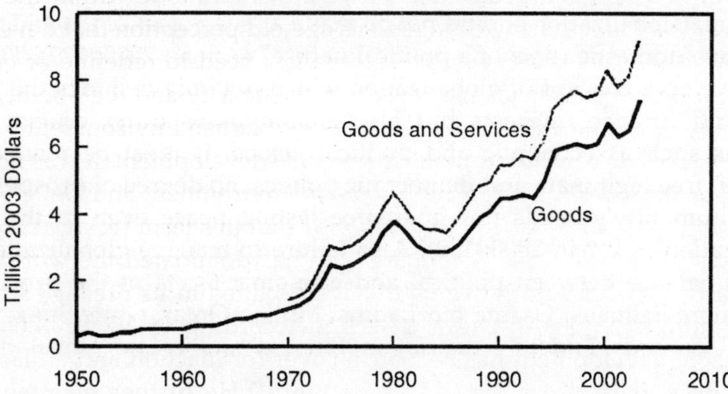


*Source* : IMF.

FIG. 1.2
**World Exports of Goods and Services as a Share of Gross World Product, 1970-2003**

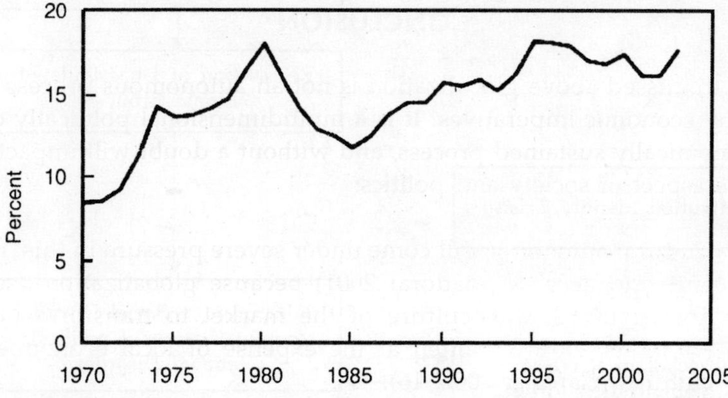


*Source* : IMF, OECD.

of hard data-based research it is difficult at this point to assess the benign or disruptive impact of these developments.

Here let us pause and ask ourselves, should we go back to medieval times, embrace Luddites or find a balanced and fair way to cope with the forces of change? 'Perception of siege is unmistakable' (Annan 2000: 127) among nationalists, culture-exclusivists, and fundamentalists who view globalization "as 'foreign invasion' and 'neo-colonialism' out to destroy local economies, cultures, traditions, and produce 'millions of mutinies'" (Naipaul

1990) which will eventually engulf and destabilize the international security system. History bears witness that international security and well being of humanity has been threatened by "power politics, hegemonic interests, suspicion, rivalry, greed, and corruption" (Annan 2000: 128) and politics of populism. Globalization should not be made a "scapegoat of ills which more often have domestic roots of a political nature" (Annan 2000: 129). The need is to develop a concept of globalization which not only includes the narrow trade and finance interests but also encompasses other crucial global concerns such as economic and political justice. It must be realized that "without free legitimate and democratic politics, no degree of prosperity can satisfy humanity's needs nor guarantee lasting peace even in the age of globalization" (Annan 2000: 130). Also failure to manage globalization, and strike a balance between political and economic facets of the process will create more Talibans, Osama bin Ladins, Mullah Omar, white Supremacists in the U.S. and Haiders (Austria) in Europe, and create global disorder (Table 1.2).

TABLE 1.2

**Authority, Social Disorder, and International Security**

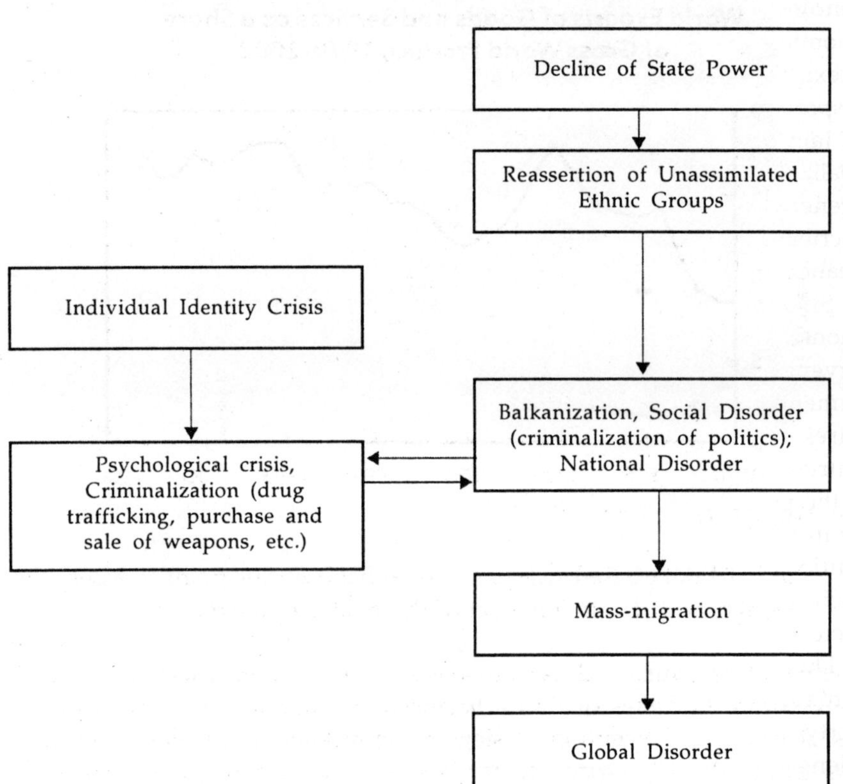

For globalization to succeed the world needs to create a network of institutions that can monitor, supervise, and enforce global standards of fairness and protection. Such institutions will require cooperation between public officials and the world's powerful organizations—both non-governmental and governmental. We must accept that institutional pluralism can coexist with diversity even in a global context. Real international security cannot be achieved by clinging to insecure ethnic, religious, and political ideological loyalties. Rich and powerful nations have to commit themselves not only to the goals of economic prosperity to their citizens but to people across the globe. Globalization will fail if it is bound to a specific ideology, country, or region. To succeed it has to be truly global. The events of September 11, 2001 might stimulate our thinking about the global consequences of an unglobal approach.

The above discussion presents a framework for essays included in this anthology. Eight essays (Dwivedi, Eden, Fuhr and Lederer, Jain, Vajpeyi and Khator, Sindzingre, Tremblay and Nikolenyi, and Vajpeyi) analyze broader issues related to globalization, technology, and good governance in a comparative perspective. Other six essays (Khator *et al.*, Li Jian, Mauceri, Nef, Orlansky *et al.*, and Sharma) are case studies highlighting the role of technology, electronic governance, role of the private-public sector in economic growth, equity and sustainable development in a changing global context, and administration reforms to enable a more accountable and transparent governance.

Jain in Chapter II discusses new concerns and issues generated by globalization, and their impact on global democracy and global governance in general and the role of information technology (IT) in particular. He prescribes several strategies to create a partnership between technology and bureaucracy.

Sindzingre in Chapter III examines various theories of development demonstrating the necessity for a central role of strong states that are able to intervene efficiently in the economy. The author also examines the opposing argument of neoclassical economics, which shows the detrimental effects and failures that have characterized state intervention in many developing countries, especially the least developed ones characterized by lack of growth, and the persistence of poverty. The paper finally explores the conditions, a state in low income countries needs in order to be "developmental". These conditions are shaped by several issues, in particular the credibility and capacity (especially redistributive) of states and bureaucracies, the historical trajectories of local political economy, and the effects of policy reforms.

Dwivedi's discussion in Chapter IV raises of the place of morality and spirituality in the well-being and happiness of the people. He maintains that poverty in the South, and voracious consumption in the North pose great challenge to global sustainability. He suggests that building bridges of collaboration between the North and the South, strengthening of cultural liberty, and having public officials with a conscience will create a new paradigm for the third millennium, a paradigm which will envision the global progress for all.

In Chapter V Eden discusses three major developments in the late twentieth Century causing uproar among commercial producers, regulators, and consumers of food. First, the global trade grew to unprecedented proportions. Secondly, the World Trade Organization (WTO) was formed to facilitate this trade, and thirdly, the development of genetically modified plants and animals for agricultural or nutritional purposes. Global acceptance of these transgenic products as the technological key to food security has been lukewarm and controversial for cultural and political reasons. Eden concludes that these concerns are part of purity and defilement (cultural), and the stability of human identity (political) hence should be regulated either by governments or by organizations such as WTO.

In Chapter VI Vajpeyi analyzes the general relationship between global technologicalization and its positive and negative impact on international political and social systems—state sovereignty, environment, terrorism, poverty alleviation, and overall nature of international security, and advances made in two major areas: (a) information technology (IT), and (b) biotechnology, and potential consequences on public policy formulation.

In Chapter VII Fuhr and Lederer explore whether non-state business actors participating in the Clean Development Mechanism (CDM) of the Kyoto Treaty induce new forms of governance in climate politics. Authors specifically focus on two research questions: (a) what are the conditions for transnationally operating business actors working jointly with international organizations and governments in less developed countries, NGOs, involving themselves with Public Private Partnerships (PPPs) and developing successfully specific CDM projects that focus on emission trade, and carbon finance, (b) what are the effects of multi-level PPPs and CDMs in terms of institutional development and do CDM projects bring about positive results towards climate protection, induce new forms of environmental governance in key countries such as Brazil, India, and China?

Khator, Glover, and Steurer in Chapter VIII analyze the pace of globalization and its impact on political, economic and social spheres of public life. Authors have taken India, and Ghana to point out the imbalance created by globalization in delivering its benefits. Globalization, without doubt, has benefited many but it has also left out a large number of people such as women, children, and the very poor around the world thus creating a new marginalized class. The paper concludes with several policy recommendations so that promises of globalization could be evenly delivered and shared.

Nef in Chapter IX discusses the political economy of globalization, exclusion, and human security in the Americas. Nef contends that the real security problem in the Americas is not necessarily military security. In fact, it may be a major contributor to the worst forms of insecurity in the region. The linkage between environmental, economic, social, and cultural insecurity is quite close to exogenous "development" and security policies, whose explicit aim is to reduce insecurity for a few in the developed core. In a closely interconnected system, insecurity in the weaker and more exposed sectors translates into greater insecurity for the whole configuration, including the seemingly secure sectors at the top of the regional regime. Nef's analysis explores these interconnections from systemic and structural point of view.

Mauceri in Chapter X focuses on how the forces of globalization reshape social capital and identity, and the implications of this transformation for democracy with an empirical focus on the Andean region. He maintains that social capital is the "glue" of civil society helping to determine the density and bonding of a broad range of social organization and relationships.

In Chapter XI Orlansky, Grottola, and Kantor analyze a very disappointing socio-economic picture in Latin Americas' lost semi-decade 1998-2003. The 2001 Argentine crisis and failure to achieve sustainable growth—even after reform process, which supposedly had removed the barriers from the "import substitution" era—cast a shadow of doubt about the plausibility of reforms. In fact, they failed to unleash the forces of development. More people in the region perceived structural reforms (liberalization, deregulation, and privatization) as obstacles to economic and social progress, and modernization. Privatization was associated with corruption. Authors examine the recent economic recovery and the significance of relative prices' changes after 2002 devaluation, the incidence of a favorable international context and the State's new role in the post-crisis period. They conclude by posing two questions: Is there a new development strategy? Does it suggest a new State intervention pattern substantially different from the one prevailing during the 1990s?

Drawing on the social choice literature of democratic institutions Tremblay and Nikolenyi in Chapter XII maintain that the future state of conflict and cooperation in global politics is a positive function of the number of consolidated democracies in the world: the more stable democracies there are, the more peaceful international relations will become. The authors argue that those democratic institutions that increase the number and degree of heterogeneity of the major political actors will be more likely to remain stable and maximize social utility of the population thus ensuring the perpetuation of the legitimate foundations of the regime. These goals can be achieved by specific political institutions and their combinations. Contemporary Afghanistan, post-colonial India, a post-communist Eastern Europe are used as case studies to assess alternative patterns of institutional designs.

Sharma in Chapter XIII discusses privatization and public-private partnership in Africa with special reference to Botswana. In the context of poor performance of public enterprises in Africa, Sharma analyzes the expansion and performance of public enterprises in Botswana, the reasons, meaning, objectives, machinery, process, monitoring and evaluation mechanisms of privatization policy. He gives particular attention to the examination of various apprehensions and critical factors for the success of the policy and concludes with some reflections on the changed role of the state in the post privatization phase.

Li Jian in Chapter XIV examines the impact of macro-economic growth on people's health and their access to health care facilities in a rural county of South-western China. Drawing upon ethnographic fieldwork in the county combined with national data, the analysis seeks to demonstrate that health equity is a critical requirement for sustainable development. Contrary to the general assumption, people's health will not automatically improve as a result of economic growth. More importantly, the health disparities that are often created by development with few provisions toward equity can erode economic growth and lock the rural people into poverty. In conclusion the discussion points out the policies implications of health inequities and their impact on overall economic growth.

## References


Akoi, T. 2002, "Aspects of Globalization in Contemporary Japan," in Berger and Huntington (eds.), 2002.

Albrow (ed.). 1990, Globalization, Knowledge and Society, London: Sage.

Annan, K. 2000, "The Politics of Globalization," in O'Meara *et. al.* (eds.) "*Globalization and the Challenges of a New Century: A Reader*," Bloomington, I.N: Indiana University Press.

Appadorai, A. (ed.), 2001, *Globalization*, London: Duke University Press.

Assadorian, E. 2005, *Global Economy Continues to Grow, Vital Signs 2005*. World Watch Institute, New York: W.W. Norton.

Ball, G. 1967, "Cosmocorporations: The Importance of Being Stateless", *Colombia Journal of World Business*, Vol. 2, No. 6.

Berger, P.L.; Huntington, S.P. (eds.), 2002, *Many Globalizations: Cultural Diversity in the Contemporary World*, New York: Oxford University Press.

Bhagwati, J. 2002, Coping with Anti-Globalization. *Foreign Affairs*, January-February.

Bhagwati, J. 2002, *Free Trade Today*, Princeton, N.J.: Princeton University Press.

Byman, D., VanEveral, S. 1998, Hypothesis on the Causes of Contemporary Deadly Conflicts, *Security Studies*, Vol. 7.

Clarke, I. 1999, *Globalization and International Relations Theory*, Oxford: Oxford University Press.

Cox, R.W. 1993, "Structural Issues of Global Governance", in Gill, S. (ed.) *Gramci, Historical Materialism, and International Relations*, Cambridge, University Press.

Cutter, W.; Bowman, J.S.; Laura, D.; Tyson, A. 2000, New World, "New Deal: A Democratic Approach to Globalization", *Foreign Affairs*, March-April.

Dougherty, D. "Cardinal of Philadelphia", Quoted by Scheiber, N. 2001, Class Act, *The New Republic*, June 25.

Esposito, J. 1992, *The Islamic Threat*, Oxford: Oxford University Press.

Falk, R. 1997, "State of Siege: Will Globalization Win Out", *International Affairs*, Vol. 73, No. 1.

Finnegan, W. 2000, "After Seattle—Anarchists Get Organized", *The New Yorker*, April 17.

Flavin, C. 2005, *Vital Signs 2005*, New York: W.W. Norton.

Foley, M.; Edwards, b. 1996, "The Paradox of Civil Society", *Journal of Democracy*, July.

Friedman, J. 1998, "Transnationalization, Socio-Political Disorder, and Ethnification as Expression of Declining Global Hegemony". *International Political Science Review*, July.

Friedman, M. 1962, *Capitalism and Freedom*, Chicago: University of Chicago Press.

Friedman, T. 2005, *The World is Flat*, New York: Ferrar, Straus, and Giroux.

Fukuyama, F. 1992, *The End of History and the Last Man*, New York: Free Press.

Fuller, G. 2002, "The Future of Political Islam", *Foreign Affairs*, March-April.

Gardner, G. 2002, "The Challenge of Johannesburg: Creating a More Secure World", in Flavin, C. *et al.* (eds.) *State of the World*, New York: W.W. Norton.

Ghosh, P. 2004, *Harmonizing Environmental Concerns and Economic Growth,* Washington, D.C.: The World Bank.

Gil, S. (ed.), 1997, *Globalization, Democratization, and Multilateralism: Multilateralism and the U.N. System,* London: Cambridge University Press.

Giles, K. 1994, *The Revenge of God: The Resurgence of Islam, Christianity and Judaism in the Modern World.* Cambridge: Polity Press.

Gilpin, R. 2000, *The Challenge of Global Capitalism: The World Economy in the 21st Century,* Princeton, N.J.: Princeton University Press.

Goldman, K. 2001, *Transforming the European Nation-State: Dynamics of Internationalization,* London: Sage.

Gurr, T.R. 1999, *Minorities at Risk: A Global View of Ethnopolitical Conflict,* Washington, D.C.: U.S. Institute of Peace Press.

Hall, T. 1998, "The Effects of Incorporation into World System on Ethnic Process: Lessons from the Ancient World for the Contemporary World", *International Political Science Review,* July.

Harvey, D. 1990, *The Conditions of Post-Modernity,* Oxford: Blackwell.

Held, D. *et. al.* 1999, *Global Transformations, Politics, Economics, and Culture.* Stanford: Stanford University Press.

Higgat, R. 1996, "Beyond Embedded Liberalism: Governing International Trade in an Era of Economic Nationalism", in Gummett, P. (ed.) *Globalization and Public Policy.* Cheltenham, U.K.; Brookfield, U.S.: E. Elgar.

Hoffmann, S. 2000, "Too Proud". *The New Republic.*

Hopkins, D. 2001, "The Religion of Globalization", in Hopkins, D.; Lorentzen, L.A. Mendieta, E.; Batstone, D. (eds.) *Religious/Globalization—Theories and Cases,* Durham, N.C.: Duke University Press.

Hsiao, H. 2002, "Coexistence and Synthesis: Cultural Globalization and Localization in Contemporary Taiwan," in Berger, Huntington (eds.), 2002.

Ikenberry, G.P. 2000, "Don't Panic—How Secure is Globalization's Future", *Foreign Affairs,* May-June.

Kortpen, D. 1995, *When Corporations Rule the World.* West Hartford, C.T.: Kumarian Press.

Kaplan, L.F. 2001, "Why Trade Won't Bring Democracy to China—Trade Barrier", *The New Republic,* July 9-16.

Kaplan, R. 2000, "The Coming Anarchy", in O'Meara, P.; Mehlinger, H.D.; Krain, M. (eds.).

Kaplan, R. 2001, *The Coming Anarchy: Shattering the Dreams of Post-Cold War,* New York: Random House.

Kennedy, P. 2001, "A Herculean Task: The Myth and Reality of Arab Terrorism," in Talbot, S.; Chanda, N. (eds.), *The Age of Terror: America and the World After September 11,* New York: Basic Books.

Khor, M. 1995, "Development, Trade and the Environment: A Third World Perspective," in Goldsmith, E. *et. al.* (eds.) *The Future of Progress: Reflections on Environment and Development,* Totnes, Devon: Green Books, Ltd.

Kitching, G. 2001, *Seeking Social Justice Through Globalization: Escaping a Nationalist Perspective,* University Park: Pennsylvania State University Press.

Klare, M.T. 2000, "Redefining Security—The New Global Schisms", in O'Meara *et. al.* (eds.).

Knox, P. 1997, Globalization and Urban Economic Change, *The Annals of the American Academy of Political and Social Science,* Vol. 17, No. 27.

Korbin, S. 1996, "Back to the Future: Neomedievalism and the Digital World Economy" *Journal of International Affairs,* Vol. 51, No. 2, pp. 367-409.

Kregel, J. 1998, "The Strong Arm of the IMF", *Report of the Jerome Levy Economic Institute of Bard College,* Vol. 8, No. 1, pp. 7-8.

LaQuain, A.A. 2002, "Urban Governance: Some Lessons Learned", in Tulchin *et. al.* 2002.

Lewis, B. 1990, "The Roots of Muslim Rage", *Atlantic Monthly,* 226(3).

Lipset, S.M. 1960, *Political Man: The Social Bases of Politics,* Garden City, N.Y.: Doubleday.

Mallaby, S. 2002, "The Reluctant Imperialists—Terrorism, Failed States, and the Case for American Empire", *Foreign Affairs,* March-April.

Mauceri, P. 2003, "Globalization, Social Capital and Democracy: The Andean Region in Comparative Perspective", Annual Meeting of APSA, August 28-31, Philadelphia, PA.
Moore, B. 1993, *Social Origins of Dictatorship and Democracy*, Boston: Beacon Press.
Melitza, M. 2000, "Ten Thousand Cultures, As Single Civilization", *International Political Science Review* January.
Mele, C. 1996. "Globalization, Culture and Neighborhood Change: Reinventing the Lower East Side of New York", *Urban Affairs Review* 32.
Naipaul, V.S. 1990. *India: A Million Mutinies*, N.Y.: Viking.
Naisbitt, J. 1994, *The Global Paradox: The Bigger the World Economy the More Powerful its Smaller Players*, London: Brealey.
Nandy, A. 1985, "An Anti-Secularist Manifesto", *Seminar*, October.
Ohame, K. 1993, "The Rise of the Region State", *Foreign Affairs* 72(2).
Reich, R.B. 1991, *The Work of Nations: Preparing for 21st Century Capitalism*, N.Y.: Simon and Schuster.
Riggs, F.W. 1998, "Ethnic Nationalism and the World System Crisis", *International Political Science Review*.
Rosenau, J.N. 1997, *Along the Domestic—Foreign Frontier, Exploring Governance in a Turbulent World*, Cambridge: University Press.
Rothkopf, D. 1997, "In Praise of Cultural Imperialism", In O'Meara *et. al.* (eds.) 2000.
Sachs, J. 2000, "International Economics: Unlocking the Mysteries of Globalization", in O'Meara *et. al.* (eds.) 2000.
Scholte, J.A. 1997, "Global Capitalism and the State", *International Affairs*, 73(3).
Shami, S. 2001, "Rehistories of Globalization: Circassian Identity in Motion", in A. Arjun (ed.) *Globalization*, London: Duke University Press.
Soros, G. 2002, "George Soros on Globalization", New York: Public Affairs, Quoted in H. Epstein and L. Chen, 'Can AIDS be Stopped,' *The New York Review of Books*, March 14, 2002: 29.
Stiglitz, J. 2000, "What I Learned at the World Economic Crisis: The Insider", *The New Republic*, April 17-24.
Sven, B. 2004, "Globalization, State Transformation and Public Security", *International Political Science Review*, July.
Taylor, A.R. 1988, "The Islamic Question in the Middle East Politics", Boulder, C.O.: Westview.
Tehranian, M. 1998, "Precapitalism and Migration in Historical Perspective", *International Political Science Review*, July.
Thompson, W.R. 1983, *Contending Approaches to World System Analysis*, California: Sage.
Tulchin, J.; Varat, C.D.; Blair (eds.), 2002, *Democratic Governance and Urban Sustainability*, Washington, D.C., Woodrow Wilson International Center.
Vajpeyi, Dhirendra, 1979, *Modernization and Social Change in India*, Delhi: Manohar.
Vajpeyi, Dhirendra, ed. 1994, "*Modernizing China*", Leiden: E.J. Brill.
Vajpeyi, Dhirendra, 1998, "Freeing of the Indian Economy: An Exercise in Privatization", in O.P. Dwivedi *et. al.* (eds.) "*Governing India*", Delhi: B.R. Publishing Corporation.
Vajpeyi, D.; Malik, Y. (eds.) 1989, "*Religious and Ethnic Minority Politics in South Asia*", Maryland: Riverdale.
Victor, D. 2006, "Recovering Sustainable Development", *Foreign Affairs*, January-February.
Wallerstein, I. 1976, "Modernization: Requiescat in Face", in L. Coser and O. Larsen (eds.), "*The Uses of Controversy in Sociology*", N.Y.: The Free Press.
Webb, A.K. 2006, "The Calm Before the Storm? Revolutionary Pressures and Global Governance", *International Political Science Review*, January.
Wilson, D. 1994, "Bureaucracy in International Organizations: Building Capacity and Credibility in a Newly Interdependent World", in A. Farazmand (ed.), "*Handbook of Bureacracy*", N.Y.: Marcel Dekker.

# Global Blues and Sustainable Development

## The Emerging Challenges for Bureaucracy, Technology, and Governance

R.B. JAIN

The advent of 21st century presented pressing issues related to governance and sustainable development in developing countries. Two such concerns: (a) Global Democracy, and (b) Global Governance—have forced governments around the world to provide a different sort of policy-making framework to meet the universal requirement of good governance. Simultaneously information technology and biotechnology revolutions have presented unprecedented governance challenges for national and international political systems. These fast changing technologies are likely to continue to affect the development paradigm, the organization of society, and the ways in which government structures operate. How policy-makers and bureaucracies respond to these challenges should be of great interest and concern to citizens in all parts of the world, especially in the developing countries. In all probability, new strategies for sustainable development and structural mechanisms both at the national and international levels may be needed to address these emerging problems. The following discussion attempts to analyze these issues, and suggests a set of strategies towards building a partnership between technology and bureaucracy to meet these global challenges.

## GLOBAL DEMOCRACY AND GLOBAL GOVERNANCE

On October 24, 1999, the One World Trust launched *Charter 99* (United Nations [UN] Day), to bring out the concept of global democracy and governance and to raise the profile of the UN Millennium. The Charter for Global Democracy was meant as a call for international accountability, justice, sustainable development and democracy. It exhorted the world leaders to set in motion a rigorous process of accountability for all agencies of global governance. At the UN Summit held in September 2000, the world leaders made a solemn commitment to reduce poverty, strengthen international peace and disarmament, protect the environment and strengthen the UN. However, it was realized that without accountability, these commitments will not be met. In order to pursue this objective, the Charter 99 addressed an open letter to the governments of the world and the people they represent, calling on them to make international decision-making democratic and accountable (One World Trust 1999).

Throughout the 20th century, there have been well meaning and sometimes eloquent calls for world government—calls which pointed to the unfairness, inequality and injustice of the present distribution of wealth, power and capacity for policy-making. These calls emphasized the dangers to peace and even to human survival. Today one in five people in the world live in absolute poverty. Only active and sustained cooperation between people of different countries could solve these global problems.

In the past, these calls were dismissed as impractical and sentimental; however, since the late 1990s, demands for international government have taken on a new energy and precision. There is now a worldwide movement for a more equal and democratic framework for global governance, represented by organizations such as the Commission on Global Governance, Earth Summit in Rio, Agenda 21, Earth Charter, Real World Coalition, Earth Action's Call for a Safer World, One Planet Initiative, Citizens' Public Trust Treaty, Hague Agenda for Peace, Jubilee 2000, the Inter-Parliamentary Union, and campaigns against landmines, support for the International Criminal Court, for codes of conduct for business and for ethical investment.

In addition, a growing scholarly literature (Lachapelle and Trent 2000; Jain 2005; Cable 1999; Aksu and Camilleri 2002) on all aspects of globalization has begun to explore how governments can regulate and democratize international affairs. There are now detailed, practical measures which set out an ambitious agenda for democracy in international decision-making known as 'global governance.' There is a profound and important reason for this historic shift. In many ways world governance does operate, but not in the conventional forums of the United Nations. In some ways, the UN has been sidelined and plays the role of a 'facilitator.' The real business of world governance is done elsewhere. Global policies are discussed and formulated behind closed doors by exclusive groups, such as the G-8, OECD, the Bank of International Settlements, the World Bank, the International

Monetary Fund, the World Trade Organization and others. These agencies are reinforced by informal networks of high officials and powerful alliances. Together they have created what can be seen as dominant and exclusive institutions of world governance. All too often they are influenced by transnational corporations which pursue their own world strategies.

Themes of 'international governance' (the way the global environmental and other policies for development are governed and administered) and its improvement primarily in the North/South context are the starting point of an increasing number of international commissions and working groups of independent experts or decision-makers. All the reports published by them suggest reforms on 'international governance' through the Consultative Group (CG) mechanism framework, which will bring donors together, who have a long-term interest in supporting developing countries. CG meetings are chaired by the World Bank. The International Monetary Fund is closely associated with the World Bank in this international framework of aid coordination. On the international level, the United Nations Development Program (UNDP) is supposed to take the institutional lead in aid coordination on the basis of its Round Table (RT) mechanism.

Thus the main challenge for international development cooperation towards sustainable development (SD) in the new century will be to bridge the economic-political divide. This will require simultaneously integrating the democracy and governance agendas into a single strategy and addressing the intricate links between economic and political reforms. The recent initiative by the World Bank on the 'Comprehensive Development Framework' (CDF) constitutes such an attempt. The CDF process stresses the necessity to devise comprehensive and coherent aid strategies based on an integrated conception of development linking economic and political challenges (Santiso 2001:394). However, these agencies of actual world governance must be made accountable. If there are to be global policies, the policy-makers would have to be answerable to the peoples of the world. How to operationalize this accountability process is one of the critical reform challenges that the governments of the world face during the post-globalization era.

The process of democratic global governance adheres to the following fundamental principles: openness and accountability; environmental sustainability; security and peace; and equality and justice. Therefore, the first aim of governments at present is to make the already existing processes of world administration and governance accountable. People everywhere would want to know the 'why,' 'what,' and 'how' of the decision-making process. Also, the decision-makers have to realize that they are answerable to the public in every country impacted by international bodies. It is also important that all decisions taken by governments ought to be compatible with public criteria for environmental sustainability. Finally, people would want global governance to be compatible with the principles of equality, human rights and economic and social justice.

## TECHNOLOGY AND GOVERNANCE

Traditionally, technology has been viewed in terms of solving problems. But technology also leaves its negative imprint on society. This dual interaction, the way in which society creates technology and its retroactive impact, is at the very centre of the ethno-technical dilemma that the governments face in all societies. Much of the current debate around the impact of science and technology concerns fears about unwanted developments. It was presumed, rightly or wrongly, that the end of the Cold War would bring an era of a safer and peaceful military climate. But the events such as the Bhopal holocaust, Chernobyl disaster, the events of 9/11, and a general rise in global terror are all reminders of the risk element in science and technological developments, which need proper regulation. There is a need to balance progress with risk. Decisions about this balance need to be made at global, supranational, national, regional and local levels across a complex web of interconnected issues. The revolutionary developments in bio-technology and information technology in recent times illustrate this dilemma very well.

## THE GROWING IMPACT OF BIO-TECHNOLOGY

This recent revolutionary progress that scientists have made in respect of bio-technologies has meant putting life to work in the service of human beings. These technologies encompass all the techniques relating to living matter used for a given purpose. They give rise to hopes, like the use of genetic engineering that opens up the possibility of transferring any gene from any living cell to another living cell (e.g., for improving crop varieties). But they also arouse fears, particularly with regard to their impact on the bio-sphere (like giving rise to genetic pollution) and their likely consequences for the human race (eugenics), or anxieties about cloning of human beings. The challenge is to see that geneticists do not use such developments to violate our greatest treasure—human dignity. However, all new knowledge is not a potential for constant worry. Biotechnologies open up vast prospects for advances in medical fields, such as 'predictive medicine,' which permits the identification of the genes that make people prone to develop a particular disease. But if the human person were to be defined only in terms of his or her genome, this would constitute a phenomenal regression with regard to human rights (Kahn 2001: 54-56).

The application of developments in the field of biotechnology has some widespread, long-term societal implications (e.g., nuclear sciences and nuclear technologies pose fundamental moral and ethical questions for all governments). Earlier, people put unlimited hope and faith in science and technology and supported them generously, but today in advanced countries they arouse concern and fear among many sections of society. In developing countries, the basic needs of society have to be met and the quality of life has to be improved. Science and technology, particularly through the enormous potential of biotechnologies, have an important role to play in hastening the current slow pace and levels of development. Thus all societies today face enormous moral and ethical challenges related to human rights in the application of scientific and technological advances particularly in the field of biotechnology, and to look upon it as a revolution to be harnessed in the service of humanity (Menon 2001: 57-59).

## INFORMATION TECHNOLOGY

A similar dilemma is posed by advances in the field of information and communication technological developments. One area generally recognized for the potential of Information Technology (IT) and its application and use by the government institutions in their various operations in realizing the goal of more performance effective and less costly government is e-governance, which involves not only the application of information and communication technology for delivery of various public services, but also designing a new process of coordination and sharing of powers, thereby reconfiguring the traditional mode of governance. There is already a firm realization in many countries, both developed and developing, that e-governance is not an option any more but an essential requirement for good governance. The advent of IT has had far-reaching impact on government departments and bodies. It has led to an increased awareness on the part of people, civil servants and political leadership of new expectations from the process of governance. Such awareness leads to demands, which are sometime just and legitimate and sometimes unjust and illegitimate. Thus both the political leadership and civil services have come under increased pressure and anxiety as to what to deliver, to whom, and how quickly (Mitra and Gupta 2003: 32-39).

However, these revolutionary developments have also created many more opportunities for the unscrupulous and the corrupt in society to use these to benefit their own sinister motives. An example of the negative impact of IT is the use of Internet, which opens up a whole new set of dimensions like the ability of political actors to share information, virtual communities to be formed, information to be shared and so on. However, as it unfolds, it continues to present new types of policy dilemmas. Contemporary debates and concerns have emerged around controlling child pornography, international terrorism, and various Internet crimes like dissemination of damaging viruses, copyright issues, national and international financial, credit cards, banking and other frauds, and the exclusion of a huge proportion of the world's population from access to new information and communication technologies (Seamus O'Tuama 2004: 369-93). How to control these elements and promote appropriate use of technologies to benefit masses are the growing challenges for governance, particularly in many developing societies where the majority of people are either ignorant or illiterate and at best are not technically savvy.

Increasing IT capacity is becoming a prerequisite for improving productivity and enhancing the welfare of society. The capacity of a society to produce, select, adapt, and commercialize knowledge is critical for trade, for competitiveness, and for the sustained growth of the economy knowledge. As the World Bank's World Development Report 1999 states:

> "Today's most technologically advance economies are truly knowledge-based . . . creating millions of knowledge-related jobs in an array of disciplines that have emerged overnight . . . the need for developing countries to increase their capacity to use knowledge cannot be overstated" (Goel, *et al.* 2004: 1).

## TECHNOLOGIES AND ISSUE OF GOVERNANCE

Notwithstanding these dilemmas, it is heartening to note that certain developments in the mode of governance in some societies have pointed several positive directions towards capacity building. Two recent shifts in attitudes strongly influence the issue of governance within technological arenas. The first shift is the decline of conventional top-down governance models and an emphasis on privatization, deregulation, downsizing of bureaucracy, and private market-based solutions to many social problems. This trend is especially evident in telecommunications or information technology (IT). The largely positive and beneficial nature of IT, coupled with the anti-statist attitudes of the late 20th century, have shifted attitudes toward technology more generally and discouraged regulation as an effective solution to the challenges that the new technology presents.

The second shift is a changing public attitude toward the conduct of scientific research and the resulting technological innovations that might best be summed up as follows: "Don't leave scientific decision-making to the scientists." The most important influence on this perspective may have been our experience with the advent of nuclear weapons. This world-changing technological development was greeted by many with great alarm, which has led to the creation of an international regime to prevent the proliferation of nuclear technology. In the United States, the 1993 Government Performance and Review Act concisely illustrates this trend toward greater societal interest in knowing the outcomes emerging from the scientific enterprise. New reporting, accountability and transparency requirements would need to be introduced, despite continuing protests from the scientific community that such norms of accountability may be impractical and may be counterproductive to innovations (www.rand.org/publications/MR/MR1139.sum.pdf., accessed on 11.2.05).

## CAPACITY BUILDING FOR GOVERNING SCIENCE AND TECHNOLOGY

As discussed above, technologies emerging from bio-technology revolutions as well as information technology are likely to present unprecedented capacity building challenges to national and international political systems. If not properly regulated, science and technology can be manipulated, ignored and discredited by unscrupulous individuals and organizations. The real challenge is curbing corruption and enforcing transparency. New government mechanisms, both on national and international levels, may be needed to address these emerging issues. The practical obstacles to governance of these technologies are many. Success in governing them requires the cooperation of stakeholders, states, non-governmental organizations (NGOs), international organizations, and the average citizens.

In order to build governance capabilities for regulating such technological development, one strategy could be to use a decentralized decision-making model involving a number of organizations and users in deciding, what technologies need regulation and which of these need Research and Development (R&D) supports, and what means to adopt to regulate such technologies. Secondly, a number of Citizen Councils can be used to deliberate upon norms, use, regulation, and governance of technology and make recommendations to higher levels of formal institutions of governance. Using the networking capacities of information technology, these bodies can share ideas and arrive at consensus on views to manage and regulate technologies. It should, however, be noted that "today's governance structures are challenged by a unique shift from collective control and hierarchical decision-making to individual control and decision-making that will mark the technologies form the dual revolutions" (www.rand.org/publications/MR/MR1139.sum.pdf., p. 7, accessed on 11.2.05). The very nature of these technologies makes regulating and controlling them particularly challenging.

Traditional 'top-down' or positive methods of governance will have little influence over how these technologies are developed, diffused and assimilated. New governance mechanisms are needed and they must emerge quickly, be flexible, and have broad buy-in. The alternative methods discussed above—standard setting bodies, citizen-councils and NGOs—present some options to policy-makers considering ways to build up capacity to deal with these challenges" (www.rand.org/publications/MR/MR1139.sum.pdf., p. 7, accessed on 11.2.05). Ultimately, because the technologies emerging from the information and biological revolutions are inherently global, success in governing the technologies is likely to depend on evolving a kind of model that involves all stakeholders—NGOs, interest organizations, citizens and related international organizations and institutions—to cooperate in capacity building and developing governance norms or structures.

O'Tuama presents a democratic model that might help in building a nation's capacity for addressing the governance of science and technology. The first of three aspects of this model include: "free inquiry." Researches in scientific and technological developments cannot be conducted by persons who are not absolutely free. The second aspect is the idea of the free market in liberalism. Regulation is seen as interference with the free market, and science and technology is an extremely important actor in the economy. Placing regulations and control on science and technology would be placing regulation and control on the free market. The third aspect suggested by O'Tuama, apart from the various mechanisms for delivering democratic decision-making like consensus conferences, citizens' juries, public inquiries, referenda etc., concerns two imperatives for realizing democracy—responsibility and deliberation. The imperative of responsibility is to refocus on the need to contextualize it in terms of contemporary reality, and embed it in a collective or democratic context through co-responsibility. The deliberative process concerns how we as citizens and as inhabitants of this planet can engage each other in democratic processes that can lead to common understandings and decisions aimed at the common good rather than vested interests (O' Tuama 2004:388-90).

## GLOBAL BLUES AND GLOBAL GOVERNANCE

As a result of technological developments and the impact of globalization, everyone in the world is linked through "our shared environment, trade and communications." People live together as neighbors, and as neighbors they must respect the rights of all persons to address common problems. A joint effort of learning and negotiation, of trial and error, will be needed. Many vital issues can best be tackled effectively at a global level, such as the environment, biodiversity and climate change; international security and disarmament; international trade, finance and labor rights; epidemics; communications; and international crime and terrorism.

The creation of democratic global governance may be complicated. But the need for it is simple and urgent. Global problems will only get worse if international decision-making is left in the hands of the present undemocratic, exclusive institutions. Therefore, there is a need to continue to press for action and public support around the world. Worldwide campaigns have led to the end of apartheid in South Africa, to the Statute for an International Criminal Court, to the ban on landmines and some debt-reduction for the world's poorest countries. The time has come to make democratic reform of international affairs government's priority, both as an end in itself and as a means of solving many serious social, economic and technological problems.

## IMPLICATIONS OF GLOBAL GOVERNANCE

The Commission on Global Governance is not an official body of the UN, but it has been endorsed by the UN Secretary General and the Carnegie Commission on Global Governance and funded by two trust funds of the United Nations Development Program (UNDP), nine national governments, and several foundations, including the Mac Arthur Foundation, and the Ford Foundation. The Commission's reports emphasized that world events, since the creation of the United Nations in 1945, combined with advances in technology, the information revolution, and the now-global awareness of impending environmental catastrophe, create a climate in which the people of the world will recognize the need for, and the benefits of, global governance.

Global governance, according to the report titled 'Our Global Neighborhood,' "does not imply world government or world federalism." Global governance is a procedure to define objectives that employ a variety of methods, none of which give the governed an opportunity to vote "yes" or "no" for the outcome. Decisions taken by administrative bodies or by bodies of appointed delegates, or by "accredited" civil society organizations are already implementing many of the recommendations published by the Commission.

## THE FOUNDATION FOR GLOBAL GOVERNANCE

The foundation for global governance is that the world is now ready to accept a "*global civic ethic*" based on "*a set of core values that can unite people of all cultural, political, religious, or philosophical backgrounds.*" This belief is reinforced by another belief: "*that governance should be underpinned by democracy at all levels and ultimately by the rule of enforceable law*" (Commission on Global Governance 1995).

The report states: "*We believe that all humanity could uphold the core values of respect for life, liberty, justice and equity, mutual respect, caring, and integrity.*" In the fine print, these lofty values lose much of their appeal. Respect for life, for example, is not limited to human life. "Respect for life" actually means equal respect for *all* life (The *Global Biodiversity Assessment:* Section 9) (Commission on Global Governance 1995), prepared under the auspices of the United Nations Environment Program, describes in great detail the biocentric view that "*humans are one strand in nature's web,*" consistent with the biocentric view that all life has equal intrinsic value. Some segments of humanity may balk at extending to trees, bugs, and grizzly bears the same respect for life that is extended to human beings. The report states that, "*Next to life, liberty is what people value most. The impulse to possess turf is a powerful one for all species; yet it is one that people must overcome.*" It also states: "*global rules of custom constrain the freedom of sovereign states,*" and "*sensitivity over the relationship between international responsibility and national sovereignty [is a] considerable obstacle to the leadership at the international level,*" and "*Although states are sovereign, they are not free individually to do whatever they want*" (Commission on Global Governance 1995: 336). Maurice Strong, a member of the Commission, said in an essay entitled *Stockholm to Rio: A Journey Down a Generation:* "*It is simply not feasible for sovereignty to be exercised unilaterally by individual nation-states, however powerful. It is a principle which will yield only slowly and reluctantly to the imperatives of global environmental cooperation*" (Commission on Global Governance 1995: 354-55).

The core value of "*justice and equity*" is the basis for sweeping changes in the UN as proposed by the Commission. The Commission has determined that: "*Although people are born into widely unequal economic and social circumstances, great disparities in their conditions or life chances are an affront to the human sense of justice. A broader commitment to equity and justice is basic to more purposeful action to reduce disparities and bring about a more balanced distribution of opportunities around the world. A commitment to equity everywhere is the only secure foundation for a more humane world order. . . . Equity needs to be respected as well in relationships between the present and future generations. The principle of intergenerational equity underlies the strategy of sustainable development*" (Commission on Global Governance 1995: 51).

"*Mutual respect*" is broadly defined as "tolerance." "*Some assertions of particular identities may in part be a reaction against globalization and homogenization, as well as modernization and secularization. Whatever the causes, their common stamp is intolerance*" (Commission on Global Governance 1995: 52). Individual achievement and personal responsibility are counter to the value of "*mutual respect*" as suggested in the UN's World Core Curriculum, authored by Robert Muller, Chancellor of the UN University and former Deputy Secretary General to three UN Secretaries General. The *Robert Muller School World Core Curriculum Manual* (November, 1986: 52) states: "*The idea for the school grew out of a desire to provide experiences which would enable the students to become true planetary citizens through a global approach to education.*" The first principle of the curriculum is to: "*Promote growth of the group idea, so that group good, group understanding, group interrelations and group goodwill replace all limited, self-centered objectives leading to group consciousness*" (Commission on Global Governance 1995).

The value of "*caring*" is institutionalized in the Commission's proposals: "*The task for governance is to encourage a sense of caring, through policies and mechanisms that facilitate co-operation to help those less privileged or needing comfort and support in the world*" (Commission on Global Governance 1995: 54). "*Integrity*" is defined to be the adoption and practice of these core values and the absence of corruption. As the world adopts these core values, the Commission believes a "global ethic" will emerge. Global governance will "*Embody this ethic in the evolving system of international norms, adapting, where necessary, existing norms of sovereignty and self-determination to changing realities*" (Commission on Global Governance 1995: 55). The effectiveness of this global ethic "*will depend upon the ability of people and governments to transcend narrow self-interests and agree that the interests of humanity as a whole will be best served by acceptance of a set of common rights and responsibilities. Without the objectives and limits that a global ethic would provide, however, global civil society could become unfocused and even unruly. That could make effective global governance difficult*" (Commission on Global Governance 1995: 55).

Among the "rights" such a global ethic would bestow upon all people are: a secure life; an opportunity to earn a fair living; and equal access to the global commons.

The right to *"a secure life"* means much more than freedom from the threat of war. *"Human security includes safety from chronic threats such as hunger, disease, and repression, as well as protection from sudden and harmful disruptions in the patterns of daily life. The Commission believes that the security of people must be regarded as a goal as important as the security of states"* (Commission on Global Governance 1995: 80). Herein lies a significant expansion of the responsibilities of the United Nations and ultimately of the individual national governments. Until now, the UN's responsibility was limited to its member states. The Commission's proposals will give to the UN responsibility for the security of individuals within the boundaries of member states (Commission on Global Governance 1995). The right to a secure life also means the right to live on a secure planet. *"Human activity . . . combined with unprecedented increases in human numbers . . . are impinging on the planet's basic life support systems. Action must be taken now to control the human activities that produce these risks. . . . In confronting these risks, the only acceptable path is to apply the 'precautionary principle'"* (Commission on Global Governance 1995: 82). Clearly, the Commission sees the UN as the global authority for protecting the environment.

The right to earn a *"fair living"* carries with it far-reaching implications. The Commission discusses at length what is "fair" and what is not. It is not fair, for example, for the developed countries, which contain 20 percent of the population, to use 80 percent of the natural resources. It is not fair for the permanent members of the Security Council to have the right of veto. In general, it is not fair for one segment of the population to be rich while another segment of the population is poor. *"Unfair in themselves, poverty and extreme disparities of income fuel both guilt and envy when made more visible by global television. They demand, and in recent decades have begun to receive, a new standard of global governance"* (Commission on Global Governance 1995: 157-59). The right to earn a fair living implies that there must be some kind of a job available from which people may earn their living. Under the auspices of a new Economic Security Council, which the Commission purports in its report, the Commission would give the UN responsibility for seeing that all people would have *"an opportunity to earn a fair living"* (Commission on Global Governance 1995: 157-59).

The foundation of global governance is a set of core values, a belief system, which contains ideas that are foreign to the experiences of many countries, and ignores other values and ideas that are precious to their experiences. The values and ideas articulated in the Commission's report are not new. They have been tried, under different names, in other societies. Often, the consequences have been devastating. These values, under new names, have been emerging in UN documents since the late 1980s, and have dominated international conferences, agreements, and treaties since 1992. This set of core values underlies *Agenda 21* adopted in Rio de Janeiro. Virtually every international treaty and agreement introduced during this decade reflects this set of core values. The Commission's recommendations to achieve global governance seek to enforce these values through the programs authorized and implemented by a global bureaucracy growing from a revitalized and restructured United Nations system.

A commitment to a strategy of sustainable development has to become the rule with regard to the exploitation of resources. The Commission recognizes that: "*sustainable development cannot be achieved solely through government action or market forces. The growing reliance on non-governmental organizations and institutions as partners with government and business in achieving economic progress is leading to more participatory development. Involving agents of civil society leads to programs and projects that are more focused on people and more productive*" (Commission on Global Governance 1995: 157-59). To ensure greater involvement by "civil society," the Commission has formalized proposals to elevate the status of NGOs. Two positive trends are being witnessed in this regard. First, under the combined pressures of public opinion and legislation, industry is today developing an industrial ecology, an innovative approach to risk prevention in terms of the environmental impact of the industrial processes. Second, the world is also witnessing the emergence of green chemistry in which biology, biochemistry and cloning converge. The precautionary principle, emphatically incorporated in 1987 Montreal Protocol, which underpins some twelve international treaties, will make manufacturers responsible for ensuring the safety of their products. This should reduce the potential risks to human health (Larbi 2001: 77-78).

## THE MACHINERY OF GLOBAL GOVERNANCE

The Commission recommends the creation of two new bodies: (1) an Assembly of the People, and (2) a Forum of Civil Society. "*What is generally proposed is the initial setting up of an assembly of parliamentarians, consisting of representatives elected by existing national legislatures from among their members, and the subsequent establishment of a world assembly through direct election by the people.*" The Forum of Civil Society would consist of "*300-600 representatives of organizations accredited to the General Assembly. . .*" (Commission on Global Governance: 257-58). The Forum would meet annually prior to the meeting of the UN General Assembly. "*The considered views of the Forum would be a qualitative change in the underpinnings of global governance*" (Larbi 2001: 77-78)

The idea of NGO participation in global governance is as old as the United Nations. Julius Huxley, who founded the United Nations Educational, Scientific, and Cultural Organization (UNESCO) in 1946, also founded the IUCN in 1948. It was the IUCN that effectively lobbied the UN General Assembly in 1968 to adopt Resolution #1296, which establishes a policy for "accrediting" certain NGOs. The IUCN is recognized by at least six different UN organizations. Moreover, it is the premier international NGO claiming a membership of 53 international NGOs, 550 national NGOs, 100 government agencies, and 68 sovereign nations.

NGO participation in global governance is an essential feature, and is, in fact, the dimension of governance that is totally new. It is no longer just an idea. It is a demonstrated fact of life which the Commission now seeks to institutionalize through legal status. It is the machinery of global governance which is organized and coordinated from the highest chambers of governance at the United Nations to the most local bodies of governance, including County Commissions, City Councils, and even to local watershed councils.

As of 1994, there were 980 accredited NGOs. These NGOs are accredited because of their demonstrated support of issues being advanced by the United Nations. A single NGO is selected to coordinate activities within each issue area. In addition to the Internet, NGO çoordination information is published by the World Resources Institute (WRI) in a publication called *Networking*. Activity of non-accredited NGOs is coordinated through membership in the IUCN. The IUCN Annual Report for 1993 claims more than 6000 "experts" in their network who serve as volunteers *"on Technical Advisory Committees, Regional Advisory Councils, Working Groups and Task Forces. Taken together, these voluntary groups are an immense strength of the Union"* (Commission on Global Governance: 257-8).

According to the Commission's report, 28,900 international NGOs are known to exist, and many are directly involved in advancing the agenda of global governance. At UNCED, for example, 7,892 NGOs were certified to participate in the "civil society forum" which preceded the actual conference. Many of the NGOs participated in the preliminary Preparatory Committee Meetings, or "Prep Coms," and were prepared and present to lobby the official delegates to the conference. This procedure is followed at virtually every global and regional conference.

This procedure is now being applied to domestic policy. Members of the international NGO community have strong national constituencies, and enormous staff and money capabilities. Global issues, such as the Biodiversity Treaty, which require national or local action, become the focus of the domestic agenda for national NGOs. The structure and mechanics of "civil society" participation in global governance is further revealed in a variety of documents originating from the UN organizations and from the IUCN, WWF, and the WRI (Jain 1995).

Most often, the term "Public/Private Partnerships" is used to describe and define "civil society" participation. At the lowest, "on-the-ground" level, NGOs are present and prepared to lobby on issues relating to a particular watershed or a particular project under consideration by a local zoning board. Public/Private Partnerships encourage the creation of "boards" or "councils" which are supposed to represent the interests of all the "stakeholders." In reality, these boards are encouraged because well-prepared NGOs are most often able to dominate the outcome. At the local level, NGOs are frequently full-time professionals, paid by a not-for-profit organization, funded through the coordinated efforts of the Environmental Grantmakers Association or the federal government. The other "stakeholders" in these partnerships are business people who work for a living and simply want to take care of the environment, but have too little time to become experts on the issues.

The recommendations of the Commission, if implemented, will bring all the people of the world into a global neighborhood managed by a world-wide bureaucracy, under the direct authority of a minute handful of appointed individuals, policed by thousands of individuals, paid by accredited NGOs, and certified to support a belief system. To many people this is unbelievable and unacceptable.

## GOVERNANCE REFORMS FOR CAPACITY BUILDING

It is clear that support for global democracy and global governance has put tremendous pressures on the capacities of countries all over the world to reconstruct and reform their system of 'governance' in order to implement the newly emerging values. This is especially so for the governments of developing countries which have been burdened with more problems arising out of the impact of globalization and technological revolutions—problems they had been unable to solve.

While the functions of the state in almost all countries, notwithstanding the privatization in response to globalization, have steadily increased, the capacity to deliver has declined over the years due to administrative cynicism, rising indiscipline, and a growing belief widely shared among the political and bureaucratic elite that the state is an arena where public office is to be used for private ends. In almost all countries people perceive bureaucracy as wooden, disinterested in public welfare, and corrupt. The issue of reforms for good governance has acquired more critical dimensions in poorer states than in the rich states because of the farmers' low economic growth and fiscal crisis. Weak governance, manifesting itself in poor service delivery, excessive regulation, and uncoordinated and wasteful public expenditure, is seen as one of the key factors impinging on growth and development in all developing societies. Thus the agenda of reform in governance should include not only reshaping the bureaucracy by adopting a comprehensive reform of civil services, but also a multi-faceted strategy based on ensuring security of tenure, increasing accountability, civil service renewal, open and responsive government, tackling corruption and strengthening the rule of law, and e-governance.

This rearrangement of roles between the market, the state and people gives more space for civil society to organize itself to effectively voice the interests of the people and of the common good and results in a more viable public-private synergy. It also gives more responsibility to civil society to take up the interests of the people whose voices would otherwise be overwhelmed and drowned by the powers of business interests over the politically powerful (Parr 1997: 1-2). One thing is clear: the state in transitional societies has to be more responsible in promoting human development, security and dignity in the aftermath of globalization.

### A Package of Capacity Building Strategies

In order to build capacity to meet the challenges of good governance for regulating technology and promoting human security, a multi-pronged strategy needs to be adopted at this juncture by all polities, especially in the many transitional polities and developing societies. Since most technologically advanced economies today are knowledge-based, the need for developing countries to increase their capacity to use knowledge cannot be overstated. Enhancing this capacity is one of the priority areas for improving productivity and increasing the welfare of societies. A World Bank Report defines knowledge economy (KE) through analysis of four areas (the so-called four pillars of the knowledge economy): (a) the policy and institutional framework, (b) an innovations system; (c) education and lifelong learning; and (d) information technology infrastructure and electronic development ("e-development") (Goel, *et al.* 2004: 1). The Innovation System is expected to serve the needs of societies to meet the challenges of emerging global blues by achieving better integration of science and technology (S&T) infrastructure with production needs, by increasing private sector participation in technology development, and by developing stronger linkages between industry, universities, and research institutions by focusing on (a) building an environment conducive to business development, (b) a framework for the generation of new ideas, and (c) enterprise level support the establishment of new KE based institutions to carry out research and development activities (Goel, *et. al.* 2004: 2).

Apart from the package of innovations discussed above, the developing countries in particular will need to take the following other steps to meet these challenges. First, on the institutional front, it is necessary to regenerate political and administrative institutions from the virtual collapse experienced in the last three decades. Restore the legitimacy and effectiveness of the legislature, bureaucracy, the judiciary and the non-state actors of civil society. As the 'sustainability of transition' has been greatly affected by the gradual incremental loss of the capacity and effectiveness of the democratic institutions in many such societies, it is necessary that a radical package of reforms to revamp the institutional framework be implemented immediately.

Second, there is an immediate need to cut down the size of the government and its expenditure. Simultaneously the bureaucracy should be revamped in its orientation, behavior and attitude. Instead of being the defender of the *status quo,* there has to be a realization that with the advent of globalization, liberalization and privatization, it has to play a major role as a catalyst of change. Apart from the changes in the traditional values and norms of the work culture, it has to demonstrate its willingness to accept new technical innovations and values of moral governance—such as achievement and competition, equity and egalitarianism and concern for broader collective social goals. The bureaucracy is also both under legal and moral obligation to exercise its authority and discretionary powers with a view to meet the norms of responsiveness and accountability. Apart from its professional norms of efficiency, effectiveness, economy and cost consciousness, the core public service values of integrity, impartiality and responsibility need to be observed if the gains of the process of liberalization are to be consolidated for protecting human security.

Third, on the economic front, it is of utmost importance that a comprehensive and concerted policy strategy based on general consensus be developed for (i) revamping public distribution system (PDS), (ii) disinvestments in public enterprises in key economic sectors like power, energy, oil, transport, telecommunication and weak industrial units, and (iii) reconsideration of subsidies (which are at best counter-productive) in agriculture, oil, and other key sectors of the economy.

Fourth, the system of governance faces a massive challenge to provide for adequate employment, health, education, shelter, and the basic facilities of sanitation and drinking water. Providing for higher outlays and spending on items like primary education and primary health-care is not the only solution. The real challenge is effective management on the part of the administration to deliver these goods at the lowest costs and in an equitable manner. These are some of the areas where the state cannot abdicate its responsibilities, notwithstanding the emphases on liberalization and privatization, increased public and foreign investments, and contracting out of the services in various industrial and other sectors of the economy and social services.

Fifth, in terms of securing accountability and transparency and a corruption-free government, it is important that effective mechanisms be developed to combat corruption at all levels of public and private sector. It is evident from the above account that combating corruption for sustainable development calls for (a) reducing opportunities and incentives for corrupt behavior and increasing the sense of accountability on the part of public officials, and (b) effective implementation of anti-corruption measures. This would imply that measures should be logically consistent with regard to phasing in of a time table for speedy investigation and conviction; a strong political commitment to implement the strategies and enforce anti-corruption measures; and people's active participation from below in enforcement of administrative, legal and judicial measures, thus mobilizing the public against corruption in public life.

Apart from the above mentioned fundamental conditions, it must be emphasized that fighting corruption requires: (a) formation of a national coordinating body that should be responsible for devising and following up a strategy against corruption, along with a citizen's board to oversee progress against corruption; (b) existence of a high powered independent prosecuting body to investigate and prosecute all such known cases of corruption; (c) setting up of special courts for trying such cases at a stretch so that the cases come to their legitimate conclusion without any delay; (d) thorough overhauling and reforming the system of electoral laws and economic regulations to minimize the temptation to indulge in corrupt practices; (e) enactment of an appropriate legislation to limit the number of Ministries and Departments both at the Centre and the States, so that the temptation of expanding ministries only for political gains could be minimized; and (f) provision of specialized technical assistance to anti-corruption agencies by organizing high-level anti-corruption workshops or strategic consulting or hiring international investigations to track down ill-gotten deposits overseas (Jain 2004b: 15-16).

Sixth, besides absorbing the values of a participatory and shared administrative system (emphasizing private-public synergy), governments have not only to observe a modicum of transparency in all their activities and concede an appropriate right of information to the people in its decision-making process, but also to secure a balance between a rule-bound administration and an administration that can effectively and quickly deliver results, particularly in developmental and social welfare activities. This poses a great challenge for most transitional and regulatory societies to dismantle the fort of their administrative state (Dwivedi and Jain 1985: Chap. 1) and embark on a system of open, decentralized and deconcentrated governance.

And finally, it is important to note that with the unleashing of trends towards the world becoming a globalized village, and global democracy and global governance, nations are now linked more strongly together through a relationship of international dependency. Thus the framework of governance of the nation-states in their structure and processes should absorb some of the emerging global values, which are essential for securing human development, human dignity and human security for their citizens and for ensuring the very survival and progress of the mankind.

## CONCLUSION

In conclusion, however, it should be remembered that for achieving good governance in the post-globalization era, no amount of planning and thinking in all these areas would be useful unless the governments at all levels of the polity are able to make hard and unpleasant decisions for 'moral governance' and have the will and capacity to implement and continuously monitor and evaluate their impact. At the same time, the political leadership in all nations has to demonstrate its strong determination to undertake reforms by first cleaning its own stable from corrupt and criminal influences, and setting ethical standards of quality governance both at the political and administrative levels.

In considering the worldwide developments at the threshold of the 21st century, this chapter has attempted to discuss some of the emerging challenges to good governance in the era of globalization and its aftermath, as well as the strategies for growth and sustainable development in many modern and transitional societies that can be built and operationalized. It is heartening that people in almost all developing countries have recognized their importance, and it is likely that the growing concerns about global democracy and global governance, fighting corruption and devising innovations for 'good governance' may turn out to be a concerted international movement, one not confined merely to the realm of academic discussions or writings in specific individual countries contexts, but instead one that entails constructive reform actions for positive results transcending the jurisdictions of national boundaries. This is the only hope for achieving universally good and capable governance to meet the challenges of the emerging global blues, and to ensure the very survival of humanity, for which we must all strive together.

## References

Aksu, Esref and Joseph A. Camilleri (eds.), 2002, *Democratizing Global Governance* (New York, Palgrave Macmillan).

Binde, Jerome (ed.) 2001, *"Keys to the 21st Century"*, Paris, UNESCO Publishing.

Cable, Vincent. 1999, *Globalization and Global Governance* (London, Royal Institute of International Affairs).

Commission on Global Governance. 1995, *"Our Global Neighborhood."* London, Oxford University Press.

Dwivedi, O.P., Jain, R.B. 1985, *"India's Administrative State"*, New Delhi, Gitanjali Publishing House.

Goel, Vinod K., Koryukina, Ekaterina, Bhalla, Mohini, and Agarwal, Priyanka. 2004, "Innovation Systems: World Bank Support of Science and Technology Development", Washington, D.C.: The World Bank Working Paper No. 32, IUCN (World Conservation Union) 1993, Annual Report.

Jain, R.B. (ed.) 1995, *"NGOs in Development Perspective,"* New Delhi, Vivek Prakashan.

Jain, R.B. 2004a, "Good Governance for Sustainable Development: Challenges and Strategies in India", *The Indian Journal of Public Administration*, Vol. 50, January. Special issue on governance.

Jain, R.B. 2004b, *"Corruption-Free Sustainable Development: Challenges and Strategies for Good Governance"*, New Delhi: Mittal Publications.

Jain, R.B. (ed.) 2005, *"Globalization & Good Governance: Pressures for Constructive Reforms"* New Delhi, Deep & Deep Publications Pvt. Ltd.

Kahn, Axel. 2001, "Biotechnologies: Towards a Brave New World?" in Jerome Binde (ed.) 2001, *"Keys to the 21st Century." Paris,* UNESCO Publishing.

Lachapelle, Guy and John Trent (eds.), 2000, *Globalization, Governance and Identity: The Emergence of New Partnerships,* (Montreal, University of Montreal Press).

Larbi, Bouguerrra Mohammad, 2001, "Chemical Pollution and Invisible Pollution: Prospect and Possible Response" in Jerome Binde, 2001.

Lei-Faur, David; Vigoda-Gadot, Eran (eds.) 2004, *"International Public Policy and Management: Policy Learning Beyond Regional, Cultural, and Political Boundaries."* New York: Marcel Dekker.

Menon, M.G.K. 2001, "Biotechnologies: Towards a Brave New World" in Binde 2001.

Mitra, R.K., Gupta, M.P. 2003, "Lessons from E-governance in India", *Indian Management,* August.

Muller, Robert (1986), The Robert Muller School World Core Curriculum Manual in UN's World Core Curriculum (The United Nations, 1986).

One World Trust, 1999, *"Charter 99: A Charter for Global Democracy"*, London, Parliament House.

O'Tuama, Seamus, 2004, "Public Policy and Public Participation in the Knowledge Society: Prospects for Decision-making in Science and Technology Policies" in David Lei-Faur and Eran Vigoda-Gadot (eds.), *"International Public Policy and Management: Policy Learning Beyond Regional, Cultural, and Political Boundaries"*, 2004, New York, Marcel Dekker.

Parr, Sakiko Fuuda, 1997, *"Sustainable Human Development in a Globalized World"*, New York, Human Development Report Office.

Santiso, Carlos, 2001, "Development Cooperation and the Promotion of Democratic Governance: Promises and Dilemmas" in *"International Politiik und Gessellchaft (International Politics and Society)"*, Bonn, Friedrich, Ebert Stiftung.

Strong, Maurice, 1995, "Stockholm to Rio: A Journey Down a Generation," Commission on Global Governance, London: Oxford University Press.

Websites:

www.governance.org

www.rand.org/publications/MR/MR1139

# 3

# A Failure or a Necessity? State Intervention and Growth in Developing Countries

ALICE SINDZINGRE

## INTRODUCTION

In the development economics literature the role of the state is often considered as detrimental to growth and poverty reduction. It is maintained that bureaucracies are bloated, engage in rent-seeking and crowd out the private sector. This conception emerged in the 1970s with the pre-eminence of the neoclassical paradigm. In neoclassical views, state intervention in the economy and the size of governments constitute distortions; they therefore introduce inefficiencies and are harmful to growth. These theoretical views have been compounded due to the influence of international financial institutions in developing countries, especially in low-income countries, such as in Sub-Saharan Africa. Since the 1980s these international financial institutions have made their financing conditional to programs aiming at reducing state intervention. The minimal role of the state was further supported by the abuses of predatory politicians and bureaucracies, dictatorships—whose intervention in economies had clear negative effects on economic growth, directly or indirectly, through the aggravation of inequality, social polarisation and civil conflict among others.

Economic theories, however, did not always conceive the state through these approaches. Before and after WWII, earlier theories of development demonstrated the necessity of strong state intervention in the economy for fostering growth. This was confirmed by the spectacular growth of the developmental states' in East Asia, where public policies and the bureaucracy played an important role. In many developing countries, the size of the public sector is, moreover, sometimes more limited than in industrialised countries.

The paper examines the theories that show the necessity for a key role of the state (which cannot be reduced to a 'market failure'), or, on the contrary, view the state as harmful for growth. It analyses the arguments of the 'founding fathers' of development economics who demonstrated the necessity of the state at low-levels of development and the role of strong states that are able to intervene efficiently in the economy. It also examines the opposing argument of neoclassical economics, which shows the detrimental effects and failures that have characterised state intervention in many developing countries, especially the least developed ones. The paper finally explores the conditions a state in low-income countries need in order to be 'developmental' in the current context of globalisation. These conditions are shaped by several issues, in particular the credibility, size, 'quality', and capacity (especially redistributive) of states and bureaucracies, the historical trajectories of local political economy and the nature of groups that predominate in the state apparatus, and the effects of policy reforms.

Section 1 of the paper analyses the conceptions of the state in the founding theories of development economics. Section 2 presents the lessening of influence of these conceptions due to the increase in power of the neoclassical (or Walrasian) model and the conceptions it has entailed as to the role of the state in development economics. Section 3 presents the elements and possible lessons that can be drawn from the economic growth of Asian 'developmental' states.

## 1. THE CRUCIAL ROLE OF THE STATE AT EARLY STAGES OF GROWTH : THE FOUNDING THEORIES OF DEVELOPMENT ECONOMICS

Many changes have occurred within development economics since WWII and within development theory the conceptions of the state and its role have undergone a dramatic evolution. One topic that has been an object of radical change is the model of the desirable role of government in the economy—the form of its intervention, the nature of government-market relations, and associated policies (Adelman 2000b). The 'founding fathers' of development economics in the 1940s and after agreed on a series of commonalities—among the most well-known are Paul Rosenstein-Rodan, Arthur Lewis, Ragnar Nurske, Gunnar Myrdal, or Albert O. Hirschman, who published a great number of books and articles that deeply influenced the discipline. They agreed that there is scope for choice in institutions, policies and in their sequencing, and that certain choices, in turn, generate the initial conditions for development. There are thus alternative trajectories in development. After WWII, under the influence of the prevailing economic paradigm at that time—and due to the constraints weighing on the governments of newly-independent states—Sub-Saharan Africa (SSA) countries pursued a natural resource intensive development strategy that was trade-led and characterised by limited industrialisation. As Adelman (2000b) put it, however, it fostered growth but with a narrow-base.

The role of governments in economic development has differed considerably among countries. In the 'developmental states' of East Asia, governments had a successful entrepreneurial role demonstrating that an adaptive mix of government and market may promote development. From the 1970s onwards the neoclassical paradigm became increasingly pre-eminent in development economics. For Adelman (2001), however, it allowed a series of fallacies, such as assigning a single cause to underdevelopment, though there are many causes: e.g. low physical or human capital, incorrect relative prices, barriers to international trade and ineffective government. Development is a non-linear, path-dependent, dynamic process. The relevant policies and institutions therefore change over time.

The thinking about the role of the state after WWII evolved in a series of phases. Government was firstly viewed as a necessary engine of development: able to exercise an entrepreneurial role in the context of limited private sectors and as the only player in an economy that has the capacity to achieve tradeoffs and impose solutions among conflicting interests. As highlighted by Paul Rosenstein-Rodan (1943), developing countries at early stages of growth are characterised by coordination failures in interdependent investments in industry which prevent positive spillovers. States at early stages of development have to address the issue of the conditions of the 'big push,' or at least the pump-priming of a regular and long-term growth. Rosenstein-Rodan showed the importance of spillovers and the importance of coordination in development. The crucial question, at the beginning of development, is the understanding of the conditions and policies able to trigger the taking-off of sustained and cumulative growth (Hoff 2000; Bardhan and Udry 1999).

The analyses by Arthur (1994) later revealed the fundamental mechanism of the path dependence of economies, the existence of increasing returns and threshold effects, and therefore the possibility of multiple—low or high—equilibria. Coordination failures may thus lock-in an economy at early stage of development in a low-equilibrium. According to these approaches, the state was viewed as the only agent in the economy capable of correcting these coordination failures and therefore moving the economy out of the low-level equilibrium trap, i.e., the poverty trap. The state was conceived as the only agent being able to fulfil the conditions of the growth process, i.e. the reallocation of factors of productivity from a low-productivity sector (traditional) to a high-productivity (industrial) sector. Non-neoclassical economists viewed resources reallocation as hampered by technological and institutional rigidities. For economists after WWII, industrialisation was not driven by technical progress, but by applying existing technology. The engineering of complementary demand could not happen if left to private sector. It had to be planned by the state (Toye 2003).

History shows that governments always take the lead in promoting institutional development (Adelman 2000a). It also shows that public investment in infrastructure, human capital and industry have been essential to development, as have government-set trade policies, the promotion of technology and the design of overall goals for economic policy. Flexibility and the credibility of government are also important for long-term growth. Governments are more efficient when they are autonomous *vis-à-vis* the pressures of elites. The opposition between states and market is a recent notion. A key historical function of the state has been the creation of well-functioning markets, such as providing the legal framework, credit and infrastructure.

## The State in Developing Countries : The Example of Sub-Saharan Africa

In some countries of Sub-Saharan Africa (SSA), for example, the formation of states after independence has been seen as an application of these theoretical perspectives, which justified the key economic role of the state. In view of the prevailing paradigm in development economics at that time, the post-independence period in SSA is the period of the 'big push', i.e., government-promoted investment programs into domestic infrastructure and inter-related industrial investments. Most SSA states implemented policies involving active government intervention. Ghana is a well-known example of such policies (Killick 1978).

A key issue was the existence of a domestic private sector, entrepreneurship and local capital, which are necessary ingredients for development. Post-independence SSA countries were confronted with problems of capital, technical and organisational skills, weak business elites, as well as political constraints. Private sectors had difficulty developing in SSA due to the colonial structure of trade that was—and still is—based on primary commodity production, with the related problems of forward linkages (processing of commodities, industries) and backward linkages (transport, domestic production of inputs). This post-colonial structure of trade is associated to a specific fiscal model, which impose serious constraints on state intervention. After independence, states intervened in the economy in order to set the conditions of accumulation for their citizens: provision of credit, nationalisations, and external borrowing to finance physical and social infrastructure. Macro-economic policies have not been focused enough on exports, resulting in a low rate of growth of export earnings.

After independence, the post-colonial state has been confronted with state-building constraints. At the end of the 1970s public employment progressively represented the largest part of total non-agricultural employment (about 70% in some countries). States became the main employers in the formal sector. Governments created state-owned enterprises (SOEs) according to analogous processes in most countries. At the end of the 1970s/beginning of the 1980s, there were thus some 200 SOEs in Senegal, 150 in Ghana and Côte d'Ivoire, 60 in Benin and 400 in Tanzania (Nellis 1986). Due to the lack of domestic entrepreneurship, especially in the industrial sector, the state and its 'big push' strategies had no other choice but to create public enterprises in almost all sectors. States likewise created state-owned financial institutions and banks (development banks, agricultural banks) that were aimed to achieve broader objectives of development. State marketing boards were similarly created as interfaces between atomised producers and international markets, while they also fulfilled other objectives, i.e. to work as mechanisms of redistribution and indirect taxation. The relationships between the private sector—local and foreign—and the state followed various models, which evolved according to exogenous and domestic determinants: for example, a private sector based on rents extracted from the public sector and occupying positions in the state (as in Côte d'Ivoire) or having developed outside the political sphere (as in Ghana).

Post-colonial state-building had to address another series of constraints that were specifically political. It had to gather centrifugal forces (based on ethnicity or political rivalries), build infrastructures (ports, roads, etc.) and fulfil social objectives. Lacking capital, it had to borrow at high interest rates for projects that could exhibit low profitability. This process inherent to states at early stages of development is one of the structural factors in the accumulation of unsustainable debt. State-building had to rely on limited resources: the share of public budgets in the GDP is indeed still relatively low, which, according to the so-called 'Wagner law,' characterises developing countries. On average, fiscal revenues represented 21% of the GDP and public spending 26% of the GDP over 1986-87 and 1985-89 respectively, compared with 23% in East Asia and around 50% in industrialised countries in 1995.

The evolution of the impact of the state on economies cannot be dissociated from the historical evolution of economic structures in developing countries. In SSA the model of the 'small open colonial economy' analysed by Hopkins (1973) persisted during the 20th century: import of manufactures and export of primary commodities, due to both external and internal processes. The great vulnerability of this model became evident at end of the 1970s when the external shocks on commodities prices and their volatility created fiscal and current account imbalances, increased public debt and seriously affected growth in low-income countries, further compounded by the debt crisis in 1982, which dried up private investment. A traditional ingredient of growth such as investment and savings also explains poor performances. SSA states received significant investment after independence, but could not sustain it nor trigger a virtuous process of growth circles involving savings and investment and a complementary increase of savings and exports (Akyüz and Gore 2001). While investment in Asia rose between the 1960s and the 1980s (from 10-15% of GDP to 30-40%), it declined in SSA and in 1990-97 was at 17% of the investment levels of the 1960s. Initially both Asia and SSA depended on capital inflows with investment depending on foreign savings. In Asia, however, the increase in investment was accompanied by a faster increase in domestic savings, while in SSA savings lagged behind investment and investment increasingly depended on external resources. Similarly, exports rose faster than GDP in Asia, but not in SSA.

The reform programs prescribed by the international financial institutions (IFIs) did not enhance investment or foster a growth process that would have linked investment, savings and exports. In SSA governments also made policy mistakes, such as increasing external borrowing or showing a lack of interest towards agriculture-based industrialisation, even though most of the countries were agricultural. In the industrial sector, the import-substitution process did not lead to the development of manufacturing exports. Domestic entrepreneurs were often not encouraged and the allocation of rents by the state was not contingent on economic performance. Growth in public spending accelerated in the 1960s because of the provision of social services and recruitment in the civil service. Above all, governments were unable to diversify economic structures, with the constraint that over the long-term the real resources available to government remained limited by the growth of export earnings that were subject to the instabilities of international markets.

## 2. A LIMITED ROLE FOR THE STATE IN DEVELOPING COUNTRIES : THEORETICAL CRITIQUES OF STATE INTERVENTION

The pre-eminence of the neoclassical perspective introduced a dramatic change in development economics in the 1980s. It represented, among other things, a reaction against 'Keynesianism'—interpreted as 'statism'—and the impact it had on economic thought and policy-making in the 1930s and 1940s. Government controls and intervention came to be viewed as inefficient (Toye 1987). In developing countries the state was progressively viewed as predatory, inducing rent–seeking and corruption. Economists advocated a limited state, viewed government economic controls as ineffective, counter-productive and costly, and recommended outward-looking trade policies. Price distortions created by governments, the anti-export bias of trade controls came to be seen as a key cause of the balance of payments constraints on economic growth. The 'right system of incentives' (i.e., governmental measures affecting the allocation of resources) was said to be the most neutral in terms of discrimination among economic activities or foreign and domestic markets. Government was considered as the problem and not anymore the solution, and the optimal policies were now to 'get prices right'.

In this perspective, government intervention was not needed because governments are said to maintain unproductive bureaucracies, fuel the expansion of public sectors, and crowd-out private sector investors. Trade liberalisation and the removal of controls were now seen as fostering growth. International trade can provide a substitute for low aggregate domestic demand: 'trade is enough.' This has been the underlying assumption of the model of export-led economic growth.

In the late 1970s the concept of 'state failure' emerged in the theoretical thinking regarding development, both for empirical reasons—the failure in growth performances in many low-income countries—and theoretical ones. The feeling was that traditional explanations of poor growth performances were insufficient (such as lack of capital, investment, and so on). For many development economists, as well as for the IFIs—the IMF and the World Bank—the failures of states thus appeared *ex-post*, after the occurrence of fiscal crises following the drop in commodity prices in the late 1970s-early 1980s. 'Failures' were obviously present but have been assessed retrospectively, as a result of many factors: economic facts (external shocks) and evolution within development economics, which added to the traditional ingredients of development institutional and political economy factors.

This evolution has been reinforced by studies in political science and political economy in low-income countries, which explained their 'failure' by history and features of local politics, such as neopatrimonialism, predation, cronyism, nepotism, patronage, clientelism or kleptocracy. These features had been mentioned for a long time within economic theories, for example by Gunnar Myrdal (1968) characterising states in developing countries as 'soft', i.e., unwilling to engage in active public policies that promote forced savings and growth. A well-known example is Ghana, which after independence was a 'laboratory', a showcase of the theories of the 'big push' and the necessity of state intervention, but progressively became an illustration of the concept of a 'vampire state' and the failure of 'statist' policies (Austin 1996; Frimpong-Ansah 1991; Rimmer 1992). For this conception of the state, economic failure in developing countries is explained by the state alone, its nature—being dominated by bloated and rentier bureaucracies—and the associated inefficiency of its policies.

In the mid-1970s, these conceptions of the state were reinforced by the theories of rent-seeking, public choice and rational choice. Government officials were perceived as rent-seekers in competition on political markets and in particular seeking public rents (political resources, or the control of natural resources) (Krueger 1974). The aim of the rules they establish is to create distortions for their sole benefit. Theories of public choice or rational choice thus reveal the 'urban bias' in political decisions, stigmatising the urban and political elites that give themselves priority through legislative measures and form interest groups exerting pressure to ensure that economic policies work in their favour (Bates 1988). The state was viewed as a bureaucracy that aims to protect its own interests before and against the interests of citizens. In these approaches, there are very few functions that the state would better fulfil and very few goods it would provide more efficiently than markets (public goods), which would justify its existence. For Bates (1999), for example, policies in SSA did not make a relevant use of human capital or build middle classes. Policies allowed the pre-eminence of traders exploiting macro-economic imbalances and price distortions, as well as ethnic divisions and statuses that prevented the middle classes from forming political opposition movements. States pursued 'extractive' policies. They did not rely on skills and human capital, but rather on the extraction of natural resources. In the case of predatory regimes (as well as in 'warlords economies'), it has even been shown that there is no interest in economic development: preventing development is a rational option as it prevents the building of institutions and wealth that could foster political changeover and opposition (Robinson 1998).

Most studies in political economy characterise states in developing countries in terms of rent, property rights, incentives or corruption; they often rely on an over-simplified concept of the state and political dynamics, especially since these studies are subject to the needs for formalisation and quantification. Politics is taken into account but is often reduced to an analysis of the interest groups and utility-maximising bureaucrats, the winners and losers of the reforms, the appropriate incentives to ensure that the elites apply these reforms, and the ingredients to build up a consensus on 'good policies.' The complexity of the representations relating to power is rarely taken into account. In support of their position, neoclassicals point out the genuine dysfunctions existing in bureaucracies and civil services in developing countries but neglect to question the complexity of their causes and therefore draw conclusions on the state in general (e.g., the Leviathan state) and the limitation of its role as a policy that is always more efficient.

The political economy and institutional explanations of state failure were completed in the 1990s by theories of the state that rely on geography. The nature and economic impact of states is explained via structural characteristics such as geography and demography. In SSA these characteristics explain state failure by its inability to provide certain public goods, such as the rule of law, contract enforcement and infrastructure. Low demographic density is indeed a key challenge in SSA, as the construction of state authority is more difficult in a context of scattered populations. As shown by Herbst (2000), precolonial states were not determined by competition over land, as land was abundant, and exit options were always possible. Thus states were built through loyalties and shaped by the costs of expanding power. After independence, boundaries were set by the colonial powers, and political leaders were affected early on by challengers and instability more than inter-state wars. A growing literature in development economics now highlights the crucial role of geography and the endogeneity of the state in relation to geography and factor endowments (Sokoloff and Engerman 2000; Engerman and Sokoloff 2002).

## Minimal State and International Financial Institutions

During the 1980s the IFIs adopted a variant of the neoclassical paradigm as a basis of their programs, known as the 'Washington consensus' (Williamson 1990). In order for developing countries to achieve long-term growth, Williamson recommended a series of ten reforms. These were fiscal discipline; reordering public expenditure priorities; tax reform; liberalising interest rates; competitive exchange rates; trade liberalisation; liberalisation of inward foreign direct investment (but not capital account liberalisation, which is a less consensual issue); privatization; deregulation (easing barriers to entry and exit); and the reform of property rights.

When the global economic crises destabilised the developing countries at the end of the 1970s—and particularly those depending on the export of primary commodities—the IFIs prescribed a series of policy reforms in exchange for financing the stabilisation and adjustment programs, which were aimed at the reduction of state intervention in the economy. In the early 1980s, the IFIs thus introduced the first generation of stabilisation and adjustment programs following the sharp drop in the prices of primary commodities (e.g., coffee, cocoa, and then oil in the mid-1980s). The theoretical paradigm of stabilisation programs considers that market forces are more efficient than state intervention (such as policies of import-substitution). Developing countries are considered to be at fault. The combination of a rentier structure and inappropriate economic policies were held responsible for the lack of growth. The aim of reforms was therefore to implement a model recommending a minimal state (Sindzingre 1998a). The variants of this model—e.g., the monetary approach to the balance of payments, the Jacques Polak's model—have formed the basis for IFIs reforms aiming at more efficient markets via liberalisation and privatization.

This model, which stigmatises state excess, has been adopted in development economics and backed by the IFIs after political science analyses have brought to the fore the inadequacies of African civil services and the fact that economic history has shed light on the lasting nature of colonial trade structures. As most economic models, this model does not use the concepts from other social sciences (McCloskey 1983), because of the progressive pre-eminence of the formal-neoclassical (North American) paradigm in development economics and the conviction that it is useless to have a theory on the state (which explains its 'under-theorisation' in development economics, Brohman 1995). States continue to be 'black boxes.' SSA states are characterised by their under-development, thereby confirming macro-economic observations. On the one hand, the link between a sizeable public sector and a mediocre economic performance remains controversial, and as is well-known, public expenditure increases with the standard of living. On the other hand, SSA countries exhibit low rates of taxation that set in motion a vicious circle of inefficiency and lack of credibility of the state. Compared to developed countries the weight of the civil service and its wage bill is not excessive in many developing countries. It may be excessive in relation to the weight of the wage bill in the public budgets. It is difficult to evaluate the productivity of bureaucracies. The staff was cut down and salaries frozen after the stabilisation reforms of the 1980s. In terms of percentage of population alone, SSA has the lowest ratio of all the developing regions (Goldsmith 1999; Schiavo-Campo *et al.* 1997a and 1997b; Lindauer and Nunberg 1994).

The application of the minimal state model, against the costly and rentier state given the limited well-being it provides for its citizens, has led the IFIs to reduce the public sector during the period of adjustment that started in the 1980s. It had mixed effects, especially in SSA, since the public sector was in some cases already 'privatised' (i.e., 'captured' by private interests) and civil servants had little sense of the state or 'public service'. Reforms that only followed an economic approach centred on macro-financial aggregates (e.g., the wage bill) were ineffective. The IFIs had to acknowledge that the quality and the ability of the bureaucracy to assume more responsibility were more important factors. They implemented a 'second generation of reforms' in the 1990s that were more micro-economic and took into consideration the motivations and incentives of civil servants (Tanzi 2000).

IFI reforms were focused on the downsizing of the state and the limiting of its intervention in the economy. As for investment, the IFIs' reform programs did not address the issue of industrial and export diversification, and did not avoid 'white elephant' projects and over-optimistic forecasts on countries' growth rates or rates of return on projects (Van Arkadie 1995). They did not address the major weaknesses of SSA states and bureaucracies: the colonial legacy, dependence on the unstable price of a few commodities for foreign exchange and budgets (e.g., coffee, cocoa, oil), and therefore a structural instability and vulnerability. Structural adjustments were based on a technical and apolitical model of the state that has difficulties to take into account the individual rationalities prevailing in developing countries. Reform programs attributed responsibilities and failures to state intervention and criticised 'bad' policies without questioning the local determinants of neo-patrimonialism (Sindzingre and Conte 2002).

In SSA for example, adjustment reforms intensified economic instability and the micro-economic uncertainties that characterise SSA economies over the *longue durée* (Berry 1993). Failure of reforms in terms of growth induced an accumulation of IFI conditionalities over time. The second decade of adjustment in the 1990s therefore witnessed a massive intrusion of IFIs and multiple donors in the policy-making of low-income countries (the game of the 'ritual dance', Kahler 1992; Van de Walle 2001). The theories of 'state failure 'and 'poor governance' justified conditionalities that increasingly affected the core of state formation and local political mechanisms. In the 1990s states had to simultaneously implement economic reform and political reform, i.e. democratisation. The economic benefits of the democratisation, however, remain mixed both at the empirical and theoretical level (Callaghy and Ravenhill 1993).

From the 1980s onwards, the IFIs' influence increased considerably in low-income countries, as a consequence of the fiscal crises that originated from the fall in the terms of trade of primary commodities and the mitigated success of reforms that created repeated lending and 'prolonged use' of IFI resources over the decades (IMF-IEO 2002). As shown by Easterly (2001), in certain countries that received more than 15 'tranches' of loans from the IFIs in the 1980-94 period, the average growth rate was zero. This led to a crisis of credibility of SSA governments, which was accentuated by the repetition of stabilisation programs in contrast with the theory that justifies IMF intervention, i.e. restoring the international credibility of developing countries' governments. During the 1990s, after more than a decade of reform programs, the IFIs often became the main creditors in SSA countries. The latter became increasingly dependent on development assistance and their autonomy in domestic policies increasingly limited, which as expected induced resistance from governments. IFI conditionalities multiplied with time as they extended their financial instruments to domains that became increasingly long-term in nature, structural, political and institutional, e.g., with the concept of governance.

For the IFIs a justification of conditionality and reform is their claim that they act as agents of modernization: economic reforms such as liberalization and privatization undermine domestic rent-seeking and rentier activity. The obvious limits of the IFIs' economic and institutional reforms, however, are that these international financial institutions have to be simultaneously external (to be credible) and intrusive to be effective (thus incurring the risk of being partisan and non-credible). Their analysis of the role of the state cannot by mandate take political dimensions into account: states tend to be analysed in term of capacity—administrative capacity, capacity-building, 'weak' states—and political dimensions in terms of governance. In development economics, many studies in the 1990s thus explored the 'political economy of policy reform,' the endogeneity of policies to political and economic structures, the determinants of 'bad policies' beyond the type of political regime, the inability of governments to use transfers in separating efficiency and distribution, or the causes of their poor credibility—which has been defined as the 'inability to commit' by the two 2004 Nobel prizes in economics, Finn Kydland and Edward Prescott.

## The State as a Supplier of Public Goods : Regulation and Stability

The minimalist model has not produced the expected result in low-income countries, especially in SSA. Growth has mostly benefited exporters of primary products and investors did not turn up. This has been associated with a theoretical change, even if the model of rent-seeking bureaucrats continues to be meaningful in development economics. During the 1990s, research demonstrating the crucial functions of the state returned in favour with institutionalist theories, as well as those on information asymmetries and market failures (for which George Akerlof, Joseph Stiglitz and Michael Spence won the Nobel Prize in 2002), in particular under the influence of Joseph Stiglitz who had occupied an important position at the World Bank (Stiglitz 1974; 1989; 1997).

The 1990s thus witnessed the emergence of a more balanced view of the state, due to both policy and theoretical reasons. The poor performances in Latin America and SSA have been interpreted as failures, either of government policies and reforms. The theoretical framework of information asymmetries and public goods assigned an enhanced role to government intervention. A consensus emerged over the fact that markets may be inefficient in the presence of externalities. States may be inefficient in terms of allocation of resources. They may, however, address better than markets the problems of externalities, coordination failures that stem from externalities, and collective action problems. Market failures (information problems, missing markets) are indeed larger in developing countries, and capacities of government to correct them are weaker. The neoclassical view of efficient economic activity focuses on freedom and on the market as the best example of a system under which people enjoy that freedom, but under certain conditions, there can be 'market failures,' such as the presence of externalities, which justifies the state. This justification, however, is conceived in a narrow sense, i.e., the state may provide public goods that cannot be provided by markets because of market failures. Beyond this mission, the state exceeds its domain and generates inefficiencies, rents, and price distortions.

This was coined as the 'post-Washington consensus,' a concept that became influential within the World Bank in the late 1990s and 'rehabilitated' the role of the state (Stiglitz 1997; World Bank 1997). In this approach, the state has the role of establishing infrastructure—educational, technological, financial, physical, environmental and social. As argued by Joseph Stiglitz, the government has six key roles: promoting education, promoting technology, supporting the financial sector, investing in infrastructure, preventing environmental degradation, creating and maintaining a social safety net. This conception of the state, however, is also affected by several limitations: it has a weak understanding of the complexity of history, politics and the unique 'path dependence' of states. The analysis relies on stylized facts and concepts where meanings and causalities would be similar and stable across time and space. There is an ambiguity in regard to the positive or normative dimension of the analysis, an ignorance of the micro-economic expectations of individuals (in particular civil servants in developing countries) and the composite nature of institutions (Sindzingre 1998b).

These functions of the state consist mainly in supplying public goods that the markets, if left to their free functioning, have no incentive to supply, i.e., the stability of the economic environment, rules that stabilise individual expectations and the correction of market failures and information asymmetries. The policies pursued by governments are not exempt from failures, errors or bad management, and there are just as many government failures as market failures. The concept of a regulating state has therefore gradually inspired development economics as well as the IFIs. In the 'post-Washington consensus' perspective, the functions of the state remain limited: they consist in providing macro-economic stability, regulation and the right incentives, rewarding performance, promoting competition, and privatising.

The IMF enhanced its view of the appropriate role of the state in promoting a 'second generation of reforms' of the civil service in developing countries, as opposed to the 'first generation,' which was focused on restoring macro-economic and financial balances. Reforms had to be focused on 'rules', 'institutions' and a 'high-quality public sector' (Tanzi 2000). This framework, however, has limitations, which are common to the 'Washington consensus' and the 'post-Washington consensus.' The nature of the state remains 'under-theorised' especially in particular, its intrinsic political dimension. As Tilly has shown, the ingredients of state formation are conflict, war, violence and banditry, an example being the creation of European states that painfully emerged from coercive exploitation (Tilly 1985). Mercantile capitalism and state-making reinforce each other according to a logic of expanding power and economies of scale. History shows that state formation is based on war making, extraction, tributes and protection rents (e.g. on merchants).

The 1990s also saw the emergence of the notion of governance within the 'donors' community. The increasing perception of public opinions in donor countries that aid is inefficient and is ending up in the bank accounts of local politicians put forward 'bad governance' as a key explanation of the weak economic performances of SSA countries (Sindzingre 2001). At the same time, the IFIs have discovered the virtues of participation and 'ownership' by the recipients of economic reforms. Since the end of the 1990s, theories of development and the related policies now focus on poverty reduction and the inclusion of the poor, their 'empowerment', participation in institutions and capacity to protect themselves from the corrupt practices of civil servants.

## The Impact of International Financial Institutions on States in Low Income Countries

According to their Articles of Agreement, the IFIs deal with states, irrespective of the nature of their political regime or legitimacy, and are not supposed to interfere in politics. The implicit model here is not that of the minimal state. The IFIs may contribute to the strengthening of these states, through their international recognition, membership of financial institutions and financial flows (Jackson and Rosberg 1982). The IFIs can sometimes help to keep political regimes in power, or overthrow them when the contents of reforms place certain governments in a difficult position. IFI lending continues even if the reforms have been implemented purely on paper. Thus, holding elections may be enough to transform a country into a 'democratic state.'

The gradual incorporation of institutions and the recognition of their endogeneity to policies in the development economics literature after the 1990s have come up against the 'field' operations of donors. Along with multilateral institutions, most aid agencies view their action as a dimension of their foreign policy and strategic interests, and a support to their private sectors (Alesina and Dollar 1998). This is why they have not contributed to the construction of developmental states and civil services in developing countries (not to mention those that were explicitly destabilised by such foreign policy interests). Furthermore, the IFIs take pride in the fact that their explicit objectives are to eliminate rents through the dismantling of state-owned enterprises and marketing boards, devaluations and the rehabilitation of government financial services. Many opposition movements have expressed their support for these objectives and have used them for political purposes.

## 3. THE LESSONS OF EAST ASIAN 'DEVELOPMENTAL STATES' : THE CONCEPT OF THE 'DEVELOPMENTAL STATE'

The concept of the 'developmental state' was coined at the end of the 1990s in order to explain the dramatic growth performance of three East Asian states—Japan, Taiwan and Korea—and later Hong Kong and Singapore. The concept and achievements of developmental states have been explored in the canonical studies by White (1988), Amsden (1989) on Korea, and Wade (1990) on Taiwan, and the reassessment by Wade (2000), Woo-Cumings (1999), and Sindzingre (2004).

What these states had in common was that growth was a result of state intervention and policies, though obviously this varied from one country to the other. The common features were the deliberate creation of price distortions, the objectives of industrial policies, a focus on education, the building of autonomous and technically competent bureaucracies and of coalitions with the private sector, and a positive impact of these policies in terms of growth, in contrast with neoclassical views that considered markets to be more efficient in all this. These 'developmental policies' not only aimed at enhancing the functioning of markets, as highlighted by Hausmann and Rodrik (2003), but also at creating suitable institutions and political conditions, such as coalitions and productive rents and sometimes collusive and corrupt practices, as shown by Kang (2002) in the case of Korea. This was supported in some Asian states by massive external inflows such as US development assistance.

### State Intervention Focused on Credible Policies and Growth

Developmental states revealed that 'statism' is not inherently rent-seeking. Specific public intervention may reinforce the efficiency of markets and the success of liberalisation programs, as well as support the public interest (Streeten 1993). In contrast with the view that economic development is achieved through competition, the ingredients of the developmental state were the economic complementarity between the state and the private sector, which was reinforced by mechanisms of credibility and reputation building, i.e., a credible state and credible policies. Developmental states sustained virtuous cycles where growth reinforces policy credibility and thus investment, as well as successful export-oriented strategies, international credibility reinforcing domestic credibility. Once the state has achieved development, state intervention may direct policies, rather than directly investing in the economy (Huff *et al.* 2001).

The model of growth of the developmental state also gained credibility as it took into account agricultural development and the increase of the size of domestic markets. As shown by Thorbecke and Wan, East Asian governments understood that at early stages of development the major mechanisms for obtaining the resources needed to escape the poverty trap and for industrialisation were the achievement of intersectoral transfers out of agriculture, the agricultural sector generating an agricultural surplus that finances industrialisation. Developmental states fostered primary education throughout rural areas, which allowed more non-farm activities, and therefore fostered migration, and the conditions for labor-intensive industry, outward-orientation and industrial policies (Thorbecke and Wan 2004).

Developmental states also focused on the dimension of production, which has been neglected by the orthodox literature in analysing the state's role in economic development. As argued by Amsden, 'market failures' caused by state intervention are less relevant when the focus is on production and not on exchange (Amsden 1997).

A key ingredient of developmental states has been industrial policies. This is revealed by the example of South Korea, where state intervention has been a major factor in that country's growth. Contrary to the orthodox theses, it has not been a market-preserving intervention. The state intervened heavily in domains such as tariffs and subsidies, e.g. subsidised interest rates. The state created rents as an instrument for industrial development, through a limited number of conglomerates (*chaebols*). In developmental states state intervention was more under the form of policies than in terms of owning a large share of the economy, recycling a large share of its resources through taxation and providing a large share of employment (Sindzingre 2006). Government strategies went beyond pure trade strategy and resorted to a long-term dynamic perspective regarding industrial development and institutional learning.

A key question is the nature of the factors that shape the role of the state and determine its effectiveness in promoting economic change. Historical trajectories play a crucial role, as well as a strong centralised state, a government having a clear conception of economic development. In SSA after independence, developmental states have been confronted with many obstacles. Nationalist policies met the hostility of Western countries in the context of the Cold War. Some SSA states had the ingredients for being developmental but rulers focused more on the politics of nation-building than economic growth. Later the IFIs stabilisation and structural adjustment programs did not reinforce state capacity. Finally, developmental states reveal that state building is a permanent process and that growth always results from interactions between economic and political domains, at both the domestic and international levels.

## CONCLUSION

In the development economics literature the role of the state tends to be considered as detrimental to growth and a source of inefficiencies. These theoretical views have been compounded by the influence of international financial institutions, especially in low-income countries such as in Sub-Saharan Africa. The reforms that they prescribed since the 1980s in exchange for financing have been mostly based on the premises of the virtues of a minimal state.

This paper has shown that economic theories did not always view the state through these approaches. The first theories of development revealed the necessity of state intervention in the economy for fostering growth at its early stages. The opposing arguments have been analysed: they highlight the failures that have affected state intervention in many developing countries, which explain the lack of growth and the persistence of poverty. Even in the framework of the market failure approach, the role of the state is limited to the provision of macroeconomic stability and regulation in order to foster stable expectations and investment.

The paper has also examined the spectacular growth of the 'developmental states' in East Asia, where public policies and the bureaucracy played an important role. The model of the developmental state supports the arguments of the first theories of development on the necessity of effective and strong states. The comparison between African and Asian states has shown that the conditions for states to foster growth are shaped by several issues, in particular the credibility of states and bureaucracies, the historical trajectories of local political economy, and the effects of policy reforms. It has finally been shown, through the examples of these different types of states, that state building is a permanent process and that growth always results from interactions between economic and political domains, at both the domestic and international levels.

## References

Adelman, I. 2000a, *Fifty Years of Economic Development: What Have We Learned?* Paris: The World Bank, Annual Bank Conference on Development Economics.

Adelman, I. 2000b, The Role of Government in Economic Development, In *Foreign Aid and Development: Lessons Learnt and Directions for the Future,* edited by F. Tarp. London: Routledge.

Adelman, I. 2001, Fallacies in Development Theory and Their Implications for Policy, In *Frontiers of Development Economics: The Future in Perspective,* edited by G.M. Meier and J.E. Stiglitz, New York: World Bank and Oxford University Press.

Akyüz, Y. and C. Gore. 2001, African Economic Development in a Comparative Perspective, *Cambridge Journal of Economics* 25 (3) May: 265-88.

Alesina, A. and D. Dollar, 1998, *Who Gives Foreign Aid to Whom and Why?* Cambridge MA: NBER working paper 6612.

Amsden, A.H. 1989, *Asia's Next Giant: South Korea and Late Industrialization,* New York: Oxford University Press.

Amsden, A.H. 1997, Editorial: Bringing Production Back in—Understanding Government's Economic Role in Late Industrialization, *World Development,* 25(4) April: 469-80.

Arthur, W.B. 1994, *Increasing Returns and Path Dependence in the Economy.* Ann Arbor: University of Michigan Press.

Austin, G. 1996, National Poverty and the 'Vampire State' in Ghana: A Review Article, *Journal of International Development*, 8(4): 553-73.

Bardhan, P., and C. Udry, 1999, Institutional Economics and the State in Economic Development, In *Development Microeconomics*, edited by P. Bardhan and C. Udry, Oxford: Oxford University Press.

Bates, R.H. 1999, The Economic Bases of Democratization, In *State, Conflict and Democracy in Africa*, edited by Richard Joseph, Boulder: Lynne Rienner.

Bates, R.H. ed. 1988, *Toward A Political Economy of Development: A Rational Choice Perspective*, Berkeley and Los Angeles: University of California Press.

Berry, S. 1993, *No Condition is Permanent: the Social Dynamics of Agrarian Change in Sub-Saharan Africa*, Madison: University of Wisconsin Press.

Brohman, J. 1995, Economism and Critical Silences in Development Studies: A Theoretical Critique of Neoliberalism, *Third World Quarterly*, 16(2) June: 297-318.

Callaghy, T.M., and J. Ravenhill eds. 1993, *Hemmed In: Responses to Africa's Economic Decline*, New York: Columbia University Press.

Easterly, W. 2001, *The Elusive Quest for Growth: Economists' Adventures and Misadventures in the Tropics*. Cambridge MA: MIT Press.

Engerman, S.L., and K. Sokoloff, 2002, *Factor Endowments, Inequality and Paths of Development among New World Economies*, Cambridge MA: NBER Working Paper 9259.

Frimpong-Ansah J.H. 1991, *The Vampire State in Africa: the Political Economy of Decline in Ghana*, London: James Currey.

Goldsmith, A.A. 1999, Africa's Overgrown State Reconsidered: Bureaucracy and Economic Growth, *World Politics*, 51, July: 520-46.

Hausmann, R., and D. Rodrik. 2003, Economic Development as Self-Discovery. *Journal of Development Economics*, 72: 603-33.

Herbst, J. 2000, *State and Power in Africa: Comparative Lessons in Authority and Control*, Princeton: Princeton University Press.

Hoff, K. 2000, *Beyond Rosenstein-Rodan: The Modern Theory of Underdevelopment Traps*, Washington D.C.: The World Bank, Annual World Bank Development Economics Conference.

Hopkins, A.G. 1973, *An Economic History of West Africa*, London: Longman.

Huff, W.G., G. Dewit, and C. Oughton, 2001, Building the Developmental State: Achieving Economic Growth Through Cooperative Solutions: A Comment on Bringing Politics Back In: *Journal of Development Studies*, 38(1), October: 147-51.

International Monetary Fund-Independent Evaluation Office, 2002, *Evaluation of Prolonged Use of IMF Resources*, Washington D.C.: International Monetary Fund.

Jackson, R.H., and C. Rosberg, 1982, Why Africa's Weak States Persist? The Empirical and Juridical in Statehood, *World Politics*, 35(1), October, 1-24.

Kahler, M. 1992, External Influence, Conditionality and the Politics of Adjustment, In: *The Politics of Economic Adjustment: International Constraints, Distributive Conflicts and the State*, edited by S. Haggard and R. Kaufman, Princeton: Princeton University Press.

Kang, D.C., 2002, *Crony Capitalism: Corruption and Development in South Korea and the Philippines*, Cambridge: Cambridge University Press.

Killick, T. 1978, *Development Economics in Action: A Study of Economic Policies in Ghana*, London: Heinemann.

Krueger, A.O., 1974, The Political Economy of the Rent-Seeking Society, *American Economic Review*, 64(3): 291-303.

Lindauer, D.L., and B. Nunberg eds. 1994, *Rehabilitating Government: Pay and Employment Reforms in Africa*, Washington D.C.: The World Bank.

McCloskey, D., 1983, The Rhetorics of Economics, *Journal of Economic Literature*, 21(2): 481-517.

Myrdal, G., 1968, *Asian Drama: An Inquiry into the Poverty of Nations*, New York: Pantheon.

Nellis, J.R., 1986, *Public Enterprises in Sub-Saharan Africa*, Washington D.C.: the World Bank, Discussion Paper 1.

Rimmer, D., 1992, *Staying Poor: Ghana's Political Economy, 1950-1990*, Oxford: Pergamon Press for the World Bank.

Robinson, J.A. 1998, Theories of 'Bad' Policy, *Policy Reform*, 2(1): 1-46.

Rosenstein-Rodan, P.N. 1943. Problems of Industrialization of Eastern and South-Eastern Europe, *Economic Journal*, 53(210-211) June-September, 202-11.

Schiavo-Campo, S., G. de Tommaso, and A. Mukherjee, 1997a, *An International Statistical Survey of Government Employment and Wages*. Washington D.C.: the World Bank, policy research working paper 1806.

Schiavo-Campo, S., G. de Tommaso, and A. Mukherjee, 1997b, *Government Employment and Pay: A Global and Regional Perspective;* Washington D.C.: the World Bank, Policy Research Working Paper 1771.

Sindzingre, A. 1998a, Crédibilité des Etats et économie politique des réformes en Afrique, *Economies et Sociétés* 4: 117-47.

Sindzingre, A. 1998b, The 1997, World Development Report: Better Policies and International Governance, *IDS Bulletin*, 29(2) April: 56-66.

Sindzingre, A., 2001, Le concept de gouvernance: éléments d'économie politique, In *Les non-dits de la bonne gouvernance*, edited by the Haut Conseil de la Coopération Internationale (HCCI). Paris: Karthala.

Sindzingre, A. 2004, *Bringing the Developmental State Back In: 'Contrasting Development Trajectories in Sub-Saharan Africa and East Asia'*, mimeo, Washington D.C.: Georges Washington University, Society for the Advancement of Socio-Economics (SASE) 16th Annual Meeting.

Sindzingre, A. 2006, *Financing the Developmental State: Tax and Revenue Issues*, mimeo, London: Overseas Development Institute, ODI Meetings Series '(Re)building Developmental States: From Theory to Practice'.

Sindzingre, A., with B. Conte. 2002, Reforms as a Domestic and International Process: Liberalisation and Industry in Côte d'Ivoire, In *Public Policy in the Age of Globalization: Responses to Environmental and Economic Crises*, edited by H. Hveem and K. Nordhaug. London: Palgrave.

Sokoloff, K.L., and S.L. Engerman, 2000, Institutions, Factors Endowments and Paths of Development in the New World, *Journal of Economic Perspectives*, 14(3) Summer: 217-32.

Stiglitz, J.E. 1974, Incentives and Risk-Sharing in Sharecropping, *Review of Economic Studies*, 41: 219-55.

Stiglitz, J.E. 1989, Markets, Market Failures and Development, *American Economic Review*, 79(2) May: 197-203.

Stiglitz, Joseph E. 1997, The Role of Government in Economic Development. In: *Annual Bank Conference on Development Economics 1996*, edited by M. Bruno and B. Pleskovic. Washington D.C.: the World Bank.

Streeten, P. 1993, Markets and States: Against Minimalism, *World Development*, 21(8): 1281-98.

Tanzi, V. 2000, *The Role of the State and the Quality of the Public Sector*, Washington D.C.: International Monetary Fund, working paper WP/00/36.

Thorbecke, E. and H. Wan Jr. 2004, *Revisiting East (and South East) Asia's Development Model*, mimeo, Ithaca: Cornell University Conference, 'Seventy Five Years of Development', May 7-9.

Tilly, C. 1985, War Making and State Making as Organized Crime, In: *Bringing the State Back In:*, edited by P. Evans, D. Rueschemeyer, and T. Skocpol, Cambridge: Cambridge University Press.

Toye, J., 1987, *Dilemmas of Development*, Oxford: Blackwell.

Toye, J., 2003, *60 Years of Development Economics*, mimeo, London: Development Studies Association.

Van Arkadie, B., 1995, The State and Economic Change in Africa, in *the Role of the State in Economic Change*, edited by H.-J. Chang and R. Rowthorn, Oxford: Clarendon Press.

Van de Walle, N. 2001, *African Economies and the Politics of Permanent Crisis, 1979-99*, Cambridge: Cambridge University Press.

Wade, R. 1990, *Governing the Market: Economic Theory and the Role of Government in East Asian Industrialisation*, Princeton: Princeton University Press.

Wade, R., 2000, *Governing the Market: A Decade Later*, London: London School of Economics, Development Studies Institute Working Paper 2000-03.

White, G., ed. 1988, *Developmental States in East Asia*, London: Macmillan.

Williamson, J., 1990, What Washington Means by Policy Reform, In *Latin American Adjustment: How Much Has Happened?*, edited by J. Williamson, Washington D.C.: Institute for International Economics.

Woo-Cumings, M., ed. 1999, *The Developmental State*, Ithaca: Cornell University Press.

World Bank, 1997, *World Development Report 1997: the State in a Changing World*, Washington D.C. : The World Bank.

# The Well-being of Nations

## Reflections on Integrating the Human and Ecosystem Well-being

O.P. Dwivedi

In all cultures philosophers and learned people have debated the nature of good life and have concluded that happiness and well-being, individually and collectively, is a main indicator of a good life. How people feel and think about their own lives as a member of their family and of the society is a good indicator of the quality of life as perceived by them. External factors such as income, educational background, family life, place of residence, and events do have influence on that feeling but these and such other demographic factors have only a modest impact on well-being of people (Diener, *et. al.* 2003); instead factors such as personality traits, peace, fulfilment, spirituality and life satisfaction play an important part in their well-being. It is not being said here that wealth does not play an important role; because not only people living in wealthy nations score higher in the measurement of their satisfaction index but also when poor people receive even a modest increase in their income, their satisfaction level grows. Nevertheless, for poor and middle-income group, that modest increase is merely a temporary phenomenon because such nominal increase might simply fulfil their basic human needs and not their desires. Furthermore, there are variations across cultures; for example, Diener *et. al.* (2005: 412) reported that Asian-American students were happier when they were closer to achieving academic goals "whereas Caucasian students were happy when engaging in an activity that was important to them at that moment." In addition, some societies produce higher levels of well-being than do others—a factor of that nation's cultural history, economic prosperity, and good governance.

## What is Well-being?

Is human well-being the same as human welfare? OECD has defined human well-being as more than the sum of individual levels of well-being which includes equality of opportunities, civil liberties, distribution of resources, and opportunities for further learning (OECD 2001: 11). Included in the human well-being are such factors as economic well-being (including such "social regrettables" as pollution, crime and divorce), social cohesion (or social capital), better health, and the quality of the environment. However, the OECD study did not consider a major variable in its definition: it is the spiritual or personal development; because virtually all activities are carried out by individuals (whether working within an organization or individually), and it is their motivation, behavior, emotional (including mental), physical health, and spirituality, all contribute to the well-being of people.

Spirituality, as a special factor, plays an important role in building the character of a person, as well as developing norms of behavior, strengthening inherited culture and values, and supports interaction within the society. Specifically, the inherited culture and religion play an important role in the well-being . It should also be noted that economic well-being can not be based on the strictly economic calculation nor can be determined simply on aggregate cost-benefit analysis or other consequential criteria (OECD 2001: 14).

Scientists prefer to use the term "subjective well-being" instead of happiness because happiness means several different things (such as joy, satisfaction, etc.) which are difficult to standardize. Subjective well-being "is the scientific name for how people evaluate their lives" (Diener 2005: 1). These evaluations can be specific (such as marital satisfaction, or satisfaction with the job), or wide-ranging (such as satisfaction with the self). Measurements include asking people how satisfied or how happy they are? From various measurements, it is seen that wealthier people are slightly happier on average compared to poor people. Also, good health plays a great part in being happy. Culture makes a difference because some cultures have a higher level of well-being than others. Spirituality and believing in religion makes people happier (Cohen 2002: 287-310). On the other hand, anxiety, anomic tendencies (such as powerlessness, social isolation, alienation, disorientation, and pessimism), and suicidal feelings relate to a low level of subjective well-being (Bulmahn 2000: 375-400). Bulmahn reported that before the merger of East Germany with the West, the number of suicidal mortality declined from more than 37 suicides per 100,000 to only 15 per 100,000 inhabitants by the mid-1990s (2000: 390).

## The Place of Spirituality in the Well-being of People

Subjective well-being is a factor of (a) life satisfaction, (b) the sense of happiness, and (c) a reduced level of anxiety and pessimism. For example, Bulmahn reports that when Eastern Germany was amalgamated with its western part, the subjective well-being of the people improved considerably as "eastern Germans are more satisfied today than in 1990, and the share of those who say they are leading a happy life has increased" (Bulmahn 2000: 391). The example of Eastern Germany shows that modernization improves the quality of life, including life satisfaction, and increases the sense of well-being of people. Of course, life satisfaction or the quality of life is seen as the expression of cognitive well-being, while happiness is an indication of emotional welfare (Bulmahn 2000: 386)

One reason that many Western scholars consider the concept of well-being as a subjective matter is because of a well-known association existing between religion and happiness although it is not known which particular aspect of religiosity connects with the life satisfaction and the well-being. And as the matter of faith and religion is a subjective matter, the concept of well-being is also seen as a subjective matter. Moreover, there are significant differences among people belonging to different faiths and religions, and hence it is rather difficult to develop a universal model of such co-relation which can be easily measured and analyzed in a scientific manner. Nevertheless, it has been argued very strongly that "religious people report being happier and more satisfied with life than irreligious people" (Myers and Diener 1995: 16). Levin and Chatters (1998) have also concluded that religion appears to constitute a therapeutic effect on mental health outcomes, which ultimately relates to satisfaction with life style. Life satisfaction can also be measured. However, between religiosity and spirituality, the major difference is whereas religiosity may refer to one's relationship with the religion as it is practiced (or the relationship with organized religion); spirituality (to paraphrase Cohen 2002) relates to satisfaction with life as spiritual people feel that their lives have purpose, have understanding about events happening around them, find comfort in their religious beliefs, are willing to help others as they were helped in the past, and believe in good *Karma*. Of course, not all religious beliefs and practices may have the same impact on the spirituality of people including its impact on their health. However, one major dimension of spirituality is that it brings goodness into this world. Myers (1992) asserted that happiness also depends on what meaning and purpose in life people attach to, their sense of humility, equanimity, grace, perspective, and lack of fear of death. These aspects help people to take care of hopelessness, depression, stress, and negative affects of events, leading to a better sense of well-being, and manage their lives through difficult experiences (Cohen 2002: 306).

## HAPPINESS AND WELL-BEING

For many years, psychologists have been doing research and writing about happiness (Hornby 1948; Diener 2005; Furnham and Cheng 2000; Veenhoven 1984). For some, happiness may imply a psychological state following the fulfilment of some desired human needs, for others, happiness indicates prosperity and progress. But when it comes to measure happiness, there exist cultural, racial, and individual differences; for example, despite their inferior living conditions, the older Blacks in the US reported a higher level of happiness than older Whites (Campbell 1976); or a study about happiness, materialism and religious experiences in the US and Singapore by Swinyard and others found that "less-materially-oriented people are happier than others—both in Singapore and in the United States" (2000). It means that materialism is not the main source of happiness; although happy people might have material possessions, they look for happiness elsewhere. That direction is towards their inner spirituality, religious thoughts, being keenly aware of a divine presence, and trying to live by certain cardinal beliefs. The following five values constitute the cardinal elements of the well-being: (1) meeting the physical/biological needs; (2) availability of freedom of action and choices; (3) opportunities to develop intellectual and/or artistic abilities; (4) a commonality of norms and values being shared with others, especially trust (includes whether people *trust* others or whether people are considered *trustworthy*, and whether they have trust in public and private institutions); and (5) satisfying spiritual needs. It is here where the Hindu concept of *Dharma* and *Karma* becomes relevant to secure a satisfying and happier world. This cardinal Hindu thought is expressed by the following verse: *Sarve Bhavantu Sukhinah; Sarvey Santu Niramayah; Sarve Bhadrani Pashyantu; Maa kashchit dukha bhaag-bhavet* [May all people be happy, may all be healthy, may we have the same feelings towards others, and may no one be miserable.] Thus, well-being is a part of happiness but cannot be measured easily compared to happiness.

## Review

But, what is this "well-being" that we all are striving for? Is it happiness? Is there such a thing? Does it not depend on whether we are healthy or sick, or whether we have money to spend, or enjoy holidays, acquire material things, avoid the hardship of old-age, escape from tension and stress, and so on? In this essay, an attempt is made to argue something singularly unique which is that the well-being of people is tied to the well-being of a nation; and as such, people not the aggregate of economic or related indices are the ultimate focus. On the spirituality plain, achieving this goal of the well-being is possible only by obtaining a true *happiness here and now* by removing among the people malice and spite from their thinking-process thereby creating inner genuine goodwill and benevolence which may result in the spirit of compassion and the joy of helping others. This is based on the Buddhist perspective, as explained by P. J. Saher (1970), which states that the well-being is a freedom from ill-will in the world, a consideration for all living beings; it is an absence of lust (*viraagataa*) in the world, and the sacrifice of pleasures that arise from objects of the senses (*kaamaanam samatikkam*); and finally, it is the seclusion of a person "who is content in himself (*sukho viveko tutthassa*), who hears and sees reality" (Saher 1970: 92). We know that the desire for sensuous pleasure and material objects dominates us, and we always try to seek the satisfaction of this desire; and when such a desire is not fulfilled, we suffer because "the greater the desire, the greater the suffering." Therefore, those who no longer hanker after social and professional prestige, honours, luxuries, and so forth, they may avoid anxiety and suffering.

## ASSESSING THE WELL-BEING OF NATIONS

Robert Prescott-Allen, in cooperation with the IUCN (the World Conservation Union), the International Development Research Centre (Ottawa), and some other United Nations agencies, prepared a country-by-country Index of the well-being of Nations (Prescott-Allen 2001: 1). His contention is that as human population and economies have grown, "it has become impossible to improve one's own well-being without affecting other people's." For example, nations with high standard of living impose excessive pressure on the global environment while those nations which place low demands on the ecosystem are desperately poor. Matters such as pollution, shortage of natural resources, and ever declining bio-diversity have not only affected the well-being of the ecosystem, but have also influenced the quality of life of people. Thus, the well-being of the ecosystem and of people is intertwined with each other, and as such development of a society and its sustenance require not only happiness of people but also a resilient and rich ecosystem.

To measure the well-being of nations, Prescott-Allen (2001) used several indicators such as the UNDP Human Development Report, the Ecological Footprint, Environmental Sustainability Index, World Resources Report, the Environmental Pressure Index, etc. A common framework of dimensions was prepared consisting of: (a) human dimensions including health and population, national and household wealth, education and culture, community and social capital, and equity; and (b) ecosystem dimensions including land and forests, water quality and diversity, air quality, species and genetic diversity, and energy and resources use. He defined: (1) human well-being as "a condition in which all members of society are able to determine and meet their needs and have a large range of choices to meet their potential"; and (2) ecosystem well-being as "a condition in which the ecosystem maintains its diversity and quality—and thus its capacity to support people and the rest of life—and its potential to adapt to change and provide a wide range of choices and opportunities for the future" (Prescott-Allen, 2001: 5).

Based on Prescott-Allen's work (2001) information is presented by selecting 28 countries representing all shades of national scores. (Table 4.1) the data illustrate the situation pertaining to the quest for well-being and sustainable environment. The range for Top point on scale is 100-81 being good in which case it is a desirable condition when all objectives have been

TABLE 4.1
**Ranking of Selected Countries Ranked by their HWI, EWI and WI Indices**

| | *Country* | *Human Well-being Index (HWI) Ranking* | *Ecosystem Well-being Index (EWI) Ranking* | *Composite Well-being Index (WI) Ranking* |
|---|---|---|---|---|
| 1 | Sweden | 79 | 49 | 64.0 |
| 3 | Norway | 82 | 43 | 62.5 |
| 7 | Canada | 78 | 43 | 60.5 |
| 12 | Germany | 77 | 36 | 56.5 |
| 18 | Australia | 79 | 28 | 53.5 |
| 24 | Japan | 80 | 25 | 52.5 |
| 27 | United States | 73 | 31 | 52.0 |
| 29 | France | 75 | 29 | 52.0 |
| 33 | UK | 73 | 30 | 51.5 |
| 38 | Netherlands | 78 | 22 | 50.0 |
| 55 | Argentina | 55 | 40 | 47.5 |
| 65 | Russian Federation | 48 | 42 | 45.0 |
| 79 | Chile | 55 | 30 | 42.5 |
| 87 | Indonesia | 36 | 48 | 42.0 |
| 89 | Egypt | 39 | 43 | 41.0 |
| 92 | Brazil | 45 | 36 | 40.5 |
| 99 | Malaysia | 46 | 33 | 39.5 |
| 116 | Philippines | 44 | 32 | 38.0 |
| 133 | Nigeria | 16 | 56 | 36.0 |
| 136 | South Africa | 43 | 27 | 35.0 |
| 143 | Kenya | 18 | 51 | 34.5 |
| 150 | Mexico | 45 | 21 | 33.0 |
| 160 | China | 36 | 28 | 32.0 |
| 167 | Pakistan | 18 | 44 | 31.0 |
| 168 | Ghana | 22 | 38 | 30.0 |
| 172 | India | 31 | 27 | 29.0 |
| 176 | Saudi Arabia | 31 | 23 | 27.0 |
| 180 | Iraq | 19 | 31 | 25.0 |

*Total countries surveyed*: 180. The highest and lowest scores for each of these three indices are 82/3, 68/14, and 64.0/25.0 respectively.

*Source* : Prescott-Allen (2001). *The Well-being of Nations: A Country-by-Country Index of Quality of Life and the Environment*. Washington, D.C.: Island Press (jointly with the International Development Research Centre of Canada, Ottawa), Table 27, pp. 267-68.

fully met, followed by 80-61 being fair where objectives have been almost met—an acceptable performance, 60-41 being medium, 40-21 being poor with undesirable condition, and 20-1 being bad or unacceptable status of people and the environment.

## ASSESSING HUMAN WELL-BEING

Of course, the well-being of nations and their people is a factor of their quality of life and the quality of environment around them. In this section, the author discusses ranking of selected countries with respect to their human well-being, ecosystem well-being and the composite well-being by combining the first two indices. Although it sounds strange to note how some cultures perceive good life, Prescott-Allen while preparing a country-by-country index of quality of life and the environment, states that different cultures aspire different things pertaining to good life. According to him, Chinese seek the five blessings as a part of good life: long life, riches, health, love of virtue, and a natural death in an old age; French seek liberty, equality and fraternity; for the British, it is health, wealth and wisdom; for Americans, it is life, liberty, and the pursuit of happiness; and finally for Indians, it is power, pleasure, morality, and final emancipation of soul (*nirvana*) (Prescott-Allen, 2001: 1). In the case of Chinese, another author has indicated that the Chinese concept of happiness and the well-being includes: "material abundance, physical health, virtuous and peaceful life, and relief from death anxiety" (Luo 2001: 409).

Despite what different people seek, when it comes to environmental quality, it is clear that those who have a high standard of living impose excessive demand on the environment, but those who are poor also place heavy demand on the environment because they lack means, infrastructure and resources to control environmental pollution. In a survey undertaken for preparing an index of quality of life and the environment (Table I), it has been shown that the five countries listed above score differently. In fact, the three wealthy countries show a better score (when human and eco-system well-being are combined) compared to the two poor nations of China and India.

In *The Well-being of Nations*, Prescott-Allen (2001) has contributed to the debate of what should be the appropriate relationship between people and the ecosystem, and the factors which are crucial for the well-being of our entire planetary system. Of course, most of the data used is for the 1996-99 period, but it gives a good perspective of where countries were at the end of the 20th Century.

## GOOD GOVERNANCE AS A FOUNDATION FOR OPERATIONALIZING THE INTEGRATION OF HUMAN AND ECOSYSTEM WELL-BEING

In the human well-being definition by Prescott-Allen (2001), it was stated that unless all members of society are able to meet their needs and also have a large range of choices and opportunities to fulfil their potential, a nation's well-being will not be achieved. However, Prescott-Allen (2001) did not discuss the ways and means of how members of society could meet such needs and achieve their potentials. Among other factors, good governance is one such vehicle which enables people to realize those needs and aspirations. I believe that good governance is a prerequisite for any society to achieve its fullest potential of good life. In this section, the role of good governance in creating conditions for both the human and environmental system well-being of nations is discussed.

There is no general agreement among nations and cultures as to what constitutes good governance because of difference in cultural norms, style of doing things, expectations of people from their governments, and the quality of environment surrounding them. Nevertheless, good governance is needed not only to deliver public services efficiently and effectively, but also to create conditions which enable people to pursue ends of life as they see fit. Let us examine in brief what good governance constitutes?

## A FRAMEWORK OF GOOD GOVERNANCE

The term "good" is a value-laden term that involves a comparison between two things or systems by using some standard of measure. A government or a system of governance is considered good if it exhibits certain fundamental characteristics. Perhaps the United Nations Development Program (UNDP) offers the most comprehensive definition and an idealistic model of good governance: Good governance is, among other things, participatory, transparent and accountable. It is also effective and equitable. And it promotes the rule of law. Good governance ensures that political, social and economic priorities are based on broad consensus in society and that the voices of the poorest and the vulnerable are heard in decision-making over the allocation of development resources (UNDP 1998: 3). The above discussion presents the following characteristics of good governance: (a) public participation in decision-making; (b) rule of law which is enforced impartially; (c) transparency for access to governing process (including institutions and information sources); (d) responsiveness of institutions to the needs of all stakeholders; (e) consensus among different and differing interests in the society; (f) equity assured to all individuals so that they may improve their well-being; (g) effective and efficient responsibility and accountability of institutions and the statecraft which meet basic needs of all by using state-controlled resources to their optimum accountability; (h) strategic vision of the leaders towards broad range long-term perspectives on sustainable human development; (i) transparency for access to governing process; and (j) stewardship of governance where governing elites dedicate their lives for service to the public, and where amoralism does not reign supreme (Dwivedi and Mishra 2007). Good governance and sustainable human development, especially for developing nations, also requires conscientious attempts at eliminating poverty, sustaining livelihoods, fulfilling basic needs, and offering an administrative system that is clean and open. It is important that these characteristics are not only enshrined in a constitutional document but also are practiced (Dwivedi, 2005: 271-73).

## THE ROLE OF SPIRITUALITY IN OPERATIONALIZING GOOD GOVERNANCE

As discussed earlier, spirituality plays an important part in happiness and well-being of people. Similarly it plays a crucial role in keeping the system of governance honest and transparent. Spirituality can lead to mastery over our baser impulses such as greed, exploitation, abuse of power, and mistreatment of people; it requires self-discipline, humility, and above all, the absence of arrogance in holding public office. Furthermore, it enables people to centre their values on the notion that there is a cosmic ordinance and divine law which must be maintained. Spirituality serves both as a model and operative strategy for the transformation of human character by strengthening the genuine, substantive will to serve the common people. If our goal is to serve and protect the common good, then spirituality can provide the incentive for public officials to serve the public with dignity and respect. Although spirituality is supposed to be an integral part of our religious traditions and beliefs, its secular dimension (which is yet to be particularly acknowledged by secular institutions) is crucial in governance, especially with respect to public service ethics and values. From this author's perspective, spirituality in governance requires officials not only in believing in *Dharma* (the concept of righteousness) but also doing good *Karma* (deeds).

How does spirituality assist the sustainability of good governance? A *spiritually oriented* public official knows that his/her *Dharma* enables him/her to serve others. In so doing, he will be fulfilling twofold duties: one to the self, whereby one seeks inner strength through spiritual action, and the other to the community-at-large whereby one works for the common good. As such, *Dharma* and *Karma* combined together regulate human conduct and cast individuals into the right character mould by inculcating in them spiritual, social and moral virtues, and thereby strengthens the ethos that holds the social and moral fabric of a society together, by maintaining order in society, building individual and group character, and giving rise to harmony and understanding. Thus, by understanding the precepts and relevance of *Dharma* and *Karma* for the management of statecraft, a common strategy for public service spirituality and good governance can be developed. Such a strategy depends much upon how those public officials together: (a) perceive a common future for their society; (b) act both individually and collectively towards protecting the common good; and (c) realize that they as individuals have a moral obligation to support their society's goal since their acts will have repercussions on the future of their society (Dwivedi 2002: 48). Finally, a morality-driven model strengthens those broad principles that ought to govern our governmental conduct, because they mark the direction towards which those who call for individual spirituality, sacrifice, compassion, justice, striving for the highest good, and specifically for public servants, considering their jobs as vocation. And, while the emphasis on secular government and liberal-democracy assigns the place of morality to the individual's conduct and behavior, it has, nevertheless, acknowledged a continuing tension between the requisites of good governance (through its public policy and programs) and the spiritual and moral standards by which they can be measured. Spirituality, deriving from such foundations thus provides an important base to the governing process. Confidence and trust in liberal-democracy can be safeguarded only when the governing process exhibits a higher moral tone, deriving from the breadth of ethical and spiritual sensitivity. Finally, for good governance, it is necessary for public officials (both elected and appointed) to know that there are correct ways of doing things and those standards and rules should be adhered to. Believing that they, having been entrusted with the stewardship of the state, owe special obligations, have special expectations, and reside in a fiduciary world, for these officials' accountability and responsibility becomes a moral question; and as such they are moved by a higher cause. It is here where their spirituality and a sense of doing their duty acquire a holistic tone; a tone which may enable them to dedicate their lives towards creating conditions for the well-being of their society. Material benefits, possessions, and official privileges are going to be transitory illusions; happiness, as the indicated by Swinyard study (2001) of the US and Singapore, will come from how they perceive their inner world, i.e., their spirituality, and their whole approach to life. Good governance as an operational arm of happiness and the well-being is possible only when our public officials behave as such.

## Observations and Reflections

*On well-being, Albert Einstein stated*: "The satisfaction of physical needs is indeed the indispensable precondition of a satisfactory existence, but in itself it is not enough. In order to be content men must also have the possibility of developing their intellectual and artistic powers to whatever extent accord with their personal characteristics and abilities" (Einstein 1950: 12). Building on the lamentation of Einstein and the previous discussion, the author presents the following seven prepositions for discussion:

### *(1) Poverty is the Greatest Challenge*

Environmental stress is less of the result of poor nations than the voracious style of consumption in the North. The pressure on natural resources increases with consumption. Consumption pressure is a factor of the number of people making demands, but it is also a factor of consumption pattern. It has been estimated that every birth in the North puts as much pressure on resources as tens of births in the South. Thus, in addition to the eradication of poverty in the South, lifestyle in the North will have to be modified. For example, the World Commission on Environment and Development has estimated that the cost of implementing Agenda 21 could be about $ 125 billion US a year until the end of the 20th century. And as most of the expenditures are related to managing commons and assisting poor nations, it helps to appreciate that "in 1990 developing nations transferred $140 billion in debt service payments, capital and interest, to creditor nations" (Ramphal 1992: 253-54). If the North can divert a part of this sum towards global environmental protection and sustainable development, our world will be a better and safer place to live. Some may argue that the establishment of the Global Environmental Facility (GEF) may have addressed this concern; however, there have been criticisms about the Facility's governing structure, its strategies, and operative procedures. Although in March 1994, a new instrument of governance for GEF was agreed upon between North and South, it has adopted, as some critics contend, "many of the failings of its administrative parents, and particularly those of the Bank" (Jordan 1994: 266).

### (2) Building Bridges of Collaboration between the North and the South

In the year 2004, the United States allocated $36 billion for homeland security, and about $360 billion for the military; contrast this with the $11.3 billion that the US sets aside for the international aid each year (Brusasco-Mackenzie 2004: 12). Billions more have been spent by the coalition of willing partners to the Iraq war. On the other hand, only $54 billion to $64 billion are needed annually to cut the world poverty in half by 2015 (Devrajan, *et al.* 2002). Clearly, there is a need to change the militaristic definition of security to the concept of "well-being" of all. The world population is about 6.4 billion and it might rise to about 8.9 billion by 2050 (WWI, 2004). If in 2003, 831 million people across the world remain hungry and malnourished, what will happen later when there will be further loss of croplands due to degradation, soil erosion, and climatic changes as expected during the first half of the 21st Century? If we take into account the water crisis facing the world, we should note that 1.1 billion people currently lack access to safe drinking water, and 2.4 billion do not have adequate sanitation, mostly in Asia and Africa. For these people, their well-being ought to be paramount rather than billions being used in militaristic ventures. Clearly a new model of development—one that could ensure human security and planetary well-being—is needed. It is also clear that while the North has been able to achieve environmental security at home, they have missed the opportunity to promote sustainability and equity since the Rio summit of 1992; and whether there will be any substantive change in this situation after the Johannesburg Summit of 2002, nothing is certain. It is here where there is an urgent need to build bridges of collaboration between North and South by specifically assisting the achievement of the UN Millennium Development Goals (MDGs).

### (3) Same Planet but Living in Different Worlds

In August 2005, when I visited a town Bindki (near Kanpur city, India) to see my mother on death-bed, electricity was available in that town (of more than 50,000 people) for only two hours a day. If it was available for all hours, people in that town would have easily consumed whatever the government controlled electricity board was ever able to supply. Demand for energy has outpaced the growth of population; for example, between 1850 and 1970, while the population on Earth just tripled but the energy consumption rose to 12-fold (Sawin 2004: 25). People in India and other Asian nations have either no access or only limited access to energy use; while at the same time, the rich people use, on average, 25 times more per person than the poor ones do (Sawin 2004: 24-41). If Chinese and Indians ever reach the same level of energy consumption akin to the Americans (who use 10 times more than the average Chinese and 20 times more than the average Indian), the energy crisis will be beyond our control. This has enormous implications for the survival of people.

### (4) Strengthen Cultural Liberty

UNDP has suggested through its Human development report (2004) that the denial of cultural liberty "can generate significant deprivations, impoverishing human lives and excluding people from the cultural connections they have reason to seek" (UNDP 2004: 13). That cultural liberty is central to people well-being because its successes and failures in social, economic and political spheres influence not only physical, social and material deprivation but also the overall well-being . About the importance of culture as a crucial dimension in development, this author stated in 1994: "If the root of such differences between the West and the South is culture, then should not 'culture' be the foundation upon which one should build alternate models of development?" (Dwivedi 1994: 143).

### (5) Needed Public Officials with Conscience

Conscience of a person depends largely on his/her character as well as spirituality. Spirituality can lead to mastery over our baser impulses such as greed, exploitation, abuse of power, and mistreatment of people. It requires self-discipline, humility, and above all, the absence of arrogance in holding public office. Furthermore, it enables people to centre their values on the notion that there is a cosmic ordinance and divine law which must be maintained. Spirituality serves both as a model and operative strategy for the transformation of human character by strengthening the genuine, substantive will to serve the common people. A spiritually-oriented public official knows that his/her duty enables him/her to serve others. In so doing, she will be fulfilling two duties: one to the self, whereby one seeks inner strength through spiritual action; and the other to the community-at-large, whereby one works for the common good. As such, personal spirituality and character regulate human conduct and cast individuals into the right character mold by inculcating them with spiritual, social, and moral virtues, and thereby strengthening the ethos that holds the social and moral fabric of a society together, by maintaining order in society, building individual and group character, and giving rise to harmony and understanding (Dwivedi 2002: 48). The public wants government officials also to show moral leadership. And those who follow righteousness in public office commit no sin. In some cases, ethical violations in public places are encouraged by the absence of fear of being caught, by a tendency to sidestep the voice of conscience, or by the view that if caught, there may be only a mild reprimand. The objective of good governance is to create an environment in which public servants as well as politicians in government are able to respond to the challenge of good governance. That challenge for public officials involves a notion of duty, as well as acting morally and accountably. If these two dimensions can be brought together in the management of the public service, it may become possible for a public servant to rise above self-interest, by placing the collective good above private interest and greed. The strengthening of such a notion creates a shared feeling or spirit of public duty among those who govern. Such a classical notion includes other values such as: probity; the universal application of objective standards; a willingness to speak the truth to Ministers; an appreciation of the wider common good over and above narrower political interest; equity; and a sustained concern for democratic ideals. Such is the duty of those who wish to be involved in the difficult and complex world of governance. This is the essence and basis of a good government.

### (6) A New Paradigm for the Third Millennium

Jorge Nef (1999) has argued that the fundamental premise of the dominant international paradigms which have emerged since the World War II (and especially since the collapse of the Soviet Union) is the notion that North is secure and the South is insure. Instead in an increasingly interdependent world, the weakness of the South increases the vulnerability of the North. There is a need to change the mental mode within the North which denies and resists any change to their age-old perception that developing nations are the problem. That is why there is a need to redefine or create a new global paradigm which is supports human security and well-being of all. And, although the UN Conference on the Human Environment, held in Stockholm, Sweden, 1972 brought into discussion the concept/term of sustainable development, 'it was not until the publication of the World Commission on Environment and Development (WCED) Report, *Our Common Future,* in 1987 that this term received a world-wide acceptance and usage. This paradigm has dominated the world scene for about two decades but appears to have declined in its prestige since the World Summit in Johannesburg in 2002 (UNESCO 2002). A new paradigm seems to be emerging, and that is going to be The Well-being of All (as referred to in Hindu Vedas: *Sarve Bhavantu Sukhinah*).

### (7) Envisioning the World-wide Progress for All

Progress in human development has been extraordinary during the past 50 years because on average people, living in developing nations, are living longer and healthier, have more to spend, are better fed, and more literate. And this has all happened during my lifetime. Life expectancy has risen, great advances have been made in primary education, and food sufficiency has been achieved in many countries. Nevertheless, wide disparities are also evident. For example, the amount spent by Europeans on mineral water in one year is enough to provide primary education in developing countries for the next 10 years because there are still 1 billion people who cannot read and write, and among them two-thirds are women; or when we talk about wealth, we should note that the income gap has risen between the top 20% nations and the bottom 20% poorer nation at the proportion of 30:1 in 1960 to 78:1 in 1994 (Dwivedi and Khator 2006). Thus, human development has not kept an even pace. Amartya Sen (1999) has defined it as the fundamental freedom that enhances people choices, and thus raises their level of well-being. From this perspective, substantive freedom includes the capacity to avoid deprivations such as starvation, under nourishment, or premature mortality. It also includes acquiring basic education and skills to be gainfully employed, as well as the freedom to participate in political, economic and social systems. It means building up capacity for people to take decisions. At the same time, it must be noted that human development and economic growth are mutually reinforcing, because for the development to be sustainable, both should accelerate in tandem. This requires: (a) citizens receiving the basic services (such as education, primary health care, adequate supply of food, clean water, and sanitation); (b) people participating in the implementation as well as design of developmental programs created in their name and for them if the resources are to benefit the most needy (especially women and other marginalized persons); (c) recognizing the need for greater cooperation between all sectors of human development including spiritual well-being; (d) being proactive in global economy because globalization disproportionately favors those who have expertise, power, and the capacity to compete in the global market (Kagia 2002: 63-65).

## References


Brusasco-Mackenzie, Margaret, 2004, "Environmental Security: A View from Europe", *Environmental Change and Security Project*, Washington, D.C.: Woodrow Wilson International Center for Scholars, issue 10, pp. 12-18.

Bulmahn, Thomas, 2000, "Modernity and Happiness—The Case of Germany," *Journal of Happiness Studies*, Vol. 1, pp. 375-400.

Campbell, A., 1976, "Subjective Measures of Well-Being", *American Psychologist*, February, pp. 117-24.

Cohen, Adam B., 2002, "The Importance of Spirituality in Well-being for Jews and Christians", *Journal of Happiness Studies*, Vol. 3, pp. 287-310.

Devarajan, S. Margaret J. Miller, and Eric V. Swanson. 2002, *Goals for Development: History, prospects and costs*, The World Bank website: http://econ.worldbank.org/files/13269_wps2819.pdf

Diener, Ed. 2005, "About Subjective Well-being (Happiness and Life Satisfaction)", http://www.psych.uiuc.edu/~ediener/faq.html, (April 28).

Diener, Ed, Shigehiro Oishi, and Richard E. Lucas. 2003, "Personality, Culture and Subjective Well-being: Emotional and Cognitive Evaluations of Life", *Annual Review of Psychology*, Vol. 54, pp. 403-25.

Dwivedi, O.P. 1994, *Development Administration: From Underdevelopment to Sustainable Development*, London, UK: Macmillan Press.

Dwivedi, O.P. 2002, "On Common Good and Good Governance" in *Better Governance and Public Policy* ed. by Dele Olowu and Soumana Sako, Bloomfield, CT, USA: Kumarian Press, pp. 35-51.

Dwivedi, O.P., 2005, "Good Governance in a Multicultural World: Oceans Apart yet World Together", in *Administrative Culture in a Global Context*, edited by Joseph G. Jabbra and O.P. Dwivedi, Toronto, Canada: de Sitter Publications, pp. 265-84.

Dwivedi, O.P. and Renu Khator, 2006, "Sustaining the Development: The Road from Stockholm to Johannesburg", in *Sustainable Development Policy and Administration*, ed. by Gedeon M. Mudacumura, Desta Mebratu, and M. Shamsul Haque, Boca Raton, Florida: Taylor & Francis, pp. 113-33.

Dwivedi, O.P. and D.S. Mishra, 2007, "Good Governance: A Model for India", in *Handbook of Globalization, Governance, and Public Administration*, ed. by Ali Farazmand and Jack Pinkowski, Boca Raton, Florida: Taylor & Francis, pp. 701-41.

Einstein, Albert, 1950, *Out of My Later Years*, New York: Philosophical Library.

Furnham, A. and H. Cheng, 2000, "Lay Theories of Happiness", *Journal of Happiness Studies*, Vol. 1, pp. 227-46.

Jordan, Andrew, 1994, "The Global Environmental Facility (GEF)", Global Environmental Change, Vol. 4, No. 3.

Kagia, Ruth, 2002, "Prospects for Accelerating Human Development in the Twenty-first century", In Ginkel, Hans van; Barrett, Brendan; Court, Julius; and Velasquez, Jerry. Ed. *Human development and the Environment: Challenges for the United Nations in the New Millennium*, Tokyo, Japan: United Nations University Press, pp. 63-75.

Levin, J.S. and L.M. Chatters, 1998, "Research on Religion and Mental Health: An Overview of Empirical Findings and Theoretical Issues", in *Handbook of Religion and Mental Health* ed. H.G. Koenig, San Diego, CA: Academic Press, pp. 33-50.

Luo, Lu, 2001, "Understanding Happiness: A Look into the Chinese Folk Psychology", *Journal of Happiness Studies*, Vol. 2:407-32.

Myers, D., 1992, *Pursuit of Happiness: Discovering the Pathway to Fulfilment, Well-being, and Enduring Personal Joy*, New York, NY: Avon Publishers.

Myers, D.G. and E. Diener, 1995, "Who is Happy?" *Psychological Science*, Vol. 6, No. 1: 10-19.

Nef, Jorgen, 1999, *Human Security and Mutual Vulnerability: The Global Political Economy of Development and Underdevelopment*, Ottawa, Canada: International Development Research Centre.

OECD, 2001, *The Well-being of Nations: The Role of Human and Social Capital*. Paris: OECD, Centre for Educational Research and Innovation.

Prescott-Allen, Robert, 2001, *The Well-being of Nations: A Country-by-Country Index of Quality of Life and the Environment*. Washington DC: Island Press.

Ramphal, Shridath, 1992, *Our Country, the Planet*, Washington DC: Island Press.

Saher, P.J., 1970, *Happiness and Immortality*. London: George Allen and Unwin.

Sawin, Janet L., 2004, "Making Better Energy Choices", in *State of the World 2004 (A Worldwatch Institute Report)*, New York, NY: WW Norton, pp. 24-41.

Sen, Amartya, 1999, *Development as Freedom: Human Capability and Global Need*, New York, NY: Alfred Knopf.

Swinyard, William R. Ah-Keng Kau and Hui-Yin Phua, 2001, "Happiness, Materialism, and Religious Experience in the US and Singapore", *Journal of Happiness Studies*, Vol. 2, pp. 13-32.

UNDP, 2004, *Human Development Report*, New York: United Nations Development Programme.

UNESCO, 2002, "Enhancing Global Sustainability", Online. Internet. http://undesdoc.unesco.org/images/0012/001253/125351e.pdf[Report of the Preparatory Committee for the World Summit on Sustainable Development, New York, 25 March, 2002].

Veenhoven, R. 1984, *Conditions of Happiness*, Dordrecht, the Netherlands: D. Reidel Publishing Company.

World Watch Institute (WWI), 2004, *State of the World*, Washington, D.C.: The World Watch Institute.

# 5

# Food Regulation, Technology and Sustainable Development

TRUDY EDEN

Although it is tempting to begin this paper with the assertion that we *now* live in an age of globalized foods, in fact, foods have been transported and traded to far reaches of the globe, if not entirely around the globe, for centuries. Despite the intimations of numerous recent newspaper and television reports and analysts, the global trade of foodstuffs is not a new phenomenon. Foods such as coffee, sugar, olive oil, wine, and dates, to name just a few, have been exchanged between different countries or cultural groups for centuries. The same is true of the cultivation of non-native foods. By the seventeenth century, sugar plants had been transported from the Middle East to the West Indies and South America. Wheat made its way over the centuries around the globe, as did fruits, vegetables, livestock, and herbs and spices. All were cultivated in those environments that suited them or were carefully manipulated to grow in new surroundings.

Food regulation is not a new phenomenon either. Social, cultural and religious groups have set standards for food production, distribution and consumption for millennia and have self-regulated trade for as long. They still do so today. Individuals do as well. Governmental regulation appeared later. For example, the ancient Romans regulated foods and the trading of them. In 1201 in England, King John put into effect the first English food law. His "Assize of Bread," designed to ensure the purity of wheat bread sold by bakers, prohibited the addition of beans or peas. In the United

States, governmental regulations to assure the purity of foods first appeared on the statue books in the seventeenth century, just a few decades after the advent of English colonization. These and subsequent laws carried on English legal traditions and many came about because of consumer demand. The best example of regulations brought about by citizen lobbies in the United States is the Pure Food and Drug Act of 1905. Had it not been for voluntary women's groups who lobbied law-makers and harassed the food producers they perceived as violators of unofficial community standards, the law would not have been passed when it was nor would it have contained the same provisions (Goodwin 1999). This is particularly true with regard to the scientific standards in the law that promised to ensure safe and pure commercially produced foods. Other countries and localities, each in their own time and in their own way have established food regulations for the safety of their citizens as well as to control the distribution or sale of foods within their borders. The regulations apply to local and/or imported foods.

Global trade and food regulation are, by now, ancient practices but they are traditions that have been shaken by novel and concurring developments in world trade and food production. First is the phenomenal growth of world trade that began in the end of the twentieth century. Second is the development of the World Trade Organization (WTO) established in 1998. Third is the creation of transgenic, or genetically modified, foods. The Food and Drug Administration (FDA) approved the first transgenic product in 1992, a tomato with a built-in shelf life known as the "Flavr Savr." It was available to the American public not long after its approval. In the 14 years since then, more than 40 transgenic crops have been produced, including cotton, maize, potatoes, soybeans, and tobacco, and are grown around the world. The United States leads other countries in the development and employment of transgenic technology.

Member countries of the WTO have different opinions about transgenic foods. Some, like the United States, take the position that if any transgenic food is "substantially similar" to a non-transgenic variety, it is safe and should be admitted to the international trade flow (Echols 2003-04). Other countries taking this position include Canada, Argentina, China and Brazil. Known as the "product" standard, it relies on chemical analysis to determine similarity or difference. Other countries, like members of the European Union, look at the *process* used to create the food. They believe that if the process involved in growing a food differs from similar foods, as it does with any transgenic food, then it is suspect and subject to a stricter standard of evaluation (Echols 1998: 525-43).

Before 1998, some transgenic products were authorized for trade within the European Union (EU), most notably soybeans developed by the Monsanto Corporation, which were allowed into the EU in 1996 without special labeling. Their introduction and use by farmers created a furor within member-nations. The objection to the soybeans and other crops led the EU to refuse entry to all transgenic products in that year and to revise their laws to require full traceability and labels of transgenic status (Winickoff *et al.* 2005: 87-89). Disputes have already been taken to the WTO by the United States, Canada, and Argentina claiming that the EU "moratorium" on transgenic products is not based on sound science, is protectionist, and is in violation of the WTO member agreement.

Commentators and experts differ in their opinions as to what the real issue in these cases is. Many people, as indicated above, see it as a case of differing scientific standards. The agreement that binds all members is the "Agreement on the Application of Sanitary and Phytosanitary Measures (known as SPS) which were part of the April WTO main agreement enacted in 1994 and pertains to dangers to animal, plant, and human health from foods and plants (Winickoff *et al.* 2005:82; Walker 1998:251; Howse 2000: 2329; Charnovitz 1999; Jasanoff 1995). Analysts outside the natural sciences think differently. For example, Marsha Echols, Professor of Law at Howard University School of Law, sees the conflict as one between tradition and change or experimentation. She also believes it to be an issue of market access for transgenic foods (Echols 1998: 525-29). Others focus on the question of labeling and therefore frame the issue as one of the consumer's right to know (Thorp and Robinson 2004: 287-98). Mark Mansour, a specialist in international food regulation, believes it is a question of unsubstantiated fears about food safety that cannot be allayed by labeling. David Winickoff, Sheila Jasanoff, Lawrence Busch, Robin Grove-White (2002: 17-29; Busch 2002: 17-29; Rich 2004: 889-914; Jensen 2006: 269-83; Aerni 2004: 307-41) and Brian Wynne, professors of bioethics, science and technology studies, sociology, environment and society, and science studies, respectively, see the dispute as an issue of risk assessment, or perhaps more correctly, improper risk assessment. As a historian of science and medicine in general and of food habits in particular, I think it is all of these but for different reasons. Let me take them one by one.

First is the issue of conflicting science. The regulators in the United States, the major proponent of "product" assessment, do not consider the process of genetic modification to be suspect. Because of this stance, all modified products are assumed to be "substantially equivalent" to their non-modified counterparts. The assumption carries along with it another assumption, that the transgenic food is safe. Despite initial easy passage, transgenic foods must go through a lengthy regulatory process to assure safety before they can be released on the market (York 2001: 435-37). The regulatory inquiry, testing and approval is believed to be, in the words of former Under Secretary of Commerce, David Aaron (2000) "transparent, science-based, politically independent and responsive to new scientific evidence." However, despite the widely-held conclusion that the embrace of transgenic foods by the United States results from its tendency to easily accept scientific and technological innovation, U.S. regulatory focus on final product is a methodology that has not advanced too far from the standards of its original Pure Food and Drug Act of 1905. It is as if transgenesis were similar to cooking or canning. A fresh food has something added to it a gene or a spice, it matters not, it is "cooked" or "canned" in laboratories and when it is done, if it almost like others of its kind, then it passes the test and is ready for consumers. The assumption is that traditional foods remain, substantially, traditional foods. At the chemical level, that may be exactly what they are.

Europeans cannot ignore the additions or changes to the recipe and just look at the end result. Why? Most commentators on the dispute, when forced to answer this question, offer the vague phrase "European culture and tradition." Europeans, they say, *like* their traditional foods, viewing them as "safer and closer to nature and naturalness." This attitude, some say, goes as far back as the Middle Ages (York 2001: 445-46). Some commentators then mention the genetic testing performed by Germans and Austrians during the Nazi era. Others cite a general European distrust of the efficiency of their regulators, so tragically revealed in recent health scandals in Europe, particularly mad cow disease, and proffer these incidents as reasons for what some see as reluctance, obstinacy or intentionally discriminatory trade practices (York 2001: 445-46).

I would like to suggest another way to look at these differences of approach that shows that the two methods and their proponents actually do not differ as significantly as it appears. It seems to me the problem here has to do with the notions of purity and contamination. The Food and Drug Administration (FDA), the major regulatory agency in the United States that is charged with ensuring a safe food supply for Americans, was created by the 1905 Pure Food and Drug Act. Its mission was, and still is among other things, to monitor the adulteration and contamination of foods by producers. According to the 1905 law and its regulatory spawn, food contaminants could be microscopic, such as bacteria, or more visible, such as cockroaches and rats. Now, insects and rodents, in the absence bacteria or other dangerous organisms, can be and are eaten safely. People in many cultures seek them out and include them as a part of their daily diet. For Americans, though, their presence in breakfast cereal, milk or baby food is contaminating and it is illegal to sell breakfast cereal, milk, or baby food with them as intended or unintended ingredients. Another example is horsemeat. If an American food producer quietly substituted horsemeat for beef in its canned stew, he would be guilty of adulterating his product and at the very least would be subject to fines and lawsuits from governmental units as well as individuals. Horsemeat is considered by Americans to be impure. Of course, in other countries, horsemeat is a highly respected food and if processed properly, a "pure" food.

Cultural notions of purity and impurity have been examined by social scientists and others, most notably the anthropologist Mary Douglas (2002), who concluded that across cultures, the notion of impurity arises when things are out of place. Purity and defilement are concepts that all cultures use to order and regulate themselves. While what is considered pure or impure by any society can and does change over time, it can be a difficult and slow process. The Pure Food and Drug Act of 1905, its successor, the

Food and Drug Act of 1938, and the myriad of subsidiary regulations that have been developed in the United States all claim to be based on science and I do not doubt that they are. But the science that labeled insects and rodents as impure contaminants in 1905 had behind it cultural notions of purity and its handmaiden cleanliness, newly empowered by the recent discovery of germs. For American scientists, cockroaches and rodents were not and still are not fit foods for humans and their presence in foods defiles them. If that presence is not revealed, in other words if they aren't listed on the label, that complicates the defilement. The Americans are not the only ones whose science is infused with cultural values. The Codex Alimentarius of the World Health Organization, which is the standard relied on by the WTO restricts such impurities. Take for example its regulation on oats, which states that they shall be free from abnormal odors, flavors, living and dead insects and mites. Of course what I am suggesting here is that not only is the purity of foods an issue, so is the purity of science. Is science, using the word of David Aaron, "transparent" and free from contamination by the people who practice it or the cultures from which they come? Historians and sociologists of science, among others, have doubted this purity some would say they have disproved it—for decades (Latour and Woolgar 1986).

To get back to transgenic foods, the difference between the process and product views of transgenic foods is one of purity. If one looks at the process, one focuses on what has been added to a traditional food. The addition to one organism of genes from another, dissimilar organism is, for many people, the process of putting things out of place. It defiles the biological purity of the traditional food. It is the 21st century version of rat or cockroach in the baby food. I would go even further to say that even if the presence of the foreign genetic material is removed before the product is sold or consumed, that product has still been defiled. Straining out the cockroaches before sale just isn't good enough. This is a myopic view but its narrowness of vision cannot be allowed to derogate its cultural significance or its importance to self, local and global food regulation. This dispute is a question of tradition; not, though, of refusing to add new ingredients to traditional foods. It is the ingredients that are at issue.

The product approach is equally myopic and equally traditional. Its advocates are practicing the equivalent of regulators who, in 1905, would have said, "Well, so this baby food has some cockroaches in it. It has been boiled and is sterile. It is 95% pure baby food so it is good enough to eat." And of course, they would have been right.

For most people, however, what they eat is more than an issue of scientific standards or sterility. Food is unlike any other commodity exchanged between peoples and nations because we put it into our bodies and it becomes our flesh, blood, and bones. In many cultures, people also believe it becomes their spirit. Furthermore, once any food has been digested, there is no turning back. This is, then, a matter of human identity, far more basic than what we wear or how we fix our hair. Like concepts of purity, these beliefs about ingestion and transubstantiation exist in all cultures across time and space. They exist side by side in countries that practice the most advanced science. They are fundamental, deep, and do not change easily. They should not be dismissed as old-fashioned or incorrect. This is not an issue of correctness. These beliefs exist; they are powerful determinants of human behavior that can and do transcend science and they must be taken into consideration if a satisfactory resolution to these trade issues is to be achieved (Eden 2001; Fischler 2000: 275-92; Caplan 2000; Buckner 1999:191-209; Counihan and Esterik 1997; Damerow 1996; Feeley-Harnik 1995: 565-82; Germov and Williams 2004; Barthes 1975; Coveney 2001).

If purity is at the bottom of the dispute over transgenic foods, then why not simply label those foods? People who have fears of defilement can, then, self-regulate and not purchase the foods. Those for whom purity is not an issue can purchase and enjoy them. The objections to labeling them are many. The groups that employ the product approach to transgenic foods, which assumes substantial similarity, apply the same philosophy to labeling. They assert that if transgenic foods are substantially similar they don't need any labeling in addition to that already required because "food technology, when tested according to the rigors of objective and transparent science, is presumed to be safe as long as there are no material differences in the quality, safety or nutritional composition of a given food product" (York 2001: 441-42). In addition, the veracity of a "NO GMO" label is viewed as almost impossible given the degree to which transgenic foods have infiltrated the [U.S.] food supply. Furthermore, many people think that such labeling would frighten consumers and prevent them from purchasing the product. Estimates show that, if labeled, transgenic products would not be purchased by a majority of consumers. Finally, labeling is expensive and, according to some transgenic food producers, too expensive to implement (York 2001: 441-42).

To stop here and see where we are, yes, this issue is one of tradition and change, but not on the superficial level that is often suggested. Yes, this is an issue of labeling and the consumer's right to know, but not necessarily because of ignorant or unreasonable fears. This brings us to the issue of risk. I have pointed out how ideas about purity and pollution can shape scientific attitudes towards the regulation of foods. These attitudes help to shape the risk assessment of a regulatory body in significant and positive but value-laden and often unacknowledged ways. In their recent law review article, David Winickoff, *et al.* (2005: 97) argue the same premise for the regulatory process—that it cannot be strictly scientific because risks have to be assessed before the science is applied and the assessment of risk always includes the framing of issues. What I described as myopic, they see as an inevitable consequence of what is included in the frame and what is excluded.

At this point, the WTO is bound to adjudicate the dispute over transgenic products under the Sanitary and Phytosanitary (SPS) Agreement, the aim of which is "regulatory harmonization." Another way of stating "regulatory harmonization" is a member-wide consensus on health and safety standards. The SPS does allow individual members the freedom to pass laws to protect human, animal or plant life or health in a non-discriminatory way and provides a means for judges of disputes to separate proper safety standards from pure regulatory measures (Winickoff *et al.* 2005: 90). However, it must be done on the basis of science. WTO adjudication of disputes under the SPS have already been criticized for leaning too heavily on one member's science at the expense of another. As a result, the WTO has been accused of being undemocratic, although the WTO has indicated its understanding that all science is intertwined with value (Winickoff *et al.* 2005: 92, 96).

Is there a way out of this circularity? Can trade be facilitated without the compromise of crucial but unscientific cultural needs? Winickoff and his co-authors believe that when WTO judges interpret the SPS agreement, they should avoid reliance on the scientific "truths" of one member over those of another. Rather, a judge should "act more as an administrative tribunal searching for transparency and procedural adequacy" (Winickoff *et al.* 2005: 107-08). In addition, the public should be allowed to participate in the risk assessment process. Public participation in the EU gave regulators useful and valuable input to assist in their risk assessment process. Winickoff *et al.* (2005: 100, 108, 118) also suggest revisions to the SPS that will facilitate this end without weakening the WTO's ability to remain anti-protectionist.

Because food is something we put into our bodies and becomes a part of us, it cannot be treated like any other commodity traded locally or globally. In the past, humans attached personal, social, and cultural rules to the foods they ate. We still do today and people of the future will retain them, change them, and create new ones. If an international regulatory process is to be a functional, not to mention successful, one, it must take into consideration factors other than those believed to arise from the practice of "pure science."

## References

Aaron, David, 2000, 'The Science and the Impact', Remarks of the under Secretary of Commerce for Trade Before the Conference on Biotechnology, The Hague, Netherlands, January 21, Washington File, U.S. Department of State, available at www.usia.gov/cgi-bin/washfile...=/products/washfiel/newsitem.shtml

Aerni, Philipp, "Risk, Regulation and Innovation: The Case of Aquaculture and Transgenic Fish," *Aquatic Sciences*, 66.

Barthes, Roland, 1975, "Toward a Psychosociology of Contemporary Food Consumption," in *European Diet From Pre-industrial to Modern Times*, ed. E. Forster, R. Forster (Baltimore: Johns Hopkins University Press).

Buckner, A., 1999, "Keeping Kosher: Eating and Social Identity among the Jews of Denmark", *Ethnology*, 38.

Busch, Lawrence, 2002, "The Homiletics of Risk," *Journal of Agricultural and Environmental Ethics*, 15.

Caplan, P., 2000, *Food, Health and Identity*, New York: Routledge.

Charnovitz, Steve, 1999, "Improving the Agreement on Sanitary and Phytosanitary Standards in Trade, Environment, and the Millennium," in Gary P. Sampson and W. Bradnee Chambers, eds., *Trade, Environment and the Millennium* (Tokyo: United Nations University Press).

Counihan C.M., Carole and Penny van Esterik, 1997, *Food and Culture*, New York: Routledge.

Coveney, J., 2001, *Food,*, *Morals, and Meaning: The Pleasure and Anxiety of Eating*, New York: Routledge.

Damerow, P., 1996, "Food Production and Social Status as Documented in Proto-Cuneiform Texts," in P. Wiessner and W. Schiefenhovel (eds.) *Food and the Status Quest*, New York: Berghahn.

Douglas, Mary, *Purity and Danger: An Analysis of the Concept of Pollution and Taboo*, (London: Routledge).

Echols, Marsha, 2003-04, "Bioethics Symposium: National and Global Implications of Genetically-Modified Organisms: Lay, Ethics & Science: the WTO Biotechnology Dispute," *Cumberland Law Review*, 34.

Echols, Marsha, 1998, "Food Safety Regulation in the European Union and the United States: Different Cultures, Different Laws," *Columbia Journal of European Law*, 4.

Echols, Marsha, 1998, "Bioethics Symposium," 445; idem, "Food Safety Regulation in the European Union and the United States: Different Cultures, Different Laws," *Columbia Journal of European Law*, 4, Summer.

Eden, Trudy, 2001, "Food Assimilation and the Malleability of the Human Body," in Janet M. Lindman and Michele L. Tarter, eds., *"A Centre of Wonders": The Body in Early America*, Ithaca, NY: Cornell University Press.

Feeley-Harnik, G., 1995, "Religion and Food: An Anthropological Perspective," *Journal of the American Academy of Religion*, 63.

Fischler, Claude, 2000, "Food, Self, and Identity," *Social Science Information*, 27, 1999.

Germov, J. and L. Williams, (eds.), *A Sociology of Food and Nutrition: The Social Appetite*. (New York: Oxford University Press, 2004).

Goodwin, Lorine Swainston, 1999, *The Pure Food, Drink, and Drug Crusaders*, 1879-1914, Jefferson, N.C.: McFarland & Company, Inc., Publishers.

Howse, Robert, 2000, "Democracy, Science, and Free Trade: Risk Regulation on Trial at the World Trade Organization," *Michigan Law Review*, 98.

Jasanoff, Sheila, 1995, "Product, Process, or Programme: Three Cultures and the Regulation of Biotechnology, in Martin Bauer, ed., *Resistance to New Technology: Nuclear Power, Information Technology, and Biotechnology*, New York: Cambridge University Press.

Jensen, Karsten Klint, 2006, "Conflict Over Risks in Food Production," *Journal of Agriculture and Environmental Ethics*, 19.

Latour, Bruno and Steve Woolgar, 1986, *Laboratory Life: The Construction of Scientific Facts*, Princeton: Princeton University Press.

Thorp, Andy and Catherine Robinson, 2004, "When Goliaths Clash: US and EU Differences Over the Labeling of Genetically Modified Organisms," *Agriculture and Human Values*, 21.

Rich, Matthew, 2004, "the Debate over Genetically Modified Crops in the United States: Reassessment of Notions of Harm, Difference, and Choice," *Case Western Reserve Law Review*, 54, Spring 2004, 889-914.

Walker, Vern R., 1998, "Keeping the WTO from Becoming the 'World Trans-Science Organization'" Scientific Uncertainty, Science Polity, and Factfinding in the Growth Hormones Dispute, *Cornell International Law Journal*, 31.

Winickoff, David, Sheila Jasanoff, Lawrence Busch, Robin Grove-White, and Brian Wynne, 2005, "Adjudicating the GM Food Wars: Science, Risk, and Democracy in World Trade Law," *Yale Journal of International Law*, 30.

York, George E.C., 2001, "Global Foods, Local Tastes and Biotechnology: The New Legal Architecture of International Agriculture Trade," *Columbia Journal of European Law*, Fall.

# Global Technologies

## Challenges and Alternatives

DHIRENDRA K. VAJPEYI

One of the most significant developments in contemporary times has been the explosive invention and adoption of new technologies and their impact on all aspects of human as well as non-human lives. The harnessing of atomic energy, the space breakthrough, the invention of cybernetic machines capable of acting as substitutes for the human brain, advances in molecular biology and genetics to provide insights into the perennial puzzles of life, "the scientific anticipation of the probable future and its chief technological aspects (futurology) are quite indicative of the technologicalization of our times" (Drucker 1957: 5; Kothari 1974; Falk 1975; Kennedy 1993; Diamond 1998; Fukuyama 1992: 14-15). It has become "an expression of faith about technologies' ability to solve all our problems. Those with such faith also assume that the new technologies now under discussion will succeed, and that they will do so quickly enough to make a big difference soon" (Diamond 2005: 504). "There is no such thing as a society without technology" (Sale 1950: 156). Both industrialized as well as less industrialized societies have adopted public policies supporting aggressive industrial/technical development as *sine qua non* for improving the quality of life "an instrument allowing its (technology) owner to exercise social control in various forms, decisively affecting mode of decision-making, and its relation to patterns of alienation characteristic of affluent societies" (Goulett 1977:11; Cutter *et. al.* 2000: 96).

Doubts and fears of philosophical and practical nature have been expressed about potentially catastrophic consequences of technological advances on man and society. "It (technology) has resulted in . . . a common world civilization. It is corroding and dissolving history, tradition, culture and values throughout the world, no matter how old, how highly developed, how deeply cherished and loved" (Drucker 1961: 17). It is also observed that technology "is no panacea for the ills of underdevelopment, even at best its promise is uncertain" (Goulet 1977: 251). With the introduction of technology new roles replace the old ones, and new expectations, sources of power and influence emerge (Parsons 1951: 513; Methene 1969: 40-58; Goldschmidt 1952: 139). These changes in turn directly challenge the normative values of the industrializing society. Students of industrialism have maintained that technology undermines societies and their members' view of nature, authority, progress, development and the very purpose of life. An increase in alienation is the price exacted of these societies. Kinship and other intimate relationships become subordinated to criteria of performance, power pervasive commercialization of friendship, of love, of procreation and partnership (Goulet 1977: 12-13; Linton 1952: 85; Boo 2004: 1-12; Wajeman 1991; Kramarac 1998).

Other related questions are: Where is this vigorous and rapid technological progress leading us, and what will be the ultimate consequences of "the inexorable march of technology?" (Friedman 2005: 7). Does it not harbor some grave dangers for man, and his natural environment? What measures must be taken now to direct this progress so that it is good and beneficial to mankind? Concerns have also been expressed in the voluminous literature which ranges from serious sociological and philosophical to counterculture movements and anti-utopian fiction (Ellul 1964; Kahn and Wiener 1967; Polyani 1957; Ferkiss 1969; Martin 1955; Vonnegut 1967; Wright 1942; Schwartz 1971; Esquivel 1996; Clarke 1986). Ellul contends that technology has become a self-developing system and has introduced an irreversible cultural mutation in the evaluation of mankind. Consequently the man is becoming dependent, if not a slave, of his own inventions. McHale (1969) observes that technological development has brought the evolutionary change in the overall biocultural evolution of humankind. The possible effects of such innovations such as cyborgs (Clarke 1964) and the widespread use of "psycho-sociological conditioning" bring about a general debasement of humankind or introduce irreversible qualitative inequalities among men and societies. Recent studies (Friedman 1998; Mansbach and Rhodes 2003; O'Meara *et al.* 2000; Tehranian 1998; Kaplan 2003) point out a correlation between global technologicalization and its negative impact on societies. According to them the power of Internet is challenging the old notion of state sovereignty and is pressurizing the old/transitional societies in several ways. The anti-globalists believe that these technologically driven societies are facing serious identity crisis both at micro and macro-levels. Technology and consumerism are responsible for the rise of religious fundamentalism

(Friedman 2003) and ethno-nationalism (Vajpeyi 2001; Kaplan 2003; Lobell and Mauceri 2004).

If these tendencies (anti-technology, and anti-globalism) and their implied life style predominate in the coming decades to the point of changing or seriously impacting the scientific, pragmatic ethos of technologicalization into something which is its opposite, and incompatible with the conditions required for the promotion and development of technological societies then we face a very serious challenge to the overall progress of our economic, political, and social systems, and a threat to the quality of human life. The Luddite solution to modern problems (health, social security, environment, poverty, etc.) will not lead us to a brave new world. However, an unregulated mad rush and reliance on "technofix" has its own consequences (Cutter *et al.* 2000: 80-81; Diamond 2005: 8). Hence a balance is needed between over-dependence on technology at the risk of compromising with core values as human beings, and ignoring the technological-scientific advances which have potential to improve the quality of human life. These issues and concerns are bound to dominate both scholarly and public policy debates for many years to come.

## II

Keeping in view the above discussion/framework, I will discuss two major areas of technological advances: (1) Information Technologies (IT)/ Communication technologies, and (2) Bio-technologies, and their impact on global political, economic, and social spheres.

### (1) Information Technologies/Communication Technologies

"A critical part in the world of 1801 was that nothing moved faster than the speed of a horse . . . . In Jefferson's day, it took six weeks to move information from Mississippi River to Washington, D.C. Three full days to make the 175 mile journey" (Ambrose 1996: 52). In 2005 it takes less than one minute to send a message from almost any city in the U.S. to almost any city in India/China. This miracle is due to the revolution in communication technology—the Internet. It changed the way people around the world communicate with each other, do business, collect information and impart education. "The diffusion of personal computers, fax machines, Windows, and dial-up modems connected to a global telephone network all came together in the late 1980s and early 1990s to create the basic platform that started the global information revolution." (Mundie 2005: 53). According to Internet usage statistics (2004) there were approximately 800,040,498 people using the Internet around the world in 2004, a net increase of 121.6 percent over the year 2000. The Middle East witnessed the largest increase (218.7 percent in 2004) between 2000 and 2004. Asia reported the highest number of Internet users (256,454,536) followed by Europe (224,462,968) and then North America (222,956,690). "We have discovered how to use pulses of electro-magnetic energy to embody and convey messages that up to now have been sent by voice, picture, and text" (Pool 1990: 7). The impact of these "technologies of freedom" on our lives is immense—both negative and positive. "Humanity finds itself at a crossroad between a dying old order and the rise of a new age. Revolutionary technologies are forcing a fundamental change in our spatial and temporal consciousness" (Rifkin 2004: 181). Following is a brief discussion of major areas which, I think, will be greatly affected by information/communication technologies:

(i) Changes in spatial patterns of economic, social and political activities (Pool 1990: vii; Rifkin 2004: 181-233; Friedman 2005; Koenig 1995; Diamond 2005; Vajpeyi 1998; 2001).
(ii) Issues related to individual liberties, privacy and safety (Fukuyama 2002; Kennedy 1993; Cornish 1996; Riffkin 2004, Bleha 2005: 111-24).

It is to be noted here that the impact of these technologies is not a one way street. Policies, economies, cultures and the social contexts also affect technologies in their acceptance, dissemination, etc. "Casualty is mutual. The same technology may cause opposite effects. Whether information media enhance or retard freedom" (Pool 1990: vii), progress and culture depends on the social, political and economic environment in which they are allowed to operate.

### *(i) Impact on Economic, Social and Political Activities*

The Internet (e-mail) has revolutionized marketing and other areas of business. "In less than a decade the World Wide Web has changed from a research enclave to the Main Street of the world . . . the web has become a booming market place. The rate of the change on the Net is amazing—nothing seems to stand still" (Mack 2000: 40). In 2004, there were 980 million Internet accounts globally. 40 percent of them were corporate accounts. The power of E-Commerce is exemplified in the Seattle based Amazon.com whose sales and profits continue to grow. The use of E-commerce by banking industry has also become very popular. In May 2004, Wells Fargo reported Internet merchant payments reached $3.8 billion domestically in the first quarter alone, up nearly 50 percent from a year before. In 2003 its international transactions were about a billion dollars (Sengstock 2004).

Another area of E-Commerce which generates a large amount of business is entertainment, especially the adult entertainment (pornography), the recording industry, and the online movie rental business (Ross 2005: 94-100). The E-Commerce has given birth to a new economic system. "The inexorable march of technology and capital has removed all barriers, boundaries, frictions and restraints to global commerce" (Friedman 2005: 202). "The dot com bubble was only one aspect of globalization and when it imploded rather than imploding globalization, it actually turbocharged it"

(Friedman 2005: 111). Internet marketing has now come on its own. U.S. consumers alone spent at least $2.3 billion over the Internet during the 1998 Christmas season. By 1999 the sum was $9 billion. More than nine million U.S. households purchased holiday gifts online in 1998, up from 2 million in 1997. Online clothing sales tripled to $330 million from 1997. While the Internet is not yet equal to other forms of marketing it has witnessed tremendous growth in the last ten years. The use of credit cards online has contributed to this growth (Mack 2005: 40). The cheerleaders of unrestricted trade and globalization feel that "developments in information technology are enabling companies to squeeze out all inefficiencies and friction from their markets and business operations" (Friedman 2005: 204). "The network commerce is too quick, too dense, and too globally encompassing to be constrained by national borders" (Rifkin 2004: 182). "The fast-moving, twenty-four hour a day, border-crossing, profit hunting system of international finance, in which vast sums of capital move in and out of a country or a stock according to perceptions of that entity's prospect" (Kennedy 1993: 55) could, however, destabilize weaker economies. Financial crisis in South-East Asia (1990s) is one such example. Volatility of the vast computer driven system of financial trading could contribute to panics and financial flight from economies which are overly dependent on international investors. "The real 'logic' of the borderless world is that nobody is in control" (Kennedy 1993: 55). Above discussion is mainly positive, and is not supported by many with similar enthusiasm. "We have all heard that the Web will transform the way we do business, that organizations that don't use the Web will perish, and that e-commerce will soon become a huge factor in the global economy. Such messages are promulgated primarily by venture capitalists with a stake in Internet business" (Cohan 2000). According to Cohan (2000), e-commerce is more likely to become a supplementary way to shop, similar to mail order, rather than the way everybody buys things. A study from the Organization for Economic Cooperation and Development (OECD) in 1998 concluded that E-Commerce will not have a significant impact on the global economy "anytime soon." The report also observed that visions of global E-Commerce must be tempered by the reality that half the world's population has never made a telephone call, much less accessed the Internet. The impact of other than Information Technologies has also drawn considerable attention and discussion. It is also to be noted that computers play the pivotal role in transmitting, collecting and analyzing the information. This overdependence on computers obviously raises several issues such as computer safety and above all concerns of privacy (computer ethics). Computer networks are vulnerable to physical damages (fires, earthquakes, floods, etc.), software sabotage by hackers and other malcontents, questions related to intellectual property and other computer crimes such as identity theft (Teich 2003: 243). The use of Internet makes it easier for HIV infected people to find easy sex (Specter 2005: 38-45).

Globalization and easy access to computers/Internet cafes and other communication technologies have also impacted various aspects of political spheres both in positive and negative manner. These technologies without boundaries provide easy access to political information, facilitate communication across continents and seem to erode the total monopoly of the sovereign states, especially non-democratic regimes over dissenting information. Usually this access to free and easy information is viewed unfavorably by ruling elites in countries such as China, Cuba, and Saudi Arabia and their response is "increased restriction and repression in a futile attempt to limit free international communication" (Pool 1990: 13). It empowers individuals, challenges nation states, traditional cultures, values, national identities, and "bonds of restraint that have historically provided some protection and cushioning for workers and communities . . . . threatening to dissolve all feudal, national and religious identities giving rise to a universal civilization" (Friedman 2005: 205). Such optimistic and positive sentiments should be viewed with some caution because this new system of diffusion has also brought many disgruntled people around the world to unite in launching extra-legal terrorist activities, has produced clash of cultures and the rise of religious fundamentalism. "Modern communications have also another effect, in making Middle Eastern Muslims more painfully aware of how badly things have gone wrong" (Lewis 2005: 47). The same is true in India (Vajpeyi 2001: 57-77) and Europe (Leiken 2005: 120-35) where they discuss martyrdom in Internet chat rooms and plot to avenge the past injustices. Thanks to the Internet and satellite systems, Al-Qaeda can solidify and revive Muslim identity and recruit suicide bombers by beaming in Osama bin-Laden into madrasas of Pakistan, Iraq and other places. A six year long study conducted by Gabriel Weimann of Haifa University, Israel pointed out the use of Internet by terrorists in several ways: to recruit supporters, raise funds, launch a worldwide campaign of fear, deliver threats, disseminate horrific images of recent actions, secure publicity, and acquire information about the adversaries.

"While Bin-Laden can't show his face but he can reach every household in the world, thanks to the Internet" (Mandelbaum 2000). Responsiveness and transparency are very crucial to good governance. A two way communication between the government and the citizens contributes to a participant political culture, strengthens political institutions and the overall efficacy of the regime. Democratic governments traditionally have maintained this two-way process by several means mainly by disseminating their policies by print media, television and personal contacts. The emergence of e-mail has tremendously facilitated this process. Citizens now enter into political and social discussions through computer generated information. Funds for political and social causes are raised, supporters are recruited via computer. Democrat candidate Howard Dean was immensely successful in his bid to the U.S. presidency (2004) in raising funds and mobilizing a large number of supporters. Both Republicans and Democrats, and for that matter independents and political groups of all shades and color have used the email to further their causes. "Public policy networks are a way for the government to keep political deliberation, decision-making and implementation alive and relevant by ongoing dialogue and negotiation between all the affected constituencies. Governance is no longer divided into discrete and separate stages but becomes a "continuous process" of engagement. . . . Politics becomes a 24-7 affair" (Rifken 2004: 232). Globally the process is becoming acceptable, however in some regional areas it is farther ahead than in others. For example in the early 1990s the European Union (EU) started to increasingly use the new decentralized information and communication technologies that were remaking commerce and social life (Rifkin 2004: 223). In 1994 the European Commission's Report on Europe's Way to the Information Society: An Action Plan recommended a series of initiatives to make EU the "first fully integrated information society in the world" by integrating several EU cross-border activities such as universities and research centers into interactive networks, teleworking network, a distance learning network, road traffic and air traffic control networks, health care networks, and a trans-European public administration network.

In 1996 a follow-up report on "Europe at the forefront of the Global Information Society: A Rolling Action Plan" put greater emphasis on extending the new technologies across industry and establishing the proper regulatory regime and stimuli to make network ways of doing business viable and effective. In this fashion the EU took bold steps to reinvent its style of governance—the polycentric governing style. Coordination rather than command becomes part of the new political scheme. Various EU government agencies and organizations were not only encouraged but required to establish high levels of interaction and networking between European level agencies, state, provincial and local governments, NGOs, business and corporate actors, educational organizations, research institutes and a variety of user groups (Luke 1995; Barry 1996: 33-34).

### *(2) Bio-Technology : Challenges and Opportunities*

The overriding objective in the application of science and technology to development is to further the modernization of developing economies and simultaneously not only to meet the basic human needs but also improve the quality of life both in developed and developing societies. Today we are faced with a variety of common global problems such as protection of the environment, population growth, development of new energy sources, alleviation of shortages of food and water, health and most devastating diseases such as HIV/AIDS, malaria and several other threatening diseases—avian flu—which could severely impact our health and the very existence of millions of people (Garrett 2005: 3-23). Diamond (2005: 8) contends that one of the reasons which might save modern world is modern medicine, and biotechnology. Biotechnology is "any technique that uses living organisms or process to make or modify products to improve plants or animals or to develop micro-organisms for specific uses" (U.S. Congress Office of Technology Assessment 1986: 4). Scientists and science fiction writers such as Arthur Clarke and Huxley have fantasized about societies which will be free of diseases, and financial anxieties. Huxley (1932) envisaged a "Brave New World" where babies will not be hatched in wombs (vitro), the drug Soma will give instant happiness, sensation will be simulated by implanted electrodes, and human behavior will be modified through drugs. It seems that the present world is almost at the doorsteps of Huxley's utopia, and Fukuyama's (2002: 7) "post-human stage of history." The ultimate question related to these developments is at what price—social, political, economic, and ethical—our societies are willing to pay." Medical technology offers us in many cases a devil's bargain: longer life, but with reduced mental capacity; freedom from depression, together with freedom from creativity or spirit; therapies that blur the line between what we achieve on our own and what we achieve because of the levels of various chemicals in our brains" (Fukuyama 2002: 8). An increasing number of governments around the world are betting that the bio-technology industry will boost their tax base, provide jobs, improve health, reduce diseases and overall create a better future for their citizens (Oliver 2000). Following is a discussion of two main scientific technologies which will have both short and long range impact on human behavior and overall quality of life.

(1) Genetic engineering: Damages and opportunities.
(2) Bio-medical advances (drugs, etc.)

## (1) Genetic Engineering

Recent scientific advances such as genomics, predictive diagnostics, genetically engineered agriculture, nuclear transfer cloning, and the manipulation of stem cells, the idea that genes carry pre-determined molecular programs or blueprints has generated intense debate both among the scientific community, religious leaders, and public policy elites. "Gene therapy research is exploring ways to treat cystic fibrosis, fragile-x syndrome, and other devastating genetic diseases. The transfer of genes between microbes, plants, and animals provides opportunities for altering life-forms and even creating new ones" (Anderson 2000: 20). Plants may be transformed into miniature factories producing medicines, perfumes, and plastics. Animals with human genes may provide hearts and other organs to human beings. It is hoped that genetic engineering will also revolutionize sustainable farming, especially in predominantly agricultural societies. The costs of importing farm machinery, pesticides, fertilizers, and tractor fuel are extremely burdensome for farmers in poorer countries. Sustainable agriculture's goal is low input production" (Anderson 2000: 21). It will help high protein, disease-resistant varieties of several crops such as corn, rice, wheat, sorghum, and cassava. However, these optimistic scenarios have been challenged by environmentalists and economists. It could be a long time before these advances will be available to the farmers in poor countries (Moffett 1994). Genes from genetically engineered crops might escape in pollen and fertilize the crops' wild relative—a weed. The hybrid weed could inherit the genetically altered crops' ability to poison hungry insects and to withstand big doses of weed-killer. Insect-proof, hard to kill weeds would damage the agriculture (Anderson 2000: 21). The potential benefits for gene therapy to humans are tremendous, however, there are also many risks and problems. Mistakes in germ-line gene therapy could cause serious deficiencies and mutations. Gene manipulation may tempt wealthy parents to "increase the intelligence of their children as well as that of all their subsequent descendants. Then we have the makings of not just a moral dilemma but a full-scale class war" (Fukuyama 2002: 17). There is no equal access to people with lesser means, and no opportunity to enhance their capacities (Kitcher 1996). It should also be noted here that genetic enhancement does not guarantee results. "The genetically enhanced will have to compete with genetically ordinary to prove themselves, giving "regular" people a chance to show they can perform as well or better" (Minerd 2000: 23)

By reducing or eliminating certain diseases, genetic research might further prolong life and produce demographic imbalance globally. Japan, Russia, and Germany are already facing reduced births. The graying population in developed countries will put tremendous pressure on these economies and social structures. Health infrastructures (machines, trained doctors, nurses, and old age assisted living facilities) will need reorganization, and a younger group of people to support the aged. In the United States the social security debate is indicative of things to come. Societies with older people will have to relax their immigration laws and allow more "guest" caretakers from Third World countries which have a surplus of young, unemployed, skilled and unskilled people. According to Fukuyama the absence of young people will also have an impact on politics. Evidence points out that women out-live men and have different attitudes on social, economic and political issues. The politics of these societies will be feminized, the pool of available military men/women will be smaller (2002: 62), and even open doors for "super-empowered angry men" (Friedman 2005: 79; Berger 2000: 419-27) which could increase the rate of violent crimes.

Spectacular breakthroughs in developing wonder drugs go hand in hand with genetic research and experimental biology. These drugs save lives, reduce pain, and make our lives less stressful. But some of these drugs such as Prozac to cure depression and Ritalin to control the unruly behavior of young children could also be used to control and abuse uncooperative segments of society (Mayer 2005: 60-71). These are ethical and political issues which could have serious consequences, and affect how we think and behave as decent human beings. They not only affect our physical well-being, but also spiritual existence—a Faustian dilemma. Predictions are "notoriously difficult and risky" and may land us in Dante's seventh level of inferno, however, these areas of scientific advance (molecular biology including neuroscience, population genetics, behavior genetics, psychology, anthropology, evolutionary biology and neuropharmacology) have implications. Hence the question: should we worry about it? Should we use the power of the state to regulate (Bush administration on stem cell research) them or adopt a *laissez-faire* approach? Opinions among scientists, theologians, secular-humanists, Luddites, and politicians differ, and a passionate debate is already taking place on these issues. The technology's most ardent proponents claim that unhindered and unregulated research will lead to a better society with zero-waste and healthy and long life, if not immortality. They along with the bio-tech industry contend that any attempt to regulate will impede advancements in science. Also no regulatory systems ever work. "No sovereign nation-state can regulate or ban . . . because the research and development will simply move to another jurisdiction" (Fukuyama 2002: 188). International arrangements to regulate undesirable use of technology such as nuclear proliferation have never worked. Determined nation-states will either find loopholes in these agreements or totally ignore them if they chose to do so. The opponents of free market approach fear that unregulated use of such technology and knowledge will erode basic core of free societies, infringe on privacy, harm the poor, the environment, and in the long-run create more unintended problems and may even "destroy the whole planet through self-replicating "grey-goo" (Loder 2005: 4). They support enlightened regulation by democratically constituted organizations/agencies represented by state, scientists, NGOs, and cultural leaders. These technologies show great promises but they also have their dark sides. Hence some safeguards are essential (Fukuyama 2002: xiii; Friedman 2005: 183; Loder 2005: 11; Diamond 2005: 506). These issues will continue to dominate the global discourse on the role of science and technology in development. Manifestly there are limitations as well as potentials to what science and technology can achieve in the realm of social action. "Science itself is neither good nor bad. It is the uses to which it is put that raise ethical questions. Genetic engineering is only a technique. We have to decide if we want to use it, and when and how. These decisions should be responsibility of all" (Enzo 1998: 21). "There can be no end of history without an end of modern natural science and technology. Not only are we not at an end of science and technology; we appear to be poised at the cusps of one of the most momentous periods of technological advance in history" (Fukuyama 2002: 15).

## References

Ambrose, Stephen, 1996, *Undaunted Courage*, New York: Simon and Schuster.

Anderson, Clifton E., 2000, "Genetic Engineering: Damages and Opportunities", *The Futurist*, March-April.

Barry, Andrew, 1996, "The European Network", *Technologies*, No. 29.

Berger, Peter L., 2000, "Four Faces of Global Culture" in O'Meara, Patrick, *et. al. Globalization and The Challenges of a New Century*. Bloomington, Indiana: Indiana University Press.

Bleha, Thomas, 2005, "Down to the Wire", *Foreign Affairs*, May-June.

Boo, Katherine, 2004, "The Best Job in Town", *The New Yorker*, July 5.

Clarke, Arthur, 1986, *July 20, 2019—Life in the 21st Century*, New York: Macmillan.

Clarke, Arthur, 1964, *Profiles of the Future*, New York: Bantam.

Cohan, Peter S., 2000, *Net Profit: How to Invest and Compete in the Real World of Internet Business*, California: Jossey—Bass Inc. Publishers.

Cornish, Edward, 1996, "92 Ways Our Lives will Change by the Year 2025", *The Cyber Future*. Maryland: World Future Society.

Cutter, W. Bowman, Joan Spiro, and Laura D' Andrea Tyson, 2000, "New World, New Deal: A Democratic Approach to Globalization", *Foreign Affairs*, March-April.

Diamond, Jared, 1998 *Guns, Germs, and Steel—The Fates of Human Societies*, New York: W.W. Norton.

Diamond, Jared, 2005, Collapse—*How Societies Choose to Fail or Succeed*, New York: Viking.

Drucker, Peter F., 1951, *Landmarks of Tomorrow*, New York: Harper and Row.

Drucker, Peter F., 1961, "The Technological Revolution", *Technology and Culture*. Fall, 17-23.

Ellul, Jaques, 1964, *The Technological Society*, New York: Vintage Books.

Enzo, Russo, 1998, *Genetic Engineering: Dreams and Nightmares*, London: Oxford University Press.

Esquivel, Laura, 1996, *The Law of Love*, New York: Crown Publisher.

Falk, Richard, 1975, *A Study of Future World*, New York: The Free Press.

Ferguson, Yale H., and Richard W. Mansbach, 2003, *The Elusive Quest Continues: Theory and Global Politics*, New Jersey: Prentice-Hall.

Ferkiss, Victor, 1969, *Technological Man*, New York: Braziller.

Friedman, J., 1998, "Transnationalization, Socio-political Disorder, and Ethnification as Expressions of Declining Hegemony", *International Political Science Review*, July; 242.

Friedman, Thomas L., 2005, *The World is Flat: A Brief History of the 21st Century*, New York: Farrar, Strauss and Giroux.

Fukuyama, Francis, 2002, *Our Posthuman Future—Consequences of the Biotechnology Revolution*, New York: Farrar, Strauss and Giroux.

Fukuyama, Francis, 1992, *The End of History and the Last Man*, New York: Free Press.

Garret, Laurie, 2005, "The Next Pandemic?" *Foreign Affairs*, July-August.

Goldschmidt, Walter R., 1952, "The Interrelation Between Cultural Factors and the Acquisition of New Technical Skills," in Bert F. Hoselitz (ed.) *The Progress of Technology*. Chicago: The University of Chicago Press.

Goulet, Denis, 1977, *The Uncertain Promise*, Washington, D.C.: Overseas Development Council.

Internet Usage Statistics—The Big Picture. 2004 August 12. http://www.Internetworldstats.com.htm.

Kahn, Herman and Anthony Weiner, 1967, *The Year 2000*, New York: Macmillan.

Kaplan, Robert, 2000, *The Coming Anarchy: Shattering the Dreams of the Post Cold War*, New York: Random House.

Kennedy, Paul, 1993, *Preparing for the 21st Century*. New York: Random House.

Kitcher, Philip, 1996, *The Lives to Come: The Genetic Revolution and Human Possibilities*, New York: Simon and Schuster.

Koenig, Dieter, 1995, "Sustainable Development: Linking Global Environmental Change to Technology Cooperation", in Dwivedi, O.P., and Dhirendra Vajpeyi (eds.). *Environmental Policies in the Third World—A Comparative Analysis*. Westport: Greenwood.

Kothari, Rajni, 1974, *Footsteps into the Future: Diagnosis of the Present World and a Design for an Alternative*, New York: The Free Press.

Kramarac, Chris (ed.), 1998, *Technology and Women's Voices*, New York: Routledge and Kegan Paul.

Leiken, Robert S., 2005, "Europe's Angry Muslims", *Foreign Affairs*, July-August.

Lewis, Bernard, 2005, "Freedom and Justice in the Modern Middle East", *Foreign Affairs*, May-June.

Linton, Ralph, 1952, "Cultural and Personality Factors Affecting Economic Growth" in Bert F. Hoselitz (ed.) *The Progress of Technology*, Chicago: The University of Chicago Press.

Lobell, Steven E. and Philip Mauceri (eds.), 2004, *Ethnic Conflict and International Politics*, New York: Palgrave-Macmillan.

Loder, Natasha, 2005, "Small Wonders", *The Economist*, January 1.

Luke, Tim, 1995, "World Order or Neo-World Orders: Power, Politics and Ideology in Informationalizing Localities" in Featherstone, M.S. and R. Robertson, *Global Modernities*, London: Sage.

Mack, Tim, 2000, "Electronic Marketing: What You Can Expect", *The Futurist*, March-April.

Mandelbaum, Michael 2000 quoted in Friedman 2005: 436.

Mansbach, Richard and Edward Rhodes, 2003, *Global Politics in a Changing World*, Boston: Houghton and Mifflin.

Martin, P.W., 1955, *Experiment in Depth: A Study of the Work of Jung, Eliot and Toynbee*, London: Routledge and Kegan Paul.

Mayer, Jane, 2005, *"The Experiment"*, The New Yorker, July 11-18.

McClleland, David C., 1961, *The Achieving Society*, New Jersey: VonNostrand.

McDermott, John, 1969, "Technology: The Opiate of the Masses", *The New York Review of Books*, July 31.

McHale, John, 1969, *The Future of the Future*, New York: Bantam.

Mesthene, Emmanuel G., 1969, "The Role of Technology in Society", *Technology and Culture*. April.

Minerd, Jeff, 2000, "Trend Analysis: Genetic Engineering Increases Human Power", *The Futurist*, March-April.

Mundie, Craig J. (Chief Technology Officer for Microsoft), 2005, Quoted by Friedman.

O'Meara, Patrick *et al.*. 2000.

Oliver, Richard W., 2000, *The Coming Bio-Tech Age: The Business of Bio-Materials*, New York: McGraw-Hill.

Parsons, Talcott, 1951, *The Social System. Glencoe*, Illinois: The Free Press.

Polyani, Karl, 1957, *The Great Transformation: The Political and Economic Origins of Our Times*, Boston: Beacon Press.

Pool, Ithiel de Sola, 1990, *Technolgies Without Boundaries*, Cambridge, Massachusetts: Harvard University Press.

Ramesh, Jairam, and Charles Weiss, Jr., 1979, *Mobilizing Technology for World Development*, New York: Praeger.

Raymond, Aron, 1963, *World Technology and Human "Destiny"*, Ann Arbor, Michigan: University of Michigan Press.

Rifkin, Jeremy, 2004, *The European Dream*, New York: Penguin.

Ross, Alex, 2005, "The Record Effect—How Technology has Transformed the Sound of Music", *The New Yorker*, January.

Sale, Kirkpatrick, 1980, *Human Scale*, New York: Coward, McCann, and Geoghegan.

Sardar, Ziauddin, 1999, *All our Futures: The Future of Future Studies*, Westport, Conneticut: Greenwood.

Sengstock, Charles, 2004, The Internet 2004 Usage Statistics, Trends and Applications, paper presented at RC35IPSA Regional Meeting, St. Petersburg, Russia, October 10.

Sorokin, Petrin, *Social and Cultural Dynamics 1937-41 (4 Volumes)*, New York: Bedminister Press.

Spectar, Michael, 2005, "The Higher Risk", The New Yorker, May 23.

Tehranian, M., 1998, "Precapitalism and Migration in Historical Perspective", *International Political Science Review*, July: 289-303.

Teich, Albert (ed.), 2003, *Technology and the Future*, New York: Thompson-Wadsworth.

U.S. Congress Office of Technology Assessment, 1986, Technology, Public Policy, and the Changing Structure of American Agriculture. Washington D.C.

Vajpeyi, Dhirendra, 2003, "Ethno-nationalism, Religious Revival and International Security"; paper presented at the Third International Symposium on Ethnic and Political Action in the Post-Cold War, August 15-20, Thrace, Greece, Democritus University of Thrace.

Vajpeyi, Dhirendra, 2001, *Deforestation, Environment and Sustainable Development—A Comparative Perspective*, London: Praeger.

Vajpeyi, Dhirendra, 1998, *Water Resource Management—A Comparative Perspective*, London: Praeger.

Vajpeyi, Dhirendra, 2001, "The Politics of Paradise: Islam, Identity and Politics in India," in Sharma, Arvind (ed.) *Hinduism and Secularism After Ayodhya*, New York: Palgrave.

Wajeman, Judy, 1991, "Feminist Critiques of Science and Technology", *Feminism Confronts Technology*, Spring.

# 7

# Emerging Modes of Governance and Climate Protection

## The Role of Green Companies in Newly Industrializing Countries

Harald Fuhr and Marcus Lederer

## INTRODUCTION

Although the Kyoto Protocol has recently been ratified by a critical mass of associated states, the effect of specific climate change policies may be severely limited due to weak environmental institutions and deficient regulatory capabilities in some key countries of the developing world. This holds in particular for some of the Newly Industrializing Countries (NICs) with their potentially harmful impact on the world's climate. Unless such deficiencies in NICs are effectively addressed, they may well offset good policies in OECD countries. One interesting mechanism, however, has helped getting those countries involved gradually, and establishing appropriate *Governance* structures. It is the Kyoto Protocol's so-called Clean-Development-Mechanism (CDM) that involves international "green" businesses as crucial actors, and focuses on the development of a market for greenhouse gas emission reductions (emission trade).

In practice, individual CDM projects result from different types of multi-level public-private partnerships (PPPs), encompassing (initially, at least) governments, international organizations (IOs), and transnational as well as national non-governmental organizations (NGOs) and transnational businesses. Given their importance in both theory and practice, it is astonishing that very little is known about the (often contradicting) motives and interests of those that become involved in such partnerships. Even less is known about the effects of such cooperative efforts at the country level, especially as they concern government policies and overall environmental *Governance*. Are individual CDM projects being pushed rashly by transnational actors into specific environments, or do CDM projects have broader, long-term impacts?

This paper explores initial research questions that are related to the two following areas:

- What are the conditions for transnational business actors, international organizations, governments, and NGOs to become jointly involved in PPPs in newly industrializing countries (NICs) to successfully develop specific CDM projects that focus on emission trade and carbon finance?
- What are the effects of such multi-level PPPs (and CDMs) in terms of institutional development and *Governance*? Do CDM projects bring about positive results for climate protection, and more generally, induce new forms of environmental *Governance* in countries with limited statehood? Do CDM projects lead to more effective (and more legitimate) environmental policy-making in such states? Does a true carbon market develop, and how sustainable are such PPPs?

Climate change, its possible consequences, and options to protect the world's climate have become important issues both for academicians and policy-makers. Yet, while issues and policies have been well studied within the OECD world (Hardy 2003; Boehmer-Christiansen and Kellow 2002; Spray 2002), there are significant gaps in research in areas and countries characterized by limited statehood. Although the Kyoto Protocol has defined "flexible mechanisms" for both developing and transition countries, it is still not known *how* decision-makers in the public and the private sectors in those countries react to, and participate effectively, in such ambitious policies. This holds in particular for some of the larger newly industrializing countries where environmental pollution and $CO_2$ emissions have already reached critical levels, but effective *Governance* to deal with these issues is poorly developed.

There is broad agreement that the protection of the world's climate is a common good that requires joint action of important producers of $CO_2$. Most of the literature that focuses on the political dimensions of such processes has analyzed the transatlantic debate and has either asked how single members, such as the United States or Russia, could become more dedicated members of the climate protection regime (Ochs and Venturelli 2003) or debated specific policy changes taking place in the major industrialized countries. It was the Kyoto Protocol that eventually came up with a variety of new modes of *Governance* in the environment. With its so-called "flexible" mechanisms, namely "International Emissions Trading," "Joint Implementation" (JI) and the "Clean Development Mechanism" (CDM) the Protocol has clearly emphasized market mechanisms to solve problems of global warming.

The CDM is of special importance, as it is the only Kyoto mechanism that explicitly includes developing countries (= non-Annex I Parties). It allows all Parties to implement projects that reduce greenhouse gas emissions in non-Annex I Parties of the Kyoto Protocol. Moreover, the mechanism is expected—through investments made, for example, in renewable energy projects—to assist these states in achieving *sustainable development* thus contributing to the ultimate objective of the Convention (Mendis and Openshaw 2004). Under the CDM Annex I Parties (industrialized countries) may use Certified Emission Reductions (CERs) generated by project activities in non-Annex I Parties to contribute to compliance with their emission commitments (Figure 7.1):

FIG. 7.1
**How does a CDM Work?**

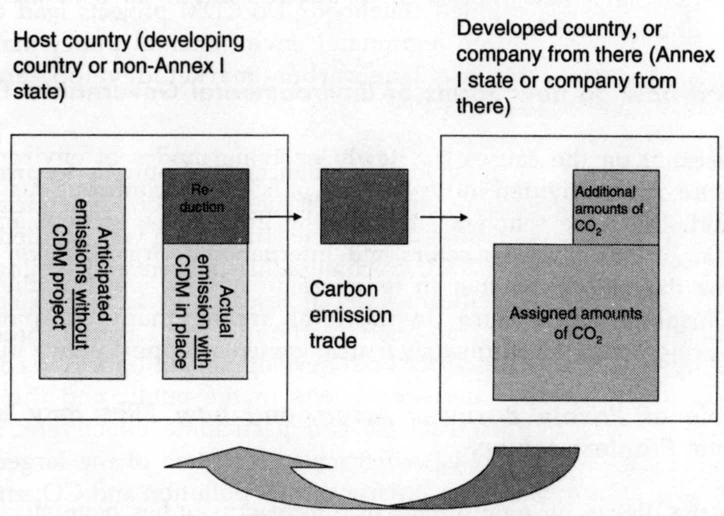


The CDM aims to establish a market where rich countries can buy emission reductions in poor countries and, while doing this, support environmental *Governance*. The market currently has a volume of 300 million tons of $CO_2$ equivalent emission reductions or emission rights traded and is expected to grow strongly in the near future (Streck 2004: 306). The value in dollar terms is somewhere up to US $ 800 billion until 2012 (OECD 2004b). It is supplemented by a secondary market that facilitates investment and risk management (Larson 2001). Meanwhile, the CDM operates in several developing countries. There are 600 to 800 projects in various stages of preparation and there are one dozen projects that have been launched successfully.

The next section will introduce two contributions from the literature which are especially important to understand: (a) the conditions under which such CDM projects evolve, and (b) their potential effects on governance in these countries. The second section will elaborate our assumptions and goals, and the third section will introduce our methodology and case studies on Brazil, China, and India.

## 1. Research Context

To better understand the political processes leading to the implementation of such mechanisms and analyze the changes they might bring about in host countries, our project is framed within *two* trends in the academic literature:

- Research on the *evolving modes of environmental and (multi-level) Governance.*
- Research on *domestic institutional change* and *political repercussions* that such new modes of *Governance* might have in areas with limited statehood.

### *Why and how do new Forms of Environmental Governance Evolve?*

Research on the causes for newly evolving modes of environmental *Governance* can be divided in *two* strands of scholarly contributions. On the one hand, there are scholars stressing the importance of new actors, in particular private business actors and International Organizations (IOs)—and how they work together in issue-oriented PPPs. On the other hand, some authors focus more on national arrangements of particular ("pioneering") states, and how such arrangements support policy diffusion.

### *The Role of Private Business Actors and how PPPs may become Effective Problem-solvers*

In the debate on new modes of *Governance* studies have stressed the importance of new actors, in particular non-state actors, who are involved in processes of political decision-making (Pierre 2000), and the shift from hierarchical forms of management to "softer" methods of coordination. Our project focuses in particular on multi-level and global environmental *Governance* in which non-state business actors interfere at all levels (Esty and Ivanova 2002; Knill and Lehmkuhl 2002). The main assumption in this literature is that with successive policy change towards privatization, liberalization and deregulation throughout the world, private business actors have acquired new forms of authority and thus have changed politics, especially international politics, and from the bottom up (Brühl *et al.* 2004:

Chap. 2; Fuhr 1998; 2001). Scholars on "private authority" point out that private agents not only exercise power by engaging in traditional lobbying and agenda-setting, but also that such power is increasingly perceived as being legitimate by governments and by the public (Cutler *et al.* 1999; Florini 2000, 15). Such views are shared by many of those working on global environmental policies. For a long time, private businesses were seen as polluters (Reed 1996, Chap. 13), and, hence, as a problem (Fuhr *et al.* 1998). Authors such as Cashore (2002) and Streck (2002) emphasize that business actors can be important contributors to environmental protection. They are supposed to play positive role due to their technical expertise, and by using their financial resources to promote efficient policy development. The underlying decision-making processes that such involvement requires, however, are analyzed rather broadly (OECD 1997; Thatcher 1998; Xu 1999), or within simple domestic or inter-state frameworks (Haas *et al.* 1993; Young 1994; Susskind 1994; Obser 1999). Moreover, empirical studies on key issues such as management problems or the role of environmental innovations are lacking. It also holds for emerging options in designing *Governance* structures for Kyoto mechanisms in general, and for JI and the CDM in particular (cf. Haites and Yamin 2000; Baumert *et al.* 2000; Lecocq 2003; Streck 2004; Browne 2004). We will try to fill this research gap by showing why and how the involvement of private business actors can contribute to the development of these new forms of *Governance*.

We can also build on the literature on *global public policy networks* or *public private partnerships* (PPPs), which describes cross-sectoral partnerships between state and non-state actors, both non-profit and for-profit (Messner 1997; Reinicke 1998; Reinicke *et al.* 2000). PPPs are regarded as practical solutions to global problems that can not be solved either by private actors, because common goods have to be provided, or by individual governments, because governments often not only lack the means but also the legitimacy to achieve successful developments on their own. This holds in particular for most countries in the developing world (OECD 2004a). Multi-level *Governance*, encompassing the involvement of private actors and international organizations, is thus seen as key both for the formulation of effective policies as well as for their implementation. In many issue areas, particularly in environmental policy-making, IOs, NGOs, and the private business sector are expected to jointly have the expertise and the necessary resources to complement traditional state action.

Recognizing the implications of global warming, the World Bank, for example, in 1999 approved the establishment of the Prototype Carbon Fund (PCF). The PCF, with the operational objective of mitigating climate change, seeks to promote the World Bank's objective of sustainable development, and, at the same time, to demonstrate the options for PPPs, and to offer a "learning-by-doing" opportunity to its stakeholders (World Bank 2004). Our study analyzes whether such evolving PPPs are successful, and under what conditions. Much of the literature on PPPs, particularly in the context of developing countries, often appears normative, stressing desirable alternatives to (traditionally weak) service provision by public agencies (Fiszbein and Lowden 1999, Vaillancourt and Rosenau 2000). Moreover, there is little information on the dynamics of such PPPs, e.g., whether PPPs are sustainable arrangements or just kick-starting transitory arrangements that need to be reintegrated into the public domain at some point in time. The same holds for the potentially positive as well as negative consequences PPPs might have for the development of public policies in states with weak regulatory capacity. It is simply assumed in the literature that partnerships replace governmental action, and that desired outputs can be delivered in a sustainable manner. The latter features, however, are at the center of our research project.

### *Environmental Policy Analysis—or How 'Best Practices' Diffuse Horizontally*

Another important (partly contradicting) scholarship for our discussion on the reasons for new modes of *Governance* to develop in environmental protection is the research carried out by scholars of comparative national environmental policy. Largely neglected by scholars of international environmental institutions, such research suggests that globalization through the diffusion of national environmental policies, rather than IOs (or any other pressure by national institutions), was responsible for the environmental successes of the last decades (Jänicke and Jörgens 1998; Jänicke and Weidner 1997; Busch and Jörgens 2004). This literature suggests that globalized environmental policy is the outcome of horizontal policy diffusion, at times—but not exclusively—pushed forward by private business actors. This research included: (i) case studies on diffusion processes and thus does not only evaluate outcomes; (ii) studies on the role of pioneering countries; and (iii) studies of international markets as a crucial factor in shaping diffusion of environmental policy (Tews and Busch 2002). Research findings indicate that lead markets, in which environmentally friendly technologies and policies have been developed initiate diffusion processes to other countries through market mechanisms, largely without being influenced by international institutions (Jänicke and Jacob 2002). Special focus is thus given to national institutional arrangements, which are seen as filters for innovation, with the individual arrangements being seen as an explanation for possible variation (Tews *et al.* 2003, 576f; Busch and Jörgens 2004).

The research on environmental policy diffusion, however, almost exclusively focuses on OECD countries, and it remains to be seen whether assumptions in this literature hold true also for areas with limited statehood—or whether the establishment of the conditions under which diffusion becomes possible depends on the involvement of international institutions. On the one hand, there are numerous indications that private sector driven innovations in environmental technologies—and the diffusion of such innovations by firms with strategic orientation—indeed provide powerful new incentives for domestic environmental adjustments, and may trigger policy change toward reducing energy consumption and/or emissions in areas with limited statehood and, in NICs (as suggested in IPCC 2000; Garcia-Johnson 2000; Jänicke and Jacob 2002). On the other hand, the literature about PPPs suggests that incentives provided by "external" actors might often be critical to get such processes started.

Keeping these two literatures in mind, we analyze whether horizontal policy diffusion can be recognized in the policy field of climate protection at all, and how private sector international and eventually national involvement with international organizations and NGOs might eventually trigger such diffusion at more sustained levels.

### *Development Studies and Public Management in Developing Countries—what kind of Domestic Institutional Change can be Expected?*

While research on environmental policies and multilateral decision-making within OECD countries is well established, the knowledge on environmental policy-making, the implementation processes, and the structural changes that can be witnessed within developing countries and NICs is scattered (Gupta 1994; Sathaye 1999). There are many publications that just highlight specific local environmental issues, often with a rather strong project focus (World Bank 1995; Chen and Lotspeich 1998), but without much analysis. They include: (i) the policy process that may lead (or not) to desired environmental action (cf. Di 1999; Lemos 1998); or (ii) the effects of economic incentives towards enforcing desired environmental rules (vs. sanctions; Dasgupta 2000). Unfortunately, there is also a lack of studies on *de-facto* 'silent' progress in some countries and missed opportunities for using CDM (cf. Haites 2004; Sims 1999; Zhang 2000).

The literature on the role of IOs, such as aid agencies, and their importance for policy change in developing countries abounds. In fact, supporters and critics agree that IOs do provide critical resources and that they are responsible for *de facto* policy change (Biersteker 1992)—for good or for bad, especially in countries demonstrating weak state capacity. In addition, development research has highlighted how bargaining preceding such change (mostly connected to structural adjustment programs) takes place among IOs, the recipient country's public administration, and concerned coalitions of reformers (Nelson 1989; Mosley *et al.* 1991; Haggard and Kaufman 1992; Heller *et al.* 1998).

While this literature on broader developmental issues is well established and critical to our research, little is known on the role that *private* international businesses play in similar avenues of policy change, in particular in the field of environmental policy making. Most authors stress the notion of a rather passive government that ultimately accepts almost any offer to invest by international businesses (Brühl *et al.* 2001). These authors highlight difficult conditions (often for both actors) and the adverse effects of networks of corruption. Such approaches neglect to analyze more deeply the various links that private actors establish with non-state actors and with local private businesses—and how such alliances create a demand for new institutional arrangements, that state and public administrators interested in fostering economic development eventually deem important to provide (Fuhr 1998; 2001; Campbell and Fuhr 2004). Hence, while IO—government relationships in rule making are rather well known, rule-making through private sector "loops" within developing countries is under analyzed.

Although the literature on (new) public management (NPM) is quite useful for analyzing emerging market incentives within the public sector, partly through cooperation with private firms (e.g., through contracting-out arrangements), it remains somewhat limited in analytical scope for our research purposes. The bulk of the literature either reviews NPM reforms and arrangements in OECD countries (Pollitt and Bouckaert 2000; Wollmann 2001), with some authors questioning the use of such concepts in states with low state capacity (Schick 2001; McCourt and Minogue 2001; Therkildsen 2000), reflects practical experiences (CLAD 2000; Bresser Pereira 1999; Luiz Abrucio and Mendes Ferreira Costa 1998), or reviews issues from a business administration point of view (Jones *et al.* 2001; Corkery *et al.* 1998).

In the issue area of environmental policy-making, and climate change in particular, our case studies provide a more thorough analysis of such private sector driven loops, and explain in more detail how they emerge, and how they influence rule setting, and, possibly, gradual institutionalization over time in countries with low state capacity. Interestingly, institutionalization of climate-related environmental policies—in our case kick-started through CDMs—could well mean "marketization," with some of the new policies being locked-in through evolving *market* mechanisms. Hence, it is possible that countries with limited statehood, who are unable to develop, manage and implement environmental policies (in general, and climate change policies in particular) may be able to "leapfrog" *straight* into new steering options and bypass traditional hierarchical and rule-based *Governance*.

## 2. Initial Hypotheses and Goals

This section frames the subsequent analysis of the involvement of certain business actors—those who participate in CDM projects—in fostering new forms of *Governance* in the realm of climate protection in selected Newly Industrializing Countries (NICs) with limited statehood. The framework is based on two main research areas identified in the review of the literature above, and includes hypothesized sequences of events to be tested (Figure 7.2). The framework addresses:

- why and how new modes of environmental *Governance* through a specific form of PPP—a CDM—evolve. Our first step is to determine the *successful emergence of private sector driven CDM projects,* since such projects, in essence, reflect the successful (and critical) involvement of business actors and other key players (such as national governments, International Organizations, and non-governmental organizations). We have four hypotheses to test.

- the *Governance* effects of such CDM projects once implemented in countries with limited statehood. Here our independent variable will be successful, private sector driven, CDM projects and we will analyze *whether and what kind of new (and sustainable) environmental rules and procedures* for effective climate protection in those countries result from the variable. We expect variance on the dependent variable and so have three hypotheses related to this dependent variable.

FIG. 7.2

**Research Areas and Variables Hypotheses**

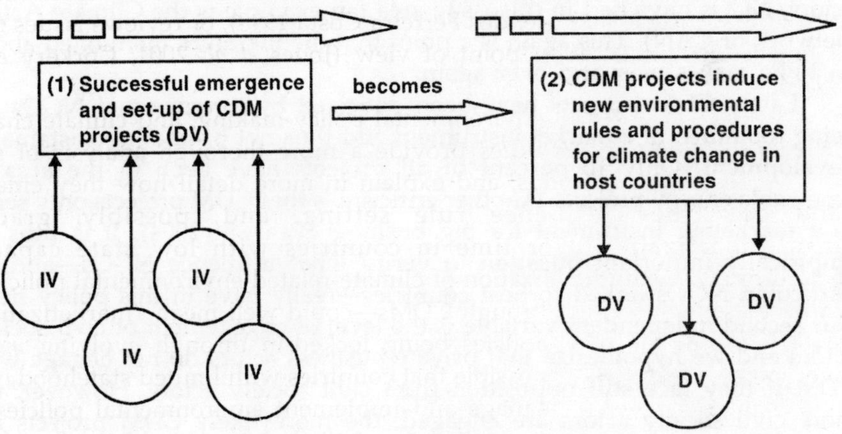


## (1) *Conditions under which the Involvement of the Business Sector is Successful*

As the establishment of CDM is nothing less than the set-up of an international market, it is generally acknowledged that CDM projects can only work effectively when the business sector is genuinely interested—and successfully engaged. However, the carbon market is by itself not yet a viable market that would induce business actors to become involved and the simple answer that profit derived from business in the market is the only incentive companies care about does not carry far in the carbon market. Consequently, there might be—as often argued—an important role to play for IOs that provide initial financial resources. In this context one can point to the World Bank which, together with some OECD countries and private sector participants, established three Carbon Funds: the "Prototype Carbon

Fund" (PCF), the "Community Development Carbon Fund" (CDCF), and the "Bio Carbon Fund" (BioCF). These funds are supposed to act as catalysts in the set up of CDM projects (Figure 7.3). They are important because they provide seed money for the development of CDM projects and because they provide expertise (i.e., help dealing with information asymmetries as well as methodological help) concerning the above mentioned secondary market. Such analysis would be consistent with the literature on other PPPs and would also be supported by many development experts who stress the role of IOs in jumpstarting policy change. Our first independent variable is the amount of financial resources provided by IO's and we hypothesize that the more financial resources and expertise are provided by IOs, the more private business actors enter CDM arrangements.

The carbon market is not only an extremely complex business, but it is also located within a political minefield. The CDM itself is sometimes labeled the "Kyoto surprise" (Werksmann 1998) as it combines rather divergent interests and motivations of the developing and the developed world (Oberthür and Ott 1999). One reason for the origin and success of CDM seems to be the mediating influence and the scrutiny civil society actors/NGOs have had in this issue area (an example is the Climate Action Network or CAN). This again is a point that the literature mentioned above on PPPs makes over and over again.

Lately CDM projects have been criticized by international NGOs for being too much of a market instrument and thus not promoting sustainable development. Only 10 percent of all projects have been in the area of renewable energy projects. Another criticism is that CDM projects only serve as a marketing instrument for big business (Pearson 2004). It is thus an empirically important question to verify what influence NGOs—and, in particular, NGOs linked to host countries—really have in this policy field. Our second independent variable is the level of engagement of civil society actors and we hypothesize that private business actors do not engage with CDM if they face stiff opposition from civil society actors. However, the more civil society actors are engaged, the more likely CDM projects are located in the area of "clean" technologies.

Another criterion for the successful establishment of CDM activities is the motivation of the business actors themselves. As has been mentioned, the market is so far rather small and seems not to be very profitable yet (Chichilnisky and Heal 2000). It is very likely that business actors do not get involved in CDM projects only for financial gains or for financial incentives provided by IOs but also for marketing reasons. It can thus be expected that primarily businesses which hope to gain from a "greener" image will participate. In fact, "greening" (formerly "brown") companies may turn out to become a clear-cut strategy to improve competitiveness (Moore and Miller 1994: Chap. IV; Kütting 2004). A good example is British Petroleum, but it has to be seen whether other companies follow suit. Following this logic our third independent variable is the level of green imaging and we hypothesize that the more a company is in need to set-up a new image as a "green company," or expects to improve competitiveness, the more likely it will engage in the carbon market.

The first two hypotheses reflect the analyses of PPPs. The third relates to this area as well, but also encompasses some corporate *Governance* issues. Following the literature on policy diffusion one could, however, also argue that possible trends in the convergence of *Governance* patterns result from the fact that governments orient their policies to what is already practiced in lead countries (Tews *et al*. 2003: 570f). As described above, it is thus lead markets and national institutional arrangements which contribute to policy diffusion and one should focus more on domestic structures and less on international factors. Our fourth independent variable is the influence of lead countries and we hypothesize that the successful setting up of CDM projects results from the emulation of lead countries. If this were the case it would logically follow that possible variations of implementing CDM projects do not depend on the influence of international actors (IOs or NGOs) but on national institutional arrangements. In the following we have summarized our four hypotheses and point out who we believe to be some of the main players (Figure 7.3).

FIG. 7.3
**CDM—Collaboration, and Emerging Private-Public Partnerships (PPPs)**

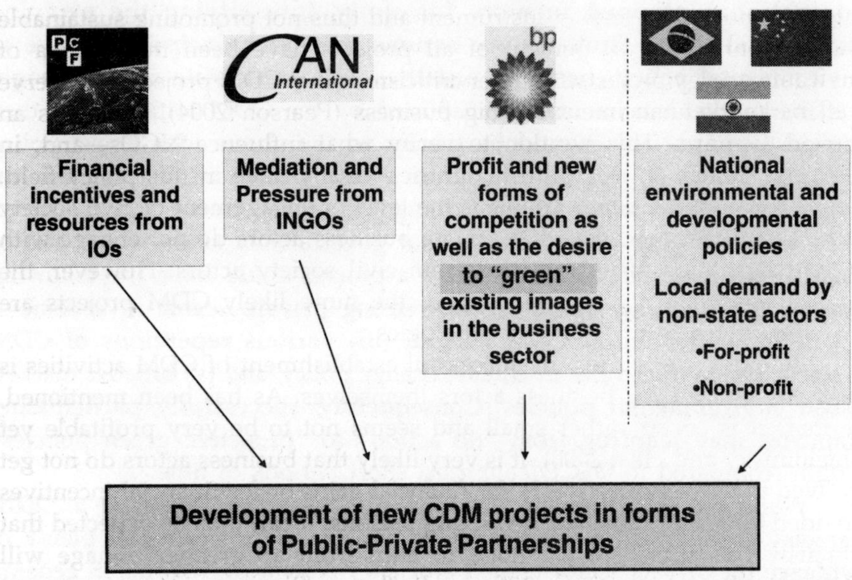


### *(2) Governance effects: new (and sustainable) environmental rules and procedures for effective climate protection in countries with limited statehood*

The successful setting up of CDM activities (independent variable) and the steady involvement of private business actors have consequences on environmental policy-making within host countries (dependent variable). As described above, a substantial part of the literature on development has so far focused only on the consequences IOs have on overall patterns of development within these countries, and on public policy-making. Concerning the role of business, in particular international business, the general assumption is that governments are passive bystanders. It is, however, also likely that the involvement in an international PPP and the opening up towards the influence of business actors may have significant repercussions, and lead to more efficiency. Such a development would also be consistent with many assumptions in the new public management literature (Jones *et al.* 2001: Chap. 4, Turner and Hulme 1997: Chaps. 5, 8). Our first dependent variable is the amount of efficient environmental policy and our fifth hypothesis is thus that the more private business actors, and corresponding PPPs, engage in areas with limited statehood through CDM, the more pressure is created to conduct a more efficient environmental policy overall.

As the development literature suggests, externally financed structural adjustment programs helped reduce state interventionism and strengthen market mechanisms in recipient countries throughout the 1990s (World Bank 1997). And, once broader liberalization and deregulation by governments became credible, private businesses, both national and international, stepped in more forcefully, intensifying the evolving institutional mesh. Similarly, we assume that the principal incentive to environmental policy change in countries with weak state capacity might well be market mechanisms, transported by the CDM initially and then carried forward. This would be similar to the above idea about policy diffusion, however, this time not from a lead market in one country but rather from a lead sector (climate change) to others. Hence, market-driven PPPs would trigger policy change that governments alone would not or could not initiate on their own. Such a process could have the following sequence: (i) setting up PPPs with strong private sector involvement; (ii) defining the initial CDM project; (iii) various repetitions of CDM projects; (iv) market-rules in climate change policy, and (v) broader market-based environmental policies. Consequently, successfully participating countries may leapfrog from "no action" to "proactive green policies" within (compared to OECD countries) short periods of time.

While the literature on new public management (Jones *et al.* 2001; Barzelay 2003), and on 'best practices' (Cabrera 1995) provides plenty of evidence for private sector-related efficiency-enhancing reforms in general, at least in specified areas of public administration we have only found narrative evidence for leapfrogging in the environment. Therefore, our second dependent variable is the amount of mechanisms underlying state policies and we hypothesize that the more Clean Development Mechanism projects are successfully established, the more likely it is that a state bureaucracy is being set-up to regulate the institutional arrangements and/

or that the introduction of market mechanisms is becoming an accepted mode of *Governance* in environmental policy-making.

Another important question is related to purposes PPPs may serve in a medium-term framework once the carbon market is well established. The above literature review does not address this question at all. It is not unlikely, and to some extent hoped for, that at one point neither the financial resources nor the ideational input of IOs and NGOs are necessary any longer for the market to efficiently function, i.e., approaching an equilibrium between demand and supply of carbon emission reductions. Chances are that the PPPs in the field of climate protection will have served their kick-starting and transitory role—and that the supervisory functions of the market may later be performed by classical state actors, such as regulatory agencies. Alternatively, PPPs may, similar to social policy reform, serve monitoring functions (Kondo 2002; Clad 2000). Our third dependent variable is the importance of PPP's and our final hypothesis is that the more mature the international carbon market becomes and the more integrated a single state is in this market, the less important the original PPPs become.

These three hypotheses can now be combined as follows (Figure 7.4):

FIG. 7.4
**CDM Projects—and their Potential Domestic Institutional Repercussions**

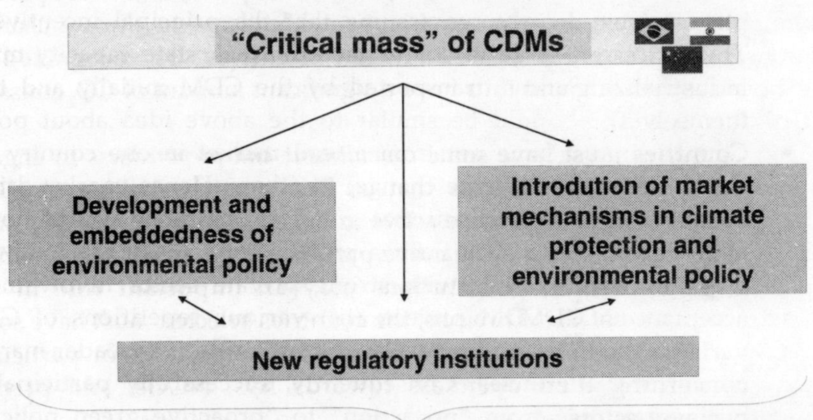


## 3. Methodology and cases

We analyze one sector (climate protection) in three countries: Brazil, China, and India. Such one-sector-multi-country-strategy allows us to verify whether evolving new modes of *Governance* in environmental policy-making is part of a global trend or whether it can be reduced to the specifics of one country. Our comparative analysis, however, takes into account in-country institutional arrangements, and specific actors and interests, to see whether they play any role in a potential diffusion of the witnessed policies.

As the changes we explore have only been taking place recently and have just started to leave their first traces within the countries examined, our methods of choice are case studies supported by inquiries through a series of field studies and through (semi-structured) interviews (with mostly open-ended questions).

Our *case selection* was guided by the following criteria:

- Focus only on areas with *limited statehood*. In our project these are countries which have weak state capabilities and capacity, particularly in environmental policy and management regulations. Policies are in place but they are not efficiently implemented or there is a great variance in local implementation. We use the Kaufmann indicators as developed by the World Bank Institute (http://www.worldbank.org/wbi/governance/data.html) to identify weak or strong state capacity. For state capacity in the field of environmental policy we rely on the data of the 2005 Environmental Sustainability Index (ESI 2005a).
- Cases must be *relevant*, that is, they must promise to be important players—may be even environmental leaders—in climate change. This criterion is satisfied when countries are recognized as industrializing and thus have a significant amount of $CO_2$ emission themselves.
- Countries must have some *commitment and preparedness* to engage with international actors that is; they must be willing to allow business actors to become active in the environment and they must allow IOs to play a substantive part. However, in order to validate whether national institutions play an important role in the acceptance of CDM projects, the countries selected must have some variance in their domestic institutional structure, in particular concerning their openness towards IOs, NGOs, and private business actors.

### *(1) Weak State Capacity*

All three cases under discussion—China, India, and Brazil—are characterized by limited statehood. This is not so much related to their monopoly on the legitimate use of force, but rather to deficiencies in state capacity in general, and in terms of environmental policy management in particular. All three countries have state capacity well below OECD standards measured in terms of "government effectiveness" compared to both OECD countries and Sub-Saharan Africa (Figure 7.5).

FIG. 7.5
**Government Effectiveness in Brazil, China, and India**

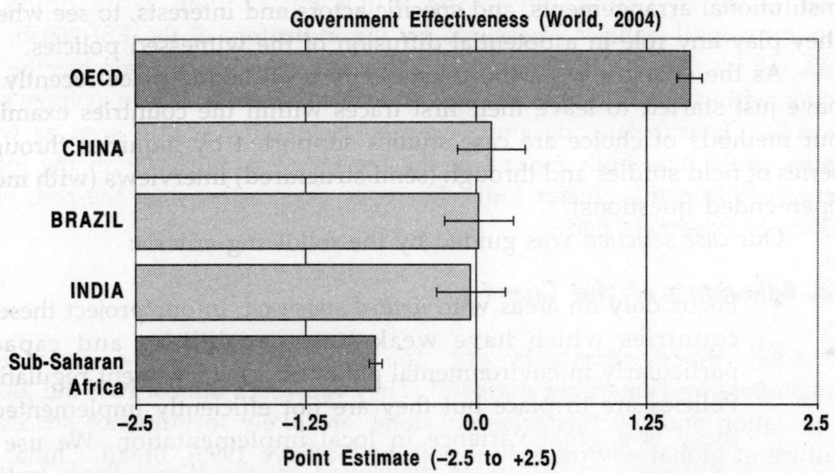


*Source* : D. Kaufmann, A. Kraay, and H. Mastruzzi 2005 : Governance Matters IV : Governance Indicators for 1996-2004. (http://www.worldbank.org/wbi/governance/[pubs/govmatters4.html).

The difference becomes even more striking once "regulatory quality" is taken into account (Figure 7.6).

FIG. 7.6
**Regulatory Quality in Brazil, China, and India**

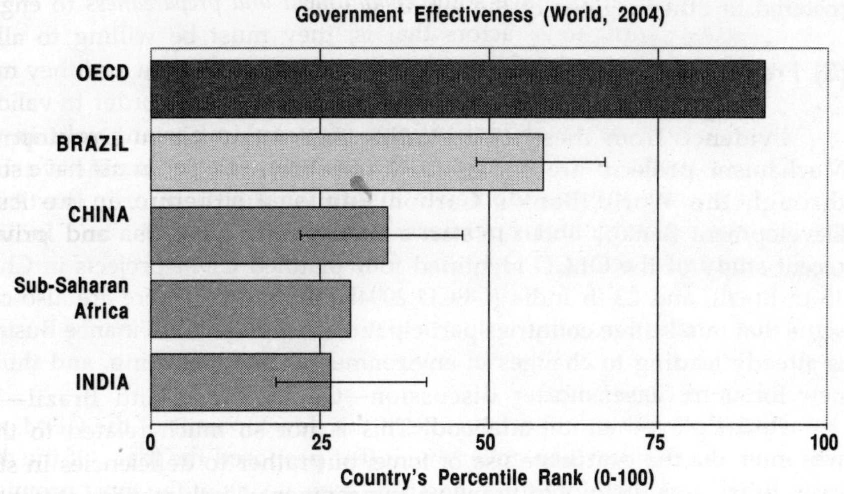


*Source* : D. Kaufmann, A. Kraay, and H. Mastruzzi 2005 : Governance Matters IV : Governance Indicators for 1996-2004. (http://www.worldbank.org/wbi/governance/[pubs/govmatters4.html).

The weak regulatory capacity of China and India in particular is interesting, with indices of India below the average of Sub-Saharan Africa, and those of China not faring much better. The same holds for environmental policies (measured by the indicators of the ESI 2005b, 123, 133, 165 for Brazil, China, and India, respectively). Brazil again has the best score, within its cluster of countries which only have an above average score overall. Nevertheless, its environmental *Governance* is still seen as weak. India and China both ranked in the cluster of countries with the lowest scores. Within this cluster India, however, does better than the rest, while China is extremely bad.

### (2) Relevance of the Cases

All three countries are "newly industrializing countries," encompassing "emerging markets". They represent almost half the globe's population and, by this criterion alone, are likely to influence success or failure of global environmental policies (Sathaye 1999). Brazil, China, and India already face severe environmental damage particularly in urban centers. All three have a very high chance of being severely affected by climate change (Chen and Lotspeich 1998). In fact, unless guided by appropriate environmental policies, catch-up growth would be extremely harmful for both local eco-systems as well as for global climate. Furthermore, these countries are expected to have most carbon market transactions. Involving this group of countries is thus key for sound climate change policies, and for the provision of the global public good of climate protection. Moreover, if PPPs can make a difference and bring about change in these critical countries, there is hope that climate protection can be fostered in other regions of the world as well.

### (3) Preparedness to Engage, and Variance in Cases

Evidence from these case studies shows that Clean Development Mechanism projects are successfully implemented by business actors, through the World Bank's Carbon Funds. Furthermore, the Asian Development Bank is about to start a similar fund for China and India. A recent study of the OECD identified four planned CDM projects in China, 15 in Brazil, and 23 in India (OECD 2004b: 40f and 6). There are also clear signs that in all three countries participation in the Carbon Finance Business is already leading to changes in environmental policy-making, and thus to new forms of *Governance*.

***Brazil*** played an important role in the development of the CDM, as it was inter alia the Brazilian government that proposed the idea. Of the three cases Brazil was therefore for a long time seen as one of the most promising countries to embrace CDM projects and has, in fact, hosted the first CDM initiative—a rural energy project which was conducted in partnership with British Petroleum (WBCSD 2004: 5). Lately, however, the government has shied away from its initial enthusiasm for reasons not yet clear to us. It is thus an open question whether Brazil could be the lead country from which diffusion to other NICs takes place. Similar to the other two cases the energy sector is seen as the most promising one.

Such facts notwithstanding, lately doubts have come up whether Brazil can still implement many CDM projects in the energy sector, as most of its electricity is derived from water power (90%) and it became obvious that such energy production does not lend itself to emission reductions. Nevertheless, domestic players in Brazil, in particular the industrial sector, are already involved in planning further CDM activities (UNIDO 2003: 7). Brazil has also developed a rather sophisticated institutional structure to deal with CDM projects, but openly acknowledges that more capacities are needed since expertise is highly concentrated. There is a strong involvement of the NGO sector in Brazilian politics as well, now even strengthened under the presidency of Lula da Silva.

***China*** ratified the Kyoto protocol in 2002, but has otherwise not been taking active steps regarding climate protection. The CDM process is sometimes seen as offering important opportunities for sustainable development particularly in the energy sector that is still coal dominated. It is, therefore, even more important that CDM projects could evolve into an important market for China, as it is estimated that China's potential share of the world's carbon trading market could be up to 50 per cent (World Bank 2004: XIII). Considering the importance of the Chinese market it is hardly surprising that several international actors (World Bank, Asian Development Bank, GTZ, but also, and of utmost interest to us, British Petroleum) are conducting studies concerning CDMs or setting up CDM projects in China.

Donors and the Chinese government seem to agree that involving China within the CDM process will not only have a significant impact on the Chinese economy but also pave the way for its new energy and environmental policies. A recent study by the World Bank stresses the importance of capacity building before CDM projects can be successfully implemented (Zhang 2004: 4). Whether such institutional change is under way already is doubtful. For example, the Chinese government was initially very hesitant to engage with the World Bank's Prototype Carbon Fund. However, in 2003 it decided to sign up as a host country. Although the country is very open to Direct Foreign Investment, there are many strings attached. China is the country in our sample which has opened up least towards IOs, and, even less towards NGOs.

***India*** does not have large primary energy reserves but faces a growing population and rapidly increasing energy demand. The government has thus pushed hard to increase the utilization of renewable energy technology. Renewable energy projects can significantly reduce GHG emissions. The country is highly attractive for CDM projects, although the projects face high upfront costs (Government of India 2003: 8). India produced $CO_2$-equivalent emissions of about 1000 billion tons in 1990 (equal to 3 per cent of global emissions). It is estimated that India would capture about 10 per cent of the global CDM market, thereby generating revenues ranging from Euro 10-300 million annually (Babu and Michaelowa 2003: 11). It is not surprising that the government pushed hard to embrace the CDM market, and has even encouraged the involvement of private business actors, despite the country's long tradition of protectionism and market-reserve policies.

The first five CDM projects were approved in 2003. Others were submitted in response to the call for tenders by the government of Sweden, Finland, and by the World Bank's three Carbon Funds (PCF, BioCF, CDCF). Two Indian financing institutions have recently set-up their own Carbon Funds. This has already brought about institutional change. The Ministry of Environment and Forest (MoEF) seems to have gained leverage in comparison to other ministries. In addition, there is traditionally a strong co-optation of and cooperation with non-governmental organizations in Indian politics. It will be interesting for our future analysis to review India's influence on the emerging carbon market, and its goal to achieve sustainable development by establishing CDM projects.

The variance in the cases can best be summarized graphically as follows (Figure 7.7).

FIG. 7.7
**Brazil, China, and India : Case Study Variance**

**Case Selection**

| | Government effectiveness index | Environmental *Governance* capacity | Involvement of IOs in CDM projects | Role of NGOs | Potential size of market | "Doing Business" climate | Commitment of host government |
|---|---|---|---|---|---|---|---|
|  | XX | XXX | XXX | XXX | X | XX | XXX |
|  | XX | X | XX | X | XXX | XX | XX |
|  | XX | XX | XX | XXX | XX | X | XX |

## CONCLUSION

This paper summarized the outline of a larger research project and presented some initial hypotheses as well as information on three case studies. Following are some initial conclusions:

(1) The private sector is one important driving force in initiating new environmental policies. Compared to other sectors (financial regulation, e-commerce, lex mercatoria), its input might not be the most important one but businesses have an important role to ensure that PPPs work effectively. The question remains, however, whether private sector involvement will lead to domestic regulatory adjustments, or to a much broader 'regulatory leapfrogging' in developing countries.

(2) PPPs in general, and in environmental policy-making in particular, are more than just discussion clubs. They appear to be good venues where new policies can be developed and adopted if needed. PPPs do not, however, just emerge or even work properly when needed. Hence, the functionalist fallacy in most of the global governance literature has to be avoided. Instead, it appears it is the financial input of International Organizations, as well as the expertise they provide, that is of utmost importance to get PPPs started. This is evidenced in many cases initially funding by the World Bank. For establishing PPPs as sustainable policy mechanisms, especially at the international level, NGO contributions and their participation is very important. However, as far as CDMs are concerned, we have not yet found a prominent role in practice. Only further research will allow for a more substantive conclusion.

(3) Finally, initial empirical evidence in Brazil, China, and India supports the notion that CDM projects are considered important business opportunities. Furthermore, a first glance at current practices seems to support our hypothesis that domestic regulatory adjustments indeed take place, and, with the setting up of CDM projects, that such change points towards adopting market-oriented instruments in managing environmental policy.

## References

Abrucio, Fernando L., and Valeriano Mendes Ferreira Costa, 1998, *Reforma do Estado e o contexto federativo brasileiro*, Pesquisas 12.

Babu, N. Yuvaraj Dinesh, and Axel Michaelowa, 2003, *Removing Barriers for Renewable Energy CDM Projects in India and Building Capacity at the State Level*, Hamburg: Hamburgisches Welt-Wirtschafts-Archiv (HWWA).

Barzelay, Michael, 2003, Introduction: "The Process Dynamics of Public Management Policy-making", *International Public Management Journal*, 6 (3), pp. 251-82.

Baumert, Kevin *et. al.* 2000, Designing the Clean Development Mechanism to Meet the Need of a Broad Range of Interests, *WRI Climate Notes* (August).

Bennis, Phyllis, 2000, (ed.), *Calling the Shots. How Washington Dominates Today's UN*, New York, Northampton, Massachusetts: Olive Branch Press.

Biersteker, Thomas J., 1992, The *"Triumph" of Neoclassical Economics in the Developing World: Policy Convergence and Bases of Governance in the International Economic Order, In Governance Without Government: Order and Change in World Politics,* edited by James N. Rosenau and Ernst-Otto Czempiel, Cambridge: Cambrigde University Press.

Boehmer-Christiansen, Sonja, and Aynsley J. Kellow, 2002, *International Environmental Policy: Interests and the Failure of the Kyoto Process*, Cheltenham: Edgar Elgar.

Bresser Pereira, Louis Carlos, 1999, *Reforma del estado para la ciudadania, La reforma gerencial brasileña en la perspectiva internacional.* Caracas: CLAD

Browne, John. 2004. Beyond Kyoto. *Foreign Affairs* 83(4).

Brühl, Tanja, Heidi Feldt, Brigitte Hamm, Hartwig Hummel, and Jens Martens, ed. 2004, *Unternehmen in der Weltpolitik, Politiknetzwerke, Unternehmensregeln und die Zukunft des Multilateralismus.* Bonn: Dietz.

Brühl, Tanja, Thomas Debiel, Brigitte Hamm, Hartwig Hummel, and Jens Martens (eds.), 2001, Die Privatisierung der Weltpolitik, Entstaatlichung und Kommerzialisierung im Globalisierungsprozess. Bonn: Dietz.

Busch, Olof-Per, and Helge Jörgens, 2004, *Globale Ausbreitungsmuster umweltpolitischer Innovationen, FFU Report [-02-2005-],* Berlin: Forschungsstelle für Umweltpolitik.

Cashore, Benjamin W., 2002, Legitimacy and the Privatization of Environmental Governance: How Non-State Market-Driven (NSMD) Governance Systems Gain Rule-Making Authority, *Governance* 15(4):503-529.

Chen, Aimin, and Richard Lotspeich, 1998, "Determinants of Industrial Residuals: Generation and Treatment: Evidence from Chinese Cities", *Ecologial Economics,* 26:97-108.

Chichilnisky, Graciela, and Geoffrey Heal, eds. 2000, *Environmental Markets: Equity and Efficiency,* New York: Columbia University Press.

CLAD, 2000, *La responsabilización en la nueva gestión pública Latinoamericana,* Caracas: CLAD.

Coninck, Helen C., and N.H. van der Linden, 2003, *An Overview of Carbon Transactions: General Characteristics and Specific Peculiarities:* ECN.

Corkery, Joan, Turkia O. Daddah, Colm O'Nuallain, and Tony Land, eds.1998, *Management of Public Service Reform, A Comparative Review of Experiences in the Management of Programmes of Reform of the Administrative Arm of Central Government. Amsterdam*: ECDPM, IOS Press.

Cutler, Claire A. 2003, *Private power and global authority: transnational merchant law in the global political economy,* Cambridge studies in international relations; 90, Cambridge, UK: Cambridge University Press.

Cutler, Claire A., Virgina Haufler, and Tony Porter, eds. 1999, *Private Authority and International Affairs,* edited by J.N. Rosenau, SUNY Series in Global Politics. Albany, NY: State University of New York Press.

Dasgupta, Nandini, 2000, "Environmental Enforcement and Small Industries in India: Reworking the Problem in the Poverty Context", *World Development,* 28:945-67.

Di, Chang X. 1999, ISO 14001: The Severe Challenge for China: An Overview of the Problems China Faced in the Implementation and Certification of ISO 14001, *In Growing Pains: Environmental Management in Developing Countries,* edited by W. Wehrmeyer and Y. Mulugetta, Sheffield: Greenleaf Publishing.

ESI, 2005a, Environmental Sustainability Index: Yale Center for Environmental Law and Policy, Yale University, Center for International Earth Science Information Network, Columbia University.

ESI, 2005b, Country Profiles: Yale Center for Environmental Law and Policy, Yale University, Center for International Earth Science Information Network, Columbia University Press, Appendix B.

Esty, Daniel C., and Maria H. Ivanova, eds. 2002, *Global Environmental Governance: Options and Opportunities,* Yale School of Forestry and Environmental Studies.

Fankhauser, Samuel, and Lucia Lavric, 2003, *The Investment Climate for Climate Investment: Joint Implementation in Transition Countries,* London: European Bank for Reconstruction and Development.

Fiszbein, Ariel, and Pamela Lowden, 1999, *Working Together for a Change, Government, Business and Civic Partnerships for Poverty Reduction in Latin America and the Caribbean,* Washington, D.C.: World Bank.

Florini, Ann. M., ed. 2000, *The Third Force. The Rise of Transnational Civil Society,* Tokyo, Washington, D.C.: Japan Center for International Exchange, Carnegie Endowment for International Peace.

Fredriksson, Per G., and Muthukumara Mani, 2002, *The Rule of Law and the Pattern of Environmental Protection,* Washington, D.C.: IMF.

Garcia-Johnson, Roni, 2000, *Exporting Environmentalism, U.S. Multinational Chemical Corporations in Brazil and Mexico*, Edited by N. Choucri, Global Environmental Accord: Strategies for Sustainability and Institutional Innovation, Cambridge, MA: MIT Press.

Greenwood, Justin, and Henry Jacek (eds.), 2000, *Organized Business and the New Global Order*, Edited by L.G. Asher Arian, William Lafferty, Theodore Lowi, Carole Pateman, Advances in Political Science: An International Series, Basingstoke: Macmillan Press.

Gupta, Joyeeta, 1997, *The Climate Change Convention and Developing Countries: From Conflict to Consensus?* Doortrecht: Kluwer Academic.

Haas, Peter, Robert O. Keohane, and Marc A. Levy, eds. 1993, *Institutions for the Earth: Sources of Effective International Environmental Protection*, Cambridge: MIT Press.

Hagem, Catherine, Steffen Kallbekken, Ottar Maestad, and Hege Westkog, 2003, *Tough Justice for Small Nations: How Strategic Behaviour can Influence the Enforcement of the Kyoto Protocol*, Oslo: CICERO.

Haggard, Stephan, and Robert R. Kaufmann, eds. 1992, *The Politics of Economic Adjustment, International Constraints, Distributive Conflicts, and the State*, Princeton: Princeton University Press.

Haites, Erik, 2004, *Estimating the Market Potential for the Clean Development Mechanism: Review of Models and Lessons Learned*, Washington, D.C.: World Bank, International Energy Agency, International Emissions Trading Association.

Haites, Erik, and Farhana Yamin, 2000, *The Clean Development Mechanism: Proposals for its Operation and Governance*, Global Environmental Change, 10:27-45.

Hardy, John T., 2003, *Climate Change: Causes, Effects, and Solutions*, Chichester, West Sussex: Wiley.

Haufler, Virginia, 1993, "Crossing the Boundary Between Public and Private", *In Regime Theory and International Relations*, edited by Volker, Rittberger, Oxford: Clarendon Press.

Heller, William B., Phil Keefer, and Mathew D. McCubbins, 1998, "Political Structure and Economic Liberalization: Conditions and Cases from the Developing World", *In the Origins of Liberty: Political and Economic Liberalization in the Modern World*, edited by Paul W. Drake and Mathew D. McCubbins. Princeton: Princeton University Press.

Heuser, Robert, and Jan de Graaf, eds. 2001, *Umweltschutzrecht der VR China, Gesetze und Analysen, Mitteilungen des Instituts für Asienkunde;* 336, Hamburg: Deutsches Übersee-Institut.

Höhne, Niklas, Carolina Galleguillos, Kornelis Blok, Jochen Harnisch, and Dian Phylipsen, 2003, *Evolution of Commitments under the UNFCCC: Involving Newly Industrialized Economies and Developing Countries*, Berlin: Federal Environmental Agency.

ICC, International Chamber of Commerce, 2004, Business perspectives on a long-term international policy approach [World Wibe Web], 2004 [cited 2004], Available from http://www.iccwbo.org/home/news_archives/2004/ICC_The_Long_term_approach_BA_2004.ppt.

IPCC, 2000, *Methodological and Technological Issues in Technology Transfer: A Special Report of IPCC Working Group III:* IPCC.

Jänicke, Martin, and Klaus Jacob, 2002, "Global Environmental Change and the Nation State: Lead Markets for Environmental Innovations", *In Proceedings of the 2001 Berlin Conference on the Human Dimensions of Global Environmental Change:* "Global Environmental Change and the Nation State," edited by Frank Biermann, Rainer Brohm and Klaus Dingwerth, Potsdam: Potsdam Institute for Climate Impact Research.

Jänicke, Martin, and Helge Jörgens, 1998, "National Environmental Policy Planning in OECD Countries: Preliminary Lessons from Cross-National Comparisons", *Environmental Politics*, 7(2): 27-54.

Jänicke, Martin, and Helmut Weidner, eds., 1997, *National Environmental Policies: A Comparative Study of Capacity-Building*, Berlin: Springer.

Jones, Laurence, James Guthrie, and Peter Steane (eds.), 2001, *Learning from International Public Management Reform (2 Vol.)*, Amsterdam: JAI Press.

Kaufmann, Daniel, Aart Kraay, and Massimo Mastruzzi, 2003, World Bank Policy Research Working Paper 3106.

Kern, Kristine, Helge Jörgens, and Martin Jänicke, 2001, *The Diffusion of Environmental Policy Innovations: A Contribution to the Globalisation of Environmenatl Policy*, Berlin: Wissenschaftszentrum Berlin für Sozialforschung.

Knill, Christoph, and Dirk Lehmkuhl, 2002, "Private Actors and the State: Internationalization and Changing Patterns of Governance", Governance 15(1): 41-63.

Kondo, Seiichi, 2002, *Transparência e responsabilização no setor público: fazendo acontecer. Brasilia:* Coleção GestãoPública.

Kütting, Gabriela, 2004, *Globalization and the Environment: Greening Global Political Economy*, Albany, NY: State University of New York Press.

Larson, Donald F. 2001, *Regulating the Clean Development Mechanism: Implications for Investors, Developing Countries, and the Environment* (PCFplus Research Paper). Washington, D.C.: World Bank.

Lecoq, Franck, 2003, "Pioneering Transactions, Catalyzing Markets, and Building Capacity: The Prototype Carbon Fund Contributions to Climate Policies", *American Journal of Agricultural Economics*, 85(3): 703-07.

Lemos, Maria C., 1998, The Politics of Pollution Control in Brazil: State Actors and Social Movements in Cleaning up Cubatao, *World Development*, 26: 75-87.

McCourt, Willy, and Martin Minogue, eds. 2001, *The Internationalization of Public Management, Reinventing the Third World State*, Cheltenham: Edward Elgar.

Mendis, Matthew, and Keith Openshaw, 2004, "The Clean Development Mechanism: Making it Operational", *Development and Sustainability*, 6:183-211.

Mendoza, Enrique C., ed., 1995, *La nueva gestión municipal en México, Analisis de experiencias innovadoras en gobiernos locales*, México: CIDE

Messner, Dirk, 1997, *The Network Society: Economic Development and International Competitiveness as a Problem for Social Governance*, London: Frank Cass.

Ministerium für Umwelt und Verkehr Baden-Württemberg, 2004, Flexible Instrumente im Klimaschutz: Emissionsrechtehandel, Joint Implementation, Clean Development Mechanism: Ministerium für Umwelt und Verkehr Baden-Württemberg, Frauenhofer Institut für Systemtechnik und Innovationsforschung.

Ministry of Non-Covemtional Energy Sources India, 2004, *Baseline for renewable energy projects under dlean development mechanism*, New Dehli: Government of India.

Moore, Curtis, and Alan Miller, 1994, Green Gold: Japan, Germany, *The United States, and the Race for Environmental Technology*, Boston: Beacon Press.

Mosley, Paul, Jane Harrigan, and John Toye, 1991 *Aid and Power: The World Bank and Policy-Based Lending*, (Vol. 2), New York.

Nelson, Joan M., ed. 1989, *Fragile Coalitions: The Politics of Economic Adjustment*, New Brunswick: Transaction Books.

Oberthür, Sebastian, and Hermann E. Ott, 1999, *The Kyoto Protocol: International Climate Policy for the 21st Century*, New York: Springer Verlag.

Oberthür, Sebastian, 1997, *Umweltschutz durch internationale Regime: Interessen, Verhandlungsprozesse, Wirkungen*, Opladen: Leske und Budrich.

Obser, Andreas, 1999, *Communicative Structuration and Governance of the Global Environment through Policy Networks of International Aid Organizations*, Baden-Baden: Nomos.

Ochs, Alexander, and Aldo Venturelli, 2003, *Towards a Transatlantic Consensus on Climate Change: High-Level Transatlantic Dialogue on Climate Change:* German Institute for International Foreign Affairs

OECD, 1997, *Climate Change: Mobilizing Global Effort*, Paris: OECD.

OECD, 2004a, New Forms of Governance for Economic Development, Paris: OECD.

OECD, 2004b, *Taking Stock of Progress under the Clean Development Mechanism* (CDM), Paris: OECD.

Ott, Herman E., 2002, *Global Climate, Yearbook of International Environmental Law*, 13.

Pearson, Ben, 2004, *Market Failure, Why the Clean Development Mechanism won't Promote Clean Development*, CDM Watch.

Pierre, Jon, ed., 2000, *Debating Governance, Authority, Steering, and Democracy*, Oxford University Press, Oxford

Pollitt, Christopher, and Geert Bouckaert, 2000, *Public Management Reform, A Comparative Analysis*, Oxford: Oxford University Press.

Princen, Thomas, and Matthias Finger, 1994, *Environmental NGOs in World Politics: Linking the Local and the Global*, London: Routledge.

Ravindranath, Nijavalli H., and Jayant A. Sathaye, 2002, *Climate Change and Developing Countries*, Dordrecht: Kluwer Academic Publishers.

Reed, David, ed. 1996, *Structural Adjustment, the Environment, and Sustainable Development*, London: Earthscan.

Reinicke, Wolfgang H., Francis Deng, Thomas Benner, and Jan. M. Witte, 2000, *Critical Choices: The United Nations, Networks, and the Future of Global Governance*, Ottawa, Canada: International Development Research Centre.

Reinicke, Wolfgang H., 1998, *Global Public Policy: Governing without Government?*, Washington D.C.: Brookings Institution Press.

Rosenau, James N., 2000, "Change, Complexity and Governance in a Globalizing Space", In *Debating Governance*, edited by Jon Pierre, Oxford: Oxford University Press.

Ruggie, John G., ed., 1993, *Multilateralism Matters: The Theory and Praxis of an Institutional Form*, New York: Columbia UP.

Sathaye, Jayant A., 1999, "Concerns about Climate Change Mitigation Projects: Summary of Findings from Case Studies in Brazil, India, Mexico and South Africa", *Environmental Science and Policy*, 2: 187-98.

Schick, Allen, 1998, Why "Most Developing Countries Should not Try New Zealand's Reforms", *World Bank Reserach Observer*, 13: 123-31.

Sims, Holly, 1999, "One-Fifth of the Sky: China's Environmental Stewardship", *World Development*, 27: 1227-45.

Sorrel, Steve, and Jim Skea, eds., 1999, *Pollution for Sale: Emissions Trading and Joint Implementation*, London: Edgar Elgar.

Spray, Sharon L., 2002, *Global Climate Change*, Lanham: Rowman & Littlefield.

Streck, Charlotte, 2002, "The Clean Development Mechanism: A Playing Field for New Partnerships", *In Proceedings of the 2001 Berlin Conference on the Human Dimensions of Global Environmental Change and the Nation State*, edited by Frank Biermann, Rainer Brohm and Klaus Dingwerth. Potsdam: Potsdam Institute for Climate Impact Research.

Streck, Charlotte, 2004, "New Partnerships in Global Environmental Policy: The Clean Development Mechanism". *Journal of Environment & Development*, 13(3): 295-322.

Susskind, Lawrence E., 1994, *Environmental Diplomacy: Negotiating More Effective Global Agreements*, Oxford, London: Oxford Univesity Press.

Tews, Kews, 2002, *Der Diffusionsansatz für die vergleichende Policy--Analyse:* Wurzeln und *Potenziale eines Konzepts, Berlin: Forschungsstelle für Umweltpolitik*, Berlin: Free University.

Tews, Kews, and Per-Olof Busch, 2002, "Governance by Diffusion? Potentials and Restrictions of Environmental Policy Diffusion", *In Proceedings of the 2001 Berlin Conference on the Human Dimensions of Global Environmental Change and the Nation State*, edited by F. Biermann, R. Brohm and K. Dingwerth. Potsdam: Potsdam Institute for Climate Impact Research.

Tews, Kews, Per-Olof Busch, and Helge Jörgens, 2003, "The Diffusion of New Environmental Policy Instruments", *European Journal of Political Research*, 42: 569-600.

Thatcher, Mark, 1998, "The Development of Policy Network Analyses: From Modest Origins to Overarching Frameworks", *Journal of Theoretical Politics*, 10:389-415.

Therkildsen, Ole, 2000, "Public Sector Reform in a Poor, Aid-dependent Country, Tanzania", *Public Administration and Development*, 20(1): 61-71.

Turner, Mark M., and David, Hulme, 1997, *Governance, Administration and Development, Making the State Work*, London: Macmillan.

UNIDO, United Nations Industrial Development Organization, 2003, CDM Investor Guide Brazil, Vienna: United Nations Industrial Development Organization (UNIDO).

Vaillancourt Rosenau, P., ed., 2000, *Public-Private Policy Partnerships*, Cambridge, MA: MIT Press.

WBCSD, World Business Council for Sustainable Development, 2004, *Engaging the Private Sector in the Clean Development Mechanism*, Geneva: World Business Council for Sustainable Development WBCSD.

Werksman, Jacob, 1998, "The Clean Development Mechanism: Unwrapping the 'Kyoto Surprise", *Review of the European Community & International Environmental Law*, 7(2): 147-58.

Willetts, Peter, ed., 1996, *The Conscience of the World, The Influence of Non-Governmental Organisations in the U.N. System*, London: Hurst and Company.

Wollmann, Hellmut, ed., 2001, "Evaluating Public Sector Reforms: An International and Comparative Perspective", *Revista Internacional de Estudos Políticos*, September, Rio de Janiero: UERJ/NUSEG.

World Bank, 1995, *National Environmental Strategies: Learing from Experience*, Washington, D.C.: The World Bank.

World Bank, 2004, *Prototype Carbon Fund, A Public-Private Partnership, Annual Report 2004*, Washington, D.C.: World Bank.

World Bank, P.R. China Ministry of Science and Technology, The Deutsche Gesellschaft für Technische Zusammenarbeit, German Technical Cooperation Unit (GTZ), Federal Ministry of Economic Cooperation and Development, and Swiss State Secretariat for Economic Affairs, 2004, *Clean Development Mechanism in China*, Washington, D.C.: The World Bank.

Xu, Xinpeng, 1999, "Do Stringent Environmental Regulations Reduce the International Competitiveness of Environmentally Sensitive Goods: A Global Perspective", *World Development*, 27: 1215-26.

Young, Oran, R., 1994, *International Governance: Protecting the Environment in a Stateless Society*, Ithaca: Cornell University Press.

Zhang, Zhong Xiang, 2000, "Decoupling China's Carbon Emissions Increase from Economic Growth: An Economic Analysis and Policy Implications", *World Development*, 28: 739-52.

Zhang, Zhong Xiang, 2004, *The World Bank's Prototype Carbon Fund and China*, Milano: Fondazione Eni Enrico Mattei.

# On the Fringes of Globalization

## The Newly Marginalized Class

RENU KHATOR, KOFI GLOVER AND ERIN STEURER

### INTRODUCTION

Over the past three decades, the pace of globalization has rapidly increased and has changed the world in many ways (Murshed 2002). The United Nations (UN) contends that the vigorous debate surrounding globalization is partly because globalization's current phase is different than it has been in any other time in history, especially since the rapid speed of communication and easy access to information have brought on qualitative changes (UN 2001).

Globalization takes on many different definitions and interpretations. For the purposes of this paper, we accept Redclift's definition and understand globalization as the "intensification of worldwide social relations that link distant localities in such a way that local happenings are shaped by events occurring many miles away and vice versa" (Redclift 2000: 47). In this context, economic globalization can be understood as "a set of processes whereby production and consumption activities shift from a local or national scale to a global scale" (O'Brien and Leichenko 2000: 225). Studies suggest that globalization has forced the "shift of power from sovereign states to technologically advanced global elites and private multinational (oftentimes non-national) interests" (UN 2001: 3). The wide disparities between and among countries has created increased vulnerability and social dislocation for many groups of the population. In addition, despite the benefits of the expansion of Information and Communications Technology (ICT), the following consequences have been felt: the world has been divided between the connected and the isolated; the labor movement across international borders has promoted the "brain drain"; and the development of new rules to integrate into the global market has led to the marginalization of certain groups, especially in poor African nations. To a certain extent, globalization has brought forth a "global village of the privileged" (UN 2001: 3). In fact, a 2002 International Monetary Fund (IMF) report stated that "the distribution of income among countries has become more unequal." The report also contends that even though there has been "unparallel growth," "far too many people are losing ground" (Grant and Nijman 2004: 467-468).

The rise in the standard of living of the few is not restricted to the developed countries; the world is witnessing not only a dichotomy of living standards between developed and developing countries, but also a dichotomy within countries themselves. In essence, two new classes have emerged because of globalization: 1.) the global super-rich, many of whose members are citizens of industrialized nations, and an increasing number of super-rich members from developing nations, and 2.) the global poor, many of whom reside in developing nations. The rise of the first class has helped exacerbate the income gap between nations and within nations, resulting in local haves and the have-nots.

Proponents of globalization argue that, as a result of globalization, people enjoy higher standards of living, unprecedented advances in communication technologies, better health, and increased life expectancies. They also argue that poverty is on the decline worldwide, mostly, if not entirely, because of globalization. For example, since 1984, the number of people that live on less than US$1 a day has declined by 200 million. For two hundred years before, the number had been steadily rising. The neoliberal argument for globalization states that the income distribution between the world's people had become more equal in the 1980s, 1990s, and the beginning of the new millennium. They also argue that, for the first time in over a century and a half, the number of people living in extreme poverty has declined. Further, the proponents of globalization attribute changes largely to the rising density of economic integration between countries. This integration is enhancing the efficiency of resource use worldwide because countries are beginning to specialize in their areas of comparative advantage. As far as the lagging regions, especially Africa, are concerned, supporters of globalization claim that the solution is to implement freer domestic and international trade and also more open financial markets, which would allow these regions to integrate deeper into the world's economy (Wade 2001). They claim that industry and technology policy play a crucial role in empowering countries to rise into higher value-added regions of global trade.

The critics of globalization, on the other hand, assert that the benefits of globalization, if any, are limited to only a small portion of the world's population. The majority of the people still live in dire poverty and globalization, in some instances, may have worsened their livelihoods. Those who had been victimized by colonial and industrial systems—women, children, the poor, and the uneducated—are still marginalized today. They cannot benefit from globalization as they are forced to bear the burden of intended or unintended negative consequences. Sadly, other groups are being added to the list of marginalized, including those without access to ICT and those on the losing side of the digital divide. The rising income inequality and increasing poverty levels worldwide are sobering examples of this disparity.

The income gap between nations has been on the rise. The following statistics provide testimony to this situation:

- In 1960, the ratio of per capita Gross Domestic Product (GDP) between richest 20 countries and poorest 20 was 18:1, but by 1995 it was 37:1 (World Bank 2000a).
- 54 countries are poorer today than they were in 1990 (UNDP 2003: 2).
- In the 1990s, the average per capita income growth in 125 developing and transition countries was less than 3% (UNDP 2003: 3).
- The world's richest 500 people have a higher combined income than the poorest 416 million people (UNDP 2005a: 4).
- There was a decline in average per capita income growth in 20 nations in Sub-Saharan Africa, 17 in Eastern Europe and the Commonwealth of Independent State (CIS), 6 in Latin America and the Caribbean, 6 in East Asia, and 5 in Arab countries (UNDP 2003: 3).
- One billion people currently live on less than US$1 per day and 2.5 billion, or 40% of the world's population, live on less than US$2 per day (UNDP 2005a: 4).
- One billion people in the developed world own 80% of the world's GDP and the remaining 20% belongs to the 5 plus billion (UN 2005: 1).
- In the last decade of the 20$^{th}$ century, the number of poor people worldwide increased by 100 million, even though total world income increased by an average of 2.5% annually (Stiglitz 2002: 5).

The income gap has widened within countries as well. Despite limited progress in reducing the share of the population living in poverty in developing countries, the absolute number of poor people has risen in every developing region except in East Asia and the Middle East (World Bank 2000a).

## THE NEWLY MARGINALIZED CLASS

The consequences of globalization are afflicting a staggering portion of the world's population, as evident in the statistics above. Along with women, the rural and the uneducated, those without access to ICT are also joining the marginalized sectors of society. There have always been "haves," or people who are fortunate enough to enjoy high standards of living, and "have-nots," or people who unfairly endure the lowest standards of living. However, under globalization, the third and fourth classes of "global super-haves" and "global have-nots" have now emerged, eclipsing the haves and further pushing down the have-nots. The global super-haves are the wealthiest people in the world and are increasing in number. Many of them are billionaire and multi-millionaire businessmen or businesswomen who have exploited the global market in their favor. On the other hand, the global have-nots are the poorest of the poor and are dependent on economic forces that are extremely far removed from their place of work. The global have-nots do not earn enough income to subsist, and the absolute number of them is increasing as well.

Poverty is not the only dividing line. Access to information and technology are further dividing haves from have-nots. Approximately 2.4% of the world's population uses the Internet, most of who live in the Organization for Economic Cooperation and Development (OECD) countries. Furthermore, approximately 90% of the Internet host computers are in the most developed countries that account for only 16% of the world's population (World Bank 2000a: 2-3). Additionally, an inordinate amount of information on the Internet is in English, so those who cannot read English are prevented from accessing much of the Internet's information sources (UN 2001).

Sumner (2001) contends that corporate globalization—the rising dominance of transnational corporations throughout the world—is adding to the marginalization of the rural sectors of society and women. In fact, corporate globalization negatively affects the majority of the world's population as it leaves no place for people who cannot afford to be consumers who would contribute to corporate profits. This is the "age of exclusion" because people who cannot afford to be consumers "have no right to exist" (Sumner 2001: 2).

Rural communities are especially vulnerable to the consequences of corporate globalization. They tend to be sparsely populated and are spatially isolated, so they do not have the same resources as their urban counterparts to manage the impacts of corporate globalization. Further, since government programs and policies tend to focus on the urban sectors of society, rural communities are usually excluded from such programs and policies, which work to marginalize them (Sumner 2001).

Corporate globalization is also weakening gender equality. For example, in Bangladesh, women make up the cheap labor force to manufacture the export goods that corporate globalization demands.

Women are considered to be "more productive, submissive, and less likely to form unions demanding better wages, working and health conditions" (Sumner 2001: 12). During the Asian financial crisis in 1997, women were the first to lose their jobs. Additionally, when economies restructure, formerly steady and well-paying manufacturing jobs outsource to areas that have lower wages and fewer health and safety laws. When these jobs move out of a rural community, women witness higher wage decreases than men due to the nature of the jobs they can find after layoffs. In fact, newly won rights for women are considered "anti-family" and are therefore taken away whenever possible under corporate globalization. Corporate globalization's privatization imperatives replace the state as the provider of particular functions and such functions fall on rural communities rather than on private corporations. Oftentimes, rural women must then pick up the slack for the social services that the state has neglected. It is thus evident that the highest burden of the consequences of privatization can be borne by rural women (Sumner 2001). Furthermore, since women were already marginalized by industrialization, now they are twice marginalized by globalization. The fact of the matter is that women in *any* country do not enjoy the same rights as men (UNDP 1995: 2).

World trade practices add to the negative effects of globalization. From 1985-2002, world trade had more than tripled, however, it has been on the decline in developing countries, leading to marginalization and a decline in employment and labor standards (Gunter and van der Hoeven 2004). The 2005 Human Development Report (HDR) testified that unfair trade policies prevent millions of people in the world's poorest nations from escaping poverty and that these policies have been perpetuating abominable inequalities (UNDP 2005b). Additionally, although trade can be a catalyst for human development and progress towards the Millennium Development Goals (MDG), current trade policies, structural forces that have been preventing poor people from market opportunities, and failures to confront national inequalities prevent progress toward the MDG. Sub-Saharan Africa, however, may be faring the worst from trade policies: although it has modestly increased exports, its marginalization in the global market has worsened. In total, the region has 689 million people, yet its world exports comprise a smaller share than Belgium's exports—a country with only 10 million people (UNDP 2005b).

In this paper, we will examine the patterns of marginalization precipitated by globalization within countries but also at the global level. Ghana and India will serve as the two case studies to demonstrate the stratification and further marginalization within countries. These two countries were chosen for a number of reasons. They both achieved independence around the same time (India in 1947 and Ghana in 1957), so each one has had roughly the same time to shake-off its colonial practices and develop its own identity. However, there appears to be a discrepancy between Asian and Sub-Saharan African countries in how they are integrating into the global economy and how they are benefiting from globalization *as a whole*. India has progressed tremendously since independence, whereas Ghana has not, yet both are witnessing the marginalization of regions within their countries and of particular classes of people. Therefore, together they will serve to demonstrate that globalization does not have uniform benefits, even in countries that have been rapidly industrializing after integrating into the global economy.

## CASE STUDY : INDIA

Thomas Friedman's book, *The World is Flat: A Brief History of the 21st Century*, begins in Bangalore, India, where the author is mesmerized by India's forceful entry into the global market. He attributes this spectacular success to India's educated class that allowed India to be in the right place at the right time, with the right opportunity. What afforded India the luxury of becoming a global "have," and what impact it has on India's own "have-nots" is the subject of this case study.

After 200 years of domination, India gained independence from Great Britain in 1947. Even though political independence came, the foundation of India's modern economy was laid in the early twentieth century when the British began to build railroads and schools and sent Indian students to study in the United Kingdom. Admittedly, these advances were made for the preservation of the British Raj; nonetheless, they proved to be instrumental in shaping policy choices. Indian leaders taught and trained in the West declared mass education and scientific training as the cornerstones of India's new democracy. They were convinced of the promise offered by science and technology and deliberately chose to build a bureaucratic-scientific alliance to shape the technology agenda of the nation. The framers of this alliance were S.S. Bhatnagar in the Council for Scientific and Industrial Research, Homi Bhabha in Atomic Energy, J.C. Ghosh and P.C. Mahalanobis in the Planning Commission and D.S. Khothari in the Defence Research and Development Organization. From this effort emerged the establishment of several Indian Institutes of Technology, known as the world's best technical training grounds today (Krishna 2001).

For economic policy, India chose centralized planning combined with public control over key sectors. Consequently, the Indian economy grew inwardly, developed a large public sector, prohibited foreign investment, and focused primarily on agriculture. The economic approach taken by India was not different from that of other newly-freed countries; however, India had a distinct advantage over others in the supply of efficient administrative service workers, entrepreneurial talent, and skilled and educated personnel to manage the political economy (Bhagwati and Srinivasan 1975: 5). During the 1950s, the Indian economy appeared sluggish with the annual growth rate of 3.5–4% per year, however, the growth was constant and stable. The growth rate even dropped to 2.5% during the early 1960s because of persistent droughts; nonetheless, the government did not let its science and technology program suffer. The alliance between scientists and bureaucrats was successful; however, there were serious limitations to its future viability: first, the research and development (R&D) initiative was funded almost entirely by the public sector and was thus subjected to red-tapism; second, there were no incentives and no competition, so creativity started to stifle over time; and third, it did not produce anything for general consumption, and hence people did not see themselves aligning with it.

Despite the shortcomings, the Indian economy of the 1970s was an enigma: its orientation was agricultural, and yet India's colleges were churning out hundreds of highly technical graduates who were feeding the economies of other countries, particularly the United States. Indian masses were hungry for consumption, but the market was devoid of products. Domestic production of electronic goods was in short supply, and whenever in supply, it was of substandard quality. Imported goods were banned or discouraged through the imposition of heavy custom duties. Finally, in the 1980s, the Government of India realized the connection between technology and social advancement and began to promote technology for the masses. It also relaxed taxation on foreign goods, thus creating controlled competition. In 1983, the Government of India adopted a Technology Policy Statement which sparked the white and green revolution that was to benefit the urban and the rural simultaneously. This was also the golden time for India's space and nuclear programs that brought the much needed recognition by the international community.

When faced by competition from China in the 1990s, India liberalized its economy and welcomed global integration. It not only removed trade barriers, but encouraged foreign capital and investment. A large number of companies, hungry for India's educated English-speaking labor (which was a major barrier in China), marched onto the Indian scene and connected Indian talent with the global market. At the same time, non-resident Indians also felt encouraged by India's relaxed business climate and entered the Indian market. The early entrants had mixed results, but their efforts opened the doors for those who had written India off for any entrepreneurial activity. By the turn of the century, the Indian economy was ready to release its pent-up, excess energy built over years by its surplus scientific talent.

During the 1990s, India allowed multinational corporations to enter the Indian market, encouraged direct foreign investment, allowed importation of technology and goods, and opened up its public sector for private competition. Needless to say, competition pushed creativity in the science and technology sectors, precipitating a new market culture (Krishna 2001). Demand for software engineers, computer scientists, and bio-scientists grew to the extent that by 1998, one could count 4,000 institutions of higher education training and more than 75,000 software professionals annually. Indian markets were unable to absorb these professionals and the stage was set for the global Information Technology (IT) market to reach India in search of cheap and quality information labor.

The legislative action came in 2000 when the Government of India passed the Information Technology Bill that created a new Ministry of Information Technology (MIT). With the vision of making "India an IT Super Power by 2008," MIT's goal was three-fold: (1) wealth creation; (2) employment generation; and (3) IT led economic growth. MIT encouraged e-governance, e-medicine, e-business and e-commerce, and promoted information literacy. The strategy proved to be successful for Indian scientists, with over 1,000 IT companies in the country, India became not only integrated but also assumed leadership positions.

The most visible connector between India and the global market is its outsourcing business. In 2003, India controlled 80% of the global outsourcing market,.offering 150,000 jobs and earning more than US $ 4.1 billion in revenue. Forrester Research estimates that "3.3 million US service-industry jobs and $ 136 billion in wages will move offshore to countries like India, Russia, China and the Philippines" (Campbell 2003: 2). India's share of this pie is estimated to be US $ 24 billion by 2008.

India is a great success story of the global haves. Several of the Fortune 500 companies are owned by Indians. The country hosts 19 billionaires who are *both citizens and residents* of India. Azim Premji is the world's 25th richest person, with a net worth of US $ 13.3 billion. His source of fortune is the software industry (Forbes.com 2006). Including family fortunes and Indian citizens who are now residents of other countries, there are 27 billionaires. This number is more than double the count in 2004. As of December 2005, the 27 individuals' collective worth was US $ 106 billion, up from the US $ 61 billion in 2004 (Karmali 2005).

India is now perceived to be a country of the haves that everyone wants to know and learn about. Several times a week, American television viewers get a taste of India through news stories or comedy skits. For the first time in 2002, more Indian-born people previously settled outside of the country returned to India than *vice versa*. Trade patterns also indicate that India is growing its world share of manufacturing exports (from 71% in 1990 to 77% in 2003) and high-technology exports (from 2% in 1990 to 5% in 2003).

However, Bangalore is only the beginning of India's story; it is not the full story. India's 1 billion people are divided among the global haves, the national haves, and the have-nots. Unfortunately, the have-nots are not only unaware of India's prowess, but have no chance of being touched by it any time soon. India ranks 127th on the Human Development Index (HDI). According to the most recent data, only 28.3% of the population is urban and the ratio of estimated female to male earned income is 0.38 (UNDP 2005a). For survey year 1999, the poorest 10% of the population held 3.9% of the income or consumption while the richest 10% held 28.5%, making the inequality measure 7.3 (UNDP 2005a).

India has made noticeable progress in reducing poverty (Kurian 2000). Owing to its economic policies, the percentage of people living below the poverty line has dropped from 51.3% in 1977-78 to 38.9% in 1987-88, and then to 29.2% in 1996-97 (Kurian 2000). However, the poor have little infrastructure to make progress in the global world. In 2003, there were only 22 phone lines per 1000 people in India, compared to 661 in the US (Warschauer 2003) and only 0.72 PCs per 100 inhabitants in comparison to 66 for the US (International Telecommunications Union 2004). India ranks seventh in digital government measured by the number of government Web sites, but very few people have access to the Internet to use these Web sites. A closer look at Bangalore reveals this paradox: 45% of the city's population is illiterate, 40% lives on US$1 per day, and only 0.5% of the people use the Internet (Warschauer 2003: 60-61).

Kurian (2000) argues that regional location, in addition to education and urbanization, also poses a significant barrier. The progressive states (Andhra Pradesh, Gujarat, Haryana, Karnataka, Kerala, Maharashtra, Punjab and Tamil Nadu) offer greater opportunities for its citizens than the backward states (Assam, Bihar, Madhya Pradesh, Orissa, Rajasthan, Uttar Pradesh, and West Bengal) because they have a greater capacity through social development, higher per capita incomes, more evolved economies, lower poverty levels, higher levels of revenue receipts, greater per capita private investment, and markedly better infrastructural facilities. Thus, the poorest of the poor are uneducated, rural women in backward states. Singh *et al.* (2003) argue that the "backward" regions are vulnerable to further economic decline because financial systems in practice by the national government are skewed in favor of progressive states (Singh, *et al.* 2003).

Over the last two decades, India has increased its ranking in science and technology areas; however, its human development rankings have remained the same, indicating that the country has put a higher priority on technology than on improving the lives of millions. A disproportionate spending on higher education, as opposed to primary education, is also disturbing, for it means that the haves will continue to have more and the have-nots will continue to be blocked at the very first step. India's education system reaches only 50% of the poor children.

Intense competition for scarce educational opportunities is disillusioning the urban middle class. While call centers have put a stop to the so called brain drain out of India, they have created a new malaise in the form of the "brain dump," by forcing higher-than-necessary skilled people to take low skill jobs in the call center industry. For the have-nots, technology is providing neither opportunities, nor hope. This new face of poverty, as Joyojeet Pal predicts, will become the major challenge for Indian policy-makers, for being forced out of the information market place; the rural poor will become the poorest of the poor. Pal (2003: 103) predicts that countries like India cannot fully materialize the promise of technology:

Since the organization of the information society is reliant principally on skill and knowledge networks, the benefits system may exponentially increase, and perhaps entrench, the gap between the haves and the have-nots if the speed of basic development does not catch up with that of technology spread.

Despite India's new status as a global have, much depends on the empowerment of the have-nots. Technology must empower the people and create a civil society. So far, technology has only increased the empowerment of those who were already empowered. Cross-national survey evidence indicates that those who use the Internet for civic engagement are those who are already engaged through conventional means (Norris 2001). Political resources on the web seem to be attracting only those who were already participating in the political process. Unless technology can give a voice to those at the margins, the promise of political development is unlikely to materialize and unless technology can touch the lives of the millions left out by industrialization, the promise of social development is only a mirage.

## CASE STUDY : GHANA

The British held Ghana as their model colony in Sub-Saharan Africa and this status was reflected in Ghana's economic growth and political development at the time of independence in 1957. In the 1950s Ghana appeared to be the richest, most successful, and politically developed Sub-Saharan African country, with the exception of the Republic of South Africa. The per capita income was among the highest and the rate of economic growth was high (Leith 1974). This outward appearance of economic development and wealth was really an illusion. The reality of the economy was that it was abysmally "fragile"; the seeming prosperity was limited geographically and in scope.

The whole economy of Ghana in the 1950s from production stage through transportation and distribution stages to the consumption stage revolved around a simple commodity, cocoa. About 70% of the income earned in Ghana depended on the handling of cocoa or the goods bought by the cocoa farmers, or the taxes on cocoa, or the imports brought into the country from the proceeds of sale of cocoa in the world market. "The whole value of [Ghana's] output, which in turn determines the people's living standards and the rate of development, depends very largely therefore on one commodity" (Kay 1972: 82). Mining, especially in gold, and timber made up the other export earning commodities. The industrial sector was non-existent. In spite of this, Ghanaians appeared to have enjoyed a more prosperous life compared to other Sub-Saharan Africans, often times because of the prosperity of cocoa production.

Cocoa was introduced into Ghana in the latter half of the nineteenth century. Climatic conditions in the south-central regions of the country proved highly favorable to cocoa growing thus the colonial government encouraged its cultivation and export as Ghana's cash crop. Unlike many other African countries where Europeans had established cash crop plantations, cocoa farming in Ghana has been exclusively an African enterprise, and in small acreages. Nevertheless, there have not been any rich or wealthy Africans arising from cocoa farming. The reason is because the colonial government and later the nationalist governments derived the largest share of government revenue from cocoa taxation. Also, during colonial times, the colonial governments had given the European trading companies monopoly over the marketing process and thus they expropriated a great part of the proceeds to themselves. When one took out government taxes and the proceeds of the European companies, the African farmer was usually left with revenue as low as 32% of the world market price (Omaboe 1966).

The second area of economic production is in resource extraction, i.e., the mining and timber sector. Investments in the extractive industry occurred in the 1880s to about 1910. These investments and cocoa as cash crops necessitated the construction of a rail line and vehicular roads into the mining and cocoa producing areas. Because these commodities were produced in the southern third of the country, infrastructural developments were united to the region. The real economic picture of Ghana was that at the time of independence, only the southern third of the country was directly linked to the world economy through mining and cocoa as a cash crop. Only this region had relatively significant infrastructural and urban development, whose urban population enjoyed the benefits of the wealth produced by the country's external trade. The northern two-thirds region remained largely rural, poor, and devoid of infrastructural development. It had no rail lines, very few roads, very few schools, little electricity, and no pipe-born water. The region benefited only slightly and indirectly from Ghana's participation in the world economy.

When the nationalist government assumed limited political and economic power in 1951, it embarked on its First Economic Development Plan (1951-56), fashioned by the neo-classical economist W. Arthur Lewis (1966). The nationalist government's ambition was "to create the basis" for a new modern and industrial society. The expert opinion was that the country was not yet prepared to undertake an industrial scheme of any consequence. The major problems of the economy were: thin stocks, all of them imported; the ports and road systems unable to handle much; price controls ineffective at keeping the economy under control; communications too poor to allow goods to flow readily to areas of shortage. Additionally, because the banking institutions were mostly for expatriate businesses, the public did not use them, and therefore there was no capital market in which the government could use monetary instruments, which it did not have in any case (Colonial Office 1948; Kay 1972). Given the status of the economy, the Lewis development plan emphasized the development of an infrastructure in order to attract foreign capital investments. One could speculate that there was perhaps some sense of naiveté that some good will toward Ghana as the first Sub-Saharan African country to achieve independence would bring with it economic investments. In its first (1951-56) and second (1960-65) Development Plans, Ghana spent 11.2% and 20.3%, respectively, of its total expenditure on productive capital investment (agriculture and industry) and 88.8% and 79.7% on non-productive capital (infrastructure and social services) (Omaboe 1966). Within almost a decade, there was a more than 144% increase in primary school enrolment, about a 153% increase in hospital beds, and a 220.5% increase in physicians, with some of these benefits going outside the more developed southern region of the country. The most notable undertaking, however, was the opening of the new and modern harbor at Tema in 1961.

The major failures of this first decade under the nationalist government were its failure to reform the school curriculum to be in consonant with the aspirations of a developing country, failure to make any progress in the expansion of the economy beyond cocoa and the extractive industries, failure to invest in research and development in agriculture as the mainstay of the economy, and the failure to make any progress in the expansion of the economy itself. There was no capitalization because cocoa taxes on producers remained high. There was actually the opposite effect, the flight of capital as a result of the high level of non-durable consumer goods which were imported into the country by the European trading companies which then expatriated the profits abroad. Non-durable goods imports totaled 58.8% of imports in 1956 and 57.8% in 1960. Tobacco, food and drink imports total 23.3% of the non-durable goods. Most analysts had concluded by 1960 that high expenditures on non-productive capital had rendered the country's development process "historically abnormal" and that the extravagant life style built around imported goods had depleted Ghana's foreign reserves (Killick 1966; Szereszweski 1966).

In 1961, the government changed course by abandoning the *laisser-faire* open economy policy and adopted a socialist economic planning mode. This shift in strategy was dictated by political as well as economic factors. The construction and maintenance of an infrastructure relatively superior to other Sub-Saharan African countries (except South Africa) and the higher level of social services bought the political support of the urban and literate population. The economic cost was a high level of deficit spending. In 1961, a group of economists from Cambridge University and the IMF criticized the government on its spending program and urged it to attempt to balance the budget. The government was advised on the necessity to discipline the economy by a compulsory savings scheme and high purchase tax on imported consumer goods (Austin 1962). The government took heed and introduced an austerity budget in July, 1961. Among some of the austere measures, the government would limit spending to government revenue and non-inflationary spending, would halt new projects financed by suppliers' credit, cut domestic demands, cut cocoa producer prices, and established import licenses based on a strict system of priorities. The government also used the occasion to redefine its economic goals which included: abandoning the colonial institutional structures and creating a new basis for a modern state and introducing more African presence and participation in the economy beyond cocoa farming; building up investment growth and capital accumulation; bringing greater government initiative in establishing industries in order to build up the nation's stocks internally, rather than the exclusive dependence on imports; and developing a skilled labor force.

The two most visible achievements during this period were the construction of the Volta Hydro-electric complex which was to be the show piece and foundation of industrialization, and the construction of several secondary schools. There was a general failure in the overall goals of the programs. The heavy taxes on the cocoa farmer, accompanied by low world market prices in the 1960s and the fact that the benefits from the cocoa taxes went to the urban population, and none to the rural areas and the farmers, caused the cocoa farmer to cut back production or smuggle his produce into neighboring countries. This caused further erosion in government revenue. Also, the governments failed to manage foreign exchange and import controls consistently (Leith 1974). The schools were built without any curriculum reform or clear policy of what role education should play in a developing Ghana. The schools continue to produce, therefore, the literate "clerky" graduates who served as clerks and shop keepers for the colonial government and trading companies but who possess no skills useful for a developing society. Even the Volta Hydro-electric complex fell far short in its scope and effect on the economy. Ali Mazrui, the doyen of African political science, criticized the project as delaying Ghana's industrialization by two decades (Mazrui 1986). By 1965, there was enough serious political unrest and economic discontent to cause a military overthrow of the government in February, 1966. A succession of military governments followed from 1966 to 1993, except for brief periods of civilian rule in 1969-72 and 1979-81. All of these governments promulgated well conceived economic development plans but none could solve Ghana's economic woes,—reduction in exports and government revenue, declines in agricultural production, lowered quantity and quality of investment, negative real interest rates, and over-valued currency. The cause, some critics suggest, were inefficient and unsustainable domestic policies and general corruption.

The failures of the various economic development programs sent the Ghanaian economy into a downward spiral from the 1960s through the 1970s. Nearly all economic indicators—GNP, per capita national income, government revenue, export revenue, agricultural production, manufacturing and electricity production—demonstrated an economy in a downward spiral. There was a decline in production in all sectors of the economy but especially in exports and food production. In 1983, the government accepted a Structural Adjustment Program (SAP) and an Economic Recovery Program (ERP) from the IMF and the World Bank as conditions of rescue. The program consists of a stabilization program and an economic adjustment program. The stabilization measures are designed to reduce short-term imbalances between supply and demand (Konadu-Agyemang 2003), by the re-alignment of interest rates, reduction in deficit spending, and the adjustment of the exchange rate, among other measures.

The adjustment program, on the other hand, emphasizes measures that will remove obstacles that impede growth and the increase in supply. These measures include the reformation of prices, restoration of production incentives, encouragement of private enterprises, rehabilitation of debilitated infrastructure, and the reformation of bureaucratic behavior and inefficiency. Ghana is one of the very few developing countries which has accepted and implemented SAP/ERP program in its entirety. While some see the program as necessary, others see it as particularly harsh on the already poorer segments of society. Of course, the wealthier and the better educated escaped the harsh conditions by migrating to the developed countries. Today, about 62% of Ghanaian health workers, doctors and nurses, live and work in Europe and North America (Ghana News Agency 2006). The specific measures include currency devaluation, raising interest rates while restricting credit, decreasing government spending while raising taxes, dismantling trade and investment regulations, privatizing public enterprises, reducing real wages and placing more emphasis on exportable agricultural and manufactured products (Konadu-Agyemang 2003). While SAP/ERP has rescued Ghana from bankruptcy, some argue that it has not brought any greater economic benefits in the form of major economic diversification or structural development. The program has halted the decline in exports but has not provided the foundation for rapid growth (Teal 2002). Some see a human face to SAP/ERP for rescuing the rural poor (Cornia 1988), while others see it as widening the gap between the relatively well-off and the poor within Ghana (Konadu-Agyemang 2003). In a recent symposium, Peter Quartey, a Research Fellow of the Institute of Statistical, Social and Economic Research (ISSER) revealed that 74% of the people in the northern regions of Ghana, which are mostly rural, are "either poor or very poor" compared to about 58% in the southern regions (Quartey 2006). He found this economic and political inequality to be associated with "impaired institutional development" perpetuated by a weak and unnecessary bureaucracy.

After 50 years of nationalist government and twenty years of SAP/ERP, Ghana is 138$^{th}$ on the HDI, at the lower end of the medium grouping. Ghana has no global super rich individuals. The urban population has risen from 30.1% in 1975 to 45.4% in 2003 and is projected to be 51.1% in 2015, a prognosis that is not favorable to a society that is agricultural and has no urban economic base. The distribution of income shows a great inequality between the relatively wealthy and the poor. The HDI shows that in 1998, the poorest 10% shared 2.1% of the income while the richest 10% shared 30%. The poorest 20% shared 5.6% while the richest 20% shared 46.6%. Ghana continues to be very dependent on imports, rising from 26% in 1990 to 52% in 2003. Ghana's exports remain largely in the primary products industry (agriculture and extractive)—84% in 2003 as opposed to 16% in merchandise, usually small cottage handicrafts. The only two areas in which Ghana can take great pride are the 98% female economic activity as percentage of male activity, and the 0.75 ratio of estimated female to male earned income. These data show that the gap between the haves and the have-nots remains at unacceptable levels. The economy itself remains the exporter of primary goods and has neither benefited nor taken advantage of the current global economy, which is driven by high technology in service and communication. In a recent lecture, Professor Aryeetey suggested that Ghana's economic structure has not changed since 1911, following the introduction of cocoa and gold mining. The structural dependence on cocoa does not create jobs; manufacturing should be the driving force of the economy to create jobs (Aryeetey 2006). For now, Ghana remains on the fringes of globalization and not a gainful participant in it.

## REFLECTIONS AND RECOMMENDATIONS

Our study of India and Ghana reveals some interesting patterns. While the two countries had similar colonial experiences, received their independence around the same time, emphasized social development, and adopted the planned economy model, they had distinct priorities for investment. Ghana invested in strengthening its agricultural production, while India invested in science and technology. Ghana invested in primary education, whereas India invested in the kind of higher education that was only available in imperial countries. Ghana produced graduates to continue to the imperial legacy; India produced scientists to feed world's hunger in research. Ghana spent its revenue primarily in developing non-productive social capital, while India invested in building its indigenous industrial edge. Ghana opened the door to foreign imports; India starved its consumers until its own industry could learn to walk on its own. Ghana sought survival; India sought nothing less than self sufficiency in food. Indian leaders built a dream of India to be the scientific power and implemented it through a scientific-bureaucratic alliance. India was fortunate to have had democratic governments throughout its independent history, but Ghana had to endure military regimes. India's investment in technology became the necessary asset that allowed India to take advantage of the information-based society dependent on technically-trained labor. It is not to say that India did not invest in agriculture or non-productive social capital or primary education; India also invested in what it conceived to be the future of the world. India's gamble is paying-off. However, India's case study reveals that not all groups are being lifted by the tides of globalization. Many people remain marginalized and new ones are joining the group. Ghana faces the challenge of integrating its economy into the global economy; India faces the challenge of integrating its marginalized groups into the mainstreams.

There are various speculations as to why there is a difference in growth and development between Asia and Africa. Some theories claim that the reasons lie in different economic policies, geopolitical connections to industrial economies, initial development conditions and resource endowments, domestic governance arrangements, and national culture and the role it plays in economic decision-making. At the policy level, the difference has been attributed to differing international trade and investment policies that each region has adopted (Aryeetey, *et al.* 2003).

The two case studies—India and Ghana—reflect the two divergent patterns of economic development in Asia and Sub-Saharan Africa, respectively. In recent decades, Asian economies have witnessed rapid economic growth primarily due to their high investment in human capital development in preceding decades. The equitable sharing of economic gains has been aided by universal literacy and improved health standards enjoyed by all citizens (Kurian 2000). The economic growth performance of Southeast Asia and Sub-Saharan Africa started diverging significantly in the 1980s as Asia's participation in the global market increased and Africa's participation decreased. The cautious approach by Sub-Saharan African countries is understandable, considering that financial globalization carries high risks since international capital flows are capricious by nature, and hence vulnerable economies can be exposed to unpredictable external forces (Aryeetey, *et al.* 2003). Furthermore, the benefits offered by globalization often cause disequilibrium. So far, the participating countries have witnessed diverging income levels, rather than converging, and this is evident in India and Ghana as well. There are clear winners and losers and income inequality tends to be a hallmark consequence of globalization. Despite the arguments presented by the proponents of globalization, the net benefits from globalization are not secure. Participating nations may reap the benefits of dynamism, but their integration into the global economy in and of itself does not guarantee these benefits (Aryeetey, *et al.* 2003).

Globalization will continue and will perhaps take place at an even faster pace in the future. How can countries participate in the process and more importantly, how can they benefit from it? Joseph E. Stiglitz, the former Chairman of President Clinton's Council of Economic Advisers (1993-97), the former Chief Economist and Senior Vice President at the World Bank (1997-2000), and the winner of the 2001 Nobel Prize in Economics, contends that globalization has been mismanaged and has thus burdened the marginalized sectors of society. However, "globalization . . . can be a force for good and [it] has the *potential* to enrich everyone in the world, particularly the poor" (Stiglitz 2002: ix-x). To enrich everyone, global systems will need to undergo some drastic changes. It is essential to revamp the international trade agreements that have been responsible for removing trade barriers and placing policies on developing countries.

On the basis of our examination, we propose the following recommendations:

### Invest in Building Infrastructure that Promotes Human Capital

Improving the human condition entails securing basic infrastructural services like power, irrigation, telecommunications, and transport. Such services will help meet the basic needs for human survival and help to bring people out of extreme poverty. Improving the accessibility to ICT will help bridge the digital divide. Many people are on the losing end of the divide precisely because ICT are inaccessible (Norris 2001). Reducing infant mortality rates and increasing life expectancy at birth are also key factors in improving the human condition as they will help curb rapid population growth rates. Reductions in population growth rates go hand in hand with improved conditions, particularly for women: educated women tend to have fewer children (UN 2006). Improving the quality of life will encourage economic growth, in effect bringing people out of poverty.

## Consider Primary Education as the First Step, not the Last

Promulgating universal literacy, especially for females, is vital to improving education and thus the status of women in society. It is important to invest strongly in primary education in particular, as there is a staggering amount of people, particularly females, without primary education. The UN finds that 115 million children do not attend primary school, and further, 3/5 of these children are girls. Education can help reduce poverty by offering everyone with opportunities to make better lives for themselves (UN 2006). However, literacy alone cannot produce the workforce necessary to offer edge in the global market place. Countries must encourage education that promotes creativity, ideas and entrepreneurship. Education appears to be linked to health in some respects as well. For example, infant mortality rates are lower for those children who have mothers with a secondary education or higher (World Bank 2005).

## Increase Access to ICT

ICT have the potential to bring many benefits to everyone. Since such a small percentage of the world's population uses the Internet, there is a lot of headway to be made in bridging the digital divide. ICT may harbor a great potential for the rural sectors by allowing them to stay engaged in their country's relations. Not providing access to ICT will ensure further marginalization and hence exacerbate the digital divide (Ekaas 2006).

## Practice Good Governance and Economic Agility

A key ingredient in India's integration into the world economy has been its democratic political system which allowed people to feel empowered and engage in global competition. India's bureaucracy also had to adapt to the changing forces. Countries must build state capacity through good governance. Their bureaucracies must become transformational bureaucracies.

## References

"Africa Accounts for 1% of Global Internet Users", *Africa News*, 21 April 2004.

Aryeetey, Ernest, *et. al.*, "Introduction: Sub-Saharan Africa and Southeast Asia in the Global Economy", *Asia and Africa in the Global Economy*, Eds. Aryeetey, Ernest, *et. al.*, New York: United Nations University Press, 2003.

Aryeetey, Ernest, "Structure of Ghana's Economy Unchanged Since 1911", *Ghana News Agency*, 18 May 2006.

Austin, Dennis, "The Political Scene in Ghana", *Political Quarterly*, 33 (1962).

Bhagwati, Jagdish N. and T.N. Srinivasan, *Foreign and Trade Regimes and Economic Development: India*, New York: Columbia University Press, 1975.

Black, Jane, "Losing ground bit by bit", *BBC News Online*, 1 Nov 1999.

Campbell, D., "Passage to India", *Business Journal*, 5.51 (2003): 1.

Colonial Office. "Report of the Commission of Enquiry into the disturbances in the Gold Coast," Colonial No. 231, London: HMSO, 1948.

Cornia, Giovanni, Richard Jolly, and Frances Stewart, *Adjustment with a Human Face*, Oxford: Claredon Press, 1988.

Davis, A., "Millions of high-tech jobs may follow hundreds of thousands already in India", Knight Ridder/*Tribune News Service*, 14 November 2003.

Ekaas, Sissel, "Present and Future Challenges for Rural Households—An FAO Perspective", Accessed on 19 May 2006, http://www.ifhe.org/fileadmin/ifhe_administrator/Information/Sisal_Ekaas.pdf.

Forbes.com,. "The World's Richest People", Accessed on 19 May 2006, http://www.forbes.com/lists/2006/10/Rank_1.html.

Friedman, Thomas L., "*The World is Flat: A Brief History of the 21st Century*", New York: Farrar, Straus, and Giroux, 2005.

*Ghana News Agency*, "62% of Ghanaian Health Workers Intent to Migrate", 9 March 2006.

Grant, Richard, and Jan Nijman, "The Re-scaling of Uneven Development in Ghana and India", *Tijdschrift voor Economische en Sociale Geografie* 95.5 (2004): 467-481.

Gunter, Bernhard and Rolph van der Hoeven, "The social dimension of globalization: A review of the literature", *International Labour Review*, 143 n., 1-2 (2004): 7-43.

Hill, Ronald Paul and Kanwalroop Kathy Dhanda, "Technological Achievement and Human Development: A View from the United Nations Development Program", *Human Rights Quarterly*, 25 (2003): 1020-1034.

International Monetary Fund (IMF), "Globalization: Threat or Opportunity?" 2002, http://www.imf.org/external/np/exr/ib/2000/041200.htm.

International Telecommunications Union, "Free Statistics", 30 July 2004. http://www.itu.int/ITU-D/ict/statistics/.

Internet World Stats, "Usage and Population Statistics—The Big Picture", 31 July 2004. http://www.Internetworldstats.com/stats.htm.

Karmali, Naazneen, "India's 40 Richest", 15 December 2005. http://www.forbes.com/global/2005/1226/057A.html.

Kay, G.B., *The Political Economy of Colonialish in Ghana, a Collection of Documents and Statistics, 1900-1960*, London: Cambridge University Press, 1972.

Kenny, Charles, "Development's False Divide", *Foreign Policy*, 134 (2003): 76-77.

Killick, Tony, "*Manufacturing and Construction*", *A Study of Contemporary Ghana*, Vol. I. Eds. W. Birmingham, *et. al.* Evanston, IL: Northwestern University Press, 1966.

Konadu-Agyemang, Kwadwo and Sesime Adanu, "The Changing Geography of Export Trade in Ghana under Structural Adjustment Programs: Some Socioeconomic and Spatial Implications", *The Professional Geographer*, 55.4 (2003): 513-27.

Konana, P and S. Balasubramanian, 2001, "*India as a Knowledge Economy: Aspirations versus Reality*", McCombs School of Business, University of Texas, Austin.

Krishna, V.V., "Changing policy cultures, phases and trends in science and technology in India", *Science and Public Policy*, 28.3 (2001): 179-94.

Kurian, N.J., "Widening Regional Disparities in India: Some Indicators", *Economic and Political Weekly*, 12 Feb. 2000: 538-50.

Leith, J. Clark, *Foreign and Trade Regimes and Economic Development*: Ghana, New York: Columbia University Press, 1974.

Lewis, W. Arthur, *Development Planning*, New York: Harper and Row Publishers, 1966.

Mazrui, Ali, *The African, A Triple Heritage*, Chicago, IL: Annenberg/CPB Project, 1986.

Murshed, S. Mansoob, "Perspectives on two phases of Globalization", *Globalization, Marginalization, and Development*, Ed. S. Mansoob Murshed, New York: Routledge, 2002.

Norris, Pippa, Digital Divide: *Civic Engagement, Information Poverty, and the Internet Worldwide*, New York: Cambridge University Press, 2001.

O'Brien, K. and Leichenko, R., "Double exposure: Assessing the Impacts of Climate Change within the Context of Economic Globalization", *Global Environmental Change*, 10 (2000): 221-32.

Omaboe, E.N. *"Economic Surveys", A Study of Contemporary Ghana*, Vol. I. Eds. W. Birmingham, *et. al.* Evanston, IL: Northwestern University Press, 1966.

Pal, J. "The Developmental Promise of Information and Communications Technology in India", Contemporary South Asia 12 (2003): 103-119.

Quartey, Peter, "Case Approach to Project Implementation Cost Scheduling and Development Credit Administration", *Ghana News Agency*, 24 June 2006.

Redclift, M. Addressing the Causes of Conflict: Human Security and Environmental Responsibilities, *RECIEL: Review of European Community and International Environmental Law.* 9 (2000) (1), 44-51.

Seshu, G. "Midnight 'Coolies' in the Sunshine Sector", India Resource Center 6 December 2003. http://www.indiaresource.org/issues/globalization/2003/midnightcoolies.html.

Singh, Nirvikar, *et. al.* "Regional Inequality in India: A Fresh Look", *Economic and Political Weekly*, 15 March 2003: 1069-1073.

Stiglitz, Joseph E., *Globalization and Its Discontents*, New York: W.W. Norton & Company, 2002.

Summit of the Americas, "Connectivity and Development", Bridging the Digital Divide in the Americas, Summit of the Americas, 20-22, April 2001.

Sumner, Jennifer, "Challenges to Sustainability: The Rural Impacts of Corporate Globalization to Rural Communities", Issues in Rural Extension, 2001, http://www.extension.usask.ca/cse/2001_archive/abstracts_papers/JenniferSumner.pdf.

Szereszewski, Robert, *"Patterns of Consumption", A Study of Contemporary Ghana*, Vol. I, Eds. W. Birmingham, *et. al.* Evanston, IL: Northwestern University Press, 1966.

Teal, Francis, "Export Growth and Trade Policy in Ghana in the Twentieth Century", *The World Economy*, 25.9 (2002): 1319-37.

Times News Network, "Call centers to be India's Biggest job-maker", *The Economic Times* Online, 18 December 2003.

United Nations (UN), "Report on 56th Session of the United Nations General Assembly Second Committee: Panel on High-Level Panel on Globalization and the State", 2 November 2001. http://unpan1.un.org/intradoc/groups/public/documents/un/unpan001917.pdf.

United Nations (UN), "Report on the World Social Situation 2005: The Inequality Predicament", 25 August 2005. http://www.un.org/esa/socdev/rwss/media%2005/cd-docs/RWSS'05%20ExecSum.pdf.

United Nations (UN), "The Millennium Development Goals—Goal 2: Achieve Universal Primary Education", Accessed on 19 May 2006. http://www.un.org/cyberschoolbus/mdgs/goal2.asp.

United Nations Conference on Trade and Development, *E-commerce and Development Report*, 2002, 2002.

United Nations Development Programme (UNDP), *Human Development Report 1995—Gender and Human Development*, New York: Oxford University Press, 1995.

United Nations Development Programme (UNDP), *Human Development Report 2003—Millennium Development Goals: A compact among Nations to end Human Poverty*, New York: Oxford University Press, 2003.

United Nations Development Programme (UNDP), *Human Development Report 2005—International Cooperation at a Crossroads: Aid, Trade, and Security in an Unequal World*, New York: United Nations Development Programme, 2005a.

United Nations Development Programme (UNDP), "Today's Technological Transformations—Creating the Network Age", Human Development Report 2001—Making New Technologies Work for Human Development, 2001, http://hdr.undp.org/reports/global/2001/en/pdf/chaptertwo.pdf.

United Nations Development Programme (UNDP), "Unfair Trade Policies Damaging Growth Prospects in Developing Countries", 7 September 2005b. http://hdr.undp.org/reports global/2005/pdf/presskit/HDR05_PR3E.pdf.

The World Bank, Poverty in an Age of Globalization. 2000a, http://www1.worldbank.org/economicpolicy/globalization/documents/povertyglobalization.pdf.

The World Bank, *World Development Report 2000/2001: Attacking Poverty,* New York: Oxford University Press, 2000b.

The World Bank, *World Development Report 2006: Equity and Development,* New York: Oxford University Press, 2005, http://wdsbeta.worldbank.org/external/default/WDSContentServer/IW3P/IB/2005/09/20/000112742_20050920110826/Rendered/PDF/322040World0Development0Report02006.pdf.

Van Winden, Willem, "The End of Social Exclusion? On Information Technology Policy as a Key to Social Inclusion in Large European Cities", *Regional Studies,* 35 (2001): 861-77.

Wade, Robert Hunter, "Is Globalization Reducing Poverty and Inequality?" *World Development,* 32 n. 4: 567-89.

Warschauer, Mark, *Technology and Social Inclusion-Rethinking the Digital Divide,* Cambridge, Mass: MIT Press, 2003.

# Political Economy of Globalization, Exclusion, and Human Insecurity in the Americas

## Historical and Structural Perspectives

JORGE NEF

## I. INTRODUCTION : THE PROBLEM OF INSECURITY IN THE AMERICAS

The debate over development, underdevelopment, dependency, and imperialism that provided a Latin American response to modernization theory was buried alive in the 1980s. In its stead the new mainstream paradigm-surrogate for studying the area (Bodenheimer 1970: 95-137) has been reconfigured. Unlike modernization, it is an amalgam of piecemeal mid-range uncritical "theories": transition, democratization, liberalization and structural adjustment. The roll back of critical thinking has gone as far as to resurrect discredited and vacuous doctrines such as national security. The dominant vogues nurtured in Northern academic and institutional environments—and often reproduced by technocrats, bureaucrats and institutional intellectuals in the periphery—tend to lack historicity, breadth, depth and heuristic value. They constitute a paradigm in which silences prevail over probing questions; a form of self-censorship. Thinking labelled "radical" has been officially trivialized and tossed away precisely at a time when both the world structure and domestic processes have experienced a dramatic reactionary tilt: the so-called "New World Order."

## 1. Interdependency, Complex Dependency, and Human Insecurity

This chapter proposes a re-examination of the political economy of marginalization and underdevelopment, looking at the last two decades from a prism of complex dependency (Nef and Rojas 1984: 101-22) and human security, more properly, insecurity (Nef 1999: 13-26). It also seeks to examine marginalization and underdevelopment in the broader context of the entirety of the Americas, rather than confining itself to the exotic "orientalism" of the other America. From this standpoint, globalization can be seen as a multifaceted process in which trans-nationalized alliances of elite sectors at the "centre" and the "periphery" partake in a regional and global strategy of accumulation and exploitation.

If this characterization of the current process sounds familiar it is because globalization has been going on in the world system since at least the 17th Century, with several waves and historical "hinges": in the 1870s, in the late 1940s, and rediscovered in the late 1990s. As a consequence of this modernizing project the social, cultural, economic and political fabric of societies has been transformed, and often torn apart, generating at times growth, but also self-sustained cycles of impoverishment, marginalization and alienation. In the present conjuncture, the political corollary of these socio-economic processes is a drive towards greater de-democratization and authoritarian tendencies throughout the hemisphere. The net result is a significant deterioration of the security of most people, and the generation of democratic deficits (Nye 2003), not only south of the Rio Grande, but also in North America.

Taken altogether the Americas constitute the richest continent in the world. Yet, rich does not mean developed, nor is the later synonymous with equitable, let alone secure. It contains two of the most prosperous countries—the US and Canada—by any standard of measurement. One of them is the global superpower and the other exhibits one of the persistently highest scores in the UN Human Development Index. These two countries, together with Brazil and Argentina, despite cyclical fluctuations, are large economies, with as of yet untapped potentials. From a cultural point of view, and in opposition to xenophobic and ethnocentric perceptions, both North and "Latin" America and the Caribbean are an outgrowth of Western civilization. The once called "new" world is an uneasy combination of three foundational meta-cultures—Indo-American, Euro-American and Afro-American—where new migratory strains from Asia and the Middle East have converged. This multicultural mosaic is unique to this part of the globe, from Alaska to Tierra del Fuego.

There are, of course great differences between the Northern and the Southern parts of the hemisphere, as there are equally dramatic contrasts within the societies of the Americas. Beyond national differences, there is also an equally abysmal and growing gap between the rich and powerful and the rest of the population within *all* the countries. In spite of these differences, by most statistical accounts and with very few exceptions (Haiti,

Honduras, Bolivia, Nicaragua), the lesser developed nations south of the Rio Grande comprise the "upper layer" of the once called Third World. Moreover, unlike the Middle East, Africa and especially Asia, the balance and diversity of resources to population is highly favorable. In this sense, taken altogether, Latin America and the Caribbean, other than by virtue of their proximity to the overdeveloped "North", appear at least statistically to have overcome the condition of critical poverty (CPRC 2005: 79-82). Moreover, every now and then business confidence cyclically fuels bullish waves of optimism among investors.

## 2. Patterns of Continuity and Change

However, distributional inequity, rooted in powerlessness and exclusion, has not only continued but it has become more pronounced than in other regions of the world. To understand the region as a whole, it makes little sense to talk about rich countries and poor countries. Underneath this abstraction lies the reality of rich people living quite well in poor countries and poor people living in misery in seemingly rich countries. What is important is to understand the processes whereby this inequity is generated and reproduced. According to a 2004 ECLA report, "Latin America is still the region of the planet with the worst [distribution] indicators, which is made worse because in some countries there is been growing income concentration" (ECLA/CEPAL 2004: 1). The same report estimated that by 2002, forty-four percent of the population was below the poverty line and over 19 percent lived in extreme poverty (ECLA/CEPAL 2004: 3). This means that two out of five Latin Americans are poor and survive under very precarious and vulnerable circumstances.

The Americas today may look quite different from how they looked at the start of the United Nations First Development Decade (1961). There are, nevertheless, some persistent and even more pronounced trends in both, the lesser developed south, as well as in the more modern and affluent north. A useful analytical exercise would be both to assess the regional patterns of continuity and change during these twenty years, and also examine how these patterns have affected the center and the periphery in the hemispheric system of North-South relations.

To begin with, poverty and exclusion are not just a Latin American trait. For all its wealth and power, dispossession has steadily grown to affect permanently nearly 14 percent of the US population, as income distribution has persistently and intentionally worsened over the last decades. "In 1979, the top 1% of the US population earned, on average, 33.1 times as much as the lowest 20%. In 2000, this multiplier had grown to 88.5" (Hogan 2005: 1). Though on a smaller scale, poverty and income inequality have also risen in Canada: in 2004, almost 13 percent lived below the poverty line. Even when economic recovery is factored in, the overall real income levels for most of Latin America and the Caribbean are still below those of 1980 (UN 1994: 42). As is the case in North America, a slow economic recovery has failed to translate itself into employment or social well-being. Nor are there signs of extreme inequalities being arrested, let alone reversed. Paraphrasing Brazilian dictator General Emilio Garrastazú-Medici's unintended irony in 1975, even in times of economic bonanza "the economy is doing well, people aren't."

In the case of the US, the profound cultural distemper of the Vietnam War, the institutional crisis crystallized in Watergate, and the post-war economic recession of the 1980s brought forty years of economic, social and political "Fordism" to an end. Though not unscathed, the country emerged from this quagmire still as a superpower with a secular democracy, a welfare state and a significant degree of distributional equity. The real challenge would emerge only a quarter century later. Paradoxically, the collapse of the Soviet Union and the end of the Cold war created the conditions of an even deeper crisis. Its precipitators were the 2000 presidential elections, the terrorist attacks of 2001 and the recent disaster of 2005.

In the post 9/11 period, the country finds itself lead by a much more radicalized, fundamentalist, and messianic leadership. The US has dramatically mutated into a warfare state ruled by a plutocratic civil-military regime. Civil society is also more fragmented, with the once discredited militarists once again on top of an unabashedly imperial agenda, attempting to solve internal contradictions by means of a perpetual war economy. As in the 1960s, the US is still engaged in a policy of regional destabilization of Cuba's nationalist regime, a policy now extended to the populist government of Venezuela, although the context and justification are different. The rhetoric for intervention has shifted from the Cold War to the War on Terror, now articulated in a new totalizing regional concept of hemispheric security (Chillier and Freeman 2005: 1-10).

## 3. The Nature of Inter-American Relations

From the perspective of inter-American affairs, the region is more integrated in a hub-and-spokes relationship with growing asymmetry in the so-called free trade arrangements of NAFTA, CFTA-DR and the still evolving FTAA. Military integration, through the Rio Treaty, and all its structural and ideological mechanisms has been a fact-of-life since at least World War II; much longer for Central America. For contemporary US elites, as was the case for their 19th Century forbearers, what lies south of the Rio Grande continues to be simultaneously a resource-rich El Dorado and a cultural and political threat. In this sense, the South is constructed as a source of "evil": drugs, illegal aliens, undesirable values, and a security menace (Huntington 2004) next door, contaminating American society.

Above and beyond threat misperceptions and prejudices, what is becoming patently clear is the growing historical and structural inter-connectivity between North and South in the Western Hemisphere. This realization points towards the need to study the Americas systemically as an integrated whole, avoiding the facile epistemological divide between two universes: one normal "up here," the other abnormal, "down there."

What I am arguing for here is, as Fagen, Karl and Trska suggested nearly two decades ago (Terry-Lynn and Fagen 1986: 218-38), the usefulness of applying aspects of the paradigm developed by experts to analyze Eastern Europe to the study of the Americas (Terry-Lynn and Fagen 1986: 4-8). This conceptual framework posited that Eastern Europe was an integrated region where the Soviet elites enjoyed relational control. Thus, the study of individual countries and of the region as a whole, started from the premise of penetrated political systems, not sovereign entities. Hardly anybody could have attempted to explain the pre-1989 processes within the subordinate countries behind the Iron Curtain without reference to the hegemonic and dominating power of the Soviet empire. In the Western Hemisphere, with relatively more permeable borders than in the East European example, asymmetrical formal and informal inter-penetration is continuously taking place. US elites, by themselves, or in alliance with their Latin American and Caribbean counterparts, exert relational control or metapower over other subordinate groups, classes, or clients in the region. This process is framed within a dominant economic, ideological and cultural matrix, as dogmatic and compelling as its Soviet counterpart. In this complex exchange system, capital, technology, and ideology flow south while profits and population flow north.

But even this characterization fails to capture the unique inter-meshing taking place in the Americas. For instance, a significant component of the so called "Hispanic population," in the US, as is the case with Amerindians, Mexicans, and Puerto Ricans did not have to cross any border. They were already there. This integrated complexity needs to be analyzed as such in its multiple and nuanced manifestations. The current ideographic and comparative paradigms do not allow for interactive and integrated analysis of this sort of conflict and its management. Rather, it obscures the analysis by superimposing theoretical assumptions as empirical facts.

## 4. Crises without Revolutions

South of the Rio Grande, a significant change from the scenario of two decades ago is that all out revolutions seem unlikely, at least for the moment. Guerrilla activity, and other forms of low intensity conflict, with the exception of the long-winded war between the FARC and the Colombian establishment, and the sporadic outbursts in Chiapas, is at is lowest point. However, the long and deep social antagonisms under the seemingly democratic and often constricted veneer have not vanished. Rather, they have resurfaced in the familiar spiral of poverty and institutional, repressive, and insurgent violence. The weak civilian governments that replaced the military dictatorships of the past, and the few election-based regimes that survived the authoritarian 1970s have been paralyzed by ineffectiveness, corruption, and low legitimacy. These dysfunctional characteristics are also descriptive of North America. Since 2000 mass mobilizations and people's coups have replaced the once common dynamics of the middle-class military coup d'état (Vilas 2004). This has occurred in Ecuador, Bolivia and Argentina, but the toppling of elected governments by other legal means (such as impeachment) has also been present. Political alienation runs high in the Americas.

A careful look at the emerging literature and the mass of statistical and qualitative data on the region renders a view that is far from optimistic. The alleged but ephemeral business and official confidence of the late 1990s and of today have little to do with social equity, political democracy, or even the state of real economic well being; nor with the actual material security for the region's inhabitants. It rather rests on the ideological illusion that a felicitous correspondence between market politics and market economics has finally emerged, preventing turbulent social change from below. And if all this epiphany fails, there is always national security and "securitization" (Chillier and Freeman 2005:1) as the policy software of last resort.

## 5. Mutual Vulnerability

Three central propositions are advanced. The first is that the repressive bureaucratic and military regimes of the past and today's limited democracies exhibit a greater degree of continuity than the proponents of transition theory and the popular media suggest. Despite the normalization supposedly taking place, persistent violence and political turmoil are not things of the past. The underlying social, economic, and international forces which have enjoyed extraterritorial power and privilege still prevail. Contrary to myth, the Americas as a whole and with few and reversible exemptions, have not undergone profound social revolutions. Worse, the very few attempts at reformism have been stunted and reversed. Their social and economic systems, from Patagonia to Alaska are mostly conservative and elitist. Regime stability has been maintained with significant levels of exclusion and official violence. The second proposition is that this kind of stability in the long-run has hampered sustainable, equitable and democratic development. In fact, the current style of modernization hinders real democracy and increases, rather than decreases, poverty and insecurity for most people in the hemisphere. The third proposition is that deficit and limited democracy is not only a Latin American phenomenon. North America, especially the US has moved in recent years down the spiral of de-democratization. As the current style of unipolar, imperial globalization (Terry-Lynn and Fagan 1986: 218-35) deepens, so do de-democratization, widespread insecurity, and mutual vulnerability. In fact, "securitization" and militarization lie at the core of human insecurity in the hemisphere.

## II. THE ROOTS OF UNDERDEVELOPMENT

Since the 16th century, the region has been subordinated to one or another more highly developed part of the world. The patterns of production, trade and finance have reflected an enduring satellite-metropolis international division of labor. The insertion of Latin America and the Caribbean in the global economy, with their boom-and-bust cycles, was firmly established by the latter part of the 19th century. The export economy was based on the overseas marketing of raw materials, the import of manufacture, and the super-exploitation of labor. The "modernization" of these commodity (and *rentier*) states has been largely anti-developmental, as endogenous development has been over-determined and distorted by external factors, has been undermined by flights of local capital, and has resulted in the marginalization and exclusion of most of the population. Nearly two centuries after formal independence, structural underdevelopment persists.

Under the above conditions, social underdevelopment has predictably endured, creating conditions favorable to the perpetuation of outward-looking and parasitic commercial elites, facilitating the emergence of a patrimonial system of labor relations once based upon slavery, indenture, paternalism and servitude. Class and racial barriers have been intertwined in highly hierarchical, rigid and exploitative social structures. The very existence of privilege has been largely a function of elites' linkages with global constituencies. Local oligarchies have objectively benefited from social inequities and foreign intervention. These structural circumstances have been imbedded in the national states and the system of inter-American relations, bringing about a vicious cycle. The key function of the regional and local political systems has been largely the maintenance of a hemispheric socio-economic order based on inequality and de-development.

Since the onset of the Cold War, the maintenance of the above-mentioned skewed and dependent pattern of development has been provided by counter-insurgency and civic action. In fact, the preservation of such inequities has been the central preoccupation of the region's security forces (Lovell 1971: 159-179). Between the 1950s and the 1960s a radical re-organization of the regional military structure and culture ensued. The change in military mission and doctrine from the defense of territorial security (external aggression) by conventional forces to fighting the "internal enemy" by Special Forces was a blow to the already precarious sovereignty of the Latin American countries. It transformed the U.S. security establishment into the head of a vertically integrated regional counter-revolutionary system, giving the local military a new self-justifying and professional mission: fighting "subversion," however loosely defined (Corbett 1972: 13-19; Corbett 1963: 275-76, 217-45; Corbett 1964). In a relatively brief period and irrespective of declared intentions, the local military and police forces (the latter through Public Safety Programs) had been turned into the dominant internal linkage groups, operating the lower rungs of the hemispheric security regime. Over the years, counter-insurgency and military security took precedence over democratic concerns. This reorientation became manifest as early as 1964, with the Johnson administration's encouragement and promotion of the Brazilian counter-revolution of 1964.

Even in the more institutionalized democracies, the economic crisis of the 1950s and 1960s led to a breakdown of consensus and civic confidence. Political deadlock eroded both the legitimacy and the effectiveness of these regimes. Labor practices inherited from the populist years reproduced and accelerated the "push-up" effect of institutionalized social conflict. The rules of the pluralistic game decomposed in the midst of rapid mass mobilization. In these countries, the existing socio-economic order, both domestic and international, ended up being maintained by resorting to naked, yet highly bureaucratized repression under a new political alliance. The latter involved a coalition between the externally linked business elites, which gave content to a conservative economic package, and the security establishments, trans-nationalized by the ideological "professionalism" of the Cold War. The military, representing a unique externally trained, indoctrinated and financed fraction of the middle class, provided the force required for keeping the population at bay. Its ideological-professional software was—and continues to be—the National Security Doctrine (Weil *et al.* 1979: 36-73; Rojas 2003).

## III. AUTHORITARIAN CAPITALISM AND THE REPRESSIVE STATE

The above-mentioned doctrine, also called "Pentagonism" by Juan Bosch (Bosch 2000: 5-14), was constructed on three notions: an internal and external enemy ("subversion"), an external "friend" (the regional security regime), and ideological frontiers. Its effect was to erode the national character of local military institutions and decisively trans-nationalize the state. The explicit articulation of this strategic posture was the Nixon Doctrine, outlined in the Rockefeller Report of 1969. The document clearly showed a shift in the normative ideal of political development, from democracy and participation to authoritarianism and order. Between 1969 and 1973, with a few notable exceptions, the number of military dictatorships steadily climbed: ten in 1969, twelve in 1970, fourteen in 1972 and fifteen in 1973.

### 1. The National Security Regime

The liberal-authoritarian projects that unfolded in the 1970s rejected the nationalist and protectionist premises of import substitution and other induced development policies. Instead, economic growth was seen as a function of a re-insertion of the countries' economies into the international division of labor as exporters of raw-materials: a return to a widened export economy. With the exception of Brazil in the late 60s and the 70s, economic modernization, far from "deepening industrialization" meant increased reliance on both the natural resource sector and heavy borrowing. The aggregate foreign debt, which in 1960 amounted to about one-third of the regional annual exports, had grown by 1970 to 1.7 times the total value of exports. Just before the oil crisis in 1973, it had climbed to 1.9 times that value. By 1993 the gap had grown to over 2.7 times (ECLA 1970-85), and finally became stable at about 1.8 times in 2002 (ECLAC 2001). The strategy of hyper accumulation also involved the creation of favorable conditions, through deregulation, denationalization and the disarticulation of labor organizations. This allowed domestic and transnational elites to increase their share.

The era of manifest National Security was not only extreme in its persistent abuses of human rights; the early neo-liberal design of its economic strategies implied the tearing down of the welfare state and import substitution industrialization policies and social safety nets developed since the 1930s. Authoritarian capitalism rejected the demand-side implications of the early Cold War liberalism of the Alliance for Progress and was more concerned with direct containment and the protection of the *status quo* than with development. Other than offering "economic miracles" financed by illusive foreign investment, the orthodox policies favored monetarism (later identified with the Chicago School) over the structuralist, Keynesian doctrine of the U.N. Economic Commission for Latin America (ECLA). These deflationary measures were far more effective as a shock therapy—by atomizing labor, freezing wages, letting prices float to world levels and privatizing the economies—than in raising living standards. They were much more effective in the short-run as weapons in a social war, defining "friends" and "foes," than as instruments of national development. On the contrary, the long-term socio-economic consequences of these policies were, by-and-large, disastrous and persistent for the region. So were their social, environmental and financial implications. In fact, far from generating stability and bringing prosperity, the combination of dictatorial rule with unrestricted free-market policies created a serious governability problem. The formula of authoritarian politics with free-markets also set the conditions for the subsequent debt crisis and recession of the 1980s.

The bureaucratic-authoritarian states that emerged in South America, patterned on the example of post-1964 Brazil, were attempts at modernizations from the top, with strong external inducement. The benefits of this new order accrued to a small alliance of domestic entrepreneurs and speculators supported by a technocratic-military middle class and their business, political and military associates in the Northern core. Its narrow base generated a persistent crisis of legitimacy that was managed by three instruments. One was military force, through strengthening the alliance between officers and the domestic socio-economic elites. Another was the inclusion of external constituencies—military, business, political and diplomatic—to compensate for lost internal support. The third was the demobilization and exclusion of the bulk of the population. Dictatorship became an intrinsic component of economic freedom (Letelier 1976: 138, 142).

The social cost for the majorities was enormous, since overall living conditions declined and the gap between "haves" and "have-nots" widened. Nor did these regimes succeed in unleashing real counter-revolutions. At best the National Security regimes provided a repressive brake against social mobilization, economic nationalism, regional integration and a perceived threat from the left. The effective operation of their neoliberal policies required large amounts of external financing, which was facilitated in the 1970s and early 1980s by massive deposits of recycled petrodollars in Western private banks.

## 2. Foreign Debt and Regime Crisis

Indebtedness, fuelled by the illusion of prosperity ensued. As both the governments and especially the private sector in the region increased their financial obligations, the failures of production and exports to keep pace with borrowing, and, most importantly with swelling interest rates, resulted in huge debt-burdens. Despite diverse ideological discourses, the hard-line military regimes in Brazil, Argentina, Chile, Uruguay and Bolivia did not behave very differently from the more populist ones in Peru, Panama or Ecuador, or those in civilian-controlled oil-producing countries (Mexico and Venezuela), or in the microstates of the Caribbean. The policies may have had different intentions, yet their effects were similar: unmanageable indebtedness and de-development throughout the region.

The crisis of the dictatorships in Brazil, Argentina, Uruguay and Chile involved the erosion of the political alliances that had permitted the implementation of the repressive socio-economic projects. Other populist military regimes like those of Peru, Ecuador and Panama quietly faded away. The main political limitations of the National Security regimes were three-fold. One was that government by force was ultimately untenable; the other was that the pretended security was based upon the insecurity of most of the population; and finally that National Security was not national. The Nicaraguan uprising of 1979 and the protracted civil wars in El Salvador and Guatemala signaled another form of transition: popular, radical and potentially anti-liberal. From a Northern optic, these endogenous developments posed a more serious threat to the maintenance of the hemispheric order than the erosion of the bureaucratic-authoritarian regimes in South America. The combined impact of economic crises, a growing inability to manage conflict among internal factions and a new political coalition in Washington concerned about the long-run effects of authoritarian solutions, created the conditions for military withdrawal. The Linowitz Report outlined a transitional strategy in 1975 (Linowitz 1975). This document was heavily influenced by the views of the Trilateral Commission (Sklar 1980: 1-55) and was critical of the previous

"Pentagonist" policy toward Latin America. It constituted the blueprint for President Carter's initiative on democratization.

## 3. Intra-elite Alliances and 'Democratic Transition' (Siat and Iriarte 1979: 23-24)

Democratic transition for most of Latin America was largely the result of intra-elite negotiation superintended by external actors. Rather than the alleged regime transition, this meant the consolidation of a non-democratic socio-economic order under a formally democratic political façade. The orderly retreat of the National Security regimes preserved many authoritarian traits. In this, the re-emerging democracies shared some of the political characteristics of older "managed democracies" such as those in Colombia, Venezuela or Mexico, which did not experience direct military rule. Such a closely watched transition to democracy had very strict limits. Although authoritarian capitalism proved to be largely a developmental failure, the radical restructuring of the economies along free-market lines by means of political repression had been profound enough to prevent a return to economic nationalism.

Likewise, the restructuring and transnationalization of the security establishment made the pursuit of nationalist and non-aligned foreign policies impossible. In this sense, the political arrangements that emerged in Latin America, as a result of re-democratization, while possessing the formal trappings of sovereignty and democracy have been neither truly democratic nor sovereign. They have produced precariously balanced civilian regimes, based on negotiations within the elites, with exclusionary political agendas, and narrow internal support. In these, the popular sectors are effectively maintained outside the political arena, while external actors, both economic and military, enjoy *de facto* veto power over the state. In addition, the countries have remained saddled with cumbersome, and in some cases unmanageable, foreign debts (Tables 9.1 and 9.2), not to mention debt-management conditionalities of IMF-inspired structural adjustment policies (SAPs).

The ultimate effects of these policies have been the perpetuation of dependence and underdevelopment. The latter express themselves in a vicious cycle of built-in vulnerability to external economic and political influences, requiring ever increasing doses of external supports. This vulnerability can be dramatically illustrated by the inability of the countries to extricate themselves from chronic indebtedness: the "debt-trap" (Martinez 1992: 65; World Bank Report 1990-94). Debt-management became the number one political concern in the regional agenda in the early 1980s. The service, both principal and interest, grew from slightly over 40 percent of the total value of annual exports in 1979, to over 65 percent in 1983. The total indebtedness figure for 1988 was over $ 400 billion, with the higher sums being those incurred by Brazil, Mexico, Argentina, Chile, Venezuela and Peru.

## Table 9.1
## Indebtedness: Selected Countries 1970-85 and 1985-2000

*(Billions of U.S. Dollars)*

| *Country* | *1970* | *1982* | *1985* | *2000* | *1970-85 growth %* | *1970-2000 growth %* | *% Annual growth to 85* | *% Annual growth to 00* |
|---|---|---|---|---|---|---|---|---|
| Argentina | 1.9 | 15.8 | 50.8 | 146.2 | 2674. | 7693 | 178.3 | 256 |
| Brazil | 13.2 | 47.6 | 107.3 | 238.0 | 3353. | 1802 | 223.5 | 60 |
| Chile | 2.1 | 5.2 | 21.0 | 37.0 | 1000. | 1760 | 66.7 | 59 |
| Mexico | 3.2 | 50.4 | 99.0 | 150.3 | 3094. | 4696 | 206.3 | 156 |
| Venezuela | 0.7 | 12.1 | 33.6 | 38.2 | 4800. | 13966 | 320.0 | 465 |

*Source* : Based upon Louis Lefever, "The Problem of Debt," *International Viewpoints*, Supplement of the *York Gazette.* York University (March 2, 1987), p. 2; also in the 2002 World Bank electronic publication: www.worldbank.org/data/wdi2002/

## Table 9.2
## Latin America: Foreign Debt 1990, 1992, 2000, and 2003 Figures

| | *Debt/GDP* | | | | *Debt Service* | | | |
|---|---|---|---|---|---|---|---|---|
| *Per capita as % of exports* | *1990* | *1992* | *1999* | *2003* | *1990* | *1992* | *2000* | *2003* |
| Argentina | 79.9 | 30.3 | 51.2 | — | 34.1 | 34.4 | 71.3 | — |
| Bolivia | 94.3 | 61.2 | 65.9 | 38.0* | 39.8 | 39.0 | 39.1 | 166.0 |
| Brazil | 28.8 | 31.2 | 40.0 | 54.0 | 20.8 | 23.1 | 90.7 | 330.0 |
| Chile | 74.7 | 48.9 | 50.7 | 67.0 | 25.9 | 20.9 | 26.0 | 178.0 |
| Colombia | 42.4 | 36.9 | 44.7 | 47.0 | 36.4 | 38.9 | 28.6 | 232.0 |
| Costa Rica | 70.9 | 58.7 | 33.6 | 36.0 | 24.5 | 20.6 | 8.2 | 77.0 |
| Dominican R. | 74.7 | 57.0 | 28.7 | 33.0 | 10.3 | 13.5 | 4.8 | 71.0 |
| Ecuador | 119.9 | 99.9 | 107.3 | 82.0 | 33.2 | 27.1 | 17.3 | 296.0 |
| El Salvador | 36.9 | 25.5 | 17.4 | 55.0 | 17.1 | 13.2 | 6.7 | 198.0 |
| Guatemala | 33.6 | 24.2 | 28.6 | 21.0 | 13.3 | 24.0 | 9.4 | 115.0 |
| Haiti | 37.0 | — | 30.6 | 29.0 | 9.5 | — | 8.0 | 214.0 |
| Honduras | 116.3 | 92.0 | 83.3 | 54.0 | 40.4 | 33.7 | 19.3 | 134.0 |
| Mexico | 44.5 | 34.1 | 33.5 | 25.0 | 27.8 | 44.4 | 30.2 | 88.0 |
| Nicaragua | 199.4 | 750.3 | 231.0 | 40.0 | 14.7 | 21.8 | 23.0 | 129.0 |
| Panama | 152.0 | 107.2 | 55.7 | 93.0 | 9.7 | 12.6 | 10.0 | 124.0 |
| Paraguay | 44.7 | 24.6 | 22.6 | 51.0 | 11.0 | 40.3 | 10,4 | 112.0 |
| Peru | 83.9 | 92.7 | 50.9 | 60.0 | 11.0 | 23.0 | 42.8 | 335.0 |
| Uruguay | 46.7 | 46.7 | 40.1 | 90.0 | 41.8 | 23.2 | 29.2 | 353.0 |
| Venezuela | 66.1 | 61.1 | 71.1 | 42.0 | 20.7 | 19.5 | 15.7 | 139.0 |

*Source* : World Bank, *World Development Report*, 1990, 1991 and 1992, *passim.* and 1994, pp. 206-07. Also 2005 Figures were calculated from data contained in The International Bank of Reconstruction and Development/The World Bank, *World Development Report 1989* and *World Development Report 1992. Development and the Environment*, (New York: Oxford University Press, 1989 and 1992). Tables used include Table 1 Basic Indicators, Table 21, Total external Debt, Table 24, Total External Debt Ratios, Table 26 Population Growth and Projections. The 1990 GNP figure for Nicaragua was estimated on the basis of the 1987 figure and an average decline of 2.5% per year. 2000 figures came from the United Nations Development Program, *Human Development Report 2002*, pp. 203-05.

* Data from debt sustainability analysis, Heavily Indebted Poor Countries initiative (HIPC). Estimates for such countries are for public and publicly guaranteed debt only, www.worlbank.org/date/wdi2005/wditex/Section4.htm.

Despite the fact that about one half of the countries had reduced their liabilities by 1990-91, the over-all debt had grown to 421 billion dollars: a 3.5 percent annual increase. By 2001 it reached 740 billion, expanding at an average annual rate of over 5 percent (ECLAC 2001). In fact, out of the seventeen most indebted countries in the world in 1992, twelve were in the Latin American region. On average, the annual interest rate payments fell from 33 percent of all exports in 1987 to 22 percent in 1991 as the "lost decade" came to an end. Between 1992 and 1999, the burden was reduced even further: countries like Brazil and Mexico decelerated their rate of indebtedness respectively from staggering annual rates of 223 percent to 60 percent, and 206 to 156. These figures are mind-boggling and unsustainable by any stretch of the imagination. Argentina accelerated its already huge rate of indebtedness from a 15-year average annual growth of 178 percent to a rate of 256 percent annually in the thirty years between 1970 and 2000. Venezuela, in turn, went from a yearly increase of 320 percent between 1970 and 1985 to a whopping 465 percent in the 1970 to 2000 period. If the debt problem is measured as inability to pay, an analysis of the ratio between exports and debt service shows figures that are equally dramatic. For instance the ratio of debt service to exports for Argentina moved from an already high 34 percent in 1990 to over 71 percent in 2000. For Brazil, the jump was from 23 to near 91 percent. In 2003, the average ratio for Latin America had climbed to an unbelievable 201 percent of exports: this means that countries are going into debt at twice the amount of their export earnings. So far, and despite economic disasters in Mexico (1994), Ecuador (1999), Argentina (2001), Brazil (2002), and Bolivia (2003) most countries in the region did not default on their debt or resort to a strategy of "debtors cartels." This policy of fiscal responsibility has been extremely hard for civil society, which had to absorb its full impact, especially after a number of governments have "nationalized" corporate debts.

The end of the cycle of National Security in the 1980s was a direct consequence of the insoluble contradictions between and within the nature of the reactionary coalitions in power and the centrality of external supports for the authoritarian regime. Given limited resources, there was a long-run impossibility of reconciling the interests of the national security bureaucracies with those of domestic and foreign business. There was also the additional problem emerging from the extreme vulnerability of the countries to external factors (e.g., the unmanageable debt burden, deteriorating terms of trade) and constituencies. As power conflicts intensified in Washington in the post-Nixon era, opposition from liberal political sectors against authoritarian regimes grew. Furthermore, the shrinkage of crucial support from international business compounded the internal erosion of power suffered by the Latin American dictatorships. Democratic transition became the alternative to popular revolt.

The conversion from dictatorship to limited democracy has to be seen in the context of the previous transition to National Security, both in the bureaucratic-authoritarian context of the Southern Cone and in the less institutionalized setting of Central America. Growing participation and dependent development could coexist only under conditions of economic expansion and for as long as such participation did not threaten the perceived interests of the local and regional elites.

## IV. THE NATURE OF THE RECEIVER STATE

The mounting debt crisis set the parameters for the emergence throughout the Americas in the mid-1980s of a new political formula: a *"receiver state,"* blending limited democracy and neo-liberal economics. The result was a highly trans-nationalized and weak state, acting in partnership with foreign creditors and international financial institutions as manager, executor and liquidator of national bankruptcy. The central function of this arrangement has been the administration of the debt combined with the implementation of structural adjustment policies geared to massive privatization and de-nationalization of the economy. This state reflects the nature of the trans-nationalized political alliances and the narrow spaces for political participation, where economic and fiscal policies have been affectively left out of the political debate. Yet these policies define the rules of the game and set the limits for social policies.

### 1. Pacts of Elites and Exclusionary Socio-economic Agendas

The various national incarnations of receivership exhibit important differences. These depend upon the nature of the transition processes, as well as on the particular coloration of the civilian management to appear in the post-authoritarian period and in the early adjustment phase. At close scrutiny, irrespective of the elected nature of the government in charge, the economic agenda has a striking resemblance with that imposed under authoritarian rule. These arrangements are not a mere transitional phase, from elite domination to genuine democracy: free and participatory politics, with effective popular control. Rather, the repressive state of the 1970s and the receiver state of the 1990s and 2000s are two different manifestations of a similar cluster of elite interests.

The receiver state expresses the consensus of a mostly transnational and conservative coalition, though at times managed by tamed conservative to center-left governments. Limited democracy with narrow mobility opportunities and exclusionary agendas provides a thin cushion to confront the deep structural problems once controlled by repression. The current modality of conflict-management, while reducing the most blatant (and uglier) human rights abuses, has left the most pressing and fundamental socio-economic and political problems largely unresolved. The combination of the transnational integration of the domestic elites (economic, military, technocratic and bureaucratic) with the demobilization and marginalization of the popular sectors does not provide a formula for stable governance, let alone democracy. In the absence of tangible rewards to buy legitimacy, insurgent, repressive, institutionalized (as well as criminal), violence has become a common expression. Institutional breakdown—as in 1999 Ecuador, or Argentina in 2001 and Colombia—has also emerged as a distinct possibility.

Despite rhetoric and the phasing out of the "old" National Security regimes, at present the Americas are not geared to a change toward substantial democratization. Formal demilitarization and return to limited democracy are not synonymous with an alteration of the *status quo*. Nor is democracy nowadays any more "real" in those countries in the hemisphere, including the United States, where civilian governments have remained in formal control. On the contrary, the prevailing discourse on democracy among the official intelligentsia throughout the Americas involves a juxtaposition of a substantially domesticated democracy with neoliberal economics (Montecinos and Markaff 1993: 7-22) and national security.

The above model amounts at best to a plutocracy with popular support, occasionally resorting to electoral rituals, backed by the security apparatus. While this "low-intensity democracy" may appeal to the consumption-intensive, high-income core groups in the Hemisphere, it is not really majority rule. It is basically the same elitist formula articulated by the Trilateral Commission in the mid-1970s that considers the root cause of the crisis of democracy to be democracy itself (Huntington *et al.* 1975: 1-5). Under a legal façade, this mode of conflict-management entrenches a corporatist pact of elites representing basically the same economic, social and political alliances that have sustained antidemocratic regimes: the power elite at the core, the military, the local bourgeoisie, and upper segments of the middle classes. Democratic development, with the qualified exception of Canada and Costa Rica, is weak and fragile at best throughout the hemisphere.

The regressive socio-economic policies implemented under authoritarian rule have been enshrined both in the pacts of transition and in *ad-hoc* constitutional mechanisms. The re-democratized regimes are constrained by other factors too. One is the weakness of the governing political alliances, since the transition arrangements effectively excluded most left-of-center and populist political forces from holding power. Another is the crucial, autonomous role played by the trans-nationalized security forces, as a parallel state to maintain the *status quo* and prevent exposure of past and present human rights abuses. Then, there are the odious massive debt obligations incurred mostly under the previous repressive regimes. They severely limit the rendering of services to those in need, while fiscal austerity inevitably leads to confrontation and increasingly repressive governmental responses. The impact of the debt service on already exiguous fiscal resources is compounded by the strict conditionalities imposed by the international financial institutions (the IMF, the World Bank, the IDB and private banks). Structural adjustments resulting from such conditionalities have gravitated against demands for reform, equity and social justice, already frozen by the previous dictatorships.

## 2. The Biophysical and Environmental Effects of Public Policies

Since the 1980s, the Americas have experienced an expanding and converging set of problems, whose common denominator is a fiscal crisis of the state. In North America, fiscal crises have been a recurring fixture, vaguely masked in neoliberal rhetoric and national security concerns. The crisis affects employment, purchasing power, well-being, housing, the safety of drinking water, the quality of sanitation, the growing incidence of old and new diseases of epidemic proportions, a deteriorating ecosystem, and a profound inability to meet health challenges. A regional health crisis is unfolding as life threatening ailments that were considered eradicated (such as malaria, Chagas, tuberculosis) are making a dramatic come back, and new morbidity and mortality factors (like HIV/AIDS) are on the rise. This has happened at a time when social safety nets and health delivery mechanisms are collapsing as a consequence of structural adjustment policies. The 1990 cholera epidemic was paradigmatic of extreme mutual vulnerability. The combination of a poverty driven disease, multiplied by the dismantling of the institutional mechanisms for disease containment and treatment, had the effect of multiplying generalized insecurity across class and national boundaries.

Environmental threats are another example of policy-driven dysfunctions. These include sewage, waste and air pollution, but also encompass a broader complexity of and multiplicity of reciprocating issues. In an earlier study (Nef and Roblas 1998: 42-62) we sketched a calamitous situation in which retro-feeding and destructive processes create a vicious cycle of vulnerabilities. Current industrial, mining, and agricultural practices, mixed with uncontrolled urbanization, create an interwoven pattern of biophysical and social stress upon the ecosystem and human populations. For instance, deforestation, with its sequel of health-related problems, accounts annually for over 40 percent of the global loss of forests. On a per capita basis, this makes Latin America the number one contributor to green depletion and loss of biodiversity. Furthermore, in the midst of an expansion of agricultural production for export, food insecurity still remains a major threat to large segments of the population, even in the statistically "rich" countries. Once again, the pressure to manage the debt and its conditionalities put a premium upon cash crops and the merciless exploitation of natural and human resources.

## 3. Structural Poverty and Inequality

Since 1980, those living below the poverty line in Latin America and the Caribbean *increased* from above 120 million to over 200 million and from 41 to 46 percent of the population (Rosinson 1994: 1-9; Altimir 1994). The

**TABLE 9.3**
**Growth of the Estimated % of Population in Poverty and Indigence in 19 Countries in Latin America, 1980-90**

| | *Poverty* | | | *Indigence* | | |
|---|---|---|---|---|---|---|
| | *1980-86* | *1986-90 %* | *Annual* | *1980-86* | *1986-90%* | *Annual* |
| Nationwide | 4.9 | 7.0 | 10.5 | 4.8 | 1.3 | 1.5 |
| Urban | 20.0 | 8.3 | 27.3 | 7.1 | 2.7 | 1.5 |
| Rural | 0.0 | 1.7 | 9.1 | 2.8 | 0.1 | 1.1 |

*Note* : The figures are calculated from Oscar Altimir, "Income Distribution and Poverty Through Crisis and Adjustment," *CEPAL Review*, No. 52 (April 1994), p. 12.

most affected have been those already vulnerable: women, children, the elderly, ethnic minorities. Though poverty and indigence have gone down to mid 1990s levels in most countries, overall deprivation is still higher than two decades ago, and rural poverty has increased steadily. Central America has been the most seriously affected by the double impact of concentration of wealth and the spread of poverty: reportedly nearly 80 percent of its inhabitants were unable to access a basic food basket and half of these were destitute. According to the same report, between 1977 and 1994, Guatemala witnessed an accelerated concentration of wealth and resources with fewer than 2 percent of the landowners owning now more than 65 percent of the total farmland. Between 1990 and 1993, after just two years of structural adjustment, the poverty rate in Honduras increased from 68 percent of the total population to 78 percent. In Nicaragua, as a result of the contra war and the implementation of the post-war austerity package, 71.3 percent of the economically active population was either unemployed, or underemployed. Illiteracy, which had been affectively reduced to 12 percent between 1979 and 1989 actually *increased* in the early 1990s in absolute and relative terms. The same was the case with infant mortality, from 50 per 1,000 in the 1980s to 71 per 1,000 in 1991 and 83 per 1,000 in 1993. Although these figures have been less dramatic in recent years, the legacy of a catastrophic decade of man-made and natural catastrophes has left its deep imprint.

Even the much-hailed economic "miracles" have not produced lasting development. The combination of entrenched elite interests, extreme free-market agendas, and structural adjustment policies, left a lasting burden of poverty and despair. The areas of health, education, and community development have suffered continuously, impacting precisely those less protected in society. Since the end of the boom of the 1970s, Brazil's only enduring feature has been the most unequal income distribution in the Western hemisphere, and one of the worst in the world, this despite the progressive administrations of Fernando Enrique Cardoso in the 1990s and more recently his laborite successor, "Lula" DaSilva. Chile's "success story" does not fare any better under close scrutiny. Between 1970 and 1987, the proportion of Chileans defined as poor increased by an average yearly rate of 7.2 percent. Meanwhile, real income per capita grew at an annual average rate of 0.3 percent. Since 1990, with a succession of democratic governments and despite the fact that the speed of impoverishment has been arrested, widespread privation persists. Despite impressive GNP annual growth rates between 4.5 and 10 percent, after Brazil, Chile has the second worst income distribution in the region.

Pauperization and expanding inequity are not limited to the cases mentioned above. They are present all over the hemisphere: throughout the Caribbean, in Argentina, Uruguay, Paraguay, Venezuela, Colombia, Peru, Bolivia, Ecuador, Panama, Costa Rica, the Dominican Republic, Haiti and particularly Mexico. Poverty and inequality have also significantly expanded in North America, following a similar policy package. As mentioned, the most affected are the rural and urban poor; but also white-collar, middle-class sectors have seen their economic opportunities and social safety nets dramatically eroded. In fact, in Latin America, as in Canada and the U.S. today, the middle classes are disintegrating with the growing gap between the extremities of wealth and poverty (Wolff 2003).

## 4. Civil-Military Relations

Beneath the civilian mantle, praetorianism has a lingering presence. Given the polarized and violent nature of political conflicts, militarization has been a long-standing feature of the Latin American state. It has also been a constant in the US. With few exceptions, the military establishment has played a disproportionately large role in most of the countries, whether under civilian executives or not. Even in supposedly exceptional cases, a careful examination reveals that direct military rule or militarized repression have always been present. This is abundantly clear in the deepening conflict in Colombia. Although, with the withering away of the Cold War the military appeared less conspicuously present in politics than in the recent past, a closer scrutiny reveals a more complex picture. True, the ending of the civil conflicts in El Salvador and Nicaragua, declining insurgent threats in Peru, as well as the effects of structural adjustment packages upon defense budgets, suggest a trend towards demilitarization. Yet, over-all budget reductions between the 1980s and the early 2000s have not been necessarily matched by personnel reductions. Rather, a small increase in personnel has taken place. But average figures are deceiving: downturns in countries with large establishments, such as Argentina (-39.8%), Chile (-9.1%), Nicaragua (-76.6%) and Peru (-12.5%) reduce the incidence of significant upturns in most other countries. Twelve out of twenty of the countries actually increased the size of their defense forces between 1985 and 2002. Colombia topped the list with 76.7 percent, followed by Venezuela (53.1%), Guatemala (40.7%), and Mexico (35.6%). The largest establishment outside that of the US, that of Brazil's, with nearly

**TABLE 9.4**
**Regional Military Balance**

| | *Defense as % of GDP/GNP* | | | *Numbers in Armed Forces per 1000* | | |
|---|---|---|---|---|---|---|
| *Country* | *1985* | *2000* | *Change* | *1985* | *2002* | *Change* |
| Argentina | 2.9 | 1.3 | -55.0 | 108.0 | 69.9 | -35.0 |
| Bolivia | 2.0 | 1.5 | -25.0 | 27.6 | 31.5 | 14.1 |
| Brazil | 0.8 | 1.3 | 62.5 | 276.0 | 287.0 | 4.0 |
| Chile | 7.8 | 4.0 | -49.0 | 101.0 | 80.5 | -8.4 |
| Colombia | 0.8 | 2.3 | 187.0 | 66.2 | 158.0 | 138.0 |
| Costa Rica | 0.7 | 1.0 | 42.9 | ** | * | |
| Cuba | 9.6 | 5.0 | -47.9 | 161.5 | 46.0 | -72.0 |
| Dominican Rep | 1.1 | 0.5 | -54.5 | 22.2 | 24.5 | 10.0 |
| Ecuador | 1.8 | 2.2 | 22.2 | 52.5 | 95.5 | 82.0 |
| El Salvador | 4.4 | 0.7 | -98.0 | 41.7 | 16.8 | -59.7 |
| Guatemala | 1.8 | 0.8 | -53.6 | 31.7 | 41.4 | -1.0 |
| Haiti | 1.5 | 1.1 | -26.7 | 6.9 | 0.0 | 100.0 |
| Honduras | 2.1 | 0.6 | -71.4 | 16.6 | 8.3 | -50.0 |
| Mexico | 0.7 | 0.5 | -28.6 | 129.1 | 192.8 | 49.0 |
| Nicaragua | 14.2 | 1.1 | -92.3 | 62.9 | 14.0 | -77.7 |
| Panama | 2.0 | 1.2 | -40.0 | 12.0 | 11.8 | -2.5 |
| Paraguay | 1.3 | n.k | n.k | 14.4 | 14.9 | 3.5 |
| Peru | 4.5 | 3.8 | -15.6 | 128.0 | 110.0 | -14.0 |
| Uruguay | 2.5 | 1.1 | -56.0 | 31.9 | 23.9 | -25.0 |
| Venezuela | 1.3 | 1.2 | -7.7 | 49.0 | 82.3 | 68.0 |
| Bahamas | * | 1.6 | * | 0.5 | 0.9 | 44.4 |
| Belize | 1.8 | 2.6 | 44.0 | 0.6 | 1.5 | 150.0 |
| Guyana | 9.7 | 1.9 | -80.4 | 6.0 | 1.6 | -73.3 |
| Jamaica | 0.9 | 0.7 | -22.2 | 2.1 | 2.8 | 33.3 |
| Trinidad-Tobago | 1.0 | 1.3 | 30.0 | 2.1 | 2.7 | 28.6 |
| Suriname | 2.4 | 3.4 | 41.7 | 2.0 | 1.8 | 10.0 |
| United States | 6.5 | 3.1 | -52.3 | 2,151.6 | 1,414.0 | -34.0 |
| Canada | 2.1 | 1.2 | -42.9 | 83.0 | 52.3 | -37.0 |

*Source* : IISS, *The Military Balance*, several issues 1989-2003; *World Resources*, 1994-95 and *SIPRI Yearbook 1993*.

270,000 grew 7 percent between 1988 and 1993, averaging an annual increase of 4 percent by 2002 (IISS 1087-1992).

Though in comparison with the G-8 nations and the Middle East, the size of the Latin American forces is relatively modest, the impact, influence and transnationalization of the security establishment, especially of its officer corps, remain extensive. The new concept of Hemispheric Security in fact encourages militarization of numerous human security issues (Chillier and Freeman 2005: 1-10). Not including some 760,000 paramilitary, and an indeterminate number of reserves, Latin America has over 1.3 million individuals under arms and spends close to nine billion dollars in defense. Given its economic base and geo-strategic, situation Latin America remains overly militarized; the externally controlled security sector is still a voracious competitor for the scarce resources needed for development. It constitutes a persistent obstacle to the sovereignty of and cooperation among nations, and continues to be the single most serious threat to political stability, integration, sustainable democracy and human rights.

With the end of the Cold War and with the threat of regional insurgency reduced, a fundamental security issue in the Americas is not so much how to protect society from external and internal "enemies" but how to safeguard the population in most countries from their security forces. In this context, we must reconsider civil-military relations, and the nature of the prevailing civil-military regimes in the emerging Inter-American order, especially in light of new strategic factors. One is the increasingly conservative, interventionist and apocalyptic mood in American politics, and the extensive post-September 11 resurgence of "Pentagonism," and the militarization of American society. Another is the lingering of often-construed border tensions, exemplified by flare-ups like the 1995 Ecuadorian-Peruvian war. A third factor is the growing militarization of social conflicts, as in Chiapas, or in the expansion of Colombia's civil strife, narco-wars in the Andean region, the re-emergence of Haiti's security establishment, the ongoing confrontation in and with Venezuela, and the involvement of Latin American forces in the Middle East conflict.

## 5. Limited Democracy and Elected Plutocracies

Current political developments in Latin America, while conveying a less repressive picture, especially by contrast with a somber record of the 1970s, present at best mixed signs. On the positive side, most of the region is ruled now-a-days by governments generated through formally free and competitive elections: what former Guyana's President Cheddy Jagan sarcastically called "5-minute democracy" (1996). In various instances, some sort of consolidation has taken place, as a second and even a third generation of elected governments have been inaugurated. There have been also sporadic, yet significant attempts to hold governments accountable to the electorate. Instances of torture, disappearances and blatant state terrorism, with notable exceptions, such as Colombia, have become less frequent. However, there are also disturbing signs. One is the persistence, and even revival, of authoritarian and oligarchic traditions. Power remains highly concentrated. Other less tangible but basic values, such as respect for human life, honest government and the reduction of discrimination and official abuse, are not widely adhered to. Corruption in both parts of the Hemisphere is widespread, deep, and fast growing (Nef 2004: 283-304).

TABLE 9.5
**Electoral Participation**

| | High Turnout | | | Low Turnout | |
|---|---|---|---|---|---|
| *Country* | *1988-91* | *1998-2001* | *Country* | *1988-91* | *1998-2000* |
| Uruguay | 96.9 | 94.6 | Peru | 56.9 | 78.6 |
| Argentina | 89.4 | 78.1 | Paraguay | 56.3 | 59.4 |
| Chile | 88.3 | 83.1 | Haiti | 52.7 | 60.5 |
| Costa Rica | 85.1 | 73.7 | Bolivia | 51.0 | 64.5 |
| Brazil | 76.6 | 81.0 | Mexico | 50.0 | 48.2 |
| Honduras | 75.7 | 78.0 | Dom Rep | 45.8 | 45.6 |
| Nicaragua | 73.3 | 76.2 | El Salvador | 44.0 | 31.1 |
| Venezuela | 72.3 | 46.5 | Colombia | 40.1 | 40.5 |
| Panama | 70.1 | 76.1 | U.S. | 36.5 | 46.5 |
| Canada | 68.3 | 54.6 | | | |
| Ecuador | 64.7 | 48.5 | | | |

*Source* : "International Institute for Democracy and Electoral Assistance (IDEA), "Voter Turnout from 1945 to Date", Stockholm, Sweden, 2003, *www.idea.int/vt/analysis.*

Limited democracies, based upon pacts of elites are distinctively exclusionary. Electoral processes, though a common sight throughout the Americas, are increasingly void of choice and even meaning. Fraud and manipulation still persist. Voters can cast the ballot but the menus and policy options are roughly the same. The socio-economic and institutional pillars of the former National Security regimes (landowners, business, foreign investors and authoritarian preserves within the military, the judiciary and the technocracy) are also those of the new democratic orchestrations. The large majority of those who perpetrated crimes against humanity is still at large, and has gone unpunished. Thus, it is hardly surprising that public apathy and cynicism throughout the hemisphere are at an all-time high, while governmental legitimacy is shrinking (Graham *et. al.* 2003). Despite the unfolding of formally contested elections during the 1990s in all of the countries and apparently normal constitutional reforms in a good number of others, these processes failed to provide real alternatives. The above-mentioned alienation of the population from the political process has resulted in extremely high rates of electoral abstention. For instance, eighty-four percent abstained in the Guatemalan referendum of 1994 and 50 percent in El Salvador's general election of March 1994. In the Colombian parliamentary elections of 1994, over 70 percent did not vote, while in the Ecuadorian congressional competition the same year, spoiled ballots received the second largest plurality. Colombia tops the list of electoral abstention, with roughly 40 percent of the voters casing their ballots in 2000 and it is followed closely by the United States. In addition, many of these contests have been tainted with serious irregularities.

## Table 9.6
## Comparative Indicators for Latin America and the Caribbean

| Country | A Corrupt (CPI) 2004 b | B GDP p. capita a | C Growth GDP 2003 | D Debt/ GPD 1999 | E Inflation (annual) 1999 | F GINI Index 1999-2002e | G Defense exp/GDP 2003 | H Forces per 1000 1999f | I HDI in 2002 c | J Population in millions 2004 | K Urban (thousand) 2002 | L EDI Index 2000 d |
|---|---|---|---|---|---|---|---|---|---|---|---|---|
| (1) | (2) | (3) | (4) | (5) | (6) | (7) | (8) | (9) | (10) | (11) | (12) | (13) |
| Argentina | 2.5 | 12,400 | 8.8 | 51.2 | -1.2 | 52.2 | 1.1 | 1.9 | 0.85 | 39.5 | 33,5 | 0.96 |
| Bolivia | 2.2 | 2,600 | 2.5 | 65.9 | 2.1 | 44.70 | — | 4.0 | 0.68 | 8.9 | 5,58 | 0.90 |
| Brazil | 3.9 | 8,100 | -0.2 | 40.0 | 4.9 | 59.25 | 1.5 | 1.8 | 0.77 | 186.01 | 43,49 | — |
| Chile | 7.4 | 10,700 | 3.3 | -1.1 | 3.3 | 57.10 | 3.5 | 5.8 | 0.83 | 15.9 | 13,45 | 0.96 |
| Colombia | 3.8 | 6,600 | 3.9 | 44.7 | 11.2 | 57.60 | 4.0 | 3.6 | 0.77 | 43.0 | 33,22 | 0.86 |
| Costa Rica | 4.9 | 9,600 | 6.5 | 33.6 | 10.0 | 46.50 | — | 2.3* | 0.83 | 4.0 | 2,23 | 0.91 |
| Cuba | 3.7 | 3,000 | — | 80.0 | 7.0 | — | — | 5.1 | 0.80 | 11.3 | 8,52 | 0.97 |
| Dominican R. | 2.9 | 6,200 | -0.4 | 28.7 | 3.0 | — | — | 2.0 | 0.73 | 8.9 | 5,73 | 0.86 |
| Ecuador | 2.4 | 3,700 | 2.7 | 107.3 | 52.3 | — | 2.4 | 4.5 | 0.73 | 13.3 | 8,18 | 0.92 |
| El Salvador | 4.2 | 4,900 | 1.8 | 17.4 | 0.5 | 53.20 | 0.1 | 2.7 | 0.72 | 6.74 | 00 | — |
| Guatemala | 2.2 | 4,200 | 2.1 | 28.6 | 4.9 | 59.87 | 0.5 | 2.6 | 0.64 | 14.7 | 4,83 | 0.74 |
| Haiti | 1.5 | 1,500 | 0.4 | 30.6 | 8.7 | — | — | 0.7* | 0.46 | 8.1 | 3,06 | — |
| Honduras | 2.3 | 2,800 | 3.0 | 83.3 | 11.6 | 55.00 | 0.8 | 1.2 | 0.67 | 6.9 | 3,70 | — |
| Jamaica | 3.3 | 4,100 | 2.3 | 57.6 | 5.9 | 37.90 | — | 1.1 | 0.76 | 2.7 | 1,49 | 0.92 |
| Mexico | 3.6 | 9,600 | 1.3 | 33.5 | 16.6 | 54.60 | 0.5 | 1.9 | 0.80 | 106.27 | 5,41 | 0.94 |
| Nicaragua | 2.7 | 2,300 | 2.3 | 231.0 | 10.9 | 43.11 | 0.9 | 3.3 | 0.66 | 5.4 | 3,04 | 0.73 |
| Panama | 3.7 | 6,900 | 4.1 | 55.7 | 1.3 | 56.40 | — | 0.5* | 0.79 | 3.1 | 1,67 | 0.95 |
| Paraguay | 1.9 | 4,800 | 2.6 | 22.6 | 6.8 | 57.77 | 0.7 | 1.4 | 0.75 | 6.4 | 3,15 | 0.90 |

| | | | | | | | | | | | | |
|---|---|---|---|---|---|---|---|---|---|---|---|---|
| Peru | 3.5 | 5,600 | 3.8 | 50.9 | 3.5 | 49.80 | 1.5 | 4.4 | 0.75 | 27.9 | 19,65 | 0.93 |
| Uruguay | .2 | 14,500 | 2.5 | 40.1 | 5.6 | 44.60 | 1.1 | 9.8 | 0.83 | 3.4 | 3,10 | 0.93 |
| Venezuela | 2.3 | 5,800 | -9.4 | 71.1 | 23.6 | — | 1.3 | 3.3 | 0.77 | 25.4 | 21.92 | 0.91 |

*Sources* : a=Gross Domestic Product per capita, GDP (thousands of U.S dollars). Central Intelligence Agency, in the 2005 *World Fact Book* electronic publication: *http://www.cia.gov/cia/publications/factbook/*, b=Transparency International's *2004 Corruption Perception Index* (CPI). c=United Nations Human Development Index Value (HDI) from *Latin America and the Caribbean: Selected Economic and Social Data 2004*, electronic publication: *http://qesdb.cdie.org/lac/LACbook/chapter01.pdf*, EFA GMR 2003, Statistical annex. d=EDI is a new composite index that incorporates indicators for the four most quantifiable EFA. The EDI for a country is the arithmetical mean of the observed values of indicators selected for each of the EFA goals. Since these are percentages, the value can vary from 0 to 1. The higher it is, the closer a country is to the goal and the greater its EFA achievement: *http://www.unesco.org/education/efa_report/zoom_regions_pdf/laamcari.pdf* , e=GINI Index. *World Bank*, World Development indicators, available as electronic publication: *http://esdb.cdie.org/cgi-bin2/broker.exe?_service=default&_program=lacprogs.pov_3.sas&sscode=WDI180800+&cty=ALLC&year=2002+&year=2001+&year=2000+&year=1999+&output=1*. PNUD *World Development Report 1999*. *= No military forces; only police and other security forces. Income figures are calculated as purchasing power parity (PPP) = Parity equivalent in US $.

For comparative purposes, the figures for North America, for all the above variables (A to L) were the following:

| *Country* | *A* *Corrupt (CPI)* | *B* *GDP p. capita* | *C* *Growth/ GDP* | *D* *Debt/ GDP* | *E* *Inflation (annual)* | *F* *Gini index* | *G* *Defense exp/GDP* | *H* *Forces per 1000* | *I* *Human Dev. Index* | *J* *Population in 1000s* | *K* *Urbaniz Index* | *L* *Education Index* |
|---|---|---|---|---|---|---|---|---|---|---|---|---|
| | *2001* | *1999* | *1999* | *1999* | *1999* | *1999* | *1999* | *2002* | *1999* | *1999* | *1999* | *1999* |
| *(1)* | *(2)* | *(3)* | *(4)* | *(5)* | *(6)* | *(7)* | *(8)* | *(9)* | *(10)* | *(11)* | *(12)* | *(13)* |
| Canada | 8.9 | 24,800 | 3.7 | 93.0* | 1.7 | 31.5 | 1.6 | 1.8 | 0.932 | 29,512 | 77.0 | 0.98 |
| USA | 7.6 | 33,100 | 4.2 | 59.3* | 2.1 | 40.8 | 3.3 | 5.1 | 0.927 | 275,636 | 77.0 | 0.98 |

*Notes* : 1. The bulk of the US—and to a lesser extent Canadian—debt is internal debt, unlike that of the LAC countries, which is *foreign* debt.

2. This table was calculated by the author on the basis of individual country data provided in the International Institute of Strategic Studies (IISS), *The Military Balance 2000-2001*, (London: Oxford University Press, 2001), pp. 25, 54, 227-51; also from the United Nations', PNUD, *Informe Sobre Desarrollo Humano 1999* (Madrid: Mundi Prensa Libros, 1999), pp. 134-241. The IISS figures for the GNP in Latin America and the Caribbean presented in this table, unlike that the World Bank used to calculate debt/GNP ratio on Table 2 above, are higher than those prepared by U.N. agencies like the World Bank and the UNDP.

Beyond ceremonial transfers of offices by electoral means and the absence of direct military rule, democracy in the Americas has not been consolidated in this decade. Transition remains incomplete and in some cases "undoing democracy" (Close 2004: 2-4) has been the dominant trend. Oligarchies throughout the continent have shown a remarkable continuity. The old practice of executive *continuismo* and dynastic-type succession (the elimination of which was central to the region's past democratic agenda) has resurfaced. There is also a remarkable continuity of policy. Neoliberal recipes have become entrenched in the conditionalities attached to debt-alleviation, regional trade agreements (such as NAFTA or MERCOSUR) and the so-called macro-economic equilibrium policies, which effectively remove fiscal, monetary and credit matters from national political debate. In addition, the "new" cold war in the context of unipolarism, with its pseudo moralistic and messianic discourse has debilitated democracy, development and security.

## V. CONCLUSIONS : THE FIRES WITHIN

A profound structural contradiction has emerged in the region's governance. If elected governments stress *democracy*, equity, majority rule and the interests of the public (the civil society), they would face relentless opposition and sabotage from domestic and international elites, leading to eventual ineffectiveness, if not outright destabilization. Thus, the more common course is to stress *liberalism* and ignore civil society and rule on behalf of the profit sector. This is what in the North American context Ralph Nader has labeled a *plutocracy*. The political cost of this option is very high in the long-run: loss of legitimacy, popular (and national) sovereignty, and an erosion of the trust between elected officials and the electorate, a central tenet of both governance and pluralist institutionalization.

Given the level of political alienation, it is not surprising that there have been popular insurrections where angered communities confronted threats to their livelihood: Chiapas (1993), Quito (2000), Buenos Aires (2001), and La Paz (2003 and 2005). These mobilizations and insurrections have had broad domestic and international implications. They are a specific Latin American expression of the anti-globalization movement, re-creating a civil society where popular organizations had been crushed by the double squeeze of military rule in the 1970s and economic restructuring in the 1990s.

A more institutional manifestation of this expanding protest movement is the series of electoral victories of populist, nationalist and left-of-center parties and candidates, especially in Argentina (Kirschner), Brazil ("Lula"), Uruguay (Vásquez), and Venezuela (Chávez), all of them at odds with Washington's conservative politics. These developments suggest that popular movements and rebellions are present in the new globalized regional order (Latin America Weekly Report 1994: 2, 1994: 62), and that the inter American monologue has been significantly brought into question.

Leftist groups and platforms have re-emerged as political options and it is likely that we may witness more such manifestations in the near future. Instability, even under the illusion of the NAFTA, CAFTA and FTAA umbrella, is more than skin-deep. On the other hand, by challenging the legitimacy of the new intra-elite and transnational arrangements, the new modes of resistance reveal the intrinsic weakness and precarious legitimacy of the post-transitional regimes.

Thus, from a long-range structural perspective, social upheavals, some of them violent, have not withered away altogether in the region, although their manifestations have changed. Our analysis strongly suggests that the politics of limited democratization with neo-liberal economics, while an improvement over the atrocious human rights record of the military dictatorships, imposes built-in constraints upon the realization of a truly stable and sustainable democratic project for and by the populace. Nor is the combination of limited democracy with neo-liberalism a guarantee against expanding corruption or popular alienation. In fact, the opposite seems to be the case. If economic recovery fails to produce a better standard of living for the majorities (as it is currently the case), or should the structural crisis deepen, it is likely that these weak and "pragmatic" civilian regimes could be overturned by equally weak, yet violently repressive civil-military regimes. After all the National Security doctrine is still the ideological "software" (or culture) of the security establishments and a regular staple in the training of Special Forces in the hemisphere. The "ommunist" subversion of yore is being replaced by a new definition of the internal enemy: "terrorism," "anarchy" or "war on drugs," or more broadly anything that threatens the investment climate, or core elites' interests. Growing military and US involvement, as in Plan Colombia, is a case in point. Certainly, the post September 11 atmosphere may have a most destabilizing effect by reviving a hard "counter-terrorist" posture to justify authoritarian rule, as it is occurring in the US itself.

As the entire region becomes more closely integrated, a potentially dysfunctional system of mutual vulnerability is taking shape. Its impact on the life of millions throughout the Americas can be catastrophic. The present course points toward scenarios where unemployment, poverty, violence, criminality, health hazards, environmental threats, addiction, refugee flows, massive population displacements, repression and environmental decay feed upon each other. The drug-trading regime is a dramatic illustration of this interconnectedness. The ties that link the drug trade together begin with peasant producers in the depressed Andean region, and continue with crime syndicates in producing, transporting, and importing areas, corrupt officials (as well as rabid "patriots"), retailers, and users, ranging from the destitute to those in high social standing. Being an essentially consumer-driven market, and operating on pure market logic, its containment requires addressing its social-psychological end economic causes—including the roots of addiction—rather than exclusively its symptoms. In a similar vein are the linkages between foreign-financed wars (like the Central American wars of the 1980s) and the gang—"Mara" phenomenon that "integrates" Central America and the US in dysfunctional webs of violence.

Under these circumstances, the linkages of mutual vulnerability between North and South (as well as within North and South), and their multiple accelerators, including the maquila-type mode of labor relations, create a spiraling lose-lose situation: a negative-score game. Without profound changes in both the South and the North of the Hemisphere, the possibility of arresting or reversing serious threats to human security will remain doubtful. Short of a radical reorganization of the pattern of governance throughout the Americas, including decision-making, accountability, and regional cooperation—for instance, the largely stagnant OAS system—multiple and critical dysfunctions are likely to increase.

As for the panacea of globalization, a term often used as synonymous with modernization and Americanization, Geoffrey Garrett has observed:

> middle-income countries have not done nearly as well under globalized markets as either richer or poorer countries, and the ones that have globalized the most have fared the worst [...] The ultimate irony facing globalization's missing middle may be that the more the free trade project flounders in Latin America, the greater will be the pressure on people in the region to migrate to the United States. Migration will, in turn, squeeze employment and wages for the American manufacturing middle class even more . . . (Garrett 2004: 85, 96).

Globalization does not involve just a series of purely random, mechanically pre-ordained stages—or teleology—operating outside the realm of concrete actor's interests, objectives and rules. Rather, this process unfolds within a system of intentional regulations (and their reciprocal value, de-regulations) that affect the very way the "game", and its outcomes, are played out. Globalization in the Americas is not exempt from these eminently political regulatory policies that actors can create and change. Politics still matters.

Regional security cannot be equated with short term business confidence, the magic of the marketplace, or with a messianic vision of "Manifest Destiny," or "wars" on terrorism or drugs, or more recently, fending off the "Hispanic threat" (Huntingtion 2004). A breakdown of democratic development, prosperity and equity, and the increase of tensions in the more volatile regions of the hemisphere would have a direct and most deleterious effect upon the well-being and security of both Americas. The weakness of democratic institutions and their inability to traverse from democratic transition and elected plutocracies to consolidation of popular rule is a critical structural flaw in the security of the Hemisphere. As a recent report from the International Institute for Democracy and Electoral Assistance in Sweden indicated:

> Latin Americans are frustrated with their democracies. Only 53 percent of the regional population is reported to support democracy, and a meagre 29 percent is said to be satisfied with how it is functioning. Political and economic reforms often fail to produce tangible improvements in the lives of ordinary citizen. . . . Key democratic institutions in the Americas are not performing to the entire satisfaction of citizens. Some segments of the population feel and are effectively excluded from politics and its processes, particularly women, youth and indigenous peoples. In many countries, democratic institutions remain weak, especially political parties and representative bodies. Politicians are mistrusted everywhere, yet the majority of Latin Americans say that political parties are vital to democracy. Once in office, Latin American governments often fail to forge the political alliances needed to govern and to facilitate needed reforms (otherwise known as a "crisis of governability").

It is becoming painfully obvious that the end of the Cold War did not automatically translate into a Fukuyama-type scenario of the "end of History", with global prosperity, peace and democracy (Fukuyama 1989: 3-18). The two-decade old democratic transition in the region cannot be made synonymous with either the entrenchment of participatory practices or with responsible government, let alone the enhancement of human dignity. The "safe," "limited," "low-intensity" and meaningless democracy brokered and embraced by Washington—and encapsulated in the famous unilateral "consensus"—is fundamentally flawed. This model, peddled by transition theorists and the neo-authoritarians in the core impedes more than facilitates the emergence of a sustainable security community for the whole region. So does the persistence of economic dogmatism and the rebirth of National Security doctrines designed to fight elusive and perpetual global conflicts. That narrowly-defined concept of *military* security is, in fact, a major cause of insecurity. This link underpins the insurmountable contradiction between globalization and militarization (Benítez-Manaut 2004: 59). In this context, real regime change throughout the hemisphere is a necessary condition for the human security of the vast majority of its people.

## References


Altimir, Oscar, 1994, "Income Distribution and Poverty through Crisis and Adjustment", *CEPAL Review*, No. 52, April.

Benítez-Manaut, Raúl, 2004, "*Mexico and the Challenges of Hemispheric Security*", Washington, D.C., The Woodrow Wilson International Center for Scholars, Latin American Program.

Bodehneimer, Suzanne, 1970, "The Ideology of Developmentalism: American Political Science Paradigm—Surrogate for Latin American Studies", *Berkeley Journal of Sociology*, No. 15.

Bosch, Juan, 2000, "*El Pentagonismo Sustituto del Imperialismo*", 3rd Edition. Santo Domingo: Editora Alfa y Omega.

Chillier, Gaston; Freeman, Laurie, 2005, "*Potential Threat: The New OAS Concept of Hemispheric Security*", A WOLA Special Report, Washington, D.C.: Washington Office on Latin America.

Close, David, 2004, "Undoing Democracy in Nicaragua", in David Close and Kalowatie Deonandan (eds.) "*Undoing Democracy, The Politics of Electoral Caudillismo*", Lanham: Lexington Books.

Corbett, Charles D., 1972, "The Latin American Military as a Socio-Political Force, Case Studies of Bolivia and Argentina", *Monographs in International Affairs*, Center for Advanced International Studies, University of Miami, Also see "Appendix F: Précis of the Counterinsurgency Course", "The Special Warfare School Fort Bragg, North Carolina", in Willard Barber and Neale Ronning, 1966, "*Internal Security and Military Power, Counterinsurgency and Civic Action in Latin America*", (Ohio: Ohio State University Press) as well as U.S. Army Special Warfare School, 1964, *Counterinsurgency Planning Guide*, Special Text No. 31-176.

ECLAC (UN Economic Commission for Latin America and the Carribean) *Anuario Estadistico* 2001, Santiago, Chile.

ECLA/CEPAL, 2004, *Panorama Economico de America Latina*, Santiago, CEPAL.

Fukuyama, Francis, 1989, "The End of History?", *The National Interest*, No. 16 (Summer).

Garrett, Geoffrey, 2004, "Globalization's Missing Middle", *Foreign Affairs*, Vol. 83, No. 6, November-December.

Graham, Carol; Sukhatenkar, Sandip, 2003, "Is Economic Crisis Reducing the Support for Markets and Democracy in Latin America? Some Evidence from the Economics of Happiness", The Brookings Institution, November.

Hogan, Jenny, 2005, *New Scientist Print Edition*, March 1.

Huntington, Samuel, 2004, "The Hispanic Threat", *Foreign Policy*, Electronic Version, March-April.

Huntington, Samuel; Crozier, Michel; Watanuki, Joji, 1975, "The Crisis of Democracy: Report on The Governability of Democracies to the Trilateral Commission", New York: *Triangle Papers*, No. 8: New York University Press. It was based upon the "Task Force Report to the Trilateral Commission," prepared for the first plenary meeting of the Commission in Tokyo, May; for a critique of this report see Alan Wolfe, 1975:559, "Capitalism Shows its Face," *The Nation*, Nov. 29.

Jagan, Cheddy, 1996, "Sustainable Development in the Americas", keynote address to the XXVII Annual Congress of the Canadian Association of Latin American and Caribbean Studies, York University, October 31st.

Karl, Terry-Lynn; Fagen, Richard, 1986, "The Logic of Hegemony: The United States as a Superpower in Central America", in Jan Triska, ed., "Dominant Powers and Subordinate States. The United States in Latin America and the Soviet Union in Eastern Europe", Durham, N.C.: Duke University Press.

*Latin America Weekly Report*, 13 January, 1994; 17 February, 1994.

Letelier, Orlando, 1976, "The 'Chicago Boys' in Chile: Economic Freedom's Awful Toll," *The Nation*, August 28.

Linowitz, Sol, 1975, "The Americas in a Changing World", New York: Quadrangle Books, Commission on United States-Latin American Relations, (Sol Linowitz, Chairman).

Lovell, John, 1971, "Military-Dominated Regimes and Political Development: A Critique of Some Prominent Views", in Monte Palmer and Larry Stern (Eds.), "*Political Development in Changing Societies: An Analysis of Modernization*", Levington: Heath Lexington Books.

Martínez, Osvaldo, 1992, "Debt and Foreign Capital, The Origins of the Crisis", *Latin American Perspectives*, Issue 76, Vol. 20, No. 1.

Montecinos, Verónica; Markoff, John, 1993, "Democrats and Technocrats: Professional Economists and Regime Transition in Latin America", *Canadian Journal of Development Studies*, Vol. XIV, No. 1.

Nef, Jorge, 2004, "Structural Correlates of Government Corruption in Latin America: Explaining and Understanding Empirical Findings" in Dele Olowu and Roy Mukwena (eds.), "*Governance in Southern Africa and Beyond*", Windhoek, Namibia: McMillan-Granberg.

Nef, Jorge, 1999, *"Human Security and Mutual Vulnerability, The Global Political Economy of Development and Underdevelopment"*, 2nd edition, Ottawa: IDRC Books.

Nef, Jorge; Robles, Wilder, 1998, "Environmental Issues, Politics, and Administration in Latin America: An Overview", in Joseph Jabbra and Onkar Dwivedi (eds.), *"Governmental Response to Environmental Challenges in Global Perspective"*, Amsterdam: IOS Press.

Nef, Jorge, Rojas, Fransisco, 1984, "Dependencia Compleja y Transnacionalización del Estado", *Relaciones Internacionales*, No. 8-9.

Nye, Joseph (ed.) 2003, "The Democracy "Deficit" in the Global Economy: Enhancing the Legitimacy and Accountability of Global Institutions", *Task Force Report 57*, The Trilateral Commission, electronic version.

Robinson, William, 1994, "Central America: Which Way After the Cold War?", *NotiSur*, Vol. 4, No. 8, February 25.

Rojas, Robinson, 2003, "Notes on the Doctrine of National Security": *rrojasdatabank.org/natsec1*.

Siat, Arturo; Iriarte, Gregorio, 1979, "De la Seguridad Nacional al Trilateralismo", *Cuadernos de Cristianismo y Sociedad*, Buenos Aires, May.

Sklar, Holly, 1980, "Managing Dependence and Democracy—An Overview", in Sklar (Ed.), *"Trilateralism: The Trilateral Commission and Elite Planning for World Management"*, Montréal: Black Rose.

The Chronic Poverty Research Center (CPRC), *The Chronic Poverty Report 2004-05*, Institute for Development Policy and Management, University of Manchester.

"The World Bank", *World Development Report*, 1990, 1991, 1992, and 1994.

United Nations, 1994, *World Economic and Social Survey*. New York: United Nations.

Vilas, Carlos, 2004, "Shaky Democracies and Popular Fury: From Military Coups to Poeples' Coups?" Tampa: LACS, *Cuadernos LACS*, No. 2.

Weil, Jean-Louis; Comblin, Joseph; Senese, Judge, 1979, "The Repressive State: The Brazilian National Security Doctrine and Latin America", *LARU Studies*, Doc. No. 3.

"World Debt Tables, External Debt of Developing Countries", 1987-88, 1989-90 and 1991-92 Editions, Vol. II, *Country Tables*, Washington.

# 10

# Globalization, Social Capital and Democracy

## The Andean Region in Comparative Perspective

PHILIP MAUCERI

In many ways, globalization has become a new interpretive framework within which a variety of social, economic and political phenomena have increasingly been interpreted and analyzed. As with other frameworks (e.g., dependency) its usefulness should be judged less by its implicit policy implications than by its ability to highlight the relationships between seemingly distinct phenomena. At its most basic level, globalization is the "widening, deepening and speeding up of global interconnectedness" across economic, technological, cultural, social and political spheres (Held *et. al.* 1999: 4). Globalization's multi-dimensional character would seem particularly well-suited to help us understand relationships and processes that impact the polity, society and economy. At the same time, because globalization encompasses such a wide range of fields and empirical phenomena, it can often be frustrating for those trying to create a simply tally sheet of costs and benefits, advances and setbacks. Adding to this difficulty is the fact that the "widening, deepening and speeding up" occur at different paces in different settings, making any attempt to "measure" its validity, virtually impossible. Still, for the analyst interested in developing a framework that is both cross-national/regional as well as multi-dimensional, globalization is a promising starting point.

The following discussion focuses on how the forces of globalization reshape social capital and identity, and the implications of this transformation for democracy, with an empirical focus on the Andean region. There have been few attempts to link the processes of globalization with social capital (Trigilia 2001: 427-43; de Haan 2000: 339-66; Carroll and Babbington 2000: 435; Fox *et al.* 2000: 399; Ekins *et al.* 1998: 863-72). On the one hand, much attention has been given to specific development policies and their impacts on local, particularly rural, patterns of social capital. Other studies focus specific civil society groups and especially the ways in which globalization has contributed to the rise of both domestic and international non-governmental organizations (NGOs). This discussion argues for a different focus. Social capital, broadly understood as civic engagement that involves both private and public/political organizations, has widespread implications for political behaviors and institutional structures. Social capital is the "glue" of civil society helping to determine the density and bonding of a broad range of social organizations and relationships. These relationships in turn affect the expectations, demands and activities of community members as they participate in politics. From Tocqueville onwards, the linkage between social capital, civil society and politics (especially democratic politics) has been argued strongly.

Nonetheless, social capital is not immutable. Like society itself, it is vulnerable to the winds of technological, economic and political change. In focusing on globalization, this analysis hopes to sketch out some of the possible links between these two ongoing processes: globalization and the development of social capital (Table 10.1). In the first part of this paper, I review the two prevailing analyses.

**Table 10.1**
**Impact of Globalization on Social Capital and Implications for Democracy**

| *Globalization Processes* | *Social Capital Outcome Scenarios* | *Democratic Challenges of Social Capital Outcomes* |
|---|---|---|
| • Market Liberalization | 1. Decline and Atomization? | • Collective Action Problems<br>• Demagoguery/Opportunism |
| • Communication Revolution | 2. Issue/Identity Transformation? | • Disjunction between issues and institutions: unresponsiveness |
| • Consumerism | | • Exclusion/Conformity |
| • Limitations on the State | | |

The first suggests a movement towards decline and atomization, while the second analysis emphasizes a transformation in the types and expressions of social capital/identity. The paper offers a brief review of the key globalization processes relevant to social organization during the last decade and their impacts on Latin America. Finally, the paper turns to the countries of the Andes, the region of Latin America that has seen the most social and political tumult during the last decade. To what extent can this tumultuous experience be traced to the challenges of globalization, and particularly to the ways in which these processes affect social organization? I argue in this section that political trends in the region suggest that globalization is pulling social capital and identity in opposed directions simultaneously. Although, one of these directions—atomization or transformation—may ultimately emerge dominant, it is not at all clear yet which. I conclude this paper with a few brief implications this discussion may have on the possibilities for deepening democratization in the region.

## SOCIAL CAPITAL AND IDENTITY

There are two largely opposite interpretations regarding the shift in social capital and identity that has occurred as a result of recent economic/ technological changes. The first might be termed the "atomization" model of social identity. Robert Putnam (1995: 65-78) argued that "civic engagement and social connectedness" were rapidly declining in the United States. Reviewing declining voter turnouts and organizational memberships in the US since the 1960s, Putnam suggests that the country is seeing its "social capital", that is the aspects of social organization that foster mutual cooperation and trust within society, eroding. The explanation for this erosion, he argues lies in a series of changes that have occurred in US society, including the entry of women into the workplace in large numbers, greater mobility of the population and the "technological transformation of leisure" (e.g., television, video games, Internet). The decline in social capital fosters collective action problems and promotes greater opportunism among both individuals and political groups, ultimately making democratic governance more difficult.

The scenario Putnam depicts of increasingly isolated individuals unconnected and uninterested in broader social and political ties and unwilling to engage in collective action, is not a new one. Marxists and non-Marxists alike have long focused on the problems of alienation and anomie. Marx's focus was primarily on the relationship between workers and both the products they produced and the production environment. In the Marxist perspective, alienation was the result of the expansion of industrial capitalism which, in the words of Pappenheim, alienated man from "his work, from himself, and from the reality of society and nature" (1995: 43). Later theorists, like Durkheim, broadened this conceptualization by refocusing the notion to a social condition experienced by individuals, with multiple causal factors. As the concept was broadened in the 1950s and 1960s to include "a lack of social integration," the "loss of social trust" and "individual isolation" it lost its Marxian referent and was used to analyze a variety of phenomena, from the rise of the student movement and revolutions to declining voter turnout (Finifter 1972). In this context, Habermas (1973: 44; 128-29) referred to alienation as the result of the growing "internal complexity" of advanced capitalist states that dissolve the "communicative organization of behavior".

What are the political implications of societies increasingly afflicted by the loss of trust and characterized by a lack of social integration and individual isolation? In reviewing the rise of new parties in Europe, Piero Ignazi provides a possible answer. He suggest that atomization/alienation has given rise to a new breed of authoritarian neoconservative parties, led by "political entrepreneurs" like Le Pen, Berlusconi, Haidar, Fortuyne who respond to the growing yearning for "order, tradition, identity and security" by emphasizing issues of immigration, morality and nationalism. As Ignazi notes,

> The defence of the national community from foreigners—hence racism and xenophobia—responds to the identity crisis produced by atomization. Moreover, the claim for more law and order, the search for a 'charismatic' leader, the seeking of harmony and security, the irritation towards representation mechanisms and procedures; all express a desire for an authoritative guide in a society where self-achievement and individualism have disrupted the protective network of traditional social bonds (Ignazi: 1996: 11).

The first vision of the links between social identity/capital and globalization suggests that as changes wrought by globalization take hold, from the expansion of communications and the flow of people and goods, to the shifts in production methods (to post-industrialism in advanced countries, and to industrial platforms/specialized agro-exports in LDCs and NICS), social identity, cohesion and trust weaken, and atomization and alienation increasingly prevails in society. Both, distrustful of the changes occurring and nostalgic for the (largely imagined) order and traditions of a previous ear, citizens turn to the charismatic authoritarian, who promises a return to order and a new era of harmony.

Under these circumstances, liberal democratic norms and institutions are increasingly called into question. Clearly, the deep institutionalization of democratic values and procedures that took place after WWII has prevented any serious threat to European democracy. New right-wing parties have had difficult winning a majority of votes at a national level, and even where they have gained a foothold in government or governing coalitions (Italy, Austria) the institutional changes adopted have only marginally affected the quality of democracy.

An alternative interpretation of the links between social capital/identity and globalization suggest that just the opposite of atomization is occurring, namely the formation of new value and identity systems based on an intensified transnational interconnectedness. Inglehart (1997: 22) has been at the forefront in sketching out a newly developing value system:

> "On this new Post-modern trajectory, economic rationality determines

human behavior less narrowly than before: the realm of the possible has expanded and cultural factors are becoming more important. An empirically demonstrable cultural shift is taking place. The great religious and ideological metanarratives are losing their authority among the masses. The uniformity and hierarchy that shaped modernity are giving way to an increasing acceptance of diversity. And the increasing dominance of instrumental rationality that characterized Modernization is giving way to a greater emphasis on value rationality and quality of life concerns."

According to Inglehart's data, the shift to post-modern values has been strongest in Europe, especially Northern Europe. The rise of postmodernization is primarily the result of two factors: the growing limits in the functional effectiveness of hierarchical bureaucratic organizations, as members of affluent societies are less willing to engage in alienating and depersonalizing work, and the greater emphasis on quality of life issues, the result of a new affluence and sense of security among citizens (Inglehart 1997: 28-31). In keeping with his neo-Weberian emphasis on cultural rather than economic change as the driving force behind shifts in sociopolitical structures and attitudes, Inglehart makes no effort to engage much of the literature that emphasizes the importance of changes in production, technology and communications spurred largely by globalization over the last two decades, even when such arguments might bolster his conclusions. For example, Robert Reich's discussion of the rise of high-value web networks employing "symbolic analysts" as the new form of corporate organization, replacing the traditional pyramid structure with strict differentiation between management and workers, provides an alternative explanation for the decline of hierarchically organized bureaucratic structures (Reich, 1992).

Whatever the specific origin of post-modern values, Inglehart makes clear they have reshaped politics in advanced industrialized countries, particularly Europe, effectively undermining traditional class cleavages and the Left-Right division, and giving rise to new Green parties. Post-material issues such as the environment, women's and gay rights, international peace and disarmament, and leisure time/services, have increasingly become central to European political debates. Moreover, although post-material issues have reshaped the terms of debate in European politics, they do not represent a threat to democracy. In fact, Inglehart (1997: 210) suggests that the focus on self-realization and individual autonomy inherent in post-materialism provides a bulwark to authoritarianism, in addition, post-materialists are more likely to engage in politics in ways that strengthen democracy. Even though "they are less likely to vote, which is a relatively elite-controlled form of participation . . . they are becoming *more* likely to engage in elite-challenging behavior (Inglehart 1997: 213). This is a conclusion shared by Pippa Norris (1999) who makes a strong case for the emergence of "critical citizens" in advanced democracies, who embrace democratic norms but remain highly skeptical of existing institutional structures.

The analyses offered by Norris (1999: 59) and Inglehart (1997: 28-31) closely parallel those offered by students of "new social movements" (NSMs) since the 1980s, i.e., the growing emergence of new social identities and cleavages among people participating in politics using non-electoral or extra-parliamentary modes of organization (Touraine 1981; Offe 1982: 817-68). Social actors previously excluded or not represented by existing institutional structures, such as women, people of color or ethnic minorities, begin to organize. Much of the NSM literature focuses on how new alliances are created among social groups around issues that transcend sectoral interests. For example, environmental organizations that include workers, students, women and minorities, all united in recognition of the danger presented to them by current systems of environmental degradation. Moreover, modes of organization emphasize autonomy from existing political groups such as parties, and employ mostly unconventional forms of political participation, from boycotts and strikes to demonstrations and sit-ins. These new collective actors thus represent a challenge to existing structures of participation, which they view as not meeting the democratic ideal of participation and representation.

More recently, the focus has shifted to what some refer to as "global civil society," or transnational links among groups that organize around specific issues. The emergence of these movement networks was facilitated by mechanisms of participation and organization that have largely been brought about through globalization. Intensified communication and transportation networks make possible the sharing of information, experiences and even outright participation, on a scale previously unimaginable. At the same time, the intense contact of ideas, peoples and products on a global scale has increasingly led to attempts to find common global foes and friends. Citing examples from Greenpeace to militant Islam, Tarrow asks, "Since we seem to be living in an increasingly interdependent world, are we becoming a single movement society?" (Tarrow 1994: 195).

The implications of this second interpretation of trends in social capital/identity for liberal democracy are mixed. As Norris notes, the rise of disaffected citizens who become disenchanted with democratic institutions, may ultimately be a positive development for democracy, if their disaffection is channeled in ways to reform institutions that narrows the gap between democratic ideals and reality. New movements may ultimately force change from the outside in ways that would not have been possible from within existing institutional structures. On the other hand, if disenchantment leads to a basic questioning of key democratic ideals, such as the protection of minorities, civil liberties or due process, such movements can begin to undermine a democratic regime, even where participants may continue to propound their democratic credentials (Norris 1999: 59).

Where do these two interpretive models lead us in evaluating the impact of globalization? Has globalization helped social capital decline or is it merely transforming social capital through different mechanisms and identities? Is social identity itself being reshaped in ways that would undermine traditional understandings of people's relationship with the polity? Much of the literature examining these questions, as we have seen, is focused on advanced industrial countries, and particularly Europe. With a greater sophistication in the applicability of survey research, as well as long established databases on political attitudes, shifts in socio-political structures are more easily detected in Europe than in underdeveloped nations. Europe also provides a case that is culturally, socially and economically more integrated than many other regions of the world, making it easier to arrive at regional generalizations. The impact of globalization and the possible reactions to changes wrought are likely to be quite different in much the rest of the world, where underdevelopment, economic inequality and social fragmentation are far higher. Before turning to the implications of globalization for social capital/identity in the Andean region, it is thus important to briefly outline the key characteristics or expressions of globalization in the Andes and Latin America as a whole.

## THE FACE OF GLOBALIZATION IN LATIN AMERICA

There are many processes that have been unleashed, or at least accelerated by globalization. The intensification of interconnectedness implied by globalization creates new pressures and vulnerabilities, as well as opportunities. Of these processes, four stand out in Latin America as having a particularly significant impact on social organization and potentially therefore on social capital and identity.

### A. Market Liberalization

The neoliberal economic restructuring that took place during the 1990s in Latin America, including privatizations, free trade agreements, liberalization of capital markets, and reductions in state spending on social support services, was in large part a reaction to the crisis of the "lost decade" of the 1980s. The neoliberal response to this crisis, was of course, not the only possible one, but given the vulnerability of the region and the pressure exerted on governments of the region by the United States, multilateral financial institutions and private investors, few other "options" were available. International financial institutions (IFIs) were able to exercise such great pressure in part because of a new found power of integrated markets and information sharing that could lead to rapid market discipline. Disapproval by the International Monetary Fund (IMF), the World Bank, or the US Treasury signaled market investors to abandon a country, a situation that could be devastating. Even though many of the policy recommendations of international financial institutions may have been sound, they were rarely accompanied by concerns regarding timing, sequencing or the support necessary to sustain them. As Joseph Stiglitz note in his incisive critique of IFIs.

The problem was that many of these policies became ends in themselves:

> rather than means to more equitable and sustainable growth. In doing so, these policies were pushed too far, too fast, and to the exclusion of other policies that were needed. . . . Fiscal austerity pushed too far, under the wrong circumstances, can induce recession, and high interest rates may impede fledgling business enterprises. The IMF vigorously pursued privatization and liberalization, at a pace and in a manner that often imposed very real costs on countries ill-equipped to incur them (Stiglitz 2002: 54).

The economic and social impacts of neoliberal austerity and restructuring in Latin America during the last decade are well-documented. Although there is some variation in intensity among countries, they broadly include :

1. *Rising Income Inequality:* Market liberalization tends to worsen income distribution to the extent that access to resources, from education to technology, and capital (especially credit) are increasingly restricted to those with market power. With the exception of Chile (which had seen significant worsening in the 1970s and 1980s), Latin America's income distribution worsened during the 1990s, with the regional Gini Index rising from .50 at the end of the 1980s to .53 in 2001 (Franko 2003: 355-56). This continued a trend begun in the 1980s, and although economists continue to debate the longer term trends, the immediate impact has been to deepen inequality in a region where inequality of wealth has traditionally been a problem (Chalmers 1997).
2. *Persistent Poverty:* In reducing the number of state employees and the state's social support for the poor, including spending on health and education, market liberalization, at least in its initial phases, tends to increase poverty. As trade liberalization and privatization take hold, unemployment and the informalization of the workforce have grown. Despite periods of significant economic growth in the last decade in several countries, including almost all of the Andean countries, reductions in poverty have been miniscule (again, with the exception of Chile). This is especially important in light of the rise in poverty experienced in the 1980s, which had effectively erased the gains made against poverty in the 1960s and 1970s (Korzeniewicz and Smith 2000: 7-54).
3. *Industrial Export Platforms:* Trade liberalization and privatization intensified competitive pressures on the industrial sector. Small

and medium sized firms increasingly closed. While larger countries (Brazil & Mexico) were better positioned to deal with these pressures, others were not. Coupled with shrinking domestic markets for their products, these pressures moved industries towards a greater export orientation, either as subcontractors to multinational firms (textiles in Colombia and Peru) or by promoting special free trade/processing zones (especially in Central America, Caribbean, Mexico). In both cases, competitive pressures forced a stagnation of wages, a reduction in the workforce, a weakening of labor union power and a greater vulnerability to changes in international markets (Benavente 1996).

4. *Agriculture, Agribusiness, Exports:* Market liberalization ha increasingly moved agriculture in Latin America away from producing for domestic consumption towards exports, especially of high value non-traditional and specialized products (e.g., flowers in Colombia & Ecuador, asparagus in Peru). The transformation has been favored by government policies searching for more export revenue and domestic and international agribusiness taking advantage of the growing liberalization of land tenure systems. Traditional small farms relying on peasant labor and producing crops for the local market, have seen both credit and government support shrink, continuing to make rural life difficult for peasants. The growth of mechanized corporate farms has reduced the need for labor, allowing agribusiness to rely mostly on temporary low-wage labor to help during harvests or periods of packing (Thrupp 1995).

In general, market liberalization has over the last decade or so led to a more intense and wide-ranging, though subordinate, insertion of Latin American economies into the global economic system. At the same time, persistent poverty and growing inequality characterize the social order, as low wage employment, informalization, scarce social services and the weakening position of labor/peasant unions, take hold.

## B. Consumerism

Popular understanding of globalization often revolve around the proliferation of celebrity images (J-Lo) or consumer brands (McDonald's), leading many to emphasize the "homogenizing" effects of globalization on culture (Friedman 2000). In fact, the manufacture of wants and their marketing to consumers has been a fundamental aspect of modern capitalism, through what Benjamin Barber termed the "infotainment telesector." As globalization has expanded the capacity of communication networks (discussed below), this inherent dynamic of modern capitalism has been transposed to the transnational level. That many of the images and product-brands consumed in the world originate in the United States is mostly a function of its market and technological dominance, allowing it to export them more effectively to the rest of the world. For example, the shopping mall, the sacred sanctuaries of consumer capitalism invented in the United States that replace the public plaza, can now be found virtually every corner of the globe.

Despite Latin America's high rates of poverty and underdevelopment, there are several factors which propel the development of a consumerist culture in the region, especially during the last decade. First and foremost has been the rapid expansion of the media in the region, as both satellite and cable, most often linked to US-based media companies such as Time-Warner, have made significant inroads into local markets, bringing with them US programming and its consumerist mentality. Second, the substantial Latino immigrant presence in the US, through personal visits home and telecommunications maintain close ties with countries of origin, exercises enormous cultural influence in the region. Communications with friends and relatives in Latin America, by relatively wealthier migrants in the US, transmit cultural images and market expectations that are usually far beyond the means of those left behind, but nonetheless influence behaviors. Lacking access to the more expensive original product, a thriving "pirate" market has developed on the streets of urban centers, that sell cheap knock-offs of North American culture, from CDs to software to clothing, to fulfil this demand. Finally, with market liberalization has come heightened market competition. Both local products and imports must compete more intensively for market share. For smaller countries in particular, where two or three brands were generally available 20-30 years ago on basic consumer items, free trade has now opened the floodgates. As in the developed world, corporations are forced to create strong brand identity and reach "target groups" through carefully crafted marketing campaigns. With fewer state controls on advertisements than in even the US, commercials, advertisements and direct marketing campaigns proliferate over the landscape, creating consumerist expectations in societies whose economies have difficulty meeting them.

## C. Communications

The "communications revolution" has been seen as a cornerstone of globalization during the past two decades, in part because the rapid expansion of communications technologies has driven a good deal of the widening and speeding up of global interconnectedness. Such technologies have generally arrived later in Latin America than in the developed world and access to them has been restricted, given their higher costs (Norris 2001). Beyond the technical improvements themselves, the importance of the communication revolution is in the rapidity with which images, ideas and information are transmitted to a broad swath of society. Three aspects of communications are important to mention for their potential impacts on social identity and organization in Latin America.

First, is the internationalization of content and ownership. The expansion of satellite and cable as well as the growing power of international media conglomerates have increasingly affected the content of programming as more channels are offered that carry foreign programs or broadcasts. While a broader exposure to different realities might create more cosmopolitan attitudes that challenge traditional modes of thought, it might also lead, as noted earlier, to frustrated expectations regarding standards of living and lack of material goods. Second, is the transformation of information transmission and reception. As has been noted in the developed world, television's particular mode of transmission—visual imagery and immediacy—creates an audience that is at once observer and participant in the action occurring on screen. At the same time, television viewing, as Putnam reminds us, is an individual rather than communal activity. Unlike reading or even listening to radio, the fast pace of change occurring on screen leaves little time for contemplation. A program (or individual) on television unable to immediately gratify and maintain interest, will lose the audience. Finally, the extensive reach of new communications technologies, and their bias towards visual imagery, creates new opportunities for social interaction and mediation, allowing people and groups to become aware of others with common interests and motivations more quickly and efficiently than otherwise possible.

## D. Limits on State Activities

A final expression of globalization worth considering is the ways in which "global interconnectedness" has impinged upon key aspects of modern state. Indeed, this is one of the most significant debates within the globalization framework, although it is beyond the scope of this paper to review this literature. Has globalization strengthened non-state actors to the point of shifting the locus of power away from the state system to multiple non-state poles? (Mathews 1997: 50-67; Carnoy 1993: 45-96). Or has globalization created a new "transgovernmental" structure with its own rules and institutions, which regulates more than abolishes state sovereignty and power? (Slaughter 1997: 183-98). A final scenario suggests the emergence of a "region state" within which largely economic forces expand the boundaries of traditional political states to encompass multiple states with fully integrated markets (Ohmae 1993: 78-88).

Elements of each of these three scenarios can be found in the changes that have affected Latin American states in the last decade. Non-state actors, both domestic and international, have clearly gained both new visibility and power in the region. The explosion in the number of active NGOs in the region since the 1980s has become a central theme of scholars in the region. But just as important has been the expansion of IGOs and MNCs, which have both led the way in promoting market liberalization and been the main beneficiaries of market-oriented reforms. Moreover, is has been the IGOs—

the World Bank, IMF, and WTO—that have had more of an impact than NGOs in proscribing or promoting specific state policies, from central bank autonomy to tariff rates. At the same time, the activities of IGOs and even many NGOs in the region have not emerged anarchically in a vacuum, but respond to the new "rules of the game" (namely the promotion of market reform and liberal democracy), established during the 1990s largely at the initiative of the United States as a hegemonic power. These transgovernmental structures and rules thus have had a regulatory and monitoring function that promotes a specific agenda, rather than a competition among multiple agendas. Both the sharp rise in intra-regional trade and the by now routine regional summits among the leaders of Latin American states also point to the tremendous degree of integration achieved in the region.

In addition to these new limitations on state activities, there has also been a fundamental transformation of the internal order of the state, brought on by the "third wave" of democratization. States facing international pressure to democratize have reduced the size and powers of the "coercive apparati" of the state—the military, intelligence agencies, police forces, while imposing new restraints on the use of state force. These restraints have often resulted in a new assertiveness and greater role for judiciaries, legislatures and other oversight bureaucracies. At the same time, efforts to democratize the state have created pressures to decentralize decision-making, sometimes involving increasing the autonomy of local governments at the expense of centralized bureaucratic control.

In short, globalization's impact on the state in Latin America has been to proscribe certain domestic policies and institutional mechanisms (particularly as regards security and economics), increase the profile of non-state actors and promote the integration of the region. For social actors in the region, as we shall see below, this has meant certain demands on, and supports from the state have become more difficult to sustain, while at the same time opening up spaces for new methods and strategies of organization.

## SOCIAL CAPITAL AND IDENTITY : GLOBALIZATION'S IMPACT IN THE ANDEAN REGION

What evidence is there on how the processes of globalization outline above have affected social capital and identity in the Andean region? An initial approach to this question (which is all that this paper offers), requires and examination of general trends that might indicate either a decline or transformation of social capital/identity. This section will review four of the most prominent political patterns to have merged in the Andean region during the last decade and explore what they tell us about globalization's impact on social capital and identity.

## A. Indigenous Movements

By far, the most notable development in Andean societies during the last decade has been the growing organization and power of indigenous groups. This represents a significant transformation of social identity and a new form of participatory expression. Nationalist and leftist organizations and parties throughout the 20th Century had successfully promoted a "peasant" (campesino) identity over an indigenous identity, subsuming ethnicity and race to class in class-oriented organization such as peasant unions (Albo 2004). While this was in part an attempt to strengthen national identity through inclusion, as well as recognition of the complexity of ethnic identity in places with significant mestizo populations, it left out the historic and cultural dimensions of identity in the region. Efforts to reclaim indigenous identity, while never completely gone, resurged during the 1970s, but it is only in the last decade or so that the focus has been on creating more explicit political organizations geared to benefit and advance group interests.

This transformation of identity discourse and the emergence of new organizations based on these identities have impacted all of the countries of the region in the same way. Ecuador's CONAIE (Confederation of Indigenous Nationalities of Ecuador) created in 1986 was probably the region's most sophisticated indigenous organization, which effectively used unconventional participation to thwart privatization of communal lands, restrict oil company explorations and limit the 500th Columbus anniversary in 1992 (Silverstone-Scher 2001). The more recent formation of a political party by CONAIE, namely, Pachakutik, is the culmination of identity transformation that has occurred and a demonstration of the power of the indigenous. In Bolivia, the creation of CONAMAQ (Council of Ayllus) in the late 1980s was an important first step in asserting a political role for the indigenous. The second place finish in the 2002 elections of indigenous presidential candidate Evo Morales, and his party's (MAS, Movimiento al Socialismo) position as the largest opposition party in Congress, represents a continuation of earlier trends. Elsewhere in the region, the experience has been more limited but nonetheless represents a shift away from peasant to indigenous organization. In Peru, largely due to the violence of Shining Path, indigenous organization has been more confined to the Amazonian areas, while in Colombia a more active indigenous organization, ONIC (Organizacion Nacional Indigena de Colombia) emerged in the 1980s and was helped by revisions in the 1991 Constitutions to extend indigenous rights (Pizarro 1999: 319). Although often the target of violence from both the FARC and paramilitary groups, indigenous groups and their leaders have become increasingly active in politics, helping elect Floro Tunubala as governor of Cauca province in 2000.

Two of the four processes of globalization mentioned earlier—communications and limits on state activities—have contributed to the transformation of identity and new organizational patterns among the indigenous. Both factors have fostered the development of contacts, information exchange and resource assistance across borders, as well as allowed the indigenous to appeal to a legal and human rights framework at the international level to advance their interests. Moreover, these transnational linkages have also helped the indigenous redefine their identity in ways that transcend local and traditional identities, creating "pan-indigenous" and internationalized perspectives on what constitutes their interests (Brysk 2000). Using new communications technologies and the integration of global media, indigenous groups pressured both foreign governments and multinational corporations to be sensitive to their rights. The increased international scrutiny of state activities has limited the possibilities of state repression of the indigenous. States that refuse to respect, in both discourse and practice, rights guaranteed by international norms and conventions, find themselves increasingly isolated.

Throughout the Andes, indigenous organizations have been important allies in the political coalitions formed to oppose neoliberal reforms. Yet just as the factors above helped empower indigenous organization, market liberalization has demonstrated the limits that globalization imposes on the development of new collective identities and social actions. With the exception of Ecuador, where indigenous groups have had some success forestalling neoliberal measures during the last decade, domestic and international interests advancing market liberalization policies have overcome this opposition. Nonetheless, the growth of new indigenous groups promoting alternative social and political agendas, even were not completely successful, represents a significant increase in social capital as well as transformation of social identity.

## B. Women, Environment, and Local Autonomy/Community Movements

Along with the indigenous movement, the last decade has seen a continued consolidation in the Andean region of several social movements that emerged in the 1970s, including women's groups, environmental organizations and movements to increase the powers of local governments or enhance community involvement. Each of these issues represents a sharp break with traditional issues and a significant shift in associational patterns. The development of these organizations was at the center of much of the new social movement's literature and those seeing a strengthening of civil society during the 1980s (Escobar and Alvarez 1992).

During the last decade, globalization has intensified the organization of people and groups around these non-traditional issues through three key processes. First, has been the expansion of transnational "advocacy networks," and particularly NGOs that have helped frame these issues, provided international connections and resources, and in many ways legitimized both domestically and internationally the issues for elites and traditional political actors. To a large degree, the global "reach" of these networks has been facilitated by the extension of communications, as well as transportation, networks that allow for the rapid exchange of ideas and peoples efficiently and at a reasonably low cost. The organization and global impact of key events such as the Rio Summit on the Environment or the Beijing Conference on Women would have been near impossible to achieve 30 or 50 years previously.

A second process of note is market liberalization. Although, as with the indigenous movements, efforts by women, environmental or community groups have not had much success reversing market reforms. Neoliberalism often has a contradictory impact. Austerity programs were an important factor in helping to mobilize these groups. Many community organizations, such as the Glass of Milk and Communal Kitchens groups in Peru, emerged precisely as a reaction to neoliberal reforms. Faced with the rising food costs and unemployment brought on by austerity policies, residents (and especially women) formed these associations as a survival strategy. In Bolivia, the Centro de Desarrollo de la Mujer Aymara (CDIMA) was formed to deal with the cultural impacts of neoliberalism on traditional Aymara practices (Lind 2000).

Yet while spurring greater organizational and social ties, as people affected negatively united both to oppose these policies as well as to deal with the consequences of neoliberalism, it is also clear that these policies deepened the problems these groups confront. For example, although much has been made of the growing "sensitivity" of IFIs to gender issues, one study found that World Bank programs continue to perpetuate gender inequalities by neglecting the unpaid labor that many women in the region engage in (Wood 2003: 209-30). In spurring the growth of "maquilas" and other free trade zones, market liberalization policies have deepened the environmental, labor and gender inequalities that nations confront, even as these challenges have sparked growing resistance. Foreign firms may be vulnerable to media pressure in their home-countries regarding the poor conditions in their factory sweatshops, but efforts to improve conditions are limited both by competitive pressures and the state's need for export generated revenue (Eckstein, *et. al.*: 28-29).

A third and final process related to globalization's impact on the transformation of social identity and capital in the Andes involves the new limits on the state. Whereas in the past, state agents faced with challenges from an array of social groups most likely would have used the police or military to repress them, or at best the centralized bureaucracy to co-opt their demands, reforms in the state structure mentioned earlier, make these options more costly. Moreover, the growing efforts at decentralization create new political spaces within which social groups can organize. This dynamic is best seen in Colombia, where both new parties and civil society groups have had the most success in organizing at the local level.

## C. The New Civilian Authoritarians : Fujimori and Chavez

A notable characteristic of Andean politics in the 1990s was the emergence of two elected civilian leaders whose support was gained from fragmented social sectors and who promised order in countries beset by chaos and decline: Alberto Fujimori in Peru and Hugo Chavez in Venezuela. Although both leaders differed considerably in their personal styles and socio-economic policies, they brought to the executive branch a disdain for democratic institutions and rules, as well as for existing social organizations, and instead offered a direct and personal relationship between the government and the governed. Moreover, both leaders tapped into a deep strain of "anti-politics" that had been developing in their respective societies, that is, a distrust and rejection of established political leaders and institutions. Alberto Fujimori used his 1992 "self-coup" to close down Peru's democratic institutions, create a new constitutional order that enhanced presidential powers, and began the process of enhancing the powers of the military and intelligence services while creating a clientelist machine personally loyal to his person. Hugo Chavez helped engineer a new constitution in 1999 that centralized power, relying increasingly on allies in the military and a network of loosely organized supporters to control the national agenda and implement his policies.

Fujimori and Chavez rose to power largely with the support of the most marginalized sectors of societies—peasants and the urban lower class—and specifically appealed to the history of oppression and inequality suffered by these sectors. Both leaders placed the blame for these problems on established socio-political elites, and especially identified with racial/ethnic characteristic of the lower classes. Yet unlike previous populist and leftist political organizations, neither Fujimori nor Chavez had an established political organization, a clear class-oriented message or a programmatic ideology. Rather, their appeals were largely direct, personal and unmediated.

The disenchantment of lower class sectors with existing democratic institutions and their attraction to Fujimori and Chavez suggest an encroaching decline in social capital and identity/organization. Fear and distrust, caused by years if not decades of corruption, economic decline, and growing insecurity (due to insurgency in Peru and violent crime and protests in Venezuela) played an important part in the gradual weakening of support for socio-political institutions. Both leaders were particularly astute in stoking these fears and resentments, blaming difficulties on an establishment that was described as the source for all of the nation's ills. Chavez, for example, played skillfully on the belief of many Venezuelans that economic difficulties had resulted because the country's wealth had been stolen by corrupt politicians. Fujimori attacked Peru's "partidocracia," a code-phrase that played up the image of traditional politicians as privileged and pampered successors of the viceroyal aristocracy. Each in turn promised a new order that would end the chaos and difficulties of the immediate past. Chavez's "Bolivarian Revolution" suggested a refoundation of the Venezuelan nation on principles that had been abandoned by the country's elites and thus a return to the promise of Simon Bolivar. Fujimori's promised order was less tied to an idealized past which given the historic lack of national integration is not surprising. Rather, Fujimori held out the hope of a Japanese engineer re-engineering Peru's economy and politics in a way that would end the internal warfare and hyperinflation of the 1980s.

Changes brought about by globalization helped lay the groundwork for civilian authoritarians. Market liberalization weakened the labor and peasant federations that had traditionally mediated much of the political activity of the lower classes. In their stead, an informalized workforce that had been atomized into competitive individualism struggled for daily survival in shrinking economies. This condition made individual appeals geared to an insecure, disengaged and atomized population particularly effective. Neither Fujimori nor Chavez demonstrated interest in creating organizational structures for workers, recognizing the traditional difficulty in organizing the urban informal sector. In addition, the growing role of the media was transforming politics as well as society, allowing politician to establish direct contact with people at an individual level without the need for a sophisticated organization capable of mobilizing people into plazas or to the polls. Even though neither Fujimori nor Chavez can be described as media "slick" in the style of US politicians, they utilized media, particularly television to transmit appeals directly and were especially astute in the transmission of visual imagery, whether it be evocations of Bolivar or indigenous clothing and music. Using state resources, both also attempted to intimidate opposition media and force the broadcast of favorable news and images.

## D. Violence : New and Old

During the last decade, the Andean region has emerged as the most violent in the hemisphere. Insurgencies (and violent state responses) in Colombia and Peru, violent social protests in Venezuela, Ecuador and Bolivia, as well as rapid surge in violent crime rates throughout the region, instilled a growing sense of insecurity and fear in societies that transcended social class and geography. Globalization has played an important part in the acceleration and deepening of violence in the region.

A major source of violence, both insurgent and criminal, has been drug-trafficking in the region. Drug-trafficking is a quintessential globalized enterprise that is multinational in both its organization and operations. In the last three decades it has expanded rapidly as the integration of financial markets and improved transportation and communication networks, have made it more efficient and flexible in meeting market demand. Powerful organized crime syndicates based in Colombia have developed relationships with other criminal groups in the Andes and beyond, creating a transnational criminal network that makes it difficult for any single state to combat (Shelley 1999: 25-51; Krauthausen 1998). Mauricio Rubio refers to the new organizations and ties among drug-traffickers and their collaborators as "perverse social capital," in which crime has created new relationships or built on existing familial networks (Rubio 1997: 805). The violence generated by drug trafficking involves disputes among traffickers, between state agents and traffickers and between those who oppose or refuse to cooperate with drug trafficking. The billions of dollars generated by drug trafficking help corrupt politicians and state officials, undermine the rule of law, distort economic development, increase international pressures (especially from the US) and provide a steady source of income not only for criminal groups, but in the case of Colombia, insurgents and paramilitary death squads that perpetuate cycles of violence. The violence and pressures that drug-trafficking engenders not only weakens the state organizationally, but undermines legitimacy as the state loses its monopoly of force and therefore its ability to provide security to its citizens.

Market liberalization and consumerism played a key role in increasing violence. Market-oriented reforms result in severe dislocations, as noted earlier, where unemployment, poverty and inequality have all increased in the region, even as consumerism has continued to penetrate society. An expanded and ever present mass media continuously demonstrates comfortable lifestyles in the developed world and an ever growing universe of consumer product brands that are tied to success, prestige and social status. As expectations and demands for improved lifestyles increase, particularly among the younger population, the ability to meet those expectations decline, giving rise to frustrations that provides fertile ground for the development of violent behaviors (Briceno-Leon and Zubillaga 2002: 22-23). Such behaviors can translate into criminal violence in an attempt to acquire material goods, or into political violence to protest and overturn the structures that lead to the gap between expectations and economic means.

As societies are wracked by growing violence, state responses have been not only ineffective but also contributed to violence, with security forces engaging in extrajudicial killings, torture or sustaining paramilitary and vigilante groups. Inadequate funding and inhuman conditions in the prison systems of the region remain a fundamental problem as does the slow pace and corruption of the judicial system. Andean states have also been pressured externally to both implement market liberalization and fight drug trafficking aggressively, often hurting a segment of the population—the rural peasantry—that finds itself unable to survive neoliberal agriculture as noted earlier, and finds itself under attack for their illicit crops.

Criminal and political violence have clearly eroded social capital in the Andean region, contributing to growing atomization and social fear and isolation. Private security measures have dramatically increased as the state demonstrates incapacity to curb violence. The privatization of security ranges from an expansion of private security guards for elites, high walls and alarms in middle class neighborhoods and the rise of paramilitary groups, engaging in "social cleansing" against criminals and others identified as "undesirables" (Guerrero 1995). High crime rates and political violence are likely to force people to avoid exposing themselves to public spaces where unexpected dangers may arise or to mingle with strangers. Rather, citizens emphasize familial relationships and private spaces that are well protected and considered safe. Often, curfews imposed by the military or police reinforce this behavior. In Colombia and Peru, insurgents attacked infrastructure, including telephone and electric lines, as well as setting up road-blocks, intimidating people and making it difficult to maintain communication.

The direct targeting of a variety of social organizations by violent groups has become all too common in the region. In Colombia and Peru, insurgents and paramilitaries targeted NGOs, local community groups, and labor and peasant federations that refused to cooperate with them, creating a stark choice for members between participating and running the risk of physical harm or else withdrawing their participation. Drug traffickers tend to view community associations as hostile and will target them unless they can be bought-off. Moreover, political leaders often play on the insecurities of a population, in what one analyst termed the "populism of fear" casting themselves as anti-system actors who criticize the political system's inability to provide security and promising to introduce "tough" reforms that often violate democratic norms (Chevigny 2003: 77). The continued focus of the media and politicians on insecurity merely deepens the sense of fear in the population and further contributes to declines in social capital.

## E. Globalization and Social Capital in the Andes: Paradoxes and Contradictions

This section has provided a brief overview of how globalization has shaped what are by far the most important political characteristics of the Andean region during the 1990s. What can these characteristics tell us about the impact of globalization on social capital in the region? The trends reviewed above appear to point in two different directions. The rise of indigenous movements and their growing political organization, along with the continued extension of new social movements founded in the 1970s and 1980s point to a clear transformation of social capital and identity in the region. Class and ideological movements have given way to ethnicity and concerns regarding the quality of democracy and social conditions: gender equality, community participation, the environment, health and nutrition. This should not be surprising insofar as it parallels developments elsewhere in the world. Still, even if the character of social capital has been transformed, that does not necessarily mean that social capital is necessarily "strong" or even "strengthening" in the region. As noted earlier, social capital is not immutable. Indeed it is doubtful whether measures of "strong" vs. "weak" social capital are useful. As Huntington noted in his chapter in the now famous Trilateral Commission report on democracy and participation, surges in participatory experiences tend to by cyclical (Crozier *et al.* 1975: 83-85). Nonetheless, much more study is required to compare the current state of associational ties, both quantitative and qualitative, with previous experiences in the region to arrive at more solid conclusions regarding the sustainability of social capital.

The two other characteristics of Andean politics reviewed in this section, the surge in violence and the rise of civilian authoritarians, suggest the second outcome from globalization, namely, atomization and alienation. Both outcomes are built on the fears and insecurities provoked by globalization processes and are reminiscent of Ignazi's observations on the emergence of extreme rightist movements in Europe. Whether these trends will persist in this decade is unclear. Newly elected presidents in Ecuador, Bolivia and Colombia have confronted escalating violence and protests, but have thus far not turned to the sort of authoritarian practices adopted in Peru and Venezuela. Still, the weak institutionalization of democratic norms in the region, in contrast to Europe, means there is less of a safety buffer to authoritarian temptations.

## CONCLUSIONS : IMPLICATIONS FOR DEMOCRACY IN THE ANDEAN REGION AND BEYOND

Each of the social capital outcome scenarios from globalization brings with them a set of challenges for democratic governance. Increased alienation and atomization make it more difficult to convince people that their interests are tied to others, inhibiting sustained collective action. As individuals seek personal gains or privileged access over social solidarity and civic engagement, the responsibilities of democratic citizenship are undermined. At the same time, political appeals to individual self-interest instead of to notions of the public good, lay the basis for demagoguery and scapegoating. Throughout the Andes, it has become all too common for officials to blame shantytown dwellers, the poor or those with darker skin tones for rising crime rates in many cities, inciting people to racism, classism and even vigilante justice. Political systems have long endured some of these practices. The danger arises when these behaviors predominate, increasing polarization and intolerance. Reduced social capital tears apart and weakens civil society, and with fewer citizens engaged in civil society associations, democratization is ultimately threatened. As Stepan and Linz note :

> A robust civil society, with the capacity to generate political alternatives and to monitor government and state can help transitions get started, help resist reversals, help push transitions to their completion, help consolidate, and help deepen democracy. At all stages of the democratization process, therefore, a lively and independent civil society is invaluable (Linz *et. al.* 1996: 9).

The second scenario of social capital outcomes brings its own challenges for democratization. The new issues and identities that a transformation of social capital brings about are unlikely to be reflected in the institutional structures of a political system that were founded at a different moment involving different issues/identities. Political institutions are unlikely to adapt quickly to these transformations and the possibilities of institutional reforms may be limited by the political interests of powerful political and economic elites. Constitutional systems that limit reforms face the challenge of being overwhelmed by new social demands, particularly in societies where democratic norms are not institutionalized. Unresponsive political institutions can result in an increase in an acceleration of unconventional participation, even violence that increases political instability. Many of the analyses of Colombia's guerrilla movements emphasize the exclusionary characteristics of the National Front (1958-74) and succeeding administrations, as a key explanation for their rapid expansion. As Colombian society changed and new civil society movements in both the countryside and cities developed, Colombia's institutional system not only remained closed to new entrants through elaborate rules and clientelist schemes, but the state used repression to eliminate challengers (Restrepo 1992: 273-92). Unresponsive systems can also lead to apathy and disengagement from "formal" politics. Voting declines and party memberships wane as political institutions appear more distant from people's daily lives and part of an "elite" game. Here too there is a danger to democracy, as Norris (1999: 268) points out:

> If the public has little faith in existing channels of representative democracy, they will not mobilize to defend the Russian Duma, the Mexican Camara de Diputados, or the Panamanian Asamblea Legislativa. In such circumstances, it becomes more likely that these institutions may fold against external forces . . . the danger remains that citizens may not stand as a bulwark to defend fledgling democratic institutions, for all their flaws, against authoritarian forces.

A second challenge to democracy posed by the transformation of social capital and identities is that they may lead to closed systems of solidarity that work to exclude and discriminate against other members of society. Ethnic or racial groups can use claims to social solidarity to acquire privileged access to economic resources. In an incisive critique of Putnam's Bowling Alone arguments, Alejandro Portes and Patricia Landolt point out how tight-knit communities and ethnic solidarity among Irish and Italian construction workers prevents the entrance of minorities into the buildings trade in New York City, while in San Francisco's Chinatown, family clans ensure conformity by controlling business opportunities (Portes and Landolt 1996). Where social capital is used to develop privileged access to resources or promote discrimination, it perpetuates inequalities and in the worst case scenarios may lead to ethnic, religious or other social conflicts.

The linkages between social capital and globalization are highly complex and like these phenomena themselves in constant flux. Yet given their implications on society and politics, and more specifically on democracy, it is an area that demands far more attention than it has received. More in-depth quantitative and qualitative studies of the linkages described in this paper are required before a complete assessment of these relationships can be reached. Moreover, further regional and cross-national analyses would be helpful in determining if the empirical trends described in the Andean regional also apply elsewhere.

## References


Albo, Xavier, 2004, Ethnic Identity and Politics in the Central Andes: The Cases of Bolivia, Ecuador and Peru in Jo-Marie Burt & Philip Mauceri (eds.) *Politics in The Andes; Identity, Conflict, Reform.* Pittsburgh: University of Pittsburgh Press.

Benavente, Jose Miguel, 1996, Changes in the Industrial Development of Latin America, *CEPAL Review.* 60.

Bowen, Sally, 2000, *The Fujimori File: Peru and its President, 1990-2000,* Lima: Peru Monitor.

Briceno-Leon, Robert and Zubillaga, Veronica, 2002, Violence and Globalization in Latin America, *Current Sociology.* 50(1).

Brysk, Alison, 2000, *From Tribal Village to Global Village: Indian Rights and International Relations in Latin America,* Stanford: Stanford University Press.

Buitrago, Francisco Leal, 1995, *En Busca de la Estabilidad Perdida,* Bogota: Tercer Mundo.

Burt, Jo-Marie, 2000, *State-Making Against Democracy: The Case of Fujimori's Peru,* In Burt and Mauceri.

Cameron, Maxwell and Mauceri, Philip, 1997, *The Peruvian Labyrinth: Polity, Society, Economy,* University Park: Penn State University Press.

Carnoy, Martin, 1997, Multinationals in a Changing World Economy: Whither the Nation-State? In Martin Carnoy *et. al. The New Global Economy in the Information Age,* University Park: Penn State University Press.

Carroll, Thomas and Bebbington, Anthony, 2000, Peasant Federations and Rural Development Policies in the Andes, *Policy Sciences.* 435.

Chalmers, Douglas *et. al.* 1997, *The New Politics of Inequality in Latin America, NY:* Oxford University Press.

Chevigny, Paul, 2003, The Populism of Fear: Politics of Crime in the Americas, *Punishment and Society.* 5(1).

Crozier, M., Huntington, S. and Watnuki, J., 1975, *The Crisis of Democracy,* NY: Trilateral Commission.

De Haan, L.J., 2000, Globalization, Localization and Sustainable Livelihood, *Sociologia Ruralis,* 40(3), 339-66.

Degregori, Carlos Ivan, 2000, *La Decade de la Antipolitica,* Lima: IEP.

Ekins, Paul and Newby, Les, 1998, Sustainable Wealth Creation at the Local Level in an Age of Globalization, *Regional Studies,* 32(9), 863-72.

Ellner, Steven and Hellinger, Daniel (eds.) 2002, *Venezuelan Politics in the Chavez Era,* Boulder: Lynne Reiner.

Escobar, Arturo and Alvarez, Sonia (eds.) 1992, *The Making of Social Movements in Latin America: Identity, Strategy and Democracy,* Boulder: Westview Press.

Finifter, Ada W., 1972, *Alienation and the Social System,* NY: John Wiley.

Fox, Jonathan and Gershman, John, 2000, The World Bank and Social Capital: Lessons from Ten Rural Development Projects in the Philippines and Mexico, *Policy Sciences,* 399.

Franko, Patrice, 2003, *The Puzzle of Latin American Development, 2nd Edition,* Lanham, MD: Rowman and Littlefield.

Friedman, Thomas, 2000, *The Lexus and the Olive Tree: Understanding Globalization,* NY: Knopf Publishing.

Gott, Richard, 2000, *In the Shadow of the Liberator: Hugo Chavez and the Transformation of Venezuela*. London: Verso Press.

Guerrero, Sandra Mateus, 1995, *Limpieza Social: La Guerra Contral la Indigencia.*
Bogota: Tema de Hoy.

Habermas, Jurgen, 1973, *Legitimation Crisis*, Boston: Beacon Press, 44, 128-29.

Held, David *et al.*, 1999, *Global Transformations: Politics, Economics and Culture*, Stanford: Stanford University Press.

Ignazi, Piero, 1996, The Crisis of Parties and the Rise of New Political Parties, *Party Politics*, 2(4).

Inglehart, Ronald, 1997, *Modernization and Post Modernization: Cultural, Economic and Political Change in 43 Societies*, Princeton: Princeton University Press.

Korzeniewicz, Roberto and Smith, William, 2000, Poverty, Inequality and Growth in Latin America: Searching for the High Road to Globalization, *Latin American Research Review*, 35(3).

Krauthausen, Ciro, 1998, *Padrinos y Mercaderes: Crimen Organizado en Italiay, Colombia*, Bogota: Planeta.

Lind, Amy, 2000, *Engendering Andean Politics: Womens Organizations, Neoliberal Reform and Political Change*, In Burt and Mauceri.

Linz, Juan J. and Stepan, Alfred, 1996, *Problems of Democratic Transition and Consolidation*: Southern Europe, South America and post-Communist Europe, Baltimore: Johns Hopkins University Press.

Lopez-Maya, Margarita and Lander, Luis, 2000, *The Struggle for Hegemony in Venezuela: Violence, Popular Protest and the Future of Democracy*, In Burt and Mauceri.

Mathews, Jessica T., 1997, Power Shift, *Foreign Affairs*. 76(1), 50-67.

McCoy, Jennifer and Smith, William, 1995, Democratic Disequilibrium in Venezuela, *Journal of InterAmerican Studies and World Affairs*.

Norris, Pippa, 1999, The Growth of Critical Citizens? In Pippa Norris (ed.), *Critical Citizens: Global Support for Democratic Governance*, Oxford: Oxford University Press.

Norris, Pippa, 2001, *Digital Divide: Information Poverty, and the Internet Worldwide*, NY: Cambridge University Press.

Offe, Claus, 1982, New Social Movements: Challenging the Boundaries of Institutional Politics, *Social Research*, Vol. 52.

Ohmae, Kenichi, 1993, The Rise of the Region State, *Foreign Affairs*. 72(2), 78-88.

Pappenheim, Fritz, 1959, *The Alienation of Modern Man*. NY: Monthly Review Press.

Pizzaro, Eduardo, 1999, Las Terceras Fuerzas en Colombia Hoy: Entre la Fragmentacio y la Impotencia, In Ricardo Penaranda and Javier Guerrero (eds.), *De las Armas a la Politica*. Bogota: Tercer Mundo.

Portes, Alejandro and Landolt, Patricia, 1996, Unsolved Mysteries: The Tocqueville Files II: The Downside of Social Capital, *The American Prospect*, 7(26).

Putnam, Robert, 1995, Bowling Alone: America's Declining Social Capital, *Journal of Democracy*, 6(1), 67-78.

Putnam, Robert 2000, *Bowling Alone: The Collapse and Revival of American Community;* NY: Simon and Schuster.

Reich, Robert B., 1992, *The Work of Nations*, NY: Vintage Press.

Restrepo, Luis Alberto, 1992, The Crisis of the Current Political Regime and its Possible Outcomes, In Charles Bergquist *et. al. Violence in Colombia: The Contemporary Crisis in Historical Perspective*, Wilmington: Scholarly Resourses.

Rubio, Mauricio, 1997, Pervers Social Capital: Some Evidence from Colombia, *Journal of Economic Issues*, 31(3).

Shelley, Louise, 1999, Transnational Organized Crime: The New Authoritarianism, In H. Richard Friman and Peter Andreas (eds.), *The Illicit Global Economy and State Power*, Lanham, MD: Rowman and Littlefield.

Silverstone-Scher, Melina, 2001, *Ethnopolitics in Ecuador: Indigenous Rights and the Strengthening of Democracy*, Coral Gables: North-South Center Press.

Slaughter, Ann-Marie, 1997, The Real New World Order, *Foreign Affairs*, 76(5), 183-98.

Stiglitz, Joseph, 2002, *Globalization and its Discontents*, NY: W.W. Norton.

Tarrow, Sidney, 1994, *Power in Movement: Social Movements, Collective Action and Politics*, Cambridge: Cambridge University Press, 195.

Thrupp, Lori Ann, 1995, *Bittersweet Harvest for Global Supermarkets: Challenges in Latin America's Agricultural Export Boom*, Washington D.C.: World Resource Institute.

Touraine, Alain, 1981, *The Voice and the Eye: An Analysis of Social Movements*, Cambridge: Cambridge University Press.

Trigilia, C., 2001, Social Capital and Local Development, *European Journal of Social Theory*, 4(4), 427-43.

Wood, Cynthia A., 2003, Adjustment with a Women's Face: Gender and Macro-economic Policy at the World Bank, In Susan E. Eckstein and Timothy.

Wickham-Crowley (eds.), *Struggles for Social Rights in Latin America*, N.Y., Routledge.

# 11

# Does Democratization Work in Argentina? Human Development and Governance (1989-2005)

DORA ORLANSKY, LEONARDO GROTTOLA AND MORA KANTOR

## INTRODUCTION

After the hyperinflationary crisis of 1989, Argentina launched an unprecedented state reform process which radically transformed the role of the state in the economic development. These reforms categorically rejected the former "import substitution" development strategy. The new reform agenda was consistent with the prevailing main-stream ideas in economics—the so-called "Conventional Wisdom" or "Orthodoxy"—supported by International Financial Institutions (IFIs), namely the IMF and the World Bank, and consisted of a bunch of policies popularly known as the "Washington Consensus" (Williamson 1993).

However, Argentina did not embrace "Washington Consensus" (WC) completely. Argentina was never able to pursue a robustly disciplined fiscal policies in 1990s. The exchange rate system adopted under Convertibility Law (peso pegged to US dollar) was far from the explicitly recommended flexible exchange rate regimes (Williamson 1993).

However, despite the absence of fiscally disciplined policies, Argentina's reform process can be considered as an example of following the WC policies, not only because IFIs recognized it as such in 1998, but also because the core elements of the reform package, summed up in the trilogy *stabilize-privatize-liberalize* (Rodrik 2006), were drastically introduced.

## ARGENTINA IN THE 1990S : PERFORMANCE OF DEVELOPMENT INDICATORS

The 2001 Argentine crisis and failure to achieve sustainable growth—even after a reform process, which supposedly had removed the barriers for growth introduced during the protectionist era of "import substitution"—cast a shadow of doubt about the plausibility of reforms. In fact, they failed to unleash the forces of development. The market-oriented reforms came under serious questioning after a major economic crisis (2001) in a country formerly presented as an example of their success.

Stiglitz (2003: 8-10) and Rodrik (2004b: 1-2 and 2004c: 3) observe that Latin America market-oriented reforms have failed to generate growth, and are, mostly linked with the increase in inequality and poverty. Under "import substitution" policy, growth was almost two times faster than under reforms. In this sense, there was convergence with developed countries, divergence starting circa 1980. The argument that sustains that reforms needed time to succeed is discussed by Stiglitz who claims that results were even worse in the second half of the 1990s, a fact that led the CEPAL to call the 1997-2002 period as the "semi-lost decade" (Rodrik 2004b: 1-2 and 2004c: 3, Stiglitz 2003: 8-10).

During the early period of reforms (1989 to 1993), almost all "development" indicators show an improvement. There was growth in GDP. High unemployment, which persisted for over a decade, improved only slightly. However the poverty level fell from 42.5% in 1990 to 16.1% in 1994. Income Distribution Gap (quotient between average income of superior and inferior deciles) and GINI Coefficient show a similar performance. In both cases there was an initial reduction of inequality between 1989 and 1992.

The second period of reforms started in 1993 and ended in 2002. Initially upward growth was registered after the 1995 Tequila crisis. It was over by 1998, the last year of moderate growth (3.9%) before the 1999-2002 slump. The critical 1999-2002 stage saw a 20% GDP reduction. The period witnessed one of the most severe economic and political crisis in Argentine history, which included simultaneous currency devaluation and debt default by the state. Unemployment rose from 9.9% in 1993 to 21.5% in 2002 (after the crisis, U rate lowered from 21.5% in 2001-02 to 12.8% in 2006). Poverty rose steadily from 1994 (16.1%) to 2001 (32.7%). In 2003 a record level of 51.7% of the population was below the poverty line. Indicators of income distribution show a worsening of the situation. The Income Distribution Gap (Quotient between average income of top and bottom deciles) enlarged the gap to 38 in 2002. GINI Coefficient started to deteriorate in 1992, which was quite high in Argentine history (0.418), to 0.461 in 1995, reaching 0.480 during 2000-02 and 0.523 in 2003 2[nd] semester. The Great Buenos Aires, GBA agglomerate illustrates the magnitude of the crisis and its devastating effects on a country historically known to have egalitarian income distribution. It shouldn't be forgotten that 1974 GINI Coefficient was 0.322, a figure equivalent to those of developed countries.

## ARGENTINA IN THE 1990S: "REFORM-BASED" DEVELOPMENT STRATEGY'S FAILURE: SOME POSSIBLE EXPLANATIONS

Growth performance from reform to crisis was unstable and unsustained; a very early stage of high rates growth that led many to believe that Argentine economy had once and for all taken-off was followed by a long-lasting recession that ended in the virtual collapse of the economy. Unemployment remained persistently high since 1993 and even during "good" GDP's evolution years. Poverty, although reduced to a third of its 1989's rate in 1994, started to increase, reaching above 20%, even before recession. Income distribution became gradually more unequal since 1993. Growth during the 1990s was accompanied by a permanently high level of unemployment and was unable to reduce poverty, let alone reduce inequality.

According to Stiglitz (2003: 16-19), Latin America's early 1990s unsustained growth can be explained as (i) a period of "catch up," familiar to those countries recovering from recession. Argentina experienced a 3% GDP reduction during 1981-90 and the economy deepened its recession in 1989 as a result of the hyperinflationary crisis; (ii) the stimulus derived from enormous (mostly short-run) capital entry, which financed a consumption boom (consumption repressed or postponed during hyperinflation), with the consequent impact of foreign indebtment not oriented to high-profitable investment. Big amounts of capital entry were partly due to the massive privatization process undertaken during reform era; (iii) an inadequate national accounting over-estimated growth led to a false image of success during the first years of reform. *Net National Product* (NNP, Stiglitz 2003) would have reflected in a more accurate manner the real situation than the usual GDP-based accounting system.

Initial improvement in poverty reduction and in income distribution indicators is attributable almost totally to the positive effects of the dramatic fall of inflation experienced as a result of the anchoring effect of Convertibility Law (1991). Nonetheless, once distortions by high inflation were removed, poverty and income distribution indicators started to worsen. Convertibility proved to be an efficient device in reducing inflation. It gained legitimacy among all social classes. Not only hyperinflation 1989 but also previous high inflation during the seventies and the eighties provide an explanation for such support. It is important to bear in mind the convertibility's high degree of legitimacy to understand 2001 crisis.

## "INSTITUTIONS MATTER" AND "GOOD GOVERNANCE" DISCOURSE

Once Washington Consensus agenda started to show some setbacks, failures or "side-effects" (in those cases still considered successful, like the Argentine one), IFIs started to amend the original reform set. The new agenda was not cleared of any policies but rather had added new items to its laundry list, which led Dani Rodrik to call it "Augmented Washington Consensus" (Rodrik 2004b). Common to these new items is their relevance to countries' institutional settings. The role of institutions, ignored by the Washington Consensus, which focused on getting the macro-economic fundamentals right, and privatizing, deregulating and liberalizing, became increasingly important in "development" policy proposals; so much so that it turned into "conventional wisdom", summed up in the phrase "institutions matter," as Fukuyama in a recent book rightly pointed out (Fukuyama 2004: 41-42). Developing countries should get institutions right in order to achieve successful reforms.

Douglass North renewed the neo-classical theoretical framework by stressing the role of institutions in economics (North 1989). The Northian paradigm strongly influenced the IFIs' institutionalist perspective. Institutions' relevance for development was also emphasized by heterodox economists like Stiglitz—who was *undoubtedly* inspired by the 1997 Asian crisis (Stiglitz 1998a)—and Rodrik (Rodrik 1999). Another institutionalist-heterodox economist, Ha-Joon Chang, argued that "good governance" discourse was adopted by the "orthodox" and the IFIs to justify the failure of its policies (Chang 2005: 2).

Chang's remarks lead us to introduce ourselves into the following section, in which we study the arguments of some of the main Washington Consensus' critics from a heterodox-institutionalist point of view.

## WASHINGTON CONSENSUS AND ITS CRITICS

Washington Consensus' academic critics have had a louder voice since the 1997 East Asian financial crisis, which exposed the drawbacks of the liberalization of capital markets. Their voice became even louder after the Argentine 2001-02 collapse. Those dissatisfied with "the policies advanced by the Washington Consensus" would agree to consider that they "... are not complete, and (...) sometimes misguided" and that development goals should be "broadened (...) to include other goals such as sustainable development, egalitarian development and democratic development" (Stiglitz 1998a: 1). This paragraph on "the critics" will be largely based on the academic work of Ha-Joon Chang, Dani Rodrik and Joseph Stiglitz, may be today's most insightful proponents of alternatives to Washington Consensus. Our aim will be to describe the main aspects of the "emerging consensus" among "the critics" in order to determine whether their perspective can contribute to the explanation of the Argentine case evolution, especially after the 2001 collapse.

## SUCCESSFUL COUNTRIES DIDN'T FOLLOW WASHINGTON CONSENSUS' PRESCRIPTIONS

The strongest case for those uncomfortable with Washington Consensus ideology is that most successful developing countries are far from being a prototype of adherence to the Consensus policies. The East Asian pattern (the "developmental" state, see Chang and Evans 2000 for an extensive use of the concept to explain the Korean case) had been the traditional example of successful heterodox policies. Stiglitz stresses that East Asian countries' development provides the strongest reasons to abandon Washington Consensus, given the fact that the group of countries that managed to reach what was perhaps the most successful development in history didn't adhere to the policies then canonized in the Consensus (Stiglitz 1998a: 2).

"That development strategy (*Washington Consensus*) stands in marked contrast to the successful strategies pursued in East Asia, where the *development state* took an active role" (Stiglitz 2004b: 1).

The fact that China, Vietnam, and India are among the most successful growth performers gathers more evidence in favour of heterodoxy. As Dani Rodrik points out: "these high-growth countries have marched to their own drummers, and the fit between their policies and the conventional policy agenda is awkward at best. China and Vietnam are of course the chief exhibits here. (...) And India, despite the folk wisdom that relates its growth acceleration to the liberalization of 1991, actually began its take-off a decade earlier, during the early 1980s and under heavy protectionism" (Rodrik 2004b: 2).

## ONE SIZE DOESN'T FIT ALL (SPECIFICITY OF INSTITUTIONS)

Institutional diversity's importance is strongly emphasized by the heterodox literature: highest growing developing countries have followed "deviated" policies and created institutional frameworks suited to local conditions.

The experience of China, a country which managed to promote investment without ensuring private property rights, has been highly influential for those who hold critical views towards Washington Consensus. By contrast, the Russian reform process, which included massive privatization and the guaranteeing of western-style private property rights, ended in a major crisis.

The motto goes as follows: the same function (we'd rather say "goal" or "objective" to avoid a misleading "functionalist" reading) can be achieved through different institutional forms in each society (or in the same society at different times) (Chang 2005: 4 and Rodrik 2006: 11). According to the critics, Washington Consensus (its augmented version, too), denies institutional diversity and consist of a "laundry-list" (an item by item enumeration) that denies institutional diversity under the assumption that the same policy agenda can work in all contexts (Rodrik 2004b: 4). The importance assigned to specificity leads these authors to examine the relationship between institutions prevailing in developed and developing countries. Since "good" institutions are "quite idiosyncratic and context-specific" (Rodrik 2004a: 6), adopting developed countries' institutions without adapting them to local conditions may not promote but hinder development ("the institutional repertoire available in the advanced countries may be inappropriate to the needs of the society in question," Rodrik 1999: 14). International power relationships assert that (so-called) "best practice" institutions (a set of institutions significantly biased to include Anglo-American ones) should be imposed on *a priori* unwilling developing countries through "governance-related conditionalities" (Chang 2005: 3 and 6). Further elaboration on this point leads to consideration of the "good governance" discourse as a way of preserving the asymmetric *status quo* between developed and developing countries (Chang 2001: 28), which means maintaining an unfair global governance structure.

## CURRENT GLOBAL GOVERNANCE STRUCTURE IS UNFAIR

Global governance institutions have been subject to criticism as a result of their undemocratic rules and the fact that their actions usually tend to favour the interest of developed countries. Of course, procedural matters are related to the quality of the decisions that are made (Stiglitz 2004a: 1 and 9). In fact, "the decision-making structures are a far cry from principles that govern democratic decision-making *within* countries" (Stiglitz 2004a: 8).

Global governance structure's unfairness becomes apparent when observing the rules governing the Bretton Woods institutions, international trade and intellectual property rights:

- *IFIs (International Financial Institutions)*: impose "global standard institutions" upon unwilling countries through "governance-related conditionalities" (Chang 2005: 6) and, due to the fact that votes are allocated on the basis of economic power (not even based on current economic standing) and a single country has veto power (at least in the case of the IMF), those countries exert very little influence not only on decisions that affect them but also on the election of decision-making authorities, which, as a result, become far from accountable (Stiglitz 2004a: 1 and 10).
- *International Trade Rules*: they restrict developing countries' access to markets as a result of the new protectionist mechanisms devised by developed countries (Stiglitz 1998b: 39). For an extensive

analysis of the role of the *WTO (World Trade Organization)*, see Chang and Evans (2000).

- *(IPRs) Intellectual property rights*: its excessive international protection restricts knowledge transmission from the developed to developing world. (Stiglitz 1998b: 40)

## AUGMENTED VERSIONS ARE EX-POST JUSTIFICATIONS OF WASHINGTON CONSENSUS' FAILURE

Critics of Washington Consensus' original version also disapprove of the Augmented one. They focus on the following weaknesses of the "augmenting" strategy: "developed countries in earlier times where institutionally *less* advanced compared to today's developing countries at similar stages of development," which means that "many institutions follow rather than lead, economic development" (Chang 2001: 1-2). Thus it would be tautological to argue that developing countries should be expected to establish institutions that they only can achieve by developing (Rodrik 2004b: 5). Enlarging the original list provides the framework to argue that original policies were right but didn't work because there was something missing; this argument could be repeated after every failure just by adding a new ingredient to the list (Chang 2005: 2; Rodrik 2004b: 5 and Rodrik 2006: 13).

## THE GOVERNMENT HAS AN IMPORTANT ROLE TO PLAY

Washington Consensus policies were based on a rejection of the state's activist role and on the promotion of a minimalist, non-interventionist state. The premise was: governments are worse than markets, the smaller the state the better the state (Stiglitz 1998a: 25). Washington Consensus-inspired reform policies were market-biased. They were unable to keep the adequate balance between state and market and often disregarded the importance of improving the public sector, since they believed in the market's capacity to solve all basic problems of society ("market fundamentalism"). This belief also led them to ignore the role of the state in a sound economy and to support trickle-down theory in spite of its failure (Stiglitz 2003: 21 and 27).

Stiglitz criticizes Washington Consensus' view on the basis of theoretical and empirical foundations.

Market-failure theory provides the arguments for an economic justification of state intervention. Market failure happens when the market is unable to allocate resources efficiently *in Pareto's terms*. Six kinds of market failure have been identified: lack of competition, public goods, externalities, incomplete markets, imperfect information and unemployment. Even if market failures were amended through state intervention and a *Pareto-efficient* resource-allocation were achieved, it might be a very unequal one. So income redistribution is another task the state should undertake once the fact that market-led income distribution can lead to unequal outcomes has been acknowledged (Stiglitz 1992: 74-85).

This alternative perspective regards the government (the state) as a catalyst and as a complement to markets (Stiglitz 1998a: 25). The "question should not be whether a particular activity should be carried on in the public or private sector, but how the two can best complement each other, acting as partners in the development effort" (Stiglitz, 1998b: 25). Government as a complement should both (1) provide resources to the market— which, if left to itself, tends to systematically underprovide in arenas such as human capital (public education, access to funding) and technology (investment in the production and adoption of new technology) (Stiglitz 1998a: 26-27); and (2) create an enabling environment for the private sector and fight poverty (Stiglitz, 1998b: 26).

The East Asian miracle is again the decisive event for Washington Consensus' critics when considering the issue of government intervention. East Asian countries showed that a successful development process, involving both poverty reduction and widespread improvements in living standards, could be achieved with the government playing a large role (Stiglitz, 1998b: 10).

## IT'S IMPORTANT TO FOCUS ON COUNTRY-SPECIFIC "BINDING CONSTRAINTS"

A development strategy that is to avoid Washington Consensus' flaws should concentrate on identifying a country's "binding constraints," which prevent the economy from growing: "countries do not need an extensive set of institutional reforms in order to start growing. The trick is to be able to identify the binding constraint on economic growth at the relevant moment in time" (Rodrik 2004a: 11). This "diagnostic approach" distinguishes two different stages: the first one in which growth is initiated (ignites, is stimulated) with minimal changes in the institutional framework and the second, subsequent one, in which the initial "growth acceleration" has to be sustained in order to follow a development path. In this second stage, high growth and institutional change feed on each other (Rodrik 2004a: 10). Only once country-specific "binding constraints" have been identified can a set of policies to overcome them be designed. If this set of policies works and manages to produce a "growth acceleration," then the process should be institutionalized in order to foster sustainability and self-reinforcing growth. Growth should be institutionalized but growth is simultaneously a pre-requisite for institutional change (Rodrik 2004c: 12 and Rodrik 2006: 17).

## ARGENTINA AFTER THE 2001-02 CRISIS

In following analysis we have used *Growth Diagnostics* approach (Haussman, Rodrik and Velasco 2005) to an explanation of 2001 Argentine crisis. Our aim will be to make use of some conceptual developments provided by Rodrik's theoretical framework: (i) "Binding constraints" as obstacles that should be removed from a country to resume growth, and (ii) the distinction between two stages, the first in which growth initiates without great institutional changes, and the second in which growth and institutional change feed each other letting major institutional transformation happen (Rodrik 2004a: 10-11; 2004c: 12 and 2006: 17).

The 2001-02 crisis brought the abandonment of Convertibility Law and a subsequent currency devaluation that led to a peso quotation (in terms of US dollars) of a third of its value under Convertibility Law and the implementation of a new exchange rate regime that could be termed as an intervened floatation. Since the second quarter of 2002 the economic cycle reverted. The GDP has grown at an average annual rate of 9% from 2003 on, output not only reaching but also surpassing 1998's GDP (highest peak before recession) in 2005, only four years after the crisis (Table 11.1). This Argentine recovery poses following questions about the causes of this "growth acceleration": Is it just a period of "catch up" or a natural consequence of favorable international context of high prices for Argentine commodities and low international interest rates? Or is it the removal of the "most binding constraint"?

The "catch up" factor cannot be dismissed as part of the explanation due to the magnitude of 2001 collapse. However, the fact that "output exceeds the pre-episode peak level of income" (Rodrik, Hausmann and Pritchett 2005: 2) (Table 11.1) rules out the hypothesis of mere recovery.

In order to examine the second proposition which emphasizes the influence of international context, a set of some of the most important commodities exported by Argentina has been selected to observe the evolution of its prices in the 90s and during the post-crisis period (Figure 11.1). Data on the international interest rate performance in recent years (considering USA-FF Interest Rate as indicator) is in Table 11.2.

The data on commodities prices provides a positive correlation between the Argentine economic cycle and agricultural commodities prices during 1993-2005 (Figure 11.1). Crude oil prices behave differently, softly fluctuating in the 1990s (15-20 US $ per barrel), reaching at their lowest in 1998 (13 US $ per barrel) to US $ 53 per barrel unprecedented price in 2005. The fact that crude oil has increased its share among Argentine exports in recent years and benefits from increasingly exorbitant prices since 2002 is a new reality that qualifies as an exceptional contribution to today's growth. However, this is not the case for the other commodities studied that also enjoyed high prices during the early 1990s. If we were to accept that current growth acceleration is only due to favorable agricultural commodities, we should explain early 90s growth the same way. Hence, if such a "determinist" point of view was adopted, Argentine GDP fluctuations would be exclusively caused by the variation in commodities prices without acknowledging the impact of other factors. Hence, commodities' price, which experienced a significant improvement since 2001, is influential but not determinant.

TABLE 11.1

**Gross Domestic Product in Argentina—From Recession to Recovery**

| *Year* | *1998* | *1999* | *2000* | *2001* | *2002(*)* | *2003(*)* | *2004(*)* | *2005(*)* |
|---|---|---|---|---|---|---|---|---|
| (1) | (2) | (3) | (4) | (5) | (6) | (7) | (8) | (9) |
| GDP (thousand pesos) | 288.123.305 | 278.369.014 | 276.172.685 | 263.996.674 | 235.235.597 | 256.023.462 | 279.141.289 | 304.815.326 |
| GDP Annual Percentage Variation | 3.9 % | -3.4 % | -0.8 % | -4.4 % | -10.9 % | 8.8% | 9% | 9.2% |
| GDP per capita (1993 pesos) (**) | 8.000 | 7.600 | 7.500 | 7.100 | 6.300 | 6.800 | 7.300 | 7.900 |

*Source* : INDEC, figures at 1993 prices (*), provincial estimates (**), calculated on the basis of INDEC's population estimates.

FIG. 11.1
**INDEC's Population Estimates**

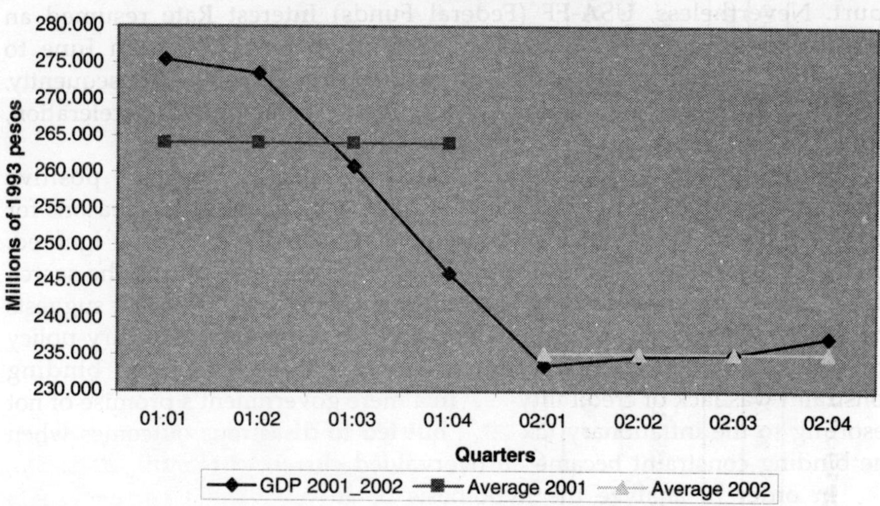


GDP anual percentage variation statistics show a 10.9% fall in 2002. It is the result of a comparison between average GDPs of the previous and following year (in this case, 2001 and 2002). So a 10.9% descent in 2002 means that average 2002 GDP was 10.9% smaller than 2001's. However, it doesn't mean the 10.9% drop happend in 2002. When observing quarterly information for 2001-02 it can be found that most of GDP's shrinking took place in 2001 (convertibility's last year) and that 2002 is in fact the first year of recovery (GDP started to grow in 2002's second quarter). In spite of recovery, average 2002 GDP kept well below 2001's, in part due to the magnitude of the previous year's decline, which explains the 10.9% fall measured by statistics.

*Source* : Damill, M. (2003) : "La reaction cumple un ano", Buenos Aires, Supleento Economico, 6 de abril de 2003 (translation by the authors).

TABLE 11.2
**USA-FF (Federal Funds) Interest Rate 2000-06 (monthly)**

| | *Jan.* | *Feb.* | *Mar.* | *Apr.* | *May* | *Jun.* | *Jul.* | *Aug.* | *Sept.* | *Oct.* | *Nov.* | *Dec.* |
|---|---|---|---|---|---|---|---|---|---|---|---|---|
| 2000 | 5.5 | 5.75 | 6 | 6 | 6.5 | 6.5 | 6.5 | 6.5 | 6.5 | 6.5 | 6.5 | 6.5 |
| 2001 | 5.5 | 5.5 | 5 | 4.5 | 4 | 3.75 | 3.75 | 3.5 | 3 | 2.5 | 2 | 1.75 |
| 2002 | 1.75 | 1.75 | 1.75 | 1.75 | 1.75 | 1.75 | 1.75 | 1.75 | 1.75 | 1.75 | 1.25 | 1.25 |
| 2003 | 1.25 | 1.25 | 1.25 | 1.25 | 1.25 | 1 | 1 | 1 | 1 | 1 | 1 | 1 |
| 2004 | 1 | 1 | 1 | 1 | 1 | 1.25 | 1.25 | 1.5 | 1.75 | 1.75 | 2 | 2.25 |
| 2005 | 2.25 | 2.5 | 2.75 | 2.75 | 3 | 3.25 | 3.25 | 3.5 | 3.75 | 3.75 | 4 | 4.25 |
| 2006 | 4.5 | 4.5 | 4.75 | 4.75 | | | | | | | | |

*Source* : Economy Ministry on the basis of US Federal Reserve Data.

International interest rate (USA-Federal Funds Interest Rate) lowered in mid-2001. The reduction was more pronounced since September 2001 and led to a rate of only 1% from June 2003 to May 2004. Such a low international interest rate must have played a part in the expansion initial spurt. Nevertheless, USA-FF (Federal Funds) Interest Rate resumed an upward tendency in June 2004. In fact, it's been 5.25% from June to September 2006. In spite of that, Argentina kept growing. Consequently, international interest rate is not a determinant of this growth acceleration, either.

Although the post-recession "catch-up" process and the positive international context described above shouldn't be dismissed as reasons for today's growth, the country's institutional framework cannot be ignored. This leads us to the "diagnostic approach" and, consequently to the search of the "most binding constraint" impeding growth. Rodrik himself suggests the answer: "Argentina's currency board, which removed monetary policy from the hands of the government, worked well when the binding constraint was lack of credibility . . ." in a mere government's promise of not resorting to the inflationary tax ". . . but led to disastrous outcomes when the binding constraint became an overvalued currency" (Rodrik 2006: 7).

In order to analyze the hypothesis of an overvalued currency as a binding constraint our analysis will include the following variables: relative prices between services and goods (as an indicator for relative prices between non-tradable and tradable goods), real exchange rates (USA, Brazil, Eurozone), exports and imports and current account (Figures 11.2, 11.3, and 11.4). Data suggest that convertibility led to an overvalued real exchange rate (*vis a vis* some of Argentina's main trade partners we take into account:

Fig. 11.2

**Commodities Prices 1993-05**

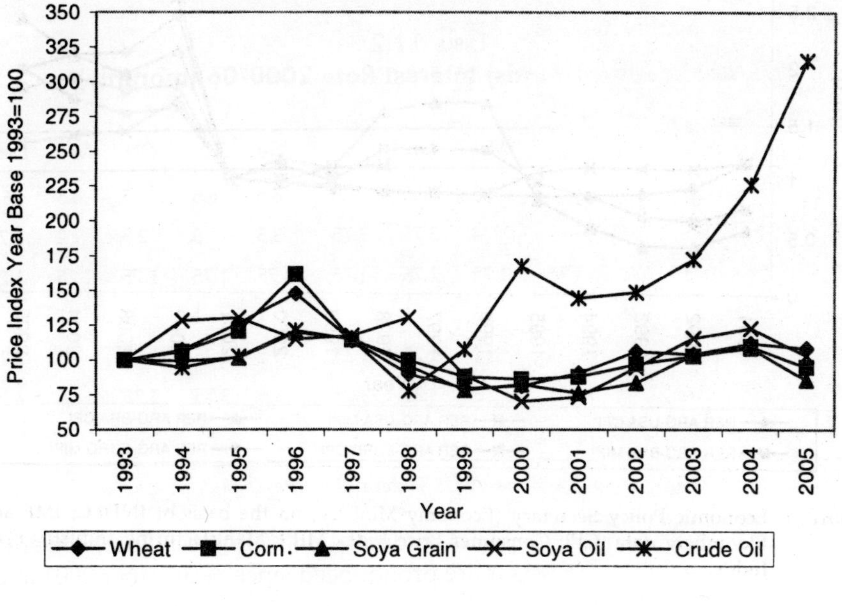

FIG. 11.3
**Relative Prices in Argentina (Services/Goods), 1995-2005**

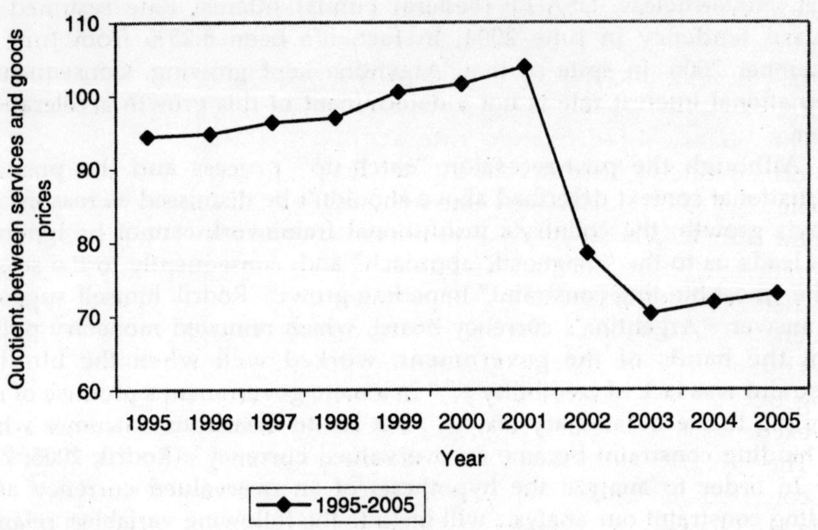


*Source* : Economic Policy Secretary (Economy Ministry) on the basis of INDEC data. 1999 = 100 Year base.

FIG. 11.4
**Real Exchange Rates**

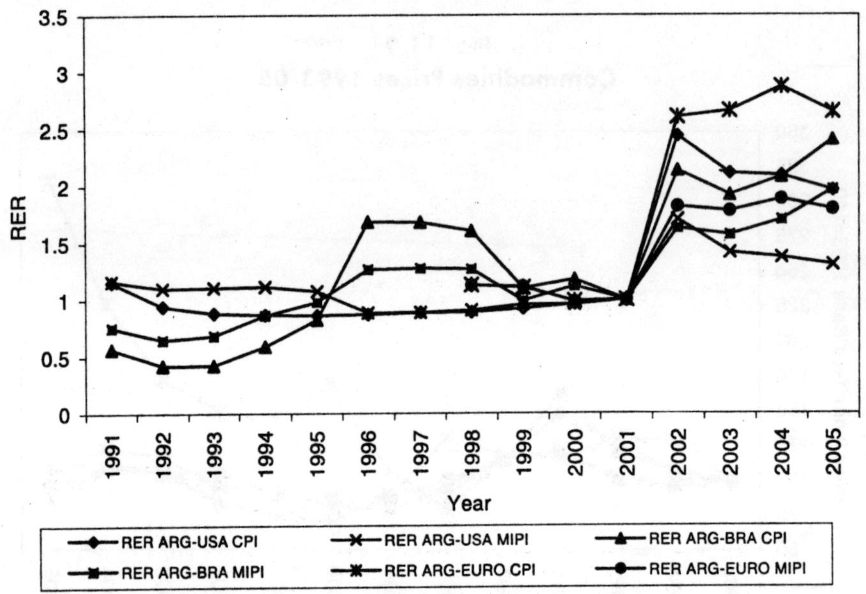


*Source* : Economic Policy Secretary (Economy Ministry) on the basis of INDEC, IMF and Bloomberg data. CPI: Consumer Price Index MIPI: Manufacturing Industry Price Index.

USA, Brazil, and Eurozone countries); a relative prices structure which privileged services over goods (non-tradable over tradable), certainly not the right incentive for an export-led growth strategy. Consequently, Argentina experienced a continuous rise in imports not matched by its exports, resulting into a trade imbalance and a permanent current account deficit.

The change of exchange rate regime that took place in 2002 transformed relative price structure to one that rewards goods over services, tradable over non-tradable, and implied a real exchange rate depreciation. The new situation encourages export-led growth and import substitution. In fact, trade balance and current account surplus were achieved and exports have risen 56% in 2002-05. It can be observed (Table 11.3) that exports augmentation is a genuine one, not exclusively attributable to a rise in their prices but also to increase in quantities exported. Manufacturing industry's strong output growth since 2003 (Table 11.4) supports the assumption of new exchange rate regime's beneficial effects on industry.

The evolution of investment is another variable that should be taken into consideration to evaluate the sustainability of growth in Argentina (Table 11.5). Recession caused a 56.3% fall in investment between 1998-2002 and a rise in investment of 127.9% took place between 2002-05. When

TABLE 11.3

**Indexes of Value, Prices and Quantities of Goods Exports**

| *Year* | *Indexes* | | |
|---|---|---|---|
| | *Value* | *Price* | *Quantity* |
| 1998 | 201.6 | 100.3 | 201.0 |
| 1999 | 177.7 | 89.1 | 199.5 |
| 2000 | 200.8 | 98.0 | 204.9 |
| 2001 | 202.3 | 94.7 | 213.7 |
| 2002 | 196.0 | 91.0 | 215.3 |
| 2003 | 225.7 | 99.7 | 226.4 |
| 2004 | 263.4 | 109.1 | 241.3 |
| 2005 | 305.0 | 110.7 | 275.5 |

*Source* : INDEC Year base 1993=100 (*) Provisional figures.

TABLE 11.4

**Manufacturing Industry Output Annual Percentage Variation**

| *1994* | *1995* | *1996* | *1997* | *1998* | *1999* | *2000* | *2001* | *2002(*)* | *2003(*)* | *2004(*)* | *2005(*)* |
|---|---|---|---|---|---|---|---|---|---|---|---|
| 4.5% | -7.2% | 6.5% | 9.2% | 1.8% | -7.9% | -3.8% | -7.4% | -11% | 16% | 12% | 7.7% |

*Source* : INDEC, based on figures at 1993 prices (*) Provisional estimations.

TABLE 11.5

**Investment in Argentina : 1994-2005**

| *Year* | *1994* | *1995* | *1996* | *1997* | *1998* | *1999* | *2000* | *2001* | *2002(*)* | *2003(*)* | *2004(*)* | *2005(*)* |
|---|---|---|---|---|---|---|---|---|---|---|---|---|
| *(1)* | *(2)* | *(3)* | *(4)* | *(5)* | *(6)* | *(7)* | *(8)* | *(9)* | *(10)* | *(11)* | *(12)* | *(13)* |
| Investment Annual Percentage Variation | 13.7% | -13.1% | 8.9% | 17.7% | 6.5% | -12.6% | -6.8% | -15.7% | -36.4% | 38.2% | 34.4% | 22.7% |
| Investment as a percentage of GDP | 20.5% | 18.3% | 18.9% | 20.6% | 21.1% | 19.1% | 17.9% | 15.8% | 11.3% | 14.3% | 17.7% | 19.8% |

*Source* : INDEC, based figures at 1993 prices.

(*) Provisional estimations.

FIG. 11.5
**Exports, Imports and Current Account in Argentina**

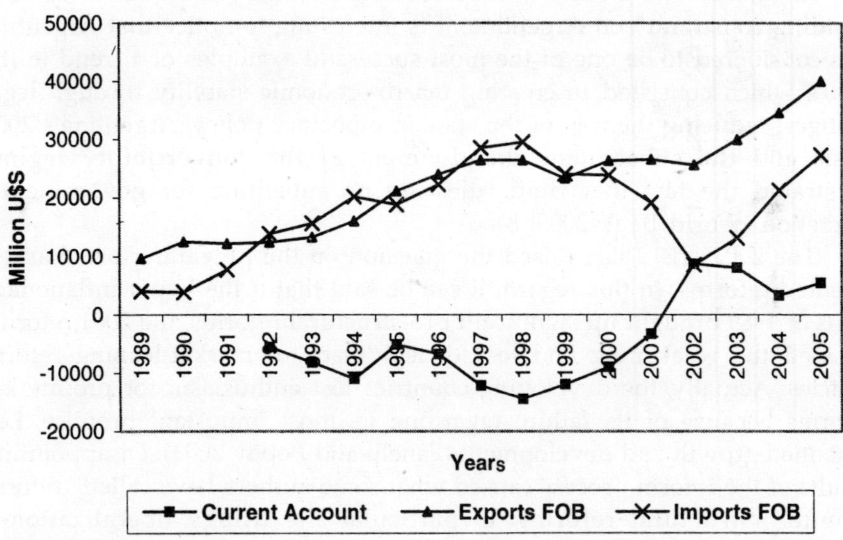


*Source* : INDEC.

measured as a percentage of GDP, investment suffered a dramatic drop during recession. The lowest level was 11.3% in 2002, to recover since then, reaching 19.8% in 2005, a figure slightly less than the pre-recession one of 2.1%.

Thus, correcting the relative prices distortion produced by exchange rate overvaluation resulting from convertibility's rigidity reveals itself as an important factor in igniting growth. The change in relative prices caused by devaluation seems to lift the barriers for growth, that peso overvaluation was imposing on the economy. According to this approach, overvalued currency could be considered Argentina's "binding constraint" for growth before 2002. Should diagnostic framework had been applied to economic policy-making in the Argentine case, the advice would have been to engineer adequate devices to an orderly exit from convertibility. Argentine authorities' obstinate attempt of sticking to convertibility led to hard landing through market devaluation with hurting side-effects: generalized contract breaking and abrupt (and unequal) income re-distribution. Since contracts were either in dollars or in pesos convertible to dollars at a 1 to 1 exchange rate, they had to be adapted to post-convertibility (since, at first, many didn't accept the restructuring decided by the government, lawsuits flourished). Contract restructuring caused income re-distribution, and inflation in 2002 (especially of food articles insofar tradable goods) brought about the unequal income re-distribution.

## RIGIDITY AND LEGITIMACY : THE ROLE OF IDEAS

In addition to Rodrik's statement on an overvalued currency as a "binding constraint" on Argentina, it is interesting to notice that Argentina was considered to be one of the most successful examples of a trend in the 1990's which consisted in creating macro-economic stability through legal changes, reducing the role of the state in monetary policy. Argentina's 2001 crisis and the subsequent abandonment of the convertibility regime illustrated the fact that rigid rules are no substitute for government's discretion (World Bank 2005: 8).

The 2001 crisis also raised the question on the prevailing pro market-oriented reforms. In this regard, it can be said that if the hyper inflationary crisis of 1989 brought up significant pro-structural reforms, the 2001 reforms stressed the weakening and loss of legitimacy of market-leaning reform policies. Actually, the developing countries lost enthusiasm for pro-market reforms because of its failure regarding its most important promise, i.e., sustained growth and development (Fanelli and Popov 2003). Disappointing results of the reform process caused what some authors have called "reform fatigue." Structural reforms, in particular the trilogy liberalization—privatization—deregulation were perceived as key issues in the deterioration of life standards (Birdsall and De la Torre 2001).

### The Government's Role after the Crisis

In fact, state reform in the 1990s was part of the process of neoliberal globalization, which has basically been defined by four characteristics: (1) the decline of the economic power of state actors; (2) the growing penetration of market forces in new spheres of activity; (3) the remarkable increase in transnational circulation of capital, goods and services; (4) the unprecedented dissemination of ideas supporting reform through networks of scientists, experts and/or distinguished professionals (*epistemic communities*) that exerted a significant influence on the government agenda setting and its international convergence (Haas 1992).

The following processes were hastily prompted: (i) privatization of state companies, social insurance and social services; (ii) outsourcing of many public sector activities; (iii) deregulation of the economy—including labor relations—and, in general, (iv) the abandonment to the role of the state as agent of development. More than 300.000 jobs were removed from the public sector payroll as a result of privatization and, although it is not easy to determine the reduction of public employment caused by outsourcing, it can be ascertained its progressive increase in the public budget.

However, in spite of the restrictive policies and the anti-state rhetoric of the 1990s, between 1991 and 2001, public employment experienced a 4.2% growth. Indeed, according to 1991 and 2001 Censuses, the volume of public employment rose from 2.221.348 to 2.313.793.

Nevertheless, public employment reduced its share in the labor market; measured as a percentage of economically active population, it fell from 16.8% in 1991 to 15.2% in 2001.

Prior to the privatization of public enterprises in the first half of the 90s, the labor market experienced the steady elimination of public sector jobs, and subsequently a much significant and relentless loss of jobs in the private sector. Therefore, those who had lost public jobs still formed both a smaller and decreasing proportion of the total number of unemployed wage-earners (1996 = 6.4%; 2001 = 4.9%; 2005 = 3.7%), as well as a low and decreasing proportion of the public employment payroll (5.0%; 4.3%; 2.1%); this pattern contrasts with the level of unemployment among wage-earners in the private sector, where one out of five, and even out of four, was unemployed (21.4%; 26%; 19.5%).

More recently, the labor market has displayed a different trend. Unemployment decreased and, although public employment increased, it did so at a low rate. As a result, if one were to compare 2005 to 2001, public employment carried less weight in the economically active population (2001: 13.7%; 2005: 13.2%) and noticeably less weight in terms of all employed wage-earners (2001: 23.5%; 2005: 19.9%).

Leading up to 2005, there was another turn from the 90s. Public employment in all the areas subject to privatization reforms—namely, transportation, construction, communications, and the supply of electricity, gas, and water—experienced substantial growth. This is a very revealing finding: it discloses the new role played by the state in the economy, largely because the increase in public employment overall was very low, to the point that there was even a decrease in the typically state-run functions, i.e., *administration* and *defense*.

In summary, although the relative impact of public employment on the labor market did not increase (but rather decrease) leading up to 2005, its revival in various areas of activity suggests a growing state intervention, as opposed to the state withdrawal experienced by the 1990s.

Following is a brief discussion of public policy actions taken by the Argentine government in the post-crisis period. Examples of government's role and intervention after the crisis can be grouped in the following categories:

*Re-statization*: It involved a process of contract renegotiation with the companies in charge of public services supply. "Re-statization" only happened in those cases of concessionaires' most flagrant unfulfilment of their obligations. Irrespective of legal forms employed, reference to "re-statization" included all situations in which private concessionaires were replaced by new created state owned companies. Such as the postal service, a railway branch in Great Buenos Aires, the water and sewers supply service for Great Buenos Aires, and the state petroleum company Enarsa (in this case, the company didn't replace the private concessionaire, it co-exists with the privatized company Repsol-YPF and other companies that operate in the Argentine market).

Price Agreements: as one of its main instruments aimed at inflation control Government's strategy included arrangements with business sector's representatives. Since Government considers prices shouldn't exceed business production costs plus a "fair and reasonable" profit, business representatives were asked to keep set prices for a period of time, established in arrangements. In general, arrangements are signed for a year. However, clauses can be modified every two months. At the time of writing, those arrangements about to expire were renewed for another year. This course of action implied a rejection of price determination through market procedures.

*Temporary restrictions on beef exports*: Due to consistent increases in beef prices government decided to restrict beef exports for 6 months in order to guarantee an adequate domestic market supply and consequently get a reduction in prices. After negotiations and agreements with representatives of cattle business sector, the measure was relaxed, establishing a quotas system for beef exports.

In conclusion, post-crisis government action has not implied a reversion of market-oriented reforms, so it shouldn't be considered a clearly stated, rationally and coherently devised, "new" development strategy. It could be more accurately described as a set of pragmatic *ad-hoc* interventions. It is not evident whether immediate post-crisis state action allows of plans, strategies or "get out of a jam" decisions imposed by circumstances.

State interventions studied here are a good example of the market failure theory (Stiglitz 1992: 74-85) as well as the idea of government as complement to markets and the one able to remedy socially unsatisfactory or unacceptable outcomes produced by markets when left to themselves.

## SUMMARY

- Since second quarter of 2002 the economic cycle reverted, and the GDP has grown at an average annual rate of 9% from 2003 onwards
- Unemployment rate decreased from 21.5% in 2002 to 12.7% in 2005.
- Population below the poverty line has also experienced a reduction during this period. From 54.3% in the second semester of 2002 to 31.4% in the first semester of 2006.
- Besides the decrease in unemployment rate and poverty level, it is relevant to emphasize the existence of employed people below the poverty line. This fact is also illustrated by the loss of purchasing power suffered by employed people after the exchange rate devaluation. Following INDEC's data, the average monthly income perceived by employed people in 2005 was $ 839, 45.9% more than in 2001. However, prices increased 74.7% during the same period.

- Indicators measuring inequality almost do not show alteration during this period. There is a visible increase in the Income Distribution Gap in 2003 which is related to the effects of the 2001-02 crisis. With regards to the GINI Coefficient, there are no significant differences either. Both values of the inequality indicators are still very high.
- It is still soon to answer if this "episode of rapid growth" Argentina is experiencing since the second quarter of 2002 will be able to lead to a sustained self-reinforcing path of economic growth and institutional change. In the near future we will be able to know if Rodrikean second stage of growth plus institutional change is about to come or this "growth acceleration" fizzles out.
- The post-crisis government action has not implied a reversion of market-oriented reforms introduced during the 1990s, therefore, it shouldn't be considered a clearly stated, rationally and coherently devised, "new" development strategy. It could be more accurately described as a set of pragmatic ad-hoc interventions.

## References


Birdsall, N., A. De la Torre, with R., Menezes, 2001, *Washington Contentious: Economic Policies for Social Equity in Latin America*, Washington, D.C.: Carnegie Endowment for International Peace and Inter-American dialogue.

Chang, H. and P. Evans, 2000, The Role of Institutions in Economic Change, Paper Prepared for the Meetings of the "Other Canon" Group Venice, Italy, 13-4 January, 2000 and Oslo, Norway, 15-6 August, 2000. Available <http://www.othercanon.org/uploads/CE4-The%20role%20of%20insitutions%20in%20economic%20change.doc>.

Chang, H., 2001, Institutional Development in Developing Countries in a Historical Perspective—Lessons from Developed Countries in Earlier Times. Available <www.st-edmunds.cam.ac.uk/vhi/research/chang.pdf>.

Chang, H., 2005, Understanding the Relationship between Institutions and Economic Development—Some Key Theoretical Issues, Article prepared for the WIDER Jubilee Conference on *WIDER Thinking Ahead: The Future of Development Economics*, Helsinki, 17-18 June 2005, Available <http://www.wider.unu.edu/conference/conference-2005-3/conference-2005-3-papers/Chang.pdf>.

Damill, M., 2003, La reactivación cumple un año, Diario Clarín, Buenos Aires, *Suplemento Económico*, 6 de abril de 2003.

Fanelli, J.M. and V. Popov, 2003, On the Philosophical, Political and Methodological Underpinnings of Reform. First Draft. Paper prepared for the Fourth Annual Global Development Conference "Globalization and Equity," Workshop on "Understanding Reform", organized by the Global Development Network (GDN), Cairo, Egypt, and January 15-21, 2003.

Fukuyama, F., 2004, *La construcción del Estado. Hacia un nuevo orden mundial en el siglo XXI*, Barcelona: Ediciones B. Barcelona (traducción: María Alonso).

Haas, P., 1992, Epistemic Communities and International Policy Coordination, *International Organization*, 46 (1): 1-35.

North, D., 1989, *Instituciones, Cambio Institucional y Desempeño Económico*, Méjico: Fondo de Cultura Económica (traducción: Agustín Bárcena).

Rodrik, D., 1999, Institutions for High-Quality Growth: What they are and How to Acquire Them, Paper Prepared for an IMF Conference on Second Generation Reforms, Revised version published in *Studies in Comparative International Development*. Available <http://ksghome.harvard.edu/~drodrik/papers.html>.

Rodrik, D. 2004a. Getting Institutions Right. Available <http://ksghome.harvard.edu/~drodrik/papers.html>.

Rodrik, D., 2004b, Rethinking Growth Policies in the Developing World, The Luca d'Agliano Lecture for 2004, Available <http://ksghome.harvard.edu/~drodrik/papers.html>.

Rodrik, D., 2004c, Rethinking Growth Strategies WIDER Annual Lecture 8, WIDER Annual Lecture 8, Available <http://www.wider.unu.edu/publications/ annual-lectures/annual-lecture-2004.pdf>.

Rodrik, D., R. Hausmann and A. Velasco, 2005, Growth Diagnostics, Available <http://ksghome.harvard.edu/~drodrik/papers.html>.

Rodrik, D., R. Hausmann and L. Pritchett, 2005, Growth Accelerations, Available <http://ksghome.harvard.edu/~drodrik/papers.html>.

Rodrik, D., 2006, Goodbye Washington Consensus, Hello Washington Confusion? Available <http://ksghome.harvard.edu/~drodrik/papers.html>.

Stiglitz, J., 1992, El papel del sector público, En *La Economía del Sector Público*, Barcelona: Editorial Antoni Bosch.

Stiglitz, J., 1998a, Más instrumentos y metas más amplias para el desarrollo. Hacia el consenso post-Washington, *Desarrollo Económico*, 151 (38): 691-722.

Stiglitz, J., 1998b, Towards a New Paradigm for Development: Strategies, Policies and Processes, 1998 Prebisch Lecture, Génova: UNCTAD, Available http://www.worldbank.org/html/extdr/extme/prebisch98.pdf.

Stiglitz, J., 2003, El rumbo de las reformas, Hacia una nueva agenda para América Latina, *Revista de la CEPAL*, 80, Available <http://www.undp-povertycentre.org/publications/economics/RumbodelasReformas_Stiglitz-CEPAL-Aug03.pdf>.

Stiglitz, J., 2004a, The Future of Global Governance, Task Force of Global Governance Working Paper Series International Policy Dialogue (IPD) Columbia University. Available <http://www0.gsb.columbia.edu/ipd/pub/Barcelona-FutureofGlobalGovernance11_8.pdf>.

Stiglitz, J., 2004b, The Post Washington Consensus, Consensus Task Force on Governance of Globalization Working Paper Series International Policy Dialogue (IPD) Columbia University. Available <http://www0.gsb.columbia.edu/ipd/pub/barcelonaintro 11_17_04.pdf>.

Williamson, J., 1993, Democracy and the "Washington Consensus", *World Development*, 21 (8): 1329-36.

World Bank, 2005, Economic Growth in the '90s: Learning from a Decade of Reform, World Bank Poverty Reduction and Economic Management (PREM).

# 12

# *Global Conflict and Conflict Resolution : Alternative Strategies to Governance*

REETA TREMBLAY AND CSABA NIKOLENYI

## INTRODUCTION

It has been well-established that the proliferation of democratic regimes promotes international peace and cooperation. According to democratic peace theory, leaders of democratic states have a number of economic, ideological and political incentives not to engage in conflictual relations but seek, instead, long-term cooperative engagement with one another. This argument logically implies that the future state of conflict and cooperation in world politics is a positive function of the number of consolidated democracies in the world: the more stable democracies, the more peaceful international relations will, overall, become.

The establishment of democratic political institutions, however, is no easy task as the rich literature on the transition to and consolidation of democracy has aptly demonstrated. Locally, specific and unique conditions may call for locally specific strategies as far as the implementation of the democratic project is concerned: one size, clearly, does not fit all (Tremblay, Nikolenyi and Otmar 2003). Notwithstanding these particular aspects of democratization, there are broader and universal concerns that all democratic institutional designers have to be worried about: namely, the *stability* and the *legitimacy* of the institutional foundation of the democratic regime, demonstrated by policies which are broadly representative and reflective of popular preferences. Such concerns are of particular significance in divided multiethnic societies where democratic political competition can easily pit the various ethnic segments, or other cleavage groups, against one another in bloody civil war. This is only avoided if the institutional design of the regime adequately accommodates their conflicting claims to resources and, of course, political power, the chief currency in politics.

Assuming, as we do in this paper, that the proliferation of democratic regimes is the key domestic political source to containing the spread of global conflict, we argue that global peace ultimately rests on the installation of successful, durable, and self-enforcing democratic regimes around the world. This, however, requires careful institutional design at the time of democratization. Drawing on the social choice literature of democratic institutions, we argue that those democratic institutions that increase the number and the degree of the preference heterogeneity of the major political actors will be both more likely to remain stable and maximize the social utility of the population, thus ensuring the perpetuation of the legitimate foundations of the regime. These goals can be achieved by specific political institutions, and their combinations, such as: separation of power horizontally, between the executive and the legislative branches of government, and vertically, between a central and sub-national levels of government via federal arrangements; proportional representation electoral rules leading to a multiparty system; and inclusive decision-making rules, such as the use of qualified majority and unanimity rules to pass key legislation. With such institutions in place, domestic democratization will prosper, making global peace an increasingly more likely prospect in the future.

The paper will start by establishing the theoretical foundation of our argument including both positive and normative theoretical considerations. This will be followed by the assessment of alternative patterns institutional designs in three very different settings: contemporary Afghanistan, post-colonial India, and post-communist Eastern Europe. By selecting such diverse contextual settings to evaluate our hypothesis, we increase the explanatory power of our argument. In fact, we believe that our argument should have universal, rather than locally- or regionally-specific, applicability.

## POSITIVE THEORETICAL CONSIDERATIONS : A SOCIAL CHOICE PERSPECTIVE ON INSTITUTIONAL DESIGN

Our theoretical point of departure is the social choice theory of democratic political institutions. McKelvey's (1972) finding is well known: under majority rule, the life-blood of democratic decision-making processes, in a two or more dimensional complex political space, it is very rare that any one alternative policy proposal can constitute a stable outcome. Unless some highly restrictive conditions regarding the spatial configuration of players' ideal points are met (Plott 1967), alternative policies will always cycle. In simple non-technical terms, this means that any alternative X can be beaten and defeated by some other alternative Y, which can be defeated by Z, which can be defeated by X again because a different majority of players can always support a new alternative over the *status quo*. The finding that majority rule generates intransitive social choice outcomes, i.e., that majority rule is chaotic, had led to pessimistic views about democracy in the social choice school.

This pessimistic finding about majority rule cycles has been aptly extended to the study of political institutions. Riker (1980) has noted that since the choice of any given political institution (by type of constitution, electoral system, etc.) reflects a social choice, they are also inherently in a state of disequilibrium: instead of institutional stability, according to Riker, the natural state of political institutions is cycling and instability! Nonetheless, there are many instances of apparently stable institutions, such as stable political regimes or constitutional structures, around the world that appear to contradict Riker's theoretical assertion. What, then, can account for the apparent stability of political institutions under democratic majority-rule?

One answer to this question has stressed the importance of the political skill of the political leadership. Ken Shepsle and Barry Weingast (1981) generated a substantial literature on agenda control that has shown how political leaders who control the sequence in which alternatives are compared and voted upon can design an agenda that will always result in the selection of their ideally most preferred outcome, i.e. their ideal point, by the majority. In the extreme case, this can mean that the majority could select a point far outside of the Pareto set of the distribution of the players' points. Clearly, this is most undesirable; for, by violating some very basic assumptions of procedural fairness, such outcomes can eventually pave the way for the disillusionment of the populace with the political leadership, leading ultimately to alienation and disenchantment with the entire political regime.

However, in an important paper, Feld, Grofman and Miller (1989) proved that the nature of the distribution of players' points in the decision-making game sets a strong limit on the effectiveness of agenda control and manipulation. More specifically, they link these limits on agenda control to the size of the yolk, a very important social choice concept that designates the generalized center of the distribution of players' ideal points. They have shown that majority rule is much more chaotic, that is to say that there are more cycles, in or near the yolk than farther away from it. Therefore, the larger the yolk, the more cycling there is, which opens up the prospect for a skillful manipulator of the agenda to exploit and divide the players to her own advantage. In contrast, the smaller the yolk, indicating that the distribution of ideal points closely approximates that configuration which would generate a majority rule equilibrium, the less the cycling that majority rule engenders, which, in turn limits and hinders the ability of the agenda-setter to control the decision process.

This argument suggests, in our context, that political institutions can be much more stable, holding all else equal, if the size of the yolk of the given distribution of ideal points in the political decision-making process is small. Alternatively, if the yolk is large, institutions, as any other collective choice outcomes, will also be subject to considerable cycling! Since the size of the yolk is, for most distribution of ideal points, an inverse function of the number of players in the decision-making game, for the most part (Feld, Grofman and Miller 1989) it follows that political institutions will be more stable when the number of players in the decision-process, *ceteris paribus*, is greater. In addition, the yolk always shrinks when the distribution of the players' ideal point in the space becomes more dispersed; therefore political institutions will also be more stable when players are more widely distributed in the n-dimensional political space. In other words, the greater the preference heterogeneity of the decision-making group, or society, the more stable its collective choices, such as its political institutions, will be!

The idea that the stability of political institutions is positively related to the number and the distribution of players' ideal points is further re-enforced by George Tsebelis' (2001, 1995) veto player theory (VPT). Tsebelis defines veto players as those political actors whose consent is necessary for the alteration of the *status quo* (SQ), and proves that the stability of SQ does not decrease when the number of veto players increases or when the spatial distance among VP increases. Therefore, VPT also leads to the prediction that political institutions in particular, and collective choices in general, are more stable when there are many, rather than few, widely dispersed, rather than closely situated, veto players involved. Of course, as the number and dispersion of veto players increases, the yolk of the group shrinks, which, as discussed above, generates more coherent collective choices, and thus institutional stability. The most important types of institutional arrangements that lead to an increase in both of these variables are:

(a) universal suffrage creating a complex electorate;
(b) proportional representation electoral systems;
(c) inclusive decision-making rules, such as qualified majority or unanimity; and
(d) horizontally and vertically divided government (such as separation of powers; bicameralism; federalism) (Colomer 2001).

Besides their own imminent stability, political institutions are also important because of the representational consequences of the outcomes that they generate. Socially efficient political institutions select outcomes that are at or very near the position of the median member of society. Such institutions maximize social utility by keeping the distance between the outcome and players' ideal points minimal. Therefore, they can play a particularly important role in a new democracy where popular satisfaction with the policy efficiency of the new regime is an especially precious commodity. In the absence of efficient outcomes the new democratic regime can fast lose popular support and legitimacy, endangering its survivability. Interestingly, the same institutions that promote the stability of collective choices also enhance social efficiency. The underlying logic of this argument is that these institutions generate outcomes that are at or very near the *n*-dimensional median of the given collective.

Colomer (2001) identifies three types of institutional regimes based on their specific institutional choices. In the rank order of the social efficiency of the outcomes that they generate, they are the following:

(1) Parliamentary majoritarian systems, which are characterized by dominant or two-party systems, and a pattern of unified government—due to the winning party controlling both the cabinet executive and a legislative majority. Collective choices in such regimes have low levels of social efficiency and are very unstable.

(2) Presidential and semi-presidential systems, which are characterized by a higher frequency of divided government due to the separation of executive and legislative powers as well as elections to these branches. Semi-presidential systems typically have a multiparty system in their legislatures, which contributes to a higher degree of stability and efficiency of their social choices than what we find in presidential regimes. In fact, at a time of same-party control of the executive and the legislature, the collective choices of a presidential system will be just as unstable and inefficient as those arrived at under a parliamentary majoritarian system. In short, collective choices are both more stable and more efficient under semi-presidential than presidential constitutions.

(3) Parliamentary proportional representation systems are characterized by the highest degree of dispersion of power. Since the executive is typically formed by multiparty coalitions and the legislature is fragmented among many political parties, it is not surprising that collective choices should be the most stable and most efficient in this regime type.

It is important to note that a federal arrangement can contribute to making the social choices generated by these three regime clusters more stable and efficient by dispersing political power vertically. However, in and of itself, federalism cannot make a difference. As Riker (1984) aptly pointed out, "there is one institutional condition that controls the nature of the [federal] bargain. . . . This is the structure of the party system, which may be regarded as the main variable intervening between the background social conditions and the specific nature of the federal bargain" (136). In short, whether federalism will promote democratic stability and efficiency depends on the type of party system that it exists under. As the examples of the communist federations showed (USSR, Czechoslovakia, Yugoslavia), federalism under a hegemonic party system can generate far lower levels of social utility than in a competitive two—(USA) or multiparty system (Germany, Austria, post-1989 India).

We can sum up the foregoing overview in the following hypothesis:

*Hypothesis*: The stability and the social utility of collective choices in democratic regimes increase as we move from parliamentary majoritarian to presidential semi-presidential, and parliamentary proportional regimes.

## NORMATIVE THEORETICAL CONSIDERATIONS AND INSTITUTIONAL DESIGN FOR DIVIDED SOCIETIES

The general concerns of democratic institutional design addressed in the previous section assume particular significance in divided multiethnic societies. In these cases, the success of any institutional arrangement of power sharing must occur within the context of the overriding constitutional values which create the basis for a normative ordering between the state and the civil society. The success of the new constitution will depend upon the extent to which the constitution-makers construct a new polity based on both similarities (the values commonly shared) and differences (the distinct identities of its varied fragments). We suggest that the notion of constructing a multicultural political community with the joint goals of a single nation and individual citizenship, on the one hand, and the representation of cultural pluralism, on the other, can only be realized and therefore needs to be analyzed within the context of the intervening role of the state in determining the content of nationalism. A state, through its legal and constitutional apparatus, along with the ideological role of the political leadership, has significant input in constructing, shaping, modifying, maintaining and containing ethnic identities. Through its legal and constitutional apparatus, the state arrogates to itself the power of naming an identity and in turn, 'profoundly affects the process by which individual and collectivized identities are constructed and maintained" (Macklem 1993: 13). Through constitutional and other political arrangements, the state denies or acknowledges differences and similarities within the civil society. The acknowledgement of differences creates a political and legal space for the communities whereby they not only define themselves but can also at the same time define their similarities and differences *vis-à-vis* the others. This is not to deny that (a) the state's legal identification of similarities and differences is generally a product of elite alliances based on ideological grounds and the exigencies of political power; and (b) in the process of political construction of an identity for its ethnic group or groups, the state selectively propagates certain historical references and symbols which satisfy its own need for cultural homogeneity and its own version of nationalism. Nevertheless, once the legal space for ethnic identity has been constructed by the state, it has far reaching consequences for the future actions and choices of both the state itself and various fragments of the civil society. Maintenance of political order or its breakdown in a particular society is directly related to the complex interplay of nation, national consciousness, and the ideology of nationalism within the legal and political framework established by the state. Its success or failure will depend on: how they import from the western liberal theory the principle of individualism and combine it with the indigenous realities and traditions; how they use the indigenous traditional symbols by emptying them of their original meanings and giving them new content; how they create a cohesive nation but not at the expense of its cultural pluralism; and how the polity can balance the state's own needs for cultural homogeneity and its own version of nationalism with that of the political and cultural claims based on ethno-nationalism.

Second, the simultaneous pursuance of the goals of a homogenous and heterogeneous nation—creating a single indivisible nation and equal citizenship, based on similarities, and ensuring the distinct identities of its population, based on differences—can effectively take place in a system whose goals are defined as multicultural rather than multinational. It is interesting to note that western discourse has only recently begun to explore the issues of citizenship, cultural pluralism and a multicultural political community. Kymlicka very convincingly points out that traditional liberal theory has always debated the issues of individual *versus* group rights and the present lack of such a discussion is a recent benign neglect. He attributes the virtual silence about the debate on national minorities to the fall of the British Empire, the rise of Cold War conflicts and the prominence of American theorists within post-war liberalism. (Kymlicka 1997:230-36) A major theoretical concern of leading North American scholars has been to show how the politics of recognition of identity and group rights can be reconciled within a liberal democratic and cohesive political community. Although these philosophical projects go much further than the studies of power-sharing in plural societies. Parekh claims that such theories fall short of being theories of multiculturalism. For Parekh, the existing theories of cultural pluralism give a coherent account of the value of culture (i.e., why human beings need a stable culture) but not of cultural diversity (i.e., the interaction of culturally differentiated groups and their presence together in public institutions; thus public policy is a product of their public mingling and a respect and understanding for previously excluded or marginalized groups). While a theory of cultural pluralism argues for the respect of diverse cultures, and public policies and political structures which allow some cultural minorities to prevent their domination by the majorities such as Kymlicka's national minorities, for Parekh, the multicultural project goes beyond these narrow goals.

In a multicultural society (which affirms the value of cultural diversity in terms of equality between groups and the realization of these values in institutions and policies) the power-sharing arrangements, as articulated in the consociation models for plural democracies and considered by some as useful in federal institutions, require two specific reformulations. First, following Brendan O'Leary's argument, it is important to acknowledge that democratic consociations can be differentiated analytically from undemocratic consociations. Second, although it is imperative that, in an ethnically divided society, the consociations require statesmanship from the political elites in terms of their pursuance of a politics of active accommodation, it must be recognized that the longevity and stability of a democratic society result from the normative entrenchment of a societal culture of accommodation of diversity. In other words, the concept of 'elite cartels' must be expanded to include the input of the political community at large.

The major critique of the consociational model of the politics of accommodation is that it is foremost concerned with maintaining stability in ethnically divided democratic societies. The models of power sharing in a consociational system rely exclusively on the political leadership to build institutions, without either cultural homogeneity or crosscutting cleavages, and to generate public policy which produces stability by constraining democratic competition. (Lijphart 1977) This political engineering on the part of the leadership presupposes a concept of a segmented citizenry responding to and behaving according to the choices of the elites. Thus, "Consociational democracy means government by elite cartel" (Lijphart 1969: 216) and for sake of stability, competitive politics are to be replaced by an accommodation of politics among the elites. There are fundamental shortcomings to this concept. The behavior of the political elites, who by virtue of their self-interest exercise restraint and pursue an accommodation of politics, does not necessarily translate into accommodative behavior of the citizenry. As a matter of fact, the power-sharing arrangements, if narrowly envisioned in this model, create segmented cultures and political exclusivity at the civil society level. Barry quite aptly points out that political leaders in their struggles with the rivals within their segments create conditions for "potential civil war or of civil war averted by effective oppression by one group or the other" (Lustcik 1997: 102). Paul Brass summarizes the inappropriateness of consociationalism for developing societies. For him, in the first place, "political accommodation in democratic societies is an art not a system, and one that has to be pursued persistently in the face of changing circumstances. Consociationalism is a device of freezing existing divisions and conflicts and reducing the art of political accommodation to formulas that can work only as long as processes of social, economic, and political change do not upset them." In addition, the success of a democracy can only be determined by this accommodation, which is often in relation to the underlying principles and goals of a political community. Moreover, if the goals of the political community are conceptualized in such a way whereby a single nation is reconciled with the pursuance of collective rights, elite accommodation *a la* consociational model can be more harmful than beneficial to the cohesiveness of the polity. Brass's second point is along similar lines. He points out, "consociational democracy inevitably violates the rights of some groups and the rights of individuals. It violates the rights of those groups in being and those that may develop in the future whose existence is not recognized by the state. It also certainty fails to provide protection to and may lead to the oppression of individuals who wish not to be identified with or wish to free themselves from identification with particular cultural groups. The use of particular consociational devices does not necessarily have this effect, but the creation of a system based on rigid segmental autonomy and isolation certainly does" (Brass 1991: 342).

Brendan O'Leary responds to some of these criticisms by pointing out that Lijphart's use of the term "elite cartel" from Ralph Dahrendorf (Society and Democracy in Germany) is "an unhappy appropriation" (2002: 4). O'Leary argues that no explanatory loss "flows from the recognition" that undemocratic consociations can be differentiated from the democratic ones in terms of the political elites' representativeness, legitimacy and accountability to the population at large. For O'Leary, "there can be non-democratic consociations in which political leaders of communities co-operate and conduct themselves according to consociational but not democratic practices. . . . It is best to regard undemocratic consociations as ones with complete or factional cartels, in which each segmental partner is controlled by an elite or faction that is not democratically controlled within its own constituency. Power may be shared among the elites with little or no reference to their bloc, and if other consociational practices prevail (autonomy, proportionality and mutual vetoes among the elites) then such a system is consociational, but it is not democratic" (2002: 5). Freeing the concept of consociations from Lijphart's usage of elite cartels and expanding it to include the regime type also allows the analyst the opportunity to analytically differentiate between the power-sharing arrangements on the one hand and creating a consociational democratic society, on the other, whose success depends as much from an elite accommodation and co-operation as from the input of the political community at large. Indeed, power sharing arrangements might be temporary and do not necessarily embody within them the consociational norms. As suggested earlier in this section, if the success of a new constitution depends upon the extent to which the constitution-makers construct a new polity based on both similarities and differences, then the constitution-making entails the conscious political engineering of a society where the polity must balance its own need for cultural homogeneity with that of the political and cultural claims based on ethno-nationalism.

The following section will present three brief case studies of experimentation with democratic institutional design.

## Case Study-1: Afghanistan

In June 2002, in conformity with the Bonn Accord, the United Nations-sponsored blueprint for democracy, peace and stability in Afghanistan, a specially convened and ethnically broad-based Loya Jhirga (traditional grand council), elected as President of Afghanistan Hamid Karzai, a Pashtun who had just completed his term as the chairman of the executive council of the interim administration. In his attempt to produce a more ethnically-balanced cabinet than his previous interim administration—an attempt to create some sort of power-sharing between different ethnic groups, President Karzai appointed 35 ministers from Afghanistan's major communities: Pashtuns, Tajiks, Hazaras, Uzbeks and some members from smaller minorities. The Bonn Accord provides for an incremental process by which temporary and provisional structures of governance are to be replaced by a democratic constitution for Afghanistan and the permanent structures of a popularly elected representative government. In the first stage (completed in June 2002), six months after taking over office, the Karzai administration was replaced by a broad-based Transitional Authority, agreed upon by an Emergency Loya Jirgha. Secondly, within eighteen months of the establishment of the Transitional Authority, a Constitutional Loya Jhirga is to be convened. The latter will establish a Constitutional Commission to prepare a new constitution for Afghanistan.

The Bonn Accord stipulates that the Afghanistan constitution of 1964 is to serve as the legal framework for the organization of the Interim government of Karzai. While the 1964 constitution enshrines equal political rights and freedoms for its citizens, it also provides Afghanistan with an administration based upon the principal of centralization. For such a pluralistic and so deeply divided society along these ethnic, linguistic and tribal lines, a centralized form of government would seem to be a sure-fire recipe for discontent and for increased demands for autonomy. It promotes the unity of the country at the expense of the rich diversity of its citizens' cultural inheritance. And this means that the Constitutional Commission, which is to be formed by the constitutional Loya Jhirga within two years, will have to pay serious attention to the need to create simultaneously a single, indivisible nation as well as a set of sub-national governments which are allowed to maintain their diversity and the plural cultural identities of their population. Federalism may be an option whereby a strong central government can be juxtaposed with strong regional units.

Moreover, federalism provides an opportunity for the framers of the constitution to mold the structure of the governments, both national and sub-national, to adjust to the specific pluralistic realities of the country. Multicultural societies such as Afghanistan require that federalism address both the territorial and the cultural projects, the latter directed to the issues of cultural representation and identity within the concept of a multicultural society. One of the tasks of a multicultural federalism is to provide cultural recognition and ensure that the deviations of minority groups from the dominant regional norms do not result in their being consigned to powerlessness and to the marginalizing of their identities. The major challenge which federalism in Afghanistan will have to face is to balance the territorial with the non-territorial requirements of the Afghani multi-cultural, multi-tribal nation. Furthermore, given Afghanistan's cultural diversity and social pluralism, the federal system will have to constantly struggle to reconcile the claims of equal citizenship with group identities and interests. Such a federal project is indeed difficult and will require an enlightened leadership and an enlightened citizenry, for there is a constant struggle to reconcile the claim of equal citizenship for all individuals with the exigencies of collective identities and interests.

Finally, as we have discussed earlier, constitutional design along federal lines, supplemented with a proportional representation electoral system, (preferably with a large district magnitude that would increase the number of political parties (Cox 1997, Lijphart 1994)), effective bicameralism, and separate executive and legislative powers would also enhance two very important qualities of this new emerging democracy: its political stability and representativeness (i.e., social efficiency). Thus, the adoption of a highly centralized interim constitutional arrangement does not strike us as a very well-thought-out proposition. Such arrangements reduce the number of veto players and undermine the stability of the *status quo*, which paves the way to political instability, which, coupled with the non-representative character of the outcomes that are associated with such institutional choices, may have disastrous consequences for the survivability of the new regime. It is important to stress, however, that a federal constitution, in and of itself, is no panacea. Unless it is accompanied by additional institutional measures that further disperse political power, most importantly a multiparty system (Riker 1984), federalism can also turn into an instrument of political centralization.

## Case Study 2: India

Historically, the Indian constitution-makers were not only sensitive to group identities but were innovative in generating a difficult and challenging non-traditional discourse on political community (Tremblay 1997). Relying on indigenous Hindu traditions, emphasizing the collective identities such as family, caste and tribe, and borrowing from "imported" liberal theory revolving around the concept of individualism, the founding fathers of the Indian state constitutionally attempted to balance contradictory principles of equal citizenship with collective rights: secularism with religious community rights, fundamental equality for all citizens with preferential privileges for backward classes/castes, and an official language with the protection of minority linguistic rights, etc. Although these contradictions in the constitution have had the adverse effect in fragmenting the society by creating narrow primordial loyalties and in generating violence as the dominant mode for the resolution of community conflicts, these present day realities of the Indian polity result from the failure of the over-loaded and over-politicized Indian state to effectively respond to the economic demands of the mobilized caste/community collectivities; from the nature of a political leadership whose interest in political power is fundamentally guided by the consideration of distribution of economic privileges to their narrowly based political constituencies; and from state repression to implement three overriding unifying principles. These principles are: (a) the Indian union is perpetual and no demands for secession would be entertained; (b) no religious consideration would form a part of the state agenda; and (c) India's territorial integrity in relation to its border states and *vis-à-vis* the neighbors would, at all costs, be protected.

Article 29 of the Indian constitution recognizes the rights of "any section of the citizens of India" who have a distinct language, script or culture "to conserve the same." While Article 350 allows any linguistic minority to "submit representation for redress of grievance to any central or state authority," Article 350-A makes it obligatory upon all regional and local governments "to provide adequate facilities for instruction in mother-tongue at the primary stage of education to children belonging to linguistic minority groups" (Brass 1990: 155). Along with the religious communities, the linguistic groups whose minority status has been recognized in the Eighth Schedule have been given the right, under Article 30, to establish and administer their educational institutions while barring the state from any discrimination against them when it grants financial support to private educational institutions. In conformity with the constitutional principles, two types of denominational schools have been organized in India by the four major religious communities: (a) religious institutions aided by a particular community (for example, Maktabs and Madrasas of the Muslims, Gurukulas, Pathshalas or Sanskrit schools of the Hindus, Gurmukhi schools of the Sikhs and Mission schools of the Christians), and (b) religious schools aided by private or government agencies (for example, Islamia schools or colleges of the Muslims, Arya Samaj or Sanatan Dharam schools of the Hindus, Khalsa schools of the Sikhs and Convent schools of the Christians). While the former category of schools impart religious education, the latter, in addition to a limited number of hours for religious instruction in the class room and during the morning assemblies, follow the secular government-prescribed curriculum. In the spirit of accommodation of religious minorities, the secular Indian constitution allows the religious communities to adhere to their personal laws in the governance of their communities in spheres such as marriage, divorce, inheritance. The 1950 constitution opted to continue the British practice to leave 'personal, or family, law to adjudication by the various communities unless the individuals concerned opted to place themselves under British law' (Austin 1993: 123). Although in the early 1950s Nehru tried to secularize the Hindu law, he faced opposition from both within and outside the Congress party. However, a series of parliamentary acts were passed which are collectively known as the Hindu code. However, no such attempt was made to modernize the Muslim personal law, generating a lot of resentment by the Hindu majority against the Muslims. The democratic egalitarian ideology of the Congress party guided the constitutional decision to provide guarantees of political representation (Articles 330-34) in Parliament and regional Legislative

Assemblies and reservation in educational and administrative institutions (Article 335) for Scheduled Castes and Tribes. (By retaining the list complied by the British government in India in 1935, the constitution placed a large number of untouchable castes and tribes on a Schedule or list. Thus, Scheduled Castes and Scheduled Tribes is a technical/formal term). Of all Central governmental jobs, 22.5 per cent are reserved for this targeted group. Of the 543 Lok Sabha seats, 78 are reserved for the Scheduled Castes and 41 for the Scheduled Tribes. The Legislative Assemblies have reserved a similar proportion of seats for this group (Hardgrave and Kochanek 1993: 190). Although these guarantees were to end in 1960, these have been renewed and expanded to the Backward Castes. Officially designated "Other Backward Castes" are generally rural and account for approximately half of India's population. In response to their political power, initially at the regional level, and now at the national level, in 1990, 27 per cent of all Central governmental jobs were reserved for the OBCs. In addition to the preferential treatment for the Scheduled Castes and Tribes, the constitution has also created flexibility for the Indian Parliament to protect the job interests of the local majorities. In defense of this provision, B.R. Ambedkar pointed out to the members of the Constituent Assembly, "You cannot allow people who are flying from one province to another, from one state to another as mere birds of passage without any roots . . . just to come, apply for posts, and so to say take the plums and walk away" (Weiner and Katzenstein 1981: 24). Thus, in India, although the constitution does not allow dual citizenship and clearly states that there would exist equality of opportunity for all citizens in matters of employment and no discrimination would be allowed on the basis of religion, race, sex, caste, descent, place of birth or residence, common citizenship has come to co-exist with regional citizenship, a necessary requirement for employment.

The institutional design of the new post-colonial Indian democracy was an interesting mix of different elements pushing towards different political equilibria. While the institutions of federalism and bicameralism dispersed political power, the retention of the British-style first-past-the-post electoral system that led to the equilibration of a predominant party system, both sowed the seeds of political instability and reduced social efficiency. Indeed, a number of traumatic domestic political events (the unresolved issue of Kashmir; the breakdown of democracy in 1977; the frequent resurgence of communal violence; the Khalistan crisis, etc.) have revealed the cracks in the foundations of India's democracy. Yet, the process of the party system fragmentation that started at the sub-national level as early as 1967 when the thereto predominant Congress Party failed to win majorities in a number of the Vidhan Sabha elections, reached the national political system by the late 1980s (Nikolenyi 2002: 1998). This fundamental transformation in the national party system, coupled with the bicameral federal design of the constitution, is bound to increase not only the stability but also the social efficiency of India's democracy. If so, the types of religious and ethnic conflicts that still resurface in the country from time to time are bound to gradually subside.

## Case Study-3: Post-Communist East Central Europe

In the post-communist democratic transitions of East Central Europe, the key institutional choice was not about federalism *versus* a unitary constitution even in those states that contained sizable ethnic minorities on their territories (in particular Romania, Slovakia, and the Baltic Republics). In fact, all three communist federations were dissolved either as a part of the transition to democracy (Soviet Union and Yugoslavia), or very shortly thereafter (Czechoslovakia). Thus, the central questions before the crafters of the new institutional mechanisms in these democracies concerned the division of powers between the executive and the legislature on the one hand, and the electoral system, by which the legislature is elected, on the other.

While all post-communist states have adopted either mixed or proportional representation electoral systems, and have as a result seen the emergence of multiparty systems, there has been more intra-regional variation with regard to power that the new constitutions allotted to the head of state *vis-à-vis* the legislature. Depending on the allocation of executive and legislative powers, three types of regimes emerged the former Soviet bloc:

(1) Presidential (Azerbaijan, Belarus, Kazakhstan, Kyrgyzstan, Tajikistan, Turkmenistan, and Uzbekistan);
(2) Semi-presidential (Albania, Armenia, Georgia, Poland, Romania, Russia, and Ukraine); and
(3) Parliamentary (Bulgaria, Croatia, Czech Republic, Estonia, Hungary, Latvia, Lithuania, Macedonia, Moldova, Slovakia and Slovenia) (Freedom House 2002).

According to our hypothesis, we expect that the level of democracy should increase as we move from type 1 to type 3. In order to test this, we have examined the democracy score that each of these states received from Freedom House in 2005.

The results clearly confirm our expectations. The post-communist state with the strongest presidency (Belarus) has the worst democracy score. In stark contrast, as we move to the groups of semi-presidential regimes, the average democracy score changes from 6.54 to 4.2 and, in the case of the parliamentary proportional regimes, it drops even further to 2.9. It is also worth noting that the standard deviation of the democracy scores of states in the third group is smaller than that in the second group, which clearly suggests that this group is far more cohesive in term of the performance of its members' democratic regimes. Nonetheless, it is worth taking note of the

TABLE 12.1
**Democratization and the Power of Post-communist Presidencies**

| *State* | *Democracy score* |
|---|---|
| **Presidential** | |
| Belarus | 6.54 |
| **Semi-presidential** | |
| Albania | 4.13 |
| Armenia | 5 |
| Georgia | 4.83 |
| Poland | 1.75 |
| Romania | 3.58 |
| Russia | 5.25 |
| Ukraine | 4.88 |
| Average | 4.2 (1.22) |
| **Parliamentary** | |
| Bulgaria | 3.25 |
| Croatia | 3.83 |
| Czech Republic | 2.33 |
| Estonia | 1.92 |
| Hungary | 1.96 |
| Latvia | 2.12 |
| Lithuania | 2.13 |
| Macedonia | 4 |
| Moldova | 4.88 |
| Slovakia | 2.08 |
| Slovenia | 1.75 |
| Serbia | 3.83 |
| Montenegro | 3.83 |
| Average | 2.9 (1.04) |

outliers, states with a democracy score that deviate from the groups-wise average by more than the standard deviation for the group:

(a) Poland is clearly more democratic than we would expect on the basis of its political institutions; and
(b) Macedonia and Moldova are less democratic than we would imagine on the basis of their parliamentary systems.

This finding also supports Linz's (1990) famous thesis about the "perils of presidentialism" in which he warns of the inherently de-stabilizing characteristics of strong presidential constitutions in a new democracy.

## CONCLUSION

In this paper, we have argued that domestic institutional design matters a great deal for the stabilization and consolidation of new democratic regimes. Therefore, so long as we assume that the proliferation of democratic regimes promotes global peace and non-violent modes of conflict resolution, we also maintain that there is a casual relationship between domestic institutional design and international peace and conflict. In sum, democratic regimes that diffuse political power through institutional channels, such a parliamentary multiparty system, bicameral legislatures and federalism, will be more stable and representative and much less subject to the manipulation of their political agendas by the leadership that can result in internationally disastrous consequences. In contrast, democratic regimes that employ institutions which concentrate rather than diffuse power, via a unitary constitution, unicameral legislature, and unified government either in its parliamentary majoritarian or the presidential form, will be much more susceptible to agenda manipulation by the leadership that can more easily cause them to be engaged in violent modes of international, as well as domestic, conflict.

### References

Barry, Brian, 1975, "Review Article: Political Accommodation and Consociational Democracy", *British Journal of Political Science*, October 5.

Bhikhu, Parekh, 1992, "The Cultural Politics of Liberal Democracy", *Political Studies*, 40, Special Volume.

Bhikhu, Parekh, 2000, "*Rethinking Multiculturalism*", MacMillan Press.

Brass, Paul R., 1990, "*The Politics of India Since Independence*", New Delhi: Cambridge University Press.

Brass, Paul R., 1991, "*Ethnicity and Nationalism: Theory and Comparison*", New Delhi: Sage Publications.

Colomer, Josep, 2001, "*Political Institutions: Democracy and Social Choice*", Oxford: Oxford University Press.

Cox, Gary W., 1997, "*Making Votes Count: Strategic Coordination in the World's Electoral Systems*", Cambridge: Cambridge University Press.

Feld, Scott; Grofman, Bernard; Miller, Nicholas, 1988, "Centripetal Forces in Spatial Voting Games: On the Size of the Yolk", *Pubic Choice* 59: 37-50.

Feld, Scott; Grofman, Bernard; Miller, Nicholas, 1989, "Limits on Agenda Control in Spatial Voting Games", *Mathematical Computer Modeling*, 12 (4/5): 405-16.

Granville, Austin, 1999, "*The Indian Constitution: Cornerstone of a Nation*", Bombay: Oxford University Press.

Hardgrave, Robert; Kochanek, Stanley, 2000, "*India: Government and Politics in a Developing Nation*", Fort Worth: Harcourt Brace Jovanovich.

Hyman, Anthony, 2002, "Nationalism in Afghanistan", *International Journal of Middle Eastern Studies*, Vol. 34.

Kymlicka, Will, 1995, "Multicultural Citizenship", Oxford: Oxford University Press.

Kymlicka, Will, 1997, "Ethnicity in the USA" in Guibernau, M.; Rex, J. (ed.), "*The Ethnicity Reader: Nationalism, Multiculturalism and Migration*", Cambridge: Polity Press.

Kymlicka, Will, 2001, "*Politics in the Vernacular*", Oxford, Oxford University Press.

Laber, Jerry; Rubin, Barnett, 1988, "*A Nation is Dying, Afghanistan Under the Soviets*", Evanston, Ill., Northwestern University Press.

Lijphart, Arend, 1969, "Consociational Democracy", *World Politics*, Volume 21.

Lijphart, Arend, 1977, "Democracy in Plural Societies: A Comparative Exploration", New Haven, Yale University Press.

Linz, Juan, 1990, "The Perils of Presidentialism", *Journal of Democracy,* 1 (1): 51-69.

Lustick, Ian S., 1997, "Lijphart, Lakatos, and Consociationalism", *World Politics,* Vol. 50, No. 1.

Maacklem, Patrick, 1993, "Ethnonationalism, Aboriginal Identity and the Law", in Levin, Michael D. (ed.), *"Ethnicity and Aboriginality: Case Studies in Ethnonationalism"*, Toronto: University of Toronto Press.

McKelvey, Richard, 1976, "Intransitivities in Multidimensional Voting Models and Some Implications for Agenda Control", *Journal of Economic Theory,* 12: 472-82.

Nikolenyi, Csaba, 1998, "The New Indian Party System; What Kind of Model?" *Party Politics,* 4: 367-80.

Nikolenyi, Csaba, 2002, "Positive Political Theory and Politics in Contemporary India: An Application of a Positive Political Model in Non-Western Politics", *Canadian Journal of Political Science,* 35(4): 881-96.

O'Leary, Brendan, 2002, "Consociation: What We Know or Think We Know and What We Need to Know", paper presented at the conference organized by the National and Ethni Conflict Group at the University of Western Ontario, London, Canada, November 8-10.

Plott, Charles, 1967, "A Notion of Equilibrium and its Possibility under Majority Rule" *American Economic Review,* 57: 787-806.

Riker, William, 1984, "Implications from the Disequilibrium of Majority Rule for the Study of Institutions", *American Political Science Review,* 74: 4732-46.

Rubin, Barnett R., 2002, *"The Fragmentation of Afghanistan: State Formation and Collapse in the International System,* New Haven", CT: Yale University Press.

Shepsle, Kenneth; Weingast, Barry R., 1981, "Structure-Induce Equilibrium and Legislative Choice", *Public Choice,* 37: 503-19.

Stepan, Alfred, 1999, "Federalism and Democracy", *Journal of Democracy,* Vol. 10, No. 4, October.

Tremblay, Reeta Chowdhari, 1996-97, "Nation, Identity and the Intervening Role of the State: A Study of the Secessionist Movement in Kashmir", *Pacific Affairs,* Vol. 69, No. 4, Winter.

Tremblay, Reeta Chowdhari, 1997, "Living Multiculturally in a Federal India" in C. Steven La Rue (ed.) *"Regional Handbook of Economic Development", Vol. 1; "India: Prospects into the 21st Century"*, Fitzroy Dearborn Publishers, Chicago.

Tremblay, Reeta Chowdhari, 2001, "Globalization and Indian Federalism", *Indian Journal of Public Administration,* April-May.

Tremblay, R.; Nikolenyi, C.; Otmar, L., 2003, "Peace and Conflict: Alternative Strategies of Governance and Conflict Resolution", *Journal of Comparative Policy Analysis: Research and Practice,* 5: 123-46.

Tsebelis, George, 1995, "Decision-making in Political Systems: Veto Players in Presidentialsm, Parliamentarism, Multicameralism, and Multipartyism", *British Journal of Political Science,* 25: 289-326.

Tsebelis, George, 2002, "Veto Players: How Political Institutions Work", Princeton: Princeton University Press.

Weiner, Myron; Katzenstein, Mary, 1981, "India's Preferential Policies: Migrants, the Middle Classes and Ethnic Equality" Chicago: University of Chicago Press.

# 13

# Privatization and Public-Private Partnership in Africa : The Case of Botswana

KESHAV C. SHARMA

## INTRODUCTION

Soon after their independence, a large number of countries on the African continent earmarked a central role to public sector for economic development. Public sector continued to expand not only as a result of creation of new public enterprises but also due to large scale nationalization of private enterprises (indigenous, foreign and multinational) motivated by ideological, political or preferred development policy and development planning considerations. By the end of the past century, due to continued poor performance of public enterprises, collapse of communism, and advocacy of Structural Adjustment Programs by donor agencies, the state and the public sector agencies in these countries started rolling back and we started witnessing a shift of emphasis from public sector to private sector. A significantly different approach towards private sector was noticeable. Private sector earlier considered to be an instrument of exploitation and creator of disparities between rich and poor, was recognized as an engine of growth. Divestiture and privatization in different forms became common. The governments of different countries started encouraging private and even foreign investment. New forms of partnership between public and private sector started to develop.

## POOR PERFORMANCE OF PUBLIC SECTOR/ENTERPRISES IN AFRICA AND EFFORTS FOR REFORMS

The performance of public enterprises in African countries has been disappointing. Many of these are incurring huge losses, have not been able to meet the objectives for which these were set-up and have been a drain on the national exchequer. Corruption, nepotism political manipulation, inefficiency and mismanagement have plagued many public enterprises. In many countries rigid adherence to ideology of socialism after independence resulted in large-scale nationalization and all pervasive public sectors.

Private enterprise was shunned as it benefited a few entrepreneurs and created a gap between the rich and the poor. Public sector over-expanded beyond its capacities and even started undertaking activities, which should have been the domain of the private sector (Grosh and Mukandala 1994; Nellis, 1996; Shirley and Nellis, 1991). UNECA (1991) identified following factors as contributing for the failure or poor performance of public enterprises in Africa: excessive control and political interference; managerial incompetence; poor financial base; low integrity and incompetence of boards of directors; managerial corruption; poor personnel policies and practices; unclear objectives; and poor industrial relations. With limited and overstretched administrative capacity, the performance of public enterprises continued to deteriorate.

Public enterprise reform became a major concern for African countries when the over expanded public sector undertakings were running in loss and were not meeting the objectives for their creation. Wide ranging reforms related to structural reorganization and management were being advocated and adopted as the problems continued to surface. Realistic appraisal of managerial capabilities, reduced political controls, greater managerial autonomy, sound composition of boards of directors, improved personnel and financial management practices, downsizing of staff, cordial industrial relations, workers' participation in management, management development and training of staff at different levels, appraisal of performance measuring techniques, effective financial controls and cordial consumer relations were advocated. Significance of developing commercialization and competitive environment in the operation of public enterprises was also realized (UN, 1989). Efforts undertaken in all these aspects did not make any significant difference in the performance of a large number of public enterprises. These could not be turned around and made productive. Gradually it was realized that essentially it was the public policy framework that needed change. The large public sector had to roll back. Many of the nationalized public undertakings had to be sold back to the private sector where they appropriately belonged and could be better managed. A consensus started to develop that apart from the national security, state should primarily be concerned with those activities that private sector is either unwilling or incapable of doing. Privatization was also visualized as an aspect of wide ranging public sector reforms needed for enhanced productivity and more efficient service delivery. Privatization became significant not only with regard to public enterprise management, but for the entire public service as it was realized that the governments could deliver public service more efficiently in some cases by using the private sector, by contracting-out and outsourcing instead of relying on and expanding public bureaucracy.

The experience of many countries indicates that privatization is most effective when it is accompanied by other reform programs that create an enabling environment for efficient private enterprises. The public sector plays a critical role in creating and supporting a market-friendly policy framework. Privatization and public sector reform must therefore go hand in hand (Republic of Botswana 1988: 39).

## EXPANSION AND PERFORMANCE OF PUBLIC ENTERPRISES IN BOTSWANA

Creation and expansion of public enterprises in Botswana was not due to ideology of socialism as was the case in many other African countries. Government in Botswana never adopted a policy of nationalization. On the contrary, the government was against the policy of nationalization all along and its development plans assured the private sector investors in this regard. Botswana, right from the time of independence in 1966, was not restrictive of the private enterprise and welcomed foreign investment. Where feasible the government was interested in joint ventures. The largest diamond mining company Debswana, a fifty-fifty joint venture between De Beers and Government of Botswana is an example of that policy. Botswana Development Corporation holds shares in a variety of firms across the economy. The creation and expansion of existing public enterprises in Botswana was a result of the positive role assumed by the Government after independence for developing the country's poor economy. As the private sector was not developed at the time of independence, the state had to come forward and undertake activities that were considered essential for economic development and social welfare. Development plans and economic policies operating in a mixed economy were governed by pragmatic considerations. Some public enterprises like Botswana Power Corporation, Water Utilities Corporation were considered essential as these were public utilities. Some public enterprises such as National Development Bank, Botswana Development Corporation were created to induce or facilitate private enterprise. Mass urban housing in the capital city was provided by Botswana Housing Corporation. Other public enterprises like Farmers' Marketing Board were created to help the agriculture; Botswana Telecommunications Corporation was created to develop telecommunications; Botswana Railways were developed to strengthen the transport network. Bank of Botswana came into being as the central bank of Botswana. Building Society as a housing finance institution and the Botswana Savings Bank as successor to the Post Office Savings Bank were among other public enterprises. Botswana's public enterprises were not to restrict or inhibit the growth of private enterprises. Public enterprise sector as a whole in Botswana is rather smaller than is typical in Africa.

With regard to the performance of public enterprises the general view is that African public enterprises have yielded a very low rate of return on the large amount of resources invested in them. Botswana's record is better than that of most public enterprises in Africa. Presenting his budget speech to the National Assembly in 2004, the Minister of Finance and Development Planning Mr. B. Gaolathe observed that, "financial performance of majority of public enterprises was satisfactory for the year 2002/2003 although there is ample scope for improvement." In 2005 Minister Gaolathe in his budget speech to the National Assembly reported that the "financial performance of the majority of public enterprises was relatively satisfactory for the year 2003/2004. Some public enterprises that recorded losses during 2002/2003 have now recorded net profits and positive return on capital employed (Budget Speech. Feb. 2005: 6). The performance of public enterprises has fluctuated during the past few years. Botswana Meat Commission running in loss for some years now for instance, was a profit-making public enterprise in the 1990s and was even identified by the United Nations Economic Commission for Africa (UNECA) as a model of success (Sharma 1994). A mixed picture of this kind and their fluctuating performance although not too depressing, establishes a need for reforms and privatization for enhanced productivity.

## Reasons for Privatization

As discussed earlier that disappointing performance of public enterprises, failure of different measures for improving their performance, and structural adjustment measures recommended by donor agencies have resulted in adoption of different forms of privatization in various African countries. Collapse of communism in the Soviet block of nations and pursuance of privatization policies in the western world have given further impetus to privatization drive all over Africa. It has been suggested that as the state with its limited administrative capacities has over-extended and overloaded itself, it should reduce and curtail the scope of its activities and contract. Increased scope of activities has resulted in inefficiency, mismanagement and corruption. With political control and interference, it has been difficult to operate these enterprises on business lines. Weak management has been difficult to develop and environment has not been conducive for the successful operation of public enterprises. Privatization policy in African countries is an outcome of these reasons (AAPAM 1987; Fadahunsi 1996; Ramanadham 1989).

Botswana's reasons for privatization are somewhat different from those of other African countries. Government here has not been pressurized to follow structural adjustment programs by international financial institutions to privatize its public enterprises. This policy in Botswana has also not been driven by budgetary constraints as in some other African countries. The impetus for privatization in Botswana has come from a desire to improve efficiency in the delivery of service, to attract direct foreign investment, and to create further opportunities for the citizen business sector. It is expected to create greater business development opportunities for the private sector as a whole. Private sector in Botswana has grown during the past years. It is now capable of delivering services both in competition with and in place of government. The financial sector is also more developed. The government realizes that private sector could undertake some functions more efficiently and the government could be left primarily with the tasks, which cannot be performed by the private sector (BOCCIM 1996; Jefferies 1998; Republic of Botswana 2003). The National Development Plan (NDP 9) follows this policy and Vision 2016 also suggests that the government must become better at costing its activities and must feel free to contract for services from the private sector in order to achieve its objectives more economically.

The privatization policy for Botswana is a product of extensive nation-wide consultation undertaken by a Task Force set-up to prepare the draft White paper on privatization in 1998. The report of the Task Force culminated in the adoption by Government in 2000 of the Privatization Policy for Botswana (Government Paper No. 1 of 2000).

## Meaning of Privatization

Defined narrowly, privatization means transferring the ownership of public enterprises to private buyers. The transfer of ownership from public to private hands is usually through selling all or some of the assets of public enterprises or other public entities to the private sector. This particular form of privatization is often termed divestiture, which may also be done by liquidation of assets. Defined broadly, privatization is much more than that; privatization encompasses all measures and policies aimed at strengthening the role of the private sector in the economy. Botswana Government has adopted the latter definition where privatization covers a very wide range of different policy actions resulting in private sector involvement in economic activities that have been previously undertaken by the public sector (GP No. 1, 7). According to the CEO of PEEPA, "privatization is not an end in itself but is a tool to shape economic policy. Privatization is a journey not a destination and must be understood in that context" (Galeforolwe 2004: 4).

## Objectives of Privatization

Privatization policy has been advocated as the means to enforce market discipline and promote efficient allocation and use of economic resources. While the reasons of privatization differ from one country to another, the objectives of privatization have often been very similar. These objectives include: promoting competition, improving efficiency and increasing productivity of enterprises; increasing direct citizen participation in the ownership of national assets; accelerating the rate of economic growth by stimulating entrepreneurship and investment; withdrawing from commercial activities which no longer need to be undertaken by the public sector; reducing the size of public sector; relieving the financial and administrative burden of Government in undertaking and maintaining a constantly expanding network of services and investments in infrastructure; and broadening and deepening the capital market (GP No. 1, 2000: 8-9).

### Machinery for Implementation of Privatization

Realizing that the management and implementation of the privatization process require an autonomous organization that has the authority, resources and technical skills to undertake the task, the Government in Botswana has established a "Public Enterprise Evaluation and Privatization Agency (PEEPA)." This entity is mandated to perform twin tasks of effective evaluation of the performance of parastatals and advice on the commercialization and privatization processes. PEEPA is at present attached to the Ministry of Finance and Development Planning but it is expected to be an autonomous entity. The Government would like it to be a company with a board of directors drawn mainly from private sector. Those chosen from the public sector will serve in their personal capacities. Members of the board will have diversified backgrounds and experiences (i.e., a lawyer, a banker, an economist, an accountant, an engineer, a businessman).

The responsibilities of PEEPA are: to identify candidates for privatization or commercialization/corporatization and decide on the appropriate course of action; to prepare a privatization master plan; to oversee all aspects of implementation of commercialization and privatization on behalf of Government; to review objectives of existing parastatals and set objectives for entities to be commercialized and/or corporatized; to assist government in setting performance targets for parastatals and other public entities; to monitor the performance of these entities in meeting their objectives and targets; to advise Government on the appointment of directors of public companies and parastatals; to monitor the performance of those directors and boards; to hire and supervise consultants on privatization and performance evaluation; to publicize its activities; and to develop and execute public education programs (GP No. 1, 2000: 21-22).

## PROCESS OF IMPLEMENTATION OF PRIVATIZATION POLICY IN BOTSWANA

### (a) Principles

The Government of Botswana has adopted the following principles for implementing the policy of privatization: privatization will be conducted for the benefit of all, not for the privileged few; privatization will be selective and, where implemented, the process will be transparent and equitable; privatization will be conducted in a way that will stimulate the development of local financial and capital markets and citizen owned businesses; different modalities of privatization will be considered as appropriate for improving the efficiency of different enterprises; measures will be taken to safeguard employee interests; the government will drive the privatization process but also hire in the expertise of different kinds required for the task (GP No. 1, 2000: 9-10).

### (b) Selecting Candidates for Privatization and Action Plans

The criteria to be adopted by the Government for considering candidates for privatization include: potential of the enterprise for improvements in efficiency and productivity; advantage of acquiring foreign participation to produce new technology and management and international link-up; the opportunity it could afford for domestic private sector growth and for citizen empowerment; contribution to stock market development; introducing competition into an otherwise monopolistic market; and extent of private sector interest in purchase and capacity for quicker investment. Action Plans prepared by PEEPA will guide the process and determine the kinds of safety nets and other support programs that will be developed on a case-by-case basis to ensure success of commercialization and privatization process. The Privatization master plan prepared by PEEPA outlines how privatization of different activities and entities can be structured, sequenced and implemented.

The Task Force (1998) recommended that the following list could be considered for privatization or commercialization: refuge collection, catering services, security services, cleaning services, landscaping and gardening, laundry services, medical equipment maintenance, mechanical and electric maintenance, ambulance and transport services in public hospitals, debt collection, tax collection, road maintenance, administration of selected tourism, management of national parks and game reserves, bore-hole drilling and maintenance, and organization of international conferences.

Public enterprises listed by the Task Force (1998) as serious candidates for privatization include: Botswana Development Corporation, National Development Bank, Botswana Building Society, Botswana Savings Bank, Botswana Motor Vehicles Insurance Fund, Botswana Power Corporation, Water Utilities Corporation, Botswana Telecommunications Corporation, Botswana Housing Corporation, Air Botswana, Botswana Meat Commission, Botswana Livestock Development Corporation, Botswana Agricultural Marketing Board, Botswana Railways, Botswana Postal Services, Botswana Vaccine Institute, and Municipal Abattoirs, and Government Ranches.

The Task Force (1998) also listed the government departments and other public entities, which could be considered for commercialization and corporatization. These include entities like Department of Architecture and Building Services, Registrar of Companies, Government Printer, Botswana Institute of Administration and Commerce (BIAC), Institute of Development Management (IDM), Botswana National Productivity Centre (BNPC), Department of Supplies, Title Deeds Office, Surveys and Mapping, Department of Information and Broadcasting, Customs Department, Department of Transport (motor Vehicles Registration), Roads Department, Birth/Death Registration, Veterinary Services, Geological Department, Department of Water Affairs, Immigration Department, Department of Civil Aviation, Central Sterilizing Unit, Department of Student Placement and Welfare, Botswana Wildlife Training Institute, Central Transport Organization (CTO), Computer Bureau, Rural Industries Promotion, Botswana Technology Centre, and Food Technology Research Service.

Reforming the Botswana public sector would require paying greater attention to maintaining lean and efficient public institutions; relating inputs (i.e., public expenditure) to outputs (i.e., provision of goods and services); avoiding redundant, conflicting or overlapping powers, responsibilities and departmental operations; rationalizing or terminating public services which are not cost effective; and monitoring more closely and evaluating the performance of Government Ministries on a continuous basis. The application of commercial principles in running government operations (commercialization) would be one way of reducing waste and improving the efficiency of allocation and utilization of economic resources. The Task Force on Privatization emphasized the need to modernize the country's public enterprises and make them operate in a business like manner. It recommended measures such as managerial autonomy, appointment of Boards of Directors exclusively on grounds of merit, performance contracts for the CEO and senior staff and performance targets (Republic of Botswana 1998: 39).

### (c) Citizen Empowerment

In order to facilitate citizen empowerment the government will promote shareholding by citizens and special access to shares by management and employees. The Government will also set up an "Investment Trust Fund" to purchase a certain percentage of shares of privatized enterprises on behalf of citizens. These shares will later be sold to citizens in small tranches over a given period. Government will also extend the Small, Medium and Micro Enterprises (SMME) "credit scheme" to small citizen investors, in order to facilitate citizen ownership of privatized enterprises. Some services (cleaning, catering, gardening, maintenance, etc.) currently produced in the public sector would provide opportunities to start many small business ventures by the same people who are presently government employees (GP 1, 2000: 11-12).

### (d) Foreign Participation

The Government realizes that there may not be enough local corporate investors with the financial resources and management expertise to acquire large state-owned enterprises. In such cases foreign participation would be necessary. As limiting foreign participation to very low levels could deter foreign investors, the government plans to adopt liberal rules for encouraging foreign participation and investment. The Government's policy is not to exclude foreign investors outright and not to impose across-the-board fixed restriction on foreign participation but to consider these on case-by-case basis. This is in keeping with government's policy to project Botswana as an investor-friendly country. Where practicable, Government will encourage and enable Botswana investors to acquire majority control. If citizen investors do not come forward to own majority of shares, concessions such as Build-Operate-Transfer (BOT) or Build-Own-Operate-Transfer (BOOT) will also be considered in cases where international expertise and technology are needed (GP 1, 2000: 12-13)

### (e) Safeguards and Safety Nets

Lay-off of some workers could be inevitable in the interest efficiency and productivity as some of these enterprises to be privatized have been over-staffed. In such cases the Government would award negotiated redundancy packages to affected employees within the established laws and policies. A program of training and skill re-orientation will be launched to facilitate the absorption of employees in other trades.

### (f) Measures for Public Education

Government realizes that privatization will only be successful when it respects and informs the public. The public needs to be regularly informed about each activity and how it will affect them. Government intends to disseminate information to the public through workshops and seminars, brochures and articles in newspapers, television and radio panel discussions, public speeches and special activities in rural areas. A national stakeholders' conference on privatization organized by PEEPA in April 2004 was an effort in that regard.

## APPREHENSIONS

Successful implementation of privatization policy will depend upon the extent to which it will be able to address adequately the anxieties and apprehensions of the people. It will have to be understood and appreciated by the public that privatization will not be a panacea for all the problems of ailing public enterprises. These enterprises may not become productive overnight simply as a result of change of ownership. In many cases competitive environment and commercialization may be an essential prerequisite for successful operation of privatized enterprises. Privatized enterprises may not become productive if these remain monopolies. The public may be subjected to inefficient and unproductive operations and may not be able to exercise control over these enterprises due to their diminished public accountability as a part of private sector. Because of underdeveloped private sector and dearth of local entrepreneurs, privatization may result in domination of foreign enterprises, multinationals or local business elite when these are offered for sale. The interests of poor and vulnerable may not be adequately guarded when these enterprises are owned by the private entrepreneurs or when the government starts applying cost recovery principles for the services rendered by the public sector. Lay-offs, retrenchment and downsizing exercises might increase unemployment and unrest. Haphazard implementation of privatization policy without adequate preparation and consultation with stakeholders and appropriate administrative machinery for implementation of the task could result in unexpected outcome. The objectives of privatization may not be realized. Privatization could also create room for corruption, in identifying the clients for buying the enterprise, fixing the price, settling the terms and conditions, etc. The experience of Zambia during the last few years demonstrates how economic liberalization and privatization could increase corruption. In that country, widespread privatization program undertaken during 1992-97, hailed by western donor countries as a model of success, revealed widespread corruption as documented by Chikulo (2000: 168-69): "Indeed, although there is no evidence to suggest an economic turn around, privatization of the economy has, instead, opened up opportunities for rampant corruption and allowed the ruling political elite to amass enormous wealth . . . small scale companies which have been bought at almost give away prices by locals, have been monopolized by politicians and their associates . . . only the well connected few reap any benefits from the government's privatization and economic liberalization program."

The Government of Botswana appears to be mindful of such apprehensions and anxieties and proposes to undertake measures (some of these have been discussed above) to preempt such possibilities. Botswana has been cautious and proposes to be selective in identifying the candidates for privatization or for resorting to a particular form of privatization. The country took time to deliberate extensively on the privatization policy before it was adopted. The recommendations of the Task Force on Privatization submitted in 1998 were widely discussed and the Government adopted the policy in 2000. Public Enterprise Evaluation and Privatization Agency (PEEPA) established as administrative machinery after the adoption of the policy has taken time to produce the Action Plan for privatization. This will be debated in the National Assembly and the public before approval and implementation. Public discussion and transparency will hopefully check the undesirable practices and corrupt practices.

## Monitoring, Evaluation and Follow-up

An effective system of regulation, continuous evaluation and close monitoring are essential to the success of privatization process. Regulation may be required to intervene to influence the economic decisions of an enterprise and continuous evaluation will be required to draw conclusions and make judgments on the outcomes or impact of the reform program. Similarly, monitoring will be essential for systematically appraising progress during the process and after privatization and to check that the objectives of privatization are being achieved. The Government has entrusted PEEPA to be responsible for these tasks with assistance from Public Enterprise Monitoring Unit (PEMU) of the Ministry of Finance and Development Planning.

## Critical Factors for Success of Policy

The Government recognizes that the success of privatization is contingent upon a number of factors: a strong political commitment to policy implementation; an appropriate legal framework; an effective supervisory or regulatory authority; reformed management systems; support of public servants and public enterprise employees; public support and transparency. It is widely recognized that privatization is a political process as well as a commercial and economic process. Therefore, public support is a major consideration in any privatization program.

## Post-privatization Phase : Changed Role of the State

The role of government will not end after the implementation of privatization plans, it will only change. The government will have to continue to safeguard public interest and monitor the performance of private sector generally and privatized undertakings in particular. The government realizes that its role will continue to change as the economy changes. The determination and commitment of Government will have to be matched by readiness and cooperation from the private sector. "The interaction between Government and the private sector will be transformed into a "smart partnership" of co-operation and complementarily that emphasizes 'win-win' situations. The drive towards diversified growth must be led by the private sector, which is expected to display the qualities of good corporate citizenship including the promotion of citizen empowerment. The public sector will progressively diminish its role in the provision of marketable goods and services and will rather seek to facilitate and, where necessary, regulate the operation of business by the private sector" (GP No. 1, 2000: 3). One could derive some satisfaction in this regard from the statement of Minister of Finance and Development Planning Gaolathe made to the National Assembly when presenting the Draft Privatization Policy for Botswana. He made it clear to the country that the privatization should not entail government discarding any of its core responsibilities which include good governance, safety and welfare of its citizens. He assured the House that the process will be carried out with a human face and efforts will be made to safeguard national interests (Mmegi 2000). Only the time will tell as to what extent these assurances will be honoured. It is hoped that a healthy public-private partnership will contribute to improved service delivery and success of privatization policy.

## References


AAPAM, 1987, *Public Enterprise Performance and Privatization Debate: A Review of Options for Africa*, New Delhi, Vikas.

Botswana Confederation of Commerce, Industry and Manpower, 1996, *Privatization in Botswana*, Gaborone

Chikulo, Bornwell C., 2000, "Corruption and Accumulation in Zambia", in K.R. Hope Sr. and B.C. Chikulo (eds.), *Corruption and Development in Africa: Lessons from Country Case Studies*, New York, Palgrave.

Fadahunsi, O. (ed.), 1996, *Privatization in Africa: The Way Forward*, Nairobi, AAPAM.

Galeforolwe, J.B., 2004, "Privatization Policy for Botswana," paper presented at a National Stakeholders' Conference on Privatization, 'Making Privatization Everyone's Business," held in Gaborone, Botswana.

Grosh, Barbara and R.S. Mukandala (eds.), 1994, *State Owned Enterprises in Africa*, Boulder, Lynne Rienner.

Jefferies, K., 1998, "Botswana's Public Enterprises", in W.A. Edge and M. Lekorwe (eds.), *Botswana Politics and Society*, Pretoria, Van Schaik Publishers.

Mmegi, 2000, 31 March-06 April.

Nellis, J.R., 1986, *Public Enterprises in Sub-Saharan Africa*, Washington, D.C.:The World Bank.

Ramanadham, V.V., (ed.), 1989, *Privatization in Developing Countries*, London, Routledge.

Sharma, K.C., 1994, "Botswana Meat Commission: A Success Story?", in S. Rasheed, Asmelash Beyene and E.E. Otobo (eds.), *Public Enterprises in Africa: Lessons from Country Case-Studies*, Ljubjana, ICPE and UNECA.

Shirley, Marry and John Nellis, 1991, *Public Enterprise in Africa*, Washington D.C. : The World Bank.

Republic of Botswana, 1998, Draft White Paper on a Privatization Policy for Botswana, Government Printer, Gaborone.

Republic of Botswana, 2000, Privatization Policy for Botswana, Government Paper No. 1 of 2000, Ministry of Finance and Development Planning, Government Printer, (Referred in the paper as GP 1).

Republic of Botswana, 2003, National Development Plan 9: 2003/04-2008/09, Gaborone, Botswana, Ministry of Finance and Development Planning.

Republic of Botswana, 2004, Budget Speech 2004 Delivered to the National Assembly on 9th February, 2004, by Hon. B. Gaolathe, Gaborone, Botswana, Government Printer.

Republic of Botswana, 2005, Budget Speech 2005 Delivered to the National Assembly on 7th February 2005 by Hon. B. Gaolathe, Minister of Finance and Development Planning, Gaborone, Botswana, Government Printer.

UN, 1989, *Role and Extent of Competition in Improving the Performance of Public Enterprises*, New York.

UNECA, 1991, *Improving Performance of Public Enterprise Management in Africa: Lessons from Country Experiences*, Dakar.

# 14

# Health, Equity and Sustainable Development : The Impact of Economic Growth on People's Health in Rural Southwestern China

LI JIAN

Since the introduction of the "Four Modernizations," China has witnessed a spectacular economic growth (Vajpeyi and Ponomarenko 2001: 91), which has brought about unprecedented changes to many sectors of Chinese society, including the rural health sector. Unlike other sectors, however, the transformation in China's rural health sector has been drastic and has affected the lives of over 900 million Chinese peasants profoundly. An in-depth understanding of the vital changes in China's rural health sector and their major impacts will shed light on the sustainability of China's economic development.

The following discussion provides a micro-level case study that highlights the interconnection between health equity and sustainable development in rural China. Drawing upon my ethnographic fieldwork in Lake Village[1] in Southwest China combined with national-level data, I examine how health disparity locks the rural households into poverty and erodes their economic achievements quickly. The central question is how health disparity functions to impoverish millions of Chinese peasants and diminish the sustainability of China's development since the country's economic reform.

Paula Braveman (2006: 167) defined health disparity as a particular type of difference in health that could be shaped by policies. According to her, health disparity does not refer to all differences in health. Rather, it is a difference in which a disadvantaged social group systematically experiences worse health or greater health risks than more advantaged social groups. Pursuing the elimination of health disparity means pursuing health equity.

Following Braveman's definition, I define health disparity as gaps in the access to health care, quality of health care, and differences in the presence of diseases between the Chinese peasants and other sectors in the Chinese society. In China, health disparity often results due to the uneven distribution of resources and it is usually unnecessary, avoidable, and unfair. Determined by their orientation and emphasis, government policies may either enhance or diminish a health disparity. Also, for the sake of my analysis, I divide the recent history of Lake Village into two phases. The first is the phase of the People's Commune, between 1958 and 1984. The second begins with the establishment of the Household Responsibility System in the village in 1985 and continues until today. At the national level, the first phase coincides with China's pre-reform era and the second stands for the post-reform period.

The paper is organized into four parts. The first part discusses the pre-reform history of the local health care system and surveys the communal socio-economic situations. The second part scrutinizes the village's health situation since 1985. In China, government policies and economic development with few provisions toward equity created remarkable health disparity in recent years. Since the 1990s, both macro and micro-data indicate that such health disparity has functioned to impoverish millions of Chinese peasants and has deprived them of access to even the most basic medical services. (WHO 2005, 6) Alarmingly, now the growing disparity has also begun to diminish the local community's participation in critical disease-prevention activities such as the schistosomiasis control program, which has resulted in the reemergence of the disease as a public health problem. Thirdly, I discuss three cases to illustrate the main patterns in which health disparity impoverishes the rural households in need of health care. The last section presents policy implications of this study and highlights the local people's perspectives on health equity and sustainable development.

## STUDY SITE AND RESEARCH METHODOLOGY

The field research for this project was conducted in Lake Village in Southwest China during the summer of 2006. Lake Village is located in the hilly region of the Southwest Plateau of China. A 15-kilometer road connected the village with Bridge Township and River County. The county seat was 20 minutes from the village by bus, about one hour by bicycle, or three to four hours on foot. Bridge Township was about half the distance.

In 2006, Lake Village had 2,086 persons living in 482 households, averaging about 4.3 persons per household. According to the village headman, the village had 982 full-time laborers and cultivated about 2,900 Mu [478 acres] of rice paddies and cornfields. In addition, the village had about 500 Mu [82 acres] of sloping fields for growing cash crops such as vegetables and fruits. Currently, about 200 young men and women worked as wage laborers outside the village, and about the same number of people did so during the slack seasons. In 2005, the average household income was 8,694 Yuan, or about 2,022 Yuan per person. On average, about 60 percent of the villagers' income came from agriculture and the rest came from trade and emigrant labor.

The village for my research site was selected for two reasons. First, it was a typical farming village in the region. Also, although the village had eradicated schistosomiasis, a parasitic disease, eight years ago, the disease had reemerged as a public health problem in the village. Because of my long-term research interest in schistosomiasis control, I found Lake Village a suitable place for my fieldwork (Li 2006a; Li 2006b; Li 2006c). During my fieldwork, I stayed in the village for four weeks and lived in the house of Mr. Song Guangyou, the owner of the village grocery store. Besides Lake Village, I also visited two nearby villages, the county schistosomiasis control station, and the county hospital.

My research methods included participant observation, key informant interviews, surveys and questionnaires, concept mapping, structured and unstructured interviews, focus groups, and home visits. Participant observation allowed me an opportunity to observe the daily activities of the peasants and provided me with some "real" sense of feeling about their health and living conditions.

While in the village, I conducted structured surveys of 50 households, and completed 16 in-depth household interviews. These interviews were about two hours long and often involved the entire family in the discussion. The households were selected based on their income status (low-income, middle-income, and upper-income groups in the village) and health status (households with members who suffered from a serious illness, and the normal households). In addition, I organized a focus group of 8 members based on the same criteria. During my fieldwork, the group had three meetings to discuss the data I obtained from interviews, surveys, and other methods. Most of the data presented in this paper were evaluated and confirmed by the focus group. The county-level statistics were collected from the local officials and the county annals.

## LAKE VILLAGE IN THE PRE-REFORM ERA : A THREE-TIERED HEALTH SYSTEM BASED ON EQUITY

As a closed society, the Chinese economy stagnated between the 1950s and the mid-1980s. The government controlled production and made decisions about distribution of resources. In cities, the state-owned companies and factories provided employment and resources. In the countryside, the People's Commune took charge of agricultural production. During this period of time, China's economic growth was remarkably slow, if compared with its neighbors. In Hong Kong, for example, per capita income grew from about $180 in 1949 to $6,000 in 1985. In Taiwan, per capita income rose from $70 to exceed $3,000 over the same period. In contrast, per capita income in China grew from $50 in 1952 to only about $200 in 1985 (Cheng 1989: 869).

Despite the slow economic growth, the Chinese government under Mao Zedong attempted to promote health equity in Chinese society and made remarkable progress. In past millennia, the Chinese peasants suffered most deeply from health disparity, bearing the bulk of China's disease burden and having minimal access to the country's medical services (*Health Research Institute 2002*: 16). After the founding of the People's Republic, Mao demanded that the health care system must "serve the rural masses" and the Chinese Communist Party waged a series of movements such as the "Patriotic Health Movement" and the "Medical Services to the Countryside Movement" to ensure national support for Mao's plan to build a new rural health system.

Mao's goal was to provide basic health care for all Chinese peasants. Following Mao's guideline, China's health spending pendulum shifted strongly toward the construction of an equity-oriented public health approach for the rural poor (Kaufman 2005: 3). Between 1950 and 1957, the government helped build some 50,000 rural health centers. By the end of 1950s, every rural county had at least one disease prevention station and every rural township had at least one health center (Li 2001: 255).

Mao's emphasis on rural health reached its climax in his "Directive on Public Health," published on June 26, 1965, in which he strongly criticized the city-biased policy of the Ministry of Health at that time. Mao pointed out that rural China was still severely short of doctors and medicine and over 500 million Chinese peasants lacked any health care. Mao concluded, "In medical and health work, we must put the emphasis on the countryside" (Mao 1976: 89).

Under this policy, China's rural health sector grew rapidly. Between 1960 and 1978, the number of patient beds and the service capacity of the rural health centers on average increased by 16.7 percent annually, 4 times higher than the overall increase in the country's health sector (Ministry of Health 2004: 66). Led by the government, the communes allocated sufficient resources to develop their Cooperative Medical System and Barefoot Doctor System in their production brigades and production teams. In less than two decades, China built a rural health care system that was based on equity, low cost, and prevention (Bezlova 1999: 2). By 1980, the system had already covered approximately 90 percent of the entire rural population (Ministry of Health 1982: 60).

To expand the rural medical personnel, the government required urban doctors to visit the countryside and train rural barefoot doctors on a regular basis. Between 1965 and 1975, 1.1 million urban health workers served in the mobile medical teams, treating rural patients and training the barefoot doctors (Xia 2003: 8). Such activities helped to improve the quality of rural health care. By the end of the 1970s, the total number of barefoot doctors had reached 1.5 million, working side by side with 3.9 million health assistants and midwives in the countryside. For the first time in Chinese history, rural China's health workers outnumbered their urban counterparts by 2 to 1 (Li 2001: 27).

Like thousands of villages in China, Lake Village benefited from such social developments. In its health sector, the village experienced three significant improvements during this time. The first was the general improvement of the villagers' living standards. After the disastrous "Great-Leap-Forward" years, the government began to allow the communes some freedom in planning their agricultural production, which made it possible for their production teams to grow more food items for local consumption. Also, in Lake Village, each household was allotted a private plot for growing vegetables or cash crops for itself. Privately owned livestock was allowed as well. These measures stimulated local agriculture, and the annual grain yields kept increasing from less than 300 kilograms in the late 1950s to more than 600 kilograms per person in the late 1980s.

With the construction of a reservoir in 1959, the villagers secured access to clean water for their household use. With the assistance of the county health education program, most households built hygienic latrines and pigpens. These and other improvements in living standards helped improve the health of the villagers. According to the county records, the local people's life expectancy increased from 35 years in 1952 to 68 years in 1982 and the infant mortality rate declined from 200 to 50 per 1000 live births during the same period of time.

The second improvement was the creation of a Three-Tiered Health System that offered the villagers access to basic health care. The first tier was made of barefoot doctors in Lake Village. In 1961, Wang Jialing and Liu Fuzhou, two village young men, were recruited by the county and were trained in the county's health school for one year. The county provided them with technical help and sent them back to open a health post in Lake Village. Wang and Liu received some additional short-term training later on and worked in the village until they retired in the early 1980s. Wang and Liu were called "barefoot doctors," because they were not fully trained doctors and because they were expected to do farm work alongside other peasants from time to time. Their responsibilities included health education, preventive work, disease surveillance, child health, and other simple outpatient care.

The Bridge People's Commune Health Center constituted the second tier, which functioned as a higher-level outpatient clinic. It had 32 health workers and 20 patient beds. Doctor Song Weiguo, who received three-year's training in the prefecture health school, headed the center. The village health post and the commune health center formed the core of the system and provided the bulk of medical services to the villagers. The River County Hospital, the final tier of the system, only treated the severely ill-patients who were referred to them by the commune centers. It had better medical equipment and its doctors received five years of medical training or more.

The Cooperative Medical System footed the villagers' medical bills. Funds from the county and the commune covered the main expenditures of the Three-Tiered Health System. In addition, the villagers needed to pay 1 Yuan per person into the system and production brigades and production teams were required to match their members' annual contributions. Wang Guoliang, a 72-year-old villager, remembered the system in this way:

> "In those years, things were easier. You didn't have much money, yet you had nothing to worry about. All you needed to do was just to live. Everything was pretty much taken care of. In case you had a bad illness, you could go to the Bridge Commune Health Center. You would pay only 5 cents for the registration fee, and the Cooperative Medical System would cover your medicine—you had to pay it first, but you could get your money back soon after. Besides, if the commune referred you to the county hospital, the Cooperative Medical System would cover your expenses there as well. . ."

Lake Village's third achievement was the eradication of a number of endemic diseases. At the national level, eradication of social ills and infectious diseases were probably China's major health achievement at the time. Those included the closure of brothels and opium dens, which made it possible to eradicate the social illness related to illicit drug use, prostitution, and sexually transmitted diseases. Relying on health education, "people's patriotism," and low-tech public health measures, the Chinese health authorities successfully reduced the national incidence of such infectious diseases as leprosy, cholera, the plague, smallpox, tuberculosis, typhoid, relapsing fever, Kaschin-beck disease, and the Keshan disease (Hesketh and Zhu 2004: 1427). Infectious diseases ranked as the second most important causes of death in 1957; they declined to 8th in 1988 in rural China (Ministry of Health 1989: 10).

*The Annals of River County* recorded that incidence of infectious diseases declined significantly during the period. Tuberculosis, for example, declined from 35 cases per 1,000 people in 1950 to 15 cases per 1000 in 1965. By the end of the 1950s, the county had already eradicated typhoid and cholera. For the Lake Villagers, however, the most important achievement was the eradication of schistosomiasis.

In China, schistosomiasis is caused by a water-borne parasite (*Schistosoma japonicum*), with a snail (*Oncomelania hupensis*) as its intermediate host. The disease begins when blood flukes enter the human body through skin penetration. Once in the human body, the female worms lay millions of eggs during their lifetime. Most eggs remain in the tissues to cause illness and the rest of the eggs pass in the feces and find their way to water. Once in the water, the eggs burst and release larvae, which infect the snail and multiply into cercariae inside their intermediate host. Eventually, the snail discharges cercariae into the water, which in turn penetrate the human skin upon contact and begin a new cycle of the disease. The symptoms of the disease include abdominal pain, fever, malnutrition, internal bleeding, diarrhea, and anemia. If the infection is acute, the patient may die in the absence of medical treatment. Chronic schistosomiasis results in liver cancer and colorectal cancer. In the late stage, as a result of the liver hardening, a large amount of fluid flows into the abdominal cavity, and the patient's belly becomes distended, and that is why schistosomiasis is often known as the "Big-belly Disease" in rural China (Li 2006c: 19).

In the 1950s, 14 townships and 67 villages in River County were endemic with schistosomiasis. In Lake Village, a 1955 study estimated that more than half of the villagers were infected and about 20 percent were in the late stage of the disease, and that schistosoma cercariae infested 90 percent of the water or marsh areas of the village.

In 1960, the County Bureau of Health established a county schistosomiasis control station to lead the countywide campaign against schistosomiasis. In the following year, all 14 endemic communes founded schistosomiasis control centers. In the next lower level, the production brigades organized schistosomiasis control teams in the village and recruited key control persons. The major strategies at the time were snail control and environment improvement. Led by the county, endemic communes mobilized mass participation in such efforts as building hygienic latrines, reconstructing irrigation systems, reclaiming swamplands, burning the weeds surrounding reservoirs and burying snails with earth. Endemic villages also organized snail-control teams to scrutinize the susceptible snail areas regularly.

To treat the patients, the county set up a schistosomiasis clinic in Lake Village in 1965. All persons aged five years and older were required to go for a stool examination. Those who were found infected were treated in the clinic. At that time, the treatment was mainly chemotherapy with Antimony Potassium Tartrate (APT). While APT was an effective parasite-killing drug, it had intoxicating side effects as well. For those who had liver or kidney problems, the drug could be lethal. To minimize the villagers' risks, the county required that the clinic must hospitalize the patients and supervise the entire two-week course of treatment. The treatment was free and the villagers needed only to pay for their meals. Besides, the production teams paid adult patients for all the days they spent in the clinic. Six months after the treatment, the clinic would conduct a follow-up examination for the patients. If any parasite eggs were found, the chemotherapy would be repeated. In addition, once every three years, the county medical team came to the village to conduct physical examinations for villagers and search for any trace of the disease in the community.

As a result of those efforts and programs, in River County, the snail habitat shrank by 80 percent and the number of infected patients declined by 95 percent. In 1995, the provincial schistosomiasis research institute conducted an evaluation study in the county and confirmed that the disease was under control. In 1998, as the prevalence of human and cattle infections was less than 2 percent and there were no reports of acute cases of human infection for three years, the provincial government announced that schistosomiasis was no longer a public health problem in River County. He Liming, a former director of the county schistosomiasis control station, recalled:

> "Before liberation, schistosomiasis devastated River County. It created more than ten widow villages, in which all men died of schistosomiasis. There used to be over 100 households and some 500 people in Riverbank Village in the 1930s, only 13 households survived in 1949. There were 16 households and some 90 people in Three-Temple Village in the 1940s. In 1949, only 27 big-belly patients were alive. The Wang family in Three-Temple Village had 18 people, 16 died of schistosomiasis. Even in the 1950s, the fluke cercariae were everywhere. If your hands or feet touched the water, you could be infected in a few seconds. How did we control the infested disease? We did it in River County, not because we had high technology or because we were rich. Our budget allowed us to spend no more than 50 cents per person per year. We did not have snail-killing chemicals. Prazequantal, the medicine we now use to treat schistosomiasis, was not available until 1986 here. How did we do it? It was because the county, the commune, and the village, all wanted to eradicate the disease. All local people were determined to win the battle. People knew what the disease had done to their family members before liberation and everyone was eager to get rid of the flukes. . ."

Retrospectively, the health sector of Lake Village improved a great deal during China's pre-reform era. The coverage of the Cooperative Medical System was low. The services provided by the barefoot doctors and the commune health center were limited. Not all patients who needed care would be referred to the county hospital. Despite that, I heard no criticisms or complaints about the Cooperative Medical System and the Three-Tiered Health System. On the contrary, I found most people spoke highly of the system.

The key point that highlighted the Three-Tiered Health System was equity. Tallied with Mao's thought, the system helped to reduce health disparity and meet the basic health needs of the villagers. The emphasis on disease prevention and health education benefited all villagers. Minor illnesses were taken care of in the village. More serious illnesses would be referred to next tier of the system. Financially protected by the Cooperative Medical System, for the first time in the village's history, the villagers found health care available and affordable. Technically, what Lake Village had was health equity based on low quality and simple technologies. However, Wang Huli, a 68-year-old-man who had just treated his rheumatism in the county hospital, looked at the system in this way:

"In those years, medical services were not as good as they are now. Neither our village health post nor the commune health center had really good medicine. Yet, they were the places we could go to. Today, the county hospital has a lot of good medicine, but a patient can die in the hospital's courtyard, if he cannot pay for their services. . ."

## LAKE VILLAGE IN POST-REFORM PERIOD: FROM HEALTH EQUITY TO HEALTH DISPARITY

To understand Lake Village's health situation today, we first need to briefly review the national scenario. For the Lake Villagers and their fellow peasants nationwide, two national events were of especial importance. In 1982, the Chinese People Congress passed a law to dismantle the People's Commune. By 1986, the Household Responsibility System had officially become the mode of agricultural production nationwide. Liberated from a controlled economy, the Chinese peasants leased their share of land and returned to an individual household farming way of life.

Despite its positive impacts on the national economy, such a reform also undermined China's Three-Tiered Health System that had operated successfully in rural China for nearly three decades. After the People's Commune was dismantled, China's rural health system lost its foundation and began to collapse. In 1993, less than 10 percent of Chinese peasants were still covered by the Cooperative Medical System, down from over 90 percent a decade ago. In 2003, 80 percent of Chinese peasants—some 640 million people—lacked any form of health insurance (World Bank 2005a: 1).

As a whole, the Chinese government reduced its health expenditure. By international standards, a country with China's per capita income would be expected to spend around 2.4 percent of its GDP on health. However, it spent only 1.9 percent (World Bank 2005b: 6). Although government health spending has risen in real terms, but has fallen sharply as a share of total government spending. For example, the government's proportion of national health care spending was 32.16 percent in 1978. By 2002, it had declined to 15.21 percent (Liu 2004: 532). (Table 14.1)

In the post-reform era, China's rural health sector faced a three-fold problem. First, the new Chinese leadership drastically changed the direction of the nation's health policy. The pre-reform health system was seen as an example of radical egalitarianism and unsuitable for a society with a market economy. The emphasis on health equity was abandoned and cities again became the focal points of government health spending. The public health and epidemic prevention were converted to a low priority. Essentially, the government adopted a *laissez-faire* policy and left the rural health sector entirely to the market (Hsiao 1995: 1047). Although the rural people lacked

**TABLE 14.1**
**Government's Share v. Individual's Share in China's National Health Spending : 1978-2002**

| *Year* | *Government health spending in real terms (100,000,000 Yuan)* | *Government's share in China's national health spending (%)* | *Individual's share in China's national health spending %)* |
|---|---|---|---|
| 1978 | 35 | 32.16 | 20.43 |
| 1979 | 41 | 32.21 | 20.34 |
| 1980 | 52 | 36.24 | 21.19 |
| 1981 | 60 | 32.27 | 23.74 |
| 1982 | 69 | 38.86 | 21.65 |
| 1983 | 78 | 37.43 | 31.45 |
| 1984 | 89 | 36.96 | 32.64 |
| 1985 | 108 | 38.58 | 28.46 |
| 1986 | 122 | 38.69 | 26.38 |
| 1987 | 127 | 33.53 | 30.31 |
| 1988 | 145 | 29.79 | 31.28 |
| 1989 | 168 | 27.27 | 34.09 |
| 1990 | 187 | 25.06 | 35.73 |
| 1991 | 204 | 22.84 | 37.50 |
| 1992 | 229 | 20.84 | 39.81 |
| 1993 | 272 | 19.75 | 42.17 |
| 1994 | 342 | 19.43 | 43.95 |
| 1995 | 387 | 17.97 | 46.40 |
| 1996 | 462 | 17.04 | 50.64 |
| 1997 | 524 | 16.38 | 52.84 |
| 1998 | 590 | 16.04 | 54.85 |
| 1999 | 641 | 15.84 | 55.85 |
| 2000 | 710 | 15.47 | 58.98 |
| 2001 | 801 | 15.93 | 59.97 |
| 2002 | 864 | 15.21 | 58.34 |

*Sources* : Health Economics Research Institute, Ministry of Health, 2003, China's Total Health Expenditure Research Report 2003. (Zhongguo Weisheng Zong Feiyong Yanjiu Baogao 2003) Zhao, Yuqing, ed. Beijing: Ministry of Health, pp. 15, and 74-77.

health insurance and their income was less than one-third of their urban counterparts, they now faced the same health care system the city dwellers utilized (Perrins 2004: 39).

Moreover, in distribution, the government spending unfairly favored cities, which worsened the existing health disparity. In 2004, the government recognized that it was unfair that only 30 percent of the total governmental health expenditure has been used for rural areas in recent years, although over 70 percent of people lived in the countryside (Xinhua 2004: 5). In reality, however, the health disparity may even be worse. In 1998, for example, the central government's total spending on health was 58.7 billion Yuan, of which only 9.3 billion Yuan or 15.9 percent were for the countryside (Zhou 2002: 4). Calculated according to the number of people, it meant that the government spent 130 Yuan on each urban person, but it only spent about 10 Yuan on each rural person. In view of hospital budgets, 50.5 percent of government expenditures in 2002 went to urban hospitals and just 7.3 percent to rural township health centers (UNPD 2005: 58).

Third, the government also reduced its subsidies to rural relief funds. For instance, the government subsidy to rural social security dropped from 100 million Yuan in 1979 to 35 million in 1992. Distributed according to the number of people, each Chinese peasant received less than 4 fen (0.5 US cent) from the government in that year. Between 1991 and 2000, the proportion of government direct investment on rural health declined from 12.5 percent to 6.6 percent. Currently, the government spends only 10 percent of its social security investment on its rural population (Chen 2005: 74).

To offset the shortage of funds in the countryside, the central government now required the local governments to be responsible for rural health. Yet, few local authorities had a financial capability to carry out such a responsibility (Wang 2004: 2). Thus, the reduced health budget of the central government directly impacted China's rural health, which resulted in shrinking in every area in the rural health sector, including health coverage, health care services, public health, health education, and disease prevention.

Viewed from Lake Village, the major negative impacts of the national-level policy changes and health budget reductions may be summed up into five categories. First, the local leadership vanished and the village became a community of disunity. In 1985, after the Bridge People's Commune was dismantled, Lake Production Brigade and its four production teams were also disbanded. A village council was founded. The council consisted of 12 persons: the village headman, the party secretary, their two deputies, and eight representatives from each of the five village units. Under the village council, each village unit had five representatives. In the past, the brigade and team leaders were paid as full-time cadres by work points. Now, the village council members received only stipends drawn from the village fees. The unit representatives were compensated only when they had meetings in the village council. As a result, the village leaders considered their positions a part-time job and spent most of their time on their own business.

In 1986, the Household Responsibility System virtually brought all villagers back to 1953, the year of Land Reform. All land and farming tools were redistributed to each household based on the number of people it had. Leasing contracts were signed for 15 years. After that neither the township nor the village would do anything for a Lake Village household, except for collecting taxes and fees. Each household changed into an economic unit and became solely responsible for its own well-being.

Under such circumstances, Lake Village lost its leadership and the social network that had once served as the foundation for the village's health sector. The cadres no longer had a genuine interest in the village's public health. To ensure their own economic well being, most households lost their incentives to participate in the village's public health activities. In the pre-reform years, the public welfare fund supported the village public health programs and protected the poorest households. As the village council abolished the fund in 1987, the village now was unable to fund any public health projects. In my survey, 42 out of the 50 households reported that the township and the village did nothing for the village's public health in the past three years.

Second, the villagers' access to health care degenerated. The Bridge Township Health Center (the former Bridge People's Commune Health Center) closed in 1988. After the collapse of the Cooperative Medical System, the center lost the main part of its subsidies and began to overcharge its patients for services. As a result, the local people considered the center too expensive, yet its quality was lower than the county hospital and another neighboring township health center. The center suffered badly from the lack of patients, which eventually resulted in the closure.

As a large village in the area, Lake Village's health post-survived and changed its name into "Lake Village Clinic." The new name was appropriate, because the post was no longer a communal health center. As it received no public funds, it was now entirely a private clinic. Wang Jialing and Liu Fuzhou, the former barefoot doctors, retired. Several local doctors leased and operated the clinic for a few years. Luo Fangguo and Wang Weiming, two men from a nearby town, had been the clinic's doctors since 2000. Luo received two-year paramedical education in the county health school. Wang was Luo's brother-in-law and he only had a high school diploma. Despite that, Wang functioned in the same way as Luo did in the clinic. Unlike the former barefoot doctors, current village doctors had little knowledge of Chinese medicine, and they only prescribed and sold western-style medicine. The registration fee (5 Yuan per person per visit) and the differences between retail and wholesale prices of the medicine accounted for the income of the clinic. For the Lake Villagers, the health care of the Three-Tiered Health System had entirely disappeared.

Thirdly, more and more villagers became unable to afford basic medical services. When sick, the villagers now had three options. For minor illness, they would take care of it by themselves. If the illness were more serious, they would visit the village clinic. For the most serious illness, the villagers would have to go to the county hospital. The average cost for a visit of the village clinic was between 20 and 50 Yuan. However, the expenses for a medical treatment in the county hospital could go far beyond the villagers' financial capacity.

Before the reform, River County Hospital's emphasis was prevention and public health. To generate income, it now concentrated on the high technologies and medical treatment. Since 1988, it purchased a number of new pieces of equipment, including an X-ray apparatus, a gastroscopic machine, and a B-ultrasonographic machine. According to He Jianguo, the vice-director of the hospital, the hospital also made progress in developing effective treatments for lung disease, stomach cancer, and lower respiratory infections. Despite such technical improvements, few peasants were able to afford health care in the county hospital. In 2006, a clinic visit to the county hospital cost between 68 and 122 Yuan, which was approximately equal to one Lake Villager's per capita income for 12 or 20 days. The cost for a hospitalization was between 3,065 and 7,200 Yuan, nearly the annual income of a household in Lake Village. Wang Zigong, a 58-year-old villager, described her experience in this way:

> "We rural people really cannot afford to be sick these days. If we catch a minor illness, we'll just lie down for a day or two. For a bad illness, if we are lucky, we may be able to buy some medicine from the village clinic for 20 or 30 Yuan and get by with it. The worst is to go to the county hospital. When my husband had his appendectomy surgery last year, for the registration fee alone, they charged us several hundred Yuan! All the money our family earned in the past years was gone. If anyone in our house were sick again, we would have to smash our wok and tear down our house. . . "

The Wang family was not alone. The cost of health care currently increased at a much faster pace than the growth of rural income, as a result, many Chinese peasants were unable to afford the most basic health care. At the national level, for example, the rural annual income increased 2.2 times between 1990 and 1999. During the same period of time, the registration fee increased 6.2 times and hospitalization expenses increased 5.1 times (National Bureau of Statistics 2000: 89; Ministry of Health 1996: 408). According to a study of 118 villages nationwide, 83 percent of rural patients were now unwilling to accept inpatient care because of financial difficulty (Han and Luo 2005: 2). Another study of 3 villages in West China found that 74 percent of the households surveyed reported that "lack of money" was the factor that prevented their family members from accepting medical services (Huang and Zhang 2006: 114).

Fourth, despite the high prices, the quality of health care available to the Lake Villagers was much lower than the services enjoyed by their urban counterparts. In Lake Village, most villagers agreed that the clinic was a useful asset of the village because it was convenient to visit. Also, if compared with the county hospital, the village clinic was more affordable.

However, a number of villagers complained about the quality of service of the clinic. Lake Village Clinic was housed in the former meeting-room of the village. Originally, it was a one-room house, now a bamboo wall portioned the room into two. The two doctors, their family members, and Doctor Wang's dogs, often ate and slept in the clinic. Sanitation conditions were often poor. The medicine was stored on an old bookshelf. According to Luo, the fixed assets of the clinic were valued at about 10,000 Yuan, including the medicine. Except for the tables, benches, and a boiling pot for sterilization, however, there was no medical equipment in the house.

Luo told me that the clinic would purchase a sphygmomanometer soon. Currently, however, questions and answers formed the two doctors' principal means of diagnosis. The clinic did not keep the medical records of their patients. Nor did the two doctors write down their prescriptions. At one time, I observed that a patient who complained about fever did not even get his body temperature examined. Doctor Luo simply sold him a dose of cold medicine and sent him home. While diagnosing, Doctor Wang's usual strategy was to question what medicine his patient usually took in the past, and then prescribed the same medicine.

Such quality issues were not just found in Lake Village. Like Luo and Wang, currently, most village doctors received very little medical education; few had more than a short-term training (UNDP 2005: 58). Thus, the medical services they provided to the peasants were beyond their training and were often questionable. Between 1998 and 1999, a study conducted in 4 township health centers and 8 village clinics in Wuxi County of Chongqing City and Min County of Gansu Province concluded that less than 2 percent of drug prescriptions were "rational." In the case of village clinics, only 0.06 percent of drug prescriptions were deemed reasonable (World Bank 2005c: 1; Zhang *et al.* 2003: 33). The education and certificate background of village doctors in rural China today is worth noting. (Table 14.2)

TABLE 14.2

**Education and Certificate Background of Village Doctors in Rural China: 2005**

| *Educational/certificate background* | *All village doctors (%)* |
|---|---|
| Four-year medical college | 1.9 |
| Three-year health school | 8.3 |
| Two-year health school | 70.6 |
| High school or no formal schooling | 19.20 |
| Certified village doctors | 80 |
| Non-certified village doctors | 20 |

*Source* : Han, Jun, and Luo Dan, 2005, Report on Rural Health Care Situation in China. (Zhongguo Nongcun Yiliao Weisheng Zhuangkuang Baogao) Beijing: Development Research Center, State Council.

Also, some villagers complained that the clinic did not offer any public health services and charged fees even for the items sponsored or required by the government. The villagers did have a ground for their complaints. In the past, a major responsibility of the village barefoot doctors was to provide public health services to the villagers free of charge. For example, in coordination with the village school, the village health post routinely provided health education to villagers by offering classes during the slack seasons. Now, the village clinic charged for all public health services, including distributing antischistosomiasis drugs and vaccinations. Not a single health education class was offered in the village during the past three years. According to the county policy, a Lake Village child must receive 7 vaccinations, for which the clinic charged a total of 164 Yuan in 2004. As a result, less than 80 percent of the village households paid for their children's vaccinations, the rest forwent those vital health services.

Besides, the Lake Villagers had a consensus that the clinic's prices of medicine were too high. Several villagers noted that the clinic often purchased medicine from a local private trader instead of the county pharmaceutical company for cheaper prices. As the government did not routinely regulate the private traders, it was possible that they could sometimes sell counterfeit or fake medicine to the clinic, which would in turn resell such medicine to the villagers.

My investigation verified that the villagers' complaints had a solid basis. The clinic did often sell medicine at a price much higher than the local retail price. A small bottle of cold medicine, for example, was sold in the clinic for 12 Yuan. The county drug store's price was 7.2 Yuan. A small box of erythromycin (12 pills) was sold for 22 Yuan in the clinic. Yet the price for the same medicine in the county drug store was 4.42 Yuan. Antiphlogistic medicine was sold for 18.2 Yuan per box (24 tablets) in the clinic. Yet, it was available at the county drug store for 12.8 Yuan. The clinic seldom issued a purchase receipt of the medicine to the patient. When a patient requested, the clinic often wrote the purchased item as "medicine," without spelling out the name of the medicine.

The price-gouging problem in Lake Village reflected worsening health disparity at the national level. A recent study indicated that rural township health centers and village clinics marked their medicine about 163 percent higher than their urban counterparts. A 2005 government publication estimated that more than 55 percent of the village clinics stored or used medicine that had gone bad, expired, or had lost curing effects (Chen 2005: 74). In Chengdu, the city authority randomly selected 10 rural health centers for investigation and found that all possessed fake medicine for sale (National Information Center 2005: 8).

Fifth, Lake Village, along with 28 villages and 6 towns in the county, saw the reemergence of schistosomiasis. Officially, the disease was brought under control in River County in 1998. In 2002, there were reports about the infection of people and cattle in the adjacent villages. In 2004, four Lake Villagers suffered from acute infection. The provincial parasitic research institute conducted an epidemiological survey in the village and confirmed the reemergence of the disease. Now the county schistosomiasis control station was taking some measures to control the disease, including mass chemotherapy and snail control by chemical means.

To many villagers, the reemergence was no surprise. The Three-Tiered Health System was gone, and infected people were not treated and perpetuated the sources of parasite eggs. The village doctors paid no attention to the endemic disease. The village snail control teams were disbanded in 1999. In the past, every winter, the villagers would burn the weeds surrounding the reservoir and drain the marsh areas outside the village. Now most men left the village for wage labor during the slack seasons. The village sanitation teams disappeared nearly ten years ago. Prior to 1995, the doctors from the county schistosomiasis control station visited the village once a year. In the past five years, they stopped by the village just once. Zhu Weimin, a doctor of the county schistosomiasis control station stated:

> "Well, no single reason can explain the reemergence of schistosomiasis. It was the result of many combined factors. We knew the disease would come back years ago, but there was nothing we could do about it. After the disease was controlled in River County, we continued to solidify our achievements and did the best we could. Year after year, the rural people got tired of it and were not interested in cooperating with us. We had to beg them to get their blood or stool samples for examination. Also, after the Three-Tiered Health System was gone, we lost our eyes and ears in the countryside. In the Household Responsibility System, it became very difficult to recruit volunteers in any village to help us with anything. Now, we have to do everything by ourselves. Snail control, for example, used to be taken care of by the endemic villages. Now, you have to pay them to do it. State funding only covers about half of our staff's salary, and the station must generate revenues to pay its members. We are county-level doctors, but we earn less money than the village doctors."

The situation was worse than what Zhu told me. At the national level, the government devoted very little to public health—only 6.3 percent of the total health expenditure, and the government funding covered only about one-third of the fiscal budget of the county-level public heath authorities (UNDP 2005: 58). To generate revenue, these institutions shifted away from their primary responsibilities. Disease prevention and health education, the beneficial yet non-profitable programs, have been weakened enormously. Currently, for example, over 60 percent of rural residents reported that they had no access to health information (Ooi 2005: 11). Essentially, the low budget reduced the prospect of preventing and controlling infectious and endemic diseases, and impaired the local health authorities' capacity to provide for the public good and prevent diseases. Table 14.3 shows the decline of the government financial allocations to the epidemic prevention institutions nationwide and the increase of the business income generated by these institutions themselves.

### Table 14.3
### Income Composition of Epidemic Prevention Institutions in China: 1990-2002

| *Year* | *Government financial allocations (%)* | *Business income generated by institutions themselves (%)* |
|---|---|---|
| 1990 | 59.21 | 40.79 |
| 1991 | 56.93 | 43.07 |
| 1992 | 53.93 | 46.07 |
| 1993 | 48.82 | 51.18 |
| 1994 | 49.98 | 50.02 |
| 1995 | 46.15 | 53.85 |
| 1996 | 43.74 | 56.26 |
| 1997 | 41.06 | 58.94 |
| 1998 | 42.74 | 57.26 |
| 1999 | 39.16 | 60.84 |
| 2000 | 38.66 | 61.34 |

*Sources* : Health Economics Research Institute, Ministry of Health, 2003, China's Total Health Expenditure Research Report 2003. (Zhongguo Weisheng Zong Feiyong Yanjiu Baogao 2003) Zhao, Yuqing, ed. Beijing: Ministry of Health, pp. 30-31.

Schistosomiasis did not just reemerge in River County. By 2006, the disease had reemerged in 150 counties in 7 provinces in which it was eradicated or controlled previously. Approximately 860,000 people were infected and some 60 million were at risk (Ross 2001: 270; Liang 2006: 139). While schistosomiasis is offered as an example to illustrate the result of weakened disease prevention, it was not just schistosomiasis that had reemerged in China. In recent years, with the loosened epidemic prevention, a number of old parasitic diseases, which made China "the Sick Man of East Asia" in the first half of the 20th century, reemerged as public health problems in China today. In 2005, some 60 species of human parasites were detected in the Chinese rural population (Wu 2005: 761). In 2005, it was estimated that 39 million Chinese people had hookworm disease, 29 million were infected by whipworms, and 85 million had ascariasis (Ministry of Health 2005: 1). As the infection rates of these diseases could have been reduced by 70 percent merely by means of mass health education, their reemergence sounded a wake-up call for the health policy-makers in China.

## HEALTH DISPARITY AND POVERTY : THREE CASES AND THEIR IMPLICATIONS

In Lake Village, the most visible impact of health disparity was poverty. After the collapse of the Cooperative Medical System, the villagers had lost their protection against illness. In River County, medical fees for a serious illness were usually catastrophic even for a well-to-do rural household. One family member's illness would often wipe out all the economic achievements the family made for many years and lock the family into poverty.

Local and national peasant sayings described the current health disparity vividly. A widespread doggerel reflected that poor peasants were deprived of access to health care: "A minor illness, you bear it; a major illness, you drag it out." A jingle said, "It takes ten years to eradicate our poverty, it takes one illness to impoverish us again." One verse protested the unreasonable medical expenses: "One appendectomy, one year's farm work is in vain." Another proverb described the villagers' view of the current medical system: "Money talks everywhere, including in a surgical operation." Of all the local people's pet phrases, "We are not afraid of poverty, we are afraid of illness" was a most common saying that I often heard in Lake Village.

Nonetheless, poverty and illness are often intertwined in Rural China. Each year, some 10 million Chinese peasants fell below China's official poverty line [680 Yuan per person per year in 2006] because of illness (National Development and Reform Committee 2006). At the national level, a Harvard study concluded that illness was the second most common cause of poverty in China, only behind lack of labor (Liu, Rao, and Hsiao 2003). In the 2003 National Health Survey, 30 percent of poor households reported that health care costs were the reason why they were in poverty (World Bank 2005b: 2). Based on a survey of 114 counties in 25 provinces, a 2004 report estimated that 41 percent of the rural poor were impoverished by illness (Chinese Red Cross Foundation 2005: 2).

Lake Village's situation coincided with the national situation. Based on my survey and the village records, of the 482 households in the village, 156 households (about 32 percent) had at least one member who suffered from an illness that required a treatment in the county hospital in the past three years. 134 households (about 28 percent) had at least one member who suffered from a chronic illness. 26 households (about 6 percent) had at least one disabled member.[2] In 2005, on average, health care accounted for about 8 percent of the annual expenditure of a normal household. However, 163 households (about 34 percent) spent more than 30 percent of their annual expenditure on medical services and drugs for their family members.

The village headman estimated that the average expenses for a patient with a severe illness were about 8,000 Yuan, or nearly the entire annual income of a household in 2005. Nevertheless, as the productivity of the households with sick members was usually lowered, few of them actually had a yearly income of 8,000 Yuan. For example, the average annual income of the 10 selected poor households with at least one chronic patient was only 3,460 Yuan. In my interviews, all the 10 households reported that they had to do everything they could to pay for their family members' medical expenses and illness was the main reason why they were deep in debt.

By and large, illness affected the Lake Villagers in two ways. In the first, an illness or injury disabled a family member. In order to treat the illness or injury, the family fell into debt. As the illness dragged on, it became impossible for the family to escape the debt prison. In the second category, a family was initially well-off. Then a member fell into a severe illness and medical fees drained the family resources and made the household poverty stricken.

In Lake Village, when a person became severely ill or injured, financially, a family would usually cope with the unfortunate incident in six ways. The family's savings constituted the first line of defense. To pay for the remaining medical fees, the family's responses included: (1) cut down its normal spending on food, clothing and other consumer goods; (2) discontinue the children's schooling to reduce the family expenditure and to get help from the children; (3) sell domestic livestock or cash crops, if available; (4) borrow from relatives, friends, and local credit union; and (5) sell the family's fixed assets such as farm tools, tractors, draft animals, and house. Depending on the situation, each family had to evaluate their trade-offs and select the solutions that they deemed the best. All these solutions would drain the family resources, affect the health of other family members, and ultimately weaken the family's productivity, which leads to its impoverishment.

All the 50 households surveyed reported that they would do anything they could to fund their members' medical treatments, if needed. However, 8 households reported that most of the above fund-raising means were not available to them. Nor were they able to raise enough funds by the above means. Thus, they would have to take so-called passive responses to illness, which included: not to seek or delay medical treatment, seek alternative treatment at a lower price, or early discharge from hospital before recovery. All the 8 households stated that they were aware of the consequences that passive responses could worsen the patient's condition and could make the treatment even more expensive in the end.

The following three cases illustrated how illness impoverished three households in Lake Village. To some degree, they reflected the common ways in which the rural households cope with severe illnesses and highlighted the main patterns through which illnesses impoverish the Chinese peasants. I selected these three cases from the 10 cases I collected in the village.

The first case involved Ying Fang, a 43-year old woman. Ying lived with her husband, their two sons, and her mother-in-law. Her family represented a poor household in the village. The family's major income came from their 4 Mu of rice paddies. The family worked hard year round and were able harvest about 2,000 kilograms of rice annually. After leaving enough for self-consumption, the family was able to earn about 3,500 Yuan from selling their rice, which was just about enough to pay for taxes and fees, fertilizers, pesticides, and some household items, such as salt and oil. To pay for electricity and their younger son's tuition, Ying's husband and older son must earn extra income by working as wage laborers whenever possible. The Ying family lived in a mud house, which Ying inherited from her parents about 10 years ago. Despite that they tried to watch every penny in their hands, the Ying family could only eke out a bare living.

In 2002, Ying was diagnosed that she had a womb tumor. The medical fees for her treatment were 6,500 Yuan and the county hospital required that the fees must be paid prior to the surgery. Because of that, Ying had to delay her treatment again and again, because the family had no savings and was unable to borrow enough money. Whenever her illness was too painful to bear, Ying would take some painkillers or go to the village doctor for an analgesic injection. Finally, in the winter of 2004, Ying's illness worsened so badly that she could not drag it on any more.

The Ying family was officially an "extremely poor household" and was eligible for social relief. When Ying's husband went to the county, however, he was told that there were no funds available at the time. He went there again several months later and received the same reply. Then, the family attempted to borrow money from the township credit union, and was told that the union could not make a loan to them, because the union assessed that her family did not have the ability to pay-off their debts. The Ying family tried to borrow money from their relatives and friends. Some offered help, but many declined. In the end, the Ying family was only able to borrow 2,800 Yuan. As they had no other options, the Ying family sold their only buffalo for 1,900 Yuan and a portion of their rice seeds for the next year for another 1,700 Yuan. Although the medical treatment was not entirely successful and Ying still suffered from the illness from time to time, the medical expenses not only made her family fall deeply into debt but also adversely affected their future agricultural production.

Ying's case showed how a serious illness deepened the poverty level of a poor household. In Lake Village, it was especially difficult for a poor family to confront illness. A poor family usually lacked savings or livestock that could be sold for cash. Besides, it often lacked good credit, which made it hard for the family to borrow money from moneylenders or even from relatives and friends. As the family had few options, it was often forced to sell their core assets such as seeds, draft animals or farming tools. Such disposal of core productive assets could lead the family to a "poverty ratchet" (Chambers 1989: 1). Ying's illness was not life threatening and the family's medical bills were not big, if compared with many of her fellow villagers. Had some financial help been available, the family might not have sold their buffalo and seeds, and thus might have had a better chance for its economic recovery.

The second case was related to Song Weimin, a 54-year-old man. Song and his wife had two daughters. The family raised vegetables and fruits in their 6 Mu of sloping fields. Before 2004, the Song family earned about 10,000 Yuan, which was one of the highest household incomes in the village. Song spent about 2,000 Yuan buying rice for his family. His two daughters studied in the township school, which added about 1,800 Yuan to the family's annual expenditure. After deducting taxes, production, and other expenses, Song normally could put 2,000 Yuan into the family's saving account each year. Although his wife suffered from gallstone (cholelithiasis) and could hardly help him with farm work, Song managed to make the family's ends meet both inside and outside the house.

In the summer of 2004, Song fell down from the roof while repairing the eaves and was severely injured. He was treated in the county hospital and the medical fees amounted to more than 30,000 Yuan. The Song family borrowed 6,000 Yuan from the township credit union, 10,000 from relatives, and sold the family's two sows, all their goats and chickens, a pair of buffalos, a horse, a cart, and everything else they could think of. Song's wife forwent her own medical treatment. His two daughters quit school. Song survived but was paralyzed due to his nerve injuries. Now he needed intensive care. Because of this accident, the Song family became one of the poorest families in Lake Village.

Song's case showed how a catastrophic accident impoverished an initially well-off family. Three points were of importance. First, although a well-to-do household had more means to pay for its medical expenses, none of such provided the family with full protection against a severe injury or illness. In the absence of health insurance, the medical expenses quickly drained the available resources and eroded the economic achievements the family made over many years. Moreover, even for a well-to-do family, the disposal of core livestock and assets would have a far-reaching impact on the household economy. In Song's case, the sales of sows, for example, eliminated a reliable source of the family's income. Third, if a family lost its bread-earner, the adverse impact of a disease or injury would often be irreversible. It would permanently affect the family's well-being. Song's case illuminated how fragile a rural household was, because the peasants lacked health insurance and social security.

The third case was about Wang Hong, a 45-year-old man. Until 2003, Wang Hong and Wu Tao, his wife, formed one of the rich households in Lake Village. In 1995, Wang found a job raising fish for an aquaculture company in a neighboring town. At home, his wife and his son took care of their fields and were able to grow enough food for the family. The Wang family lived frugally and saved about 10,000 Yuan out of Wang's wages. The family planned to open a grocery store and had purchased furniture and grocery goods.

Then, beginning in the fall of 1999, Wang began to feel a pain in his abdomen. Wu observed that her husband lost his normal appetite, frequently felt fatigue, and defecated four to five times a day, with occasional blood stools. He also had fever from time to time. Wang talked to several friends and learned that the county hospital's registration and check up fees amounted to more than 300 Yuan. To avoid medical expenses, Wang only bought some stomach medicine from the village clinic and never visited the county hospital, hoping that his illness would be gone by itself. In April 2002, Wang's belly began to swell. In May, the county schistosomiasis control station diagnosed that he had schistosomiasis. The doctor told Wu that her husband's disease was at a late stage and the parasites had already dug many nests in his liver, hardening it so badly that they could not cure him.

Wu took her husband to the provincial hospital. While the surgical operation alleviated Wang's condition, medical expenses devastated the family. The Wang family sold their half-ton tractor, a fishing boat, and all their store furniture. The grocery items were sold at sacrificial prices. Yet, Wu still had to borrow money from relatives and friends. To minimize the debt, Wang insisted on an early discharge from the hospital. Despite that, the family already owed a debt of over 50,000 Yuan. Back home, Wang remained very sick, yet unable to seek additional treatment. Today, the Wang family worried about not only Wang's illness but also the family's huge debts.

Wang's case rendered an important lesson for his fellow villagers. Except for an acute case of intensive infection (Wang's was not), schistosomiasis was a disease that can be easily treated by chemotherapy with prazequantel. Had Wang's disease been diagnosed early enough, one course of treatment should have cured him. Wang's disease should have been treated years ago and his medical expenses should have been less than 200 Yuan. Yet, Wang forwent medical examination. He was certainly not alone. Based on my interviews, it seemed to me that few Lake Villagers in Wang's situation would be able to avoid his tragedy. Retrospectively, it was the large medical fees that prevented many Chinese peasants from an early diagnosis of their illness and victimized them in the end.

## CONCLUSION

China's rural health care system was held up as a model by "Health for All by the Year 2000" at the World Health Organization's 1978 Alma Ata Conference. Ironically, by 2000, China ranked 188 out of 191 countries in terms of fairness in governmental financial contribution to health (World Health Organization 2000: 191). To a large degree, Lake Village reflects what has happened to China's rural health sector and how China's economic development has affected the health of its rural people since the country's economic reform.

After the collapse of the Cooperative Medical System and the Three-Tiered Health System, an unrestrained market took control of China's rural health sector. In addition to its urban bias, the government carried out a *laissez-faire* health policy in the following decades. As a result, health equity vanished and health disparity grew. For most rural people, health care quickly became unaffordable and access became increasingly inequitable. Today, health disparity has made it nearly impossible for millions of poor peasants to receive the medical services they need. When they do, they end up impoverishing themselves. At present, as more than 80 percent of the

Chinese peasants are not protected by health insurance, illness represents a major barrier for sustainable development in rural China.

The Lake Village case has illuminated three important points. Above all, it shows that contrary to the general assumption, people's health will not automatically improve as a result of economic growth. "When the river rises the boat goes up" is not the case as far as the Chinese rural health sector is concerned. In the pre-reform era, health equity improved substantially in China despite the country's slow economic growth. Although China has made significant economic growth since the 1980s, such a growth has not been matched by an increased government investment in rural health. Nor has it helped to promote China's health equity. On the contrary, despite the country's economic growth, China's rural health care degenerated.

Moreover, the case illustrates that health equity is an essential requirement for sustainable development in rural China. Clearly, China's economic development cannot be sustained when millions of Chinese peasants are affected by poor health and inadequate access to health care. Few would argue for a return to the era of the People's Commune. Despite that, in rural China, what has been lacking is health equity. To improve China's rural health, the government should not only increase its health expenditure but also utilize resources in such a way that it helps to diminish health disparity. For example, government spending should target reducing the gaps between rural and urban health sectors. Although many urban people have health insurance and enjoy higher incomes, they pay less for health care and receive more from the government subsidies. To narrow the gap, the government must prioritize the rural needs in its allocation of health funds, with an emphasis on equal health coverage and equal access to health care. That was what I often heard while in Lake Village. For the villagers, what mattered most was health equity, and quality must be improved based on equity.

Finally, this case study suggests that the government has a responsibility to do social good by prioritizing public health and strengthening disease prevention. Such a role must not be entirely left to the market. In China, a public health measure will likely fail without the participation of the government. The collapse of the Cooperative Medical System was a historical example. The reemergence of schistosomiasis offered a new case in point. Indeed, how could one expect River County Schistosomiasis Control Station to do its job, when the government funding was not enough to cover half of its staff's salaries? In Lake Village, virtually everyone I talked with believed that the government should do more for the peasants and doubted the wisdom of letting the market take full control of China's rural health sector.

The Chinese government has now recognized the problems in China's rural health sector and is currently experimenting with remedial programs. The New Cooperative Medical Scheme (NCMS) offers an example. The program is presently being experimented in over 300 counties and will be implemented nationwide by 2010. On a voluntary basis, the NCMS will require that each family pay 10 Yuan for each of its members. This annual contribution will be matched by a subsidy of 10 Yuan from the local governments (township, county, and province) and an additional subsidy of 10 Yuan from the central government if the family lives in the poorer provinces.

Questions about the NCMS do remain. Can each of the parties afford their contribution of 10 Yuan per person? Some scholars have doubts about the local government's capability to pay their share, as they have little taxing power to raise the funds. Also, an annual input of 30 Yuan per person (about US $3.80) seems too low, considering the sky-high prices for health care in China today. Also, little was said about the role of the village doctors. Barefoot doctors played an essential role in China's former Three-Tiered Health System. To improve rural health, the government needs to integrate the village doctors into the program so that they may contribute more to the rural health sector today as their predecessors did historically.

Despite these and other questions, the NCMS represents a positive policy improvement by the Chinese government. It reflects the government's recognition of the fact that China's economic development cannot be sustainable, when millions of Chinese peasants lacked health insurance and their economic achievements can be wiped out by an illness overnight. While watching carefully, let us hope that the NCMS will help, together with other programs, make health care available and affordable to millions of households in rural China.

## Notes

1. To ensure the local people's privacy, I have changed the name of the village in which I conducted my research. The names of the villages, the township and the country has also been changed.
2. The three surveyed groups overlapped. A family with a member suffered from a disability or a chronic illness. The same disabled member suffered from a chronic illness as well.

## References

Bezlova, Antoaneta, 1999, Shamans Return as Mao's Barefoot Doctors Fade Away, *Asia Times*, October 6, 2.

Braveman, Paula, 2006, Health Disparity and Health Equity: Acronyms Terms Concepts and Measurement, *Annual Review of Public Health*, Vol. 27: 167-94.

Chambers, R., 1989, Editorial Introduction: Vulnerability, Coping and Policy, *IDS Bulletin*, v. 20(2):1-7.

Chen, Ying, 2005, An Analysis of New Rural Medical Cooperative System, *Chinese Medical Ethics*, V. 18, No. 2/100 issue): 73-75.

Cheng, Chu-yuan, 1989, The New China: Comparative Economic Development in Mainland China, Taiwan and Hong Kong by Alvin Rabushka, *Economic Development and Cultural Change*, Vol. 37(4), 869-76.

Chinese Red Cross Foundation, 2005, *Pay Attention to the Health of Poor Peasants and Children*, (Guanzhu Pinkun Nongmin He Ertong De Jiankang), Beijing: CRCF Press, August 10, 2005.

Han, Jun, and Luo Dan, 2005, *Report on Rural Health Care Situation in China*, (Zhongguo Nongcun Yiliao Weisheng Zhuangkuang Baogao) Beijing: Development Research Center, State Council.

Health Research Institute, 2002, *From Barefoot Doctors to Rural Doctors*, (Cong Chijiao Yisheng Dao Xiangcun Yisheng), Kunming Medical University, Kunming: Yunnan People's Publishing House.

Hesketh, Therese, and Wei Xing Zhu, 2004, Effect of Restricted Freedom on Health in China, *British Medical Journal*, Vol. 329:1427.

Hsiao, William C.L., 1995, The Chinese Health Care System: Lessons for Other Nations, *Social Science and Medicine*, Vol. 41(8):1047-55.

Huang, Ying, and Zhang Dayong, 2006, An Analysis on Health Care Current Status and Medical Safety Issues among the Peasants in Poor Regions: An Investigation of the Rural Households in the Kalaqing Banner in Inner Mongolia, *Soft Science of Health*, Vol. 20(2):113-15.

Kaufman, Joan, 2005, *China: The Intersections between Poverty, Health Inequity, Reproductive Health and HIV/AIDS*, New York, Palgrave Macmillan Ltd.

Li, Changmingal, 2001, *Selected Rural Health Documents: 1950-2000*, (Nongcun Weisheng Wenjian Huibian) Beijing: Ministry of Health Press.

Li, Jian, 2006a, Excreta Disposal, Agricultural Use of Night Soil, and the Pandemic of Schistosomiasis in the Yangtze River Valley: 1905-1949, *Journal of Changsha University of Electric Power*, In Press.

Li, Jian, 2006b, Medical Anthropology and Schistosomiasis Control: Theoretical Trends, Ethnographic Fieldwork, and Case Studies, *The Chinese Journal of Schistosomiasis Control* (The flagship journal of the Preventative Medicine Association of the People's Republic of China), Vol. 18(2): 157-60.

Li, Jian, 2006c, Reemergence of Big-Belly Disease (Schistosomiasis) in China, *Anthropology News*, American Anthropological Association, Vol. 47(3): 19-20.

Liang, Song, Changhong Yang, Bo Zhong, and Dongchuan Qiu, 2006, Re-emerging Schistosomiasis in Hilly and Mountainous Areas of Sichuan, China, *Bulletin of the World Health Organization*, 84(2): 139-44.

Liu Y., 2004, China's Public Health Care System: Facing the Challenges, *World Health Organization Bulletin*, 82:532-538.

Liu, Yi, Rao Kequin, William Hsiao, 2003, Medical Expenditure and Rural Impoverishment in China, *Journal of Health, Population and Nutrition*, Vol. 21(3): 216-22.

Mao, Zedong, 1976, *Selected Works of Mao Tse-tung*, (Mao Zedong Xuanji), Beijing: People's Publishing House.

Ministry of Health, 1989, Forty-Year National Health Statistics 1949—1988, (Jianguo Sishinian Quanguo Weisheng Tongji Zhiliao: 1949—1988), Beijing: Ministry of Health, P.R. China.

Ministry of Health, 1982, *China Health Year Book 1982*, (Zhongguo Weisheng Nianjian), Beijing: People's Health Publishing House.

Ministry of Health, 1996, *China Health Year Book 1996*, (Zhongguo Weisheng Nianjian) Beijing: People's Health Publishing House.

Ministry of Health, 2004, *China Health Year Book 2004*, (Zhonguo Weishen Nianjian), Beijing: China Xiehe Medical University Press.

Ministry of Health, 2005, Investigation Report on Important Human Parasitic Diseases in China, (Quanguo Renti Jishengchong Bin Xianzhuang Diaocha Baogao), Beijing: Ministry of Health Press on May 16, 2005.

National Bureau of Statistics, 2000, *Chinese Statistics Abstract*, (Zhongguo Tongji Zeyao),. Beijing: Statistics Publishing House.

National Development and Reform Committee, 2006, *Guiding Principles for Pharmaceutical Industries in the 11th Five-Year Plan*, (Yiyao Hangye "Shiyiwu" Fazhan Zhidao Yijian), Beijing: National Development and Reform Committee.

National Information Center, 2005, Current Situation of Rural Pharmaceutics in Our Country, Reference for Chinese Mayors (Shizhang Juece Yaocan), Beijing, China Association of Mayors, No. 9 (December 22, 2005).

Ooi, Elaine Wee-Ling, 2005, *The World Bank's Assistance to China's Health Sector*, Washington, D.C.: The World Bank.

Perrins, Robert J., 2004, *China: Facts and Figures Annual Handbook*, Vol. 29, Gulf Breeze, Florida: Academic International Press.

Ross, Allen G.P., *et al.*, 2001, Schistosomiasis in the People's Republic of China: Prospects and Challenges for the 21st Century, *Clinical Microbiology Review*, 14(2):270-95.

United Nations Development Program, 2005, *China Human Development Report*: 2005, Geneva: United Nations (UNDP).

Vajpeyi, Dhirendra K. and Alyona Ponomarenko, 2001, *Deforestation in China. In: Deforestation, Environment, and Sustainable Development: A Comparative Analysis*, Dhirendra K. Vajpeyi, ed. pp. 91-109, Westport, Conn.: Praeger.

Wang, Dongbing, 2004, New Cooperative Medical System: Move Forward with Expectations and Worries, (Hezhuo Yiliao: Daizhe Yilu He Xiwang Qianxing, Jiankang Bao) *Health Daily*, August 24: p. 2.

World Bank, 2005a, Rural Health Insurance—Rising to the Challenge, Beijing: Rural Health in China: WB Briefing Notes Series No. 6, May 2005.

World Bank, 2005b, China's Health Sector—Why Reform is Needed, Beijiing: Rural Health in China: WB Briefing Notes Series No. 3, April 2005.

World Bank, 2005c, China's Health Care Delivery, Beijing: Rural Health in China: WB Briefing Notes Series No. 4. February 2005.

World Health Organization, *WHO Report 2000*, (2005) Geneva: WHO Press.

Wu, Guan-ling, 2005, Medical Parasitology in China: A Historical Perspective, *Chinese Medical Journal*, Vol. 118(9):759-61.

Xia, Xinzhen, 2003, A Historical Analysis on Village Cooperative Medical System, *Modern China*, Vol. 9:1-12.

Xinhua, 2004, Official: China to Make More Input in Health Care in Rural Areas, *People's Daily*, November 6, 5.

Zhang X, Feng Z. and Zhang L., 2003, Analysis on Quality of Prescription of Township Hospitals in Poor Areas, *Journal of Rural Health Service Management*, Vol. 23(12):33-35.

Zhou, Yanyu, 2002, Remarkable Disparities: The Great Challenges the Chinese Health Sector are Confronting, *China Reform*, Vol. 4.

# Index